The World We

The World We Have Won is a major study of transformations in erotic and intimate life since 1945. We are living in a world of transition, in the midst of a long, unfinished but profound revolution that has transformed the possibilities of living our sexual diversity and creating intimate lives. This book provides a balance sheet of the changes that have transformed our ways of being, from welfarism to the Pill, and women's and gay liberation, from globalization, consumerism and individualization to changing patterns of family life and new forms of intimacy. Some commentators, across the political spectrum, respond to these challenges with a deep cultural pessimism or moral conservatism. This book rejects such views and proposes an alternative perspective. Building on many years of innovative research, Jeffrey Weeks analyses the long term trends and the more immediate contingencies that have shaped sexuality and intimacy. He argues that this is a world we are increasingly making for ourselves, part of the long process of the democratization of everyday life. Unless we grasp this we cannot understand the problems and anxieties, but also the opportunities and hopes, in this world we have won.

This highly controversial and readable book will prove an enlightening challenge to a wide range of readers. It will also appeal to both undergraduate and postgraduate students taking modules in sexuality, gender, intimacy and family studies across a range of disciplines including sociology, history and cultural studies.

Jeffrey Weeks works at London South Bank University where he has been Professor of Sociology, Executive Dean of Arts and Human Sciences, and Director of SPUR: the Social Policy and Urban Regeneration Research Institute. He has an international reputation for his work on the history and social organization of sexuality and intimate life. Recent books include *Making Sexual History* (2000), *Same Sex Intimacies* (with Heaphy and Donovan, 2001) and *Sexuality* (second edition, 2003).

The World We Have Won
The Remaking of Erotic and Intimate Life

Jeffrey Weeks

Routledge
Taylor & Francis Group

LONDON AND NEW YORK

First published 2007
by Routledge
2 Park Square, Milton Park, Abingdon, Oxon OX14 4RN

Simultaneously published in the USA and Canada
by Routledge
270 Madison Avenue, New York, NY 10016

Routledge is an imprint of the Taylor & Francis Group, an informa business

Typeset in New Century Schoolbook and Frutiger
by Keystroke, 28 High Street, Tettenhall, Wolverhampton
Printed and bound in Great Britain
by Antony Rowe Ltd, Chippenham, Wiltshire

British Library Cataloguing in Publication Data
A catalogue record for this book is available from the British Library

Library of Congress Cataloging in Publication Data
Weeks, Jeffrey, 1945-
The world we have won : the remaking of erotic and intimate
life / Jeffrey Weeks.
p. cm.
Includes bibliographical references and index.
ISBN 978-0-415-42200-0 (hard cover) — ISBN 978-0-415-42201-7 (paper cover)
1. Sex—History—20th century. 2. Sex—History—21st century.
3. Sexual ethics—History. 4. Sexual orientation—History.
5. Sex and law—History. 6. Social history—1945- I. Title.
HQ16.W44 2007
306.709′045—dc22
2006039266

ISBN10: 0–415–42200–0 (hbk)
ISBN10: 0–415–42201–9 (pbk)
ISBN10: 0–203–95680–X (ebk)

ISBN13: 978–0–415–42200–0 (hbk)
ISBN13: 978–0–415–42201–7 (pbk)
ISBN13: 975–0–203–95680–9 (ebk)

For Mark
With love and thanks

Contents

Preface

This is a book about the present, about how we live now, but it is also a story about the transformations in erotic and intimate life since 1945. Without understanding the present we are in a poor position to take hold of the future. Without a sense of history, and an understanding of the ways we lived then, we have no benchmarks by which to measure what has changed, no means of grasping the magnitude of the dramatic shifts that have taken place over the past sixty years in this world we have won.

The title is an obvious play on Peter Laslett's famous book, *The World We Have Lost* (1965) which from the 1960s helped revolutionize our understanding of the English past of individualism and family life. But the phrase, 'the world we have lost' has had a resonance way beyond the specific scholarly intention of the author, evoking a nostalgia for a more settled and ordered moral culture than we apparently have today. A past of tradition, authority, sexual restraint, family discipline, neighbour-liness and good behaviour, where youthful unruliness could easily be curbed by a good clip around the ears by the local bobby, is counterposed to the apparent amoral uncertainty, or even (according to taste and moral urgency) the chaos of today, where families disintegrate, marriage is apparently in fatal decline, youth is more or less feral, 'anything goes' sexually, perversity is normalized, and 'respect' has all but disappeared. This latter, morally conservative critique may well be a (small) minority one today, yet echoes of the position can be traced even among self-styled progressives, especially those of a communitarian position and among those who lament the decline of social capital. While distancing themselves from the political conservatism that underpins much of the critique, leading radical scholars, such as Zymunt Bauman (2003), polemicise against the dangers and threats of 'liquid life', 'liquid love' and 'dark times', which while theoretically a million miles from the laments of conservative writers such as Melanie Phillips (1999) or Christie Davies (2006) come up with a similar cultural pessimism.

Against such settled pessimism, even despair, I want to offer not so much optimism as a realistic and forward-looking appreciation of the changes in sexual and intimate life that are transforming everyday life and the rapidly globalizing world we inhabit. We are living, as I argue in

Chapter 1, in the midst of a long, unfinished but profound revolution that has transformed the possibilities of living sexual diversity and creating intimate lives. The book provides a balance sheet of the changes that have transformed our ways of being sexual, intimate and familial, building on some thirty years of research and writing in these areas. I am with C. Wright Mills in saying, 'I have tried to be objective. I do not claim to be detached.' So I should make a declaration of interest. I believe the long revolution to have been overwhelmingly beneficial to the vast majority of people in the West, and increasingly to people living in the global South whose lives are also being transformed dramatically – and I say that while acknowledging the major problems that remain: fears, anxieties, prejudices, the play of power, and the power of privilege, discrimination and exploitation, desires stimulated and hopes deferred. It often feels that two steps forward are followed by one step backward. But the momentum is positive, and largely due to one essential feature of this new world: grass-roots agency is central to the direction we are moving in. Increasingly the contemporary world is a world we are making for ourselves, part of the long process of the democratization of everyday life. The social, cultural and moral revolutions of our times are fundamentally revolutions from below, and their future outcomes lie in our own hands to an extraordinary degree. Unless we grasp this we cannot understand not only the problems and anxieties but the challenges and opportunities in this world we are remaking.

This book engages fully with contemporary debates about intimacy and eroticism in the contemporary (whether, depending on your starting point, it is seen as 'postmodern', 'late modern', 'reflexive', 'story telling' or 'risk' laden) world, informed by a broad range of theory as well as my own empirical research over a number of years. But it seeks to do this while analysing specific moments in the convoluted journey since 1945. I judge that year to be a good symbolic starting point because it was, in many ways, the birth of the welfare world which has done so much to reshape attitudes towards sexuality and personal life. It is the nodal birth year for the baby boomers who have been the main architects of the contemporary world. It also happens to be my birth year, so that the analysis in this book is also in part an archaeology of my own life, and inevitably my own experiences, as well as the product of the extensive research on sexuality and intimate life that I have conducted since the 1970s, feed back into the narrative.

The first chapter, 'A different world', is concerned with connections. Connected lives are reflective and reflexive lives; that is, lives lived in growing self-consciousness of who we are, where we come from and what we may become. An outstanding feature of this world we inhabit, I argue, is that it has increasingly been made by active human endeavour. The sexual and intimate revolutions of our time are largely the result of these grass-roots transformations – literally the world we have made together. For connected lives are also lives lived reciprocally, with Others who shape what we are in the ties that not only bind but bond, and make us

human. Connected lives are lives that link the global and the local, bridging distances and linking questions of sexuality and intimacy to issues
of rights and responsibilities, to social justice. In a move across time
from the present to 1945 I suggest links between past and present, but
also the importance of understanding the ways we live in a new world,
and the necessity of fully encountering the historic presence.

Chapter 2, 'Cultures of restraint', focuses on the world as it was in
the 1940s and 1950s, shaped by a dominant culture of sexual restraint
even as people struggled to meet the promise of a new world at the end
of a devastating war, with the hope of radical social change. The chapter
is framed by a case study of the Rhondda Valleys in South Wales, where
I was born, in an apparently homogeneous working-class culture, dominated by a specific gendered and highly restrictive sexual pattern, where
nevertheless there is evidence of a pragmatic morality that points to the
future. The chapter then explores the wider continuities across Britain
of family and sexual life in the wake of a growing sense of security
and burgeoning affluence. The political and moral strictures on the need
for large families that harks back to the changes in fertility patterns in
the interwar years become increasingly redundant as the post-war baby
boom powers ahead. A new emphasis on the importance of pleasure in
marriage increasingly sexualizes women, within sharply defined limits.
The paradoxical result in the 1950s, however, is a strengthening of
narrow familial and heterosexual values, not a liberalization of attitudes.
In particular, male homosexuality becomes a target for social intervention, and the old 'queer world' as it had been inherited from the
nineteenth century begins to fade. A newly public subjectivity, that of
the 'respectable homosexual', emerges in social life and political discourse. And yet more significantly, the baby boomers become the focus
of anxieties which point to the fragility of this period that later conservatives looked back on as a golden age of social capital, community
and family stability.

Chapters 3 and 4 are concerned with 'The great transition'. In them
I argue that the period between the 1960s and the 1990s may best be
understood as a prolonged period of transition. The 'sexual revolution'
of the 1960s is given its due attention, especially as, through 'the Pill'
and generally improved contraception, it offered new opportunities for
women to express their sexuality, and for a growing divorce between
sexuality and reproduction. It also, of course, became the focus of conservative anathemas, the apparent source of what Fukuyama (1999)
called the 'Great Disruption'. But the changes of the 1960s are seen as
one aspect of a complex and wide-ranging series of transformations.
In these chapters I argue for the importance of four key shifts. The first
is a democratization and informalization of personal relationships that
sees the gradual development of profound caesuras: between sex and
reproduction, between sexual relationships and marriage, between marriage and parenting. Second, we see the development of a highly conscious
sense of sexual agency, especially on the part of women and increasingly

lesbians and gay men. The Women's Liberation and Gay Liberation movements are the most dramatic manifestation of this, with continuing if contested impact into the 2000s. Third, I suggest there is a profoundly important reshaping of the boundaries between public and private. We can see this in the 'permissive' legal reforms of the period, but also in feminist interventions on violence and pornography, new concerns with childhood, and in the moral conservatism, albeit inconsistently applied, of the Thatcher years. Finally, a heightened sense of 'risk' is dramatized by the HIV/AIDS crisis from the early 1980s. This casts a sharp searchlight on to shifting and uncertain mores. Yet despite the dramas and increasing sense of uncertainty around sexual values of a period that apparently moves from cultural revolution to backlash over a generation or so, in the midst of a profound reshaping of the economy and the birth of an avid new consumerism, I argue that the underlying trends show a consistent story: of liberalization, secularization and growing agency.

In Chapters 5 and 6 we move explicitly to the present. I suggest that the spectre of sexual diversity haunts the contemporary world. Behind this is an awareness of the changing meanings of erotic life, fuelled both by dramatic social change and by changing understandings about what constitutes sexuality, emphasizing the ways in which sexual meanings, identities, enactments are cultural artefacts, and culturally specific. There are no rights and wrongs in sexuality *per se*. To understand the erotic we must grasp the complexity of social forces which shape it. In Chapter 5 I explore three dimensions of diversity – lifestyle diversity, ethnic, racial and faith diversity, and life course diversity – and their implications for erotic and intimate life. This leads on to an analysis of different critiques of the new individualism, and I challenge the growing attempt to link it to the much proclaimed perils of neo-liberalism. Chapter 6 explores some of the 'contradictions' in contemporary sexuality, which feed into a sense of uncertainty and unease: the 'choice relationship', the shifting meanings of masculinity and femininity, and the complex challenge to the gender order represented by the public emergence of transgendered movements, new subjectivities and the continued institutionalization of heteronormativity, tensions between the generations, and the would-be 'technological fix', and the challenges all these pose to sexual values and to the question of sexual authority. With the decline of traditional value systems there has been a pluralization of authorities, and a proliferation of sexual voices and narratives. It is tempting to celebrate diversity as a good in itself, which in many ways it is. Yet the development of a live and let live society is challenged by the survival of homophobia, racism, conflicts over faith and the like, but also by the intractability of gender conflicts. At the same time, the profound changes that remade the sexual world both necessitate and open the way to new forms of sexual or intimate citizenship.

Following on from this, Chapter 7 engages with recent debates about, and empirical shifts in, marriage, family life and friendship, and the norms, values and commitments that underpin them. An emphasis on individual autonomy, and the individualization of moral choice, is, I argue, a characteristic feature of the contemporary world, but it is closely linked to values of reciprocity and mutual care, which are lived out in ordinary everyday life. I challenge currently fashionable theories about deficits in 'social capital', and argue that, on the contrary, despite huge and potentially disruptive changes in everyday life, there are both strong continuities in values and behaviour, and new sources of social capital that sustain life experiments. One important aspect of this is rise of a 'friendship ethic', especially among LGBT (lesbian, gay, bisexual and transgendered) people, which underpins various ways of doing family, and which poses genuine challenges to heteronormative values. This leads to a detailed discussion of same-sex marriage as an encapsulation of wider shifts in sexual and relational values. I suggest that far from being an accommodation either to heteronormativity or neo-liberalism, the rise and rise of same-sex unions suggest a 'querying/queering' of traditional institutions, and throws new light on debates about rights, commitment and recognition.

Finally, Chapter 8 puts the changes in Western society into a wider perspective. It is tempting to concentrate on the micro shifts in everyday life that are transforming sexualities and intimacy, and to forget the wider context, but of course changes that have been described and analysed in the book are the result not simply of individual or collective agency, however vital and central these have been, but of wider shifts that have made new forms of agency possible. Underpinning the changes has been the long, complex but irreducible process known as globalization. This is the focus of the final chapter. A globalized world is one in which Western categorizations of sexuality increasingly interact and interpenetrate with those operating in other sexual cultures, and in which new categorizations emerging worldwide – whether being universalized or asserted in opposition to one another – are increasingly interconnected across cultures. Globalization today points to a world in which the nature and experience of risk has changed. The spread of the HIV/AIDS epidemic since the 1980s to become a global pandemic is a vivid and tragic illustration of this. Risks have changed their forms, giving rise to new forms of conflict – over, for example, the reproductive rights of women in non-industrialized societies, or the rights of women to escape restrictive and violent family and communal relationships. These can become central to political differences on a global scale, such as the postulated conflict between Western and Islamic values. Conflicts over sexuality have become integral to the emergence of fundamentalist politics both within Western societies and elsewhere around the world. And yet processes of engagement between cultures and movements across national boundaries have in turn given rise to new discourses of human rights on a global scale, which are already having a significant impact on sexual politics within specific countries, not least Britain. This chapter explores the impact of these discourses in shaping notions of global sexual justice, and the radical humanism that I argue is becoming an increasingly urgent necessity for the world we are making.

Writing about sexuality and personal life no longer carries the stigma of marginalization it did when I first ventured into the field in the 1970s. On the contrary, what was once a thinly populated area of theoretical and research activity has now become a teeming metropolis of production, with many thousands of books and articles and vast areas of cyber-space dedicated to exploring the erotic. This reflects a wider shift, a move of the terrain of sexuality from the margins of political concern to very near the centre. By exploring the wider changes which have transformed the world since the Second World War we can begin to understand the remaking of sexual lives. By understanding the remaking of sexuality we can throw light on otherwise obscure social processes. This book is a contribution to that dual task.

Acknowledgements

This book is a culmination of many years of research and thinking about sexualities and intimacy, and even more years of trying to live them. So my debts to my families, friends, students and colleagues are greater than ever.

My first thanks must go to Deian Hopkin, Vice Chancellor of London South Bank University. With great generosity he provided me with the intellectual space during the academic year of 2005 to 2006 which allowed me to break the back of this book. He was not the only but certainly an indispensable begetter. Without that space and support it might have taken several more anguished years of trying to write while being an active dean. I must also warmly thank my colleagues at LSBU who picked up the slack while I was writing, and especially Mike Molan and Stina Lyon, without whose stalwart labours nothing would have been possible.

I owe so many thanks for so much support and help over the years that to list people seems invidious. But I must thank especially the following for indispensable support – in research, administrative, social, practical, moral and intellectual ways: Richard Allen, Dennis Altman, Maks Banens, Meg Barker, Henning Bech, Chetan Bhatt, Sue Bruley, Claire Callender, Bob Cant, Eric Chaline, Andrew Cooper, Emmanuel Cooper, Catherine Donovan, Ros Edwards, Richard Ekins, Debbie Epstein, Clare Farquhar, Jane Franklin, Val Gillies, Harry Goulbourne, Bev Goring, Lesley Hall, Jane Harmer, Gert Hekma, Kate Hudson, Brian Heaphy, Janet Holland, Dave King, Don Kulick, Jane Lewis, Karin Lutzen, Derek McGhee, Mary McIntosh, Anamika Majumdar, Rommel Mendes-Leite, Martin Mitchell, Anosua Mitra, Gareth Owen, Ken Plummer, Kevin Porter, Paula Reavey, Robert Reynolds, Tracey Reynolds, Diane Richardson, Philippe Rougier, Lynne Segal, Steven Seidman, Becky Shipman, Carol Smart, Donna Thomson, Randolph Trumbach, Matthew Waites, Simon Watney, Jane Williams, and the late and much missed Tamsin Wilton.

My students, at undergraduate, Masters and Ph.D. level, have provided indispensable sounding-boards at various times for most of the ideas in this book, and I thank them for their patience, their feedback, and the enormous stimulation I gained from them. Various parts of the book got their first airing at academic conferences, seminars and workshops in the UK and in many other parts of the world, from the Baltic to Australia. I thank all those who invited me and all participants for their comments and their engagement with my ideas. I can only hope that they got as much out of these excursions as I did.

I want to thank Gerhard Boomgaarden, Senior Editor at Routledge, for his confidence in me over several books now, and his colleagues, especially Ann Carter, for speeding this book through the editorial and production process.

The year I spent completing this book was special for me in many ways, but one of the particular joys was the kindness and support I received from the McNestry and Prime families. My warmest thanks to Ann and Joe, Tim, Pauline and Christopher McNestry, and to Marie and Richard Prime and their children, Hannah, Frank and Manny. My own blood family helped make me what I became. They remain part of me in inextricable and vital ways, even after many years of living away. My thanks as ever to Robert, Paula, Rhys, Geraint and Kier; to Dennis, Karen, Paul, Lauren, Sian and Chloe, and to Margaret, Robert and their boys. Above all, I want to express once again my gratitude and love to my mother, who has been a tower of strength through all the ups and downs of our lives, and the living embodiment of the cherished Welsh mam.

Micky Burbidge has been a stalwart friend and support for forty years as I write, an indispensable part of my own personal community. My deepest thanks.

Mark McNestry, my life partner, has done so much to help me live my life well that words seem inadequate to express my thanks. The dedication of this book to him is but a small token of an enduring gratitude.

A different world

Behind the deceptive stability of language ('a kiss is just a kiss'),
the meaning of experience and the experience of meaning change.
(Simon 2003: 27)

If the history of our present is more accidental than we may
like to believe, the future of our present is also more open than
it sometimes appears.
(Rose 1999: x)

Connections

A little time ago I noticed an advertisement in *The Economist* magazine
for a senior post at the heart of the United Kingdom government: director
of the Strategy Unit in the Cabinet Office. The specific post in question
may be immaterial (though it suggests a central shaping role), but what
really caught my eye was the rubric at the end:

The Cabinet Office is committed to providing equal opportunities
for all, irrespective of age, disability, ethnicity, gender, marital
status, religion, sexuality, transgender and working patterns.
(*The Economist*, 20 March 2004: 21)

Gender, marital status, sexuality, transgender . . . It's not so much the
pious aspirations, the devotion to current standards of equality and
diversity norms and legislation, that strikes one, it's the casualness
and comprehensiveness of the list that catches the eye. The heir to a state
machinery that in the first half of the twentieth century had upheld
'the strictest rules against sex in the world at that time' (Szreter 2002:
415), that had been deeply implicated, over a long and frequently bloody
and anguished history of sexual and moral surveillance and disciplin-
ing, was now putting itself in the vanguard of cultural enlightenment and
progressive legal reform, culminating in marriage-like civil partnerships
for same-sex couples and a Gender Recognition Act to give a new legal
status to transgendered people.
    It would be nice to think that this was a wave of enlightenment that
was carrying the world before it. Alas, other states, other mores. At about

the same time, in another jurisdiction, there was a very different cultural maelstrom. President George W. Bush, the American President riding to his second term, spoke firmly to his conservative heartland about a different moral agenda. At the heart of this was his fervent opposition to the very notion of same-sex marriage, and his willingness to support a constitutional amendment outlawing it. At the same time that the UK was witnessing a burst of sexual liberalism, its closest ally was suffering one of its regular bouts of moral regression. This may be seen in turn as part of a rising tide of absolutist politics in various parts of the world, in which sexuality had become the focus of political mobilization by conservative forces. Sexual issues are no longer peripheral in global discourse but central to key concerns: from fundamentalism to the impact of AIDS, from relations between men and women to attitudes towards sexual diversity, and especially homosexuality. Sexual meanings and values are highly contested. But at the same time as conservative forces see sexual change as a sign of moral decay, in many parts of the world transformations of sexuality and intimacy have come to signal real gains. Take the issue that seemed marginal scarcely a decade ago: same-sex marriage. For moral conservatives in the USA this has become a touchstone issue that has to be addressed by any successful conservative leader, and Bush chose to use it ruthlessly to court his evangelical base. But in this at least Bush was addressing the *Zeitgeist*, if in a socially conservative fashion. Elsewhere, same-sex unions, whether legally the same as marriage or not, were becoming normalized. The British legislation to authorize civil partnerships while not called marriage was as near as damn it to it (apart from the name, the only difference seemed to be that marriage requires sexual consummation, while same-sex civil partnerships do not: an ironic commentary on the ways in which the lives of gay and lesbian people had long been defined by their sexuality, but apparently now were not). The new UK legislation received the support of a Conservative leader, Michael Howard, who barely fifteen years before, in another incarnation, had led the introduction of the notorious section 28, banning the promotion of homosexuality as a 'pretended family relationship'. What, if not family relationships, were being offered to same-sex couples, offering as civil partnerships did rights over pensions, benefits, tax and childcare, as well as responsibilities for mutual care and financial support?

In the first six months after the first civil partnerships in December 2005, over 6000 were contracted. Special companies, each with glossy websites, now offer a range of appropriate clothes, wedding gifts, venues, food, drink, celebration planning, honeymoon destinations, gifts, followed by etiquette books, personal advisers and the whole panoply of rites and rituals that accompany well-embedded social events such as traditional weddings, where the private commitment is offered a public apotheosis. What seemed unthinkable thirty years ago, impossible twenty years ago, improbable (at least in famously slow-moving Britain) ten years ago, is now up and running with only the rumblings of the evangelical religious and the occasional jokes about who does the dishes and wears the trousers to remind us of an earlier time when *heterosexual* marriage was the only access to sanctioned sexuality and respectability, and when homosexuals were 'the most evil men in Britain'.

Attitudes have surely changed in fundamental ways. We are living now, clearly, in a different world. But what sort of different world?

We are living, I am suggesting throughout this book, in a world of transition, in the midst of a long, convoluted, messy, unfinished but profound revolution that has transformed the possibilities of living our sexual diversity and creating intimate lives. Most of the time we do not even notice the changes that are made for us and that we make for ourselves in everyday life, except when an issue hurtles to the front of our consciousness, as the introduction of the contraceptive pill did in the 1960s, the eruption of Women's Liberation and Gay Liberation did in the 1970s, the cataclysm of HIV/AIDS did in the 1980s, apparently endemic sexual abuse and violence did in the 1990s, and same-sex marriage has in the early years of the new millennium. Even then, it is tempting to see each issue in isolation, losing the connections, missing the unfolding processes, forgetting the history. But it is only by having a handle on the links, the tendencies, the interconnections of past and present in our present history and our historic present that we can measure the gains and losses, the successes and failures, the possibilities and the intransigencies, the pleasures and dangers. A history of the present, which is what I offer in the following pages, allows us to question our current certainties and uncertainties, about who we are, what we know, how we should live, by bringing us face to face with our various, complicated, intertwined pasts. A sense of the past holds the present to account, denaturalizing and relativizing it, demonstrating that it is a historical creation, suggesting its contingency.

I want to offer a balance sheet of the changes that have transformed our ways of being sexual, intimate, familial, using my sense of history, my sociological preoccupations, my understanding of politics, and inevitably my personal sensibilities and values. I believe the long revolution to have been overwhelmingly beneficial to the vast majority of people in the West, and increasingly to people living in the global South whose lives are also being transformed dramatically – and I say that while acknowledging fully the major problems – inequalities of power and resources, prejudice, discrimination, racism, violence and ignorance that continue to limit life chances across the globe. For above all the long revolution has given rise to discourses of individual autonomy, rights and sexual justice that have set new standards for judging sexual wrongs, and can empower new forms of agency. Increasingly the ways we live now are part of a world we are making for ourselves, built on the creativity, inventiveness and mutual involvement of millions of people.

In the crisis years of the 1980s generated by the terrible toll of the HIV/AIDS crisis, and the threat it posed to so many lives, Susan Sontag (Sontag and Hodgkin 1991) wrote a story called 'The way we live now', which in turn echoed the title of a novel by Trollope. Sontag's story was about connections, about the links between people that propelled the spread of the HIV virus but also locked disparate people together in what could be seen as a dance of death but was also more hopefully a dance of life. For it is through complex links that we affirm our common humanity, make ourselves human. People of my generation, the baby boomers, have been perhaps the main beneficiaries of the changes in personal lives that I describe in the following pages. Perhaps we also bear the scars. For subsequent generations it may all seem so easy, so predestined, so obvious. But we have had to learn, often the hard way, not only about the delights of autonomy but also about the pains of moral choice, the necessity of reciprocity, and the importance of the connections we weave: between our various selves, across the various forms of difference, across the global links and the local loyalties, and between rights and obligations, needs and desires, risks and opportunities, justice and continuing forms of injustice. 'Connected lives': that is what I really want to talk about in the world we live in now. Connected lives, I shall argue, are reflexive lives; that is, lives lived in growing self-consciousness of who we are, where we come from, and what we can become. The sexual and intimate revolutions of our time are largely the result of grass-roots transformations – literally the world *we* have made together. For connected lives are also lives lived reciprocally, with Others who shape what we are in the ties that not only bind but bond, and make us human. Connected lives are lives that link the global and the local, bridging distances and linking questions of sexuality and intimacy to issues of rights and responsibilities, to social justice.

In this world of connections I want to show how and why things have changed largely for the better, but I want to do this without falling into the traps that other writers on these themes have fallen into.

Trap number one is to believe in the transformation as automatic or inevitable, a journey from the darkness of sexual repression into sexual freedom, a sort of Whig interpretation of sexual history. I have been accused of this myself in previous writings (see Waters 1999, Houlbrook 2005), and if the argument is that there has been progress in the ways we deal with questions of pleasure, desire, diversity and choice then I can only plead guilty as charged. Who in their right senses would not prefer living today than fifty years ago? Despite the horrors that afflict so many parts of the world, from endemic war and ethnic cleansing (and the frequent association with them of sexual degradation and rape) to poverty, disease and transnational trade in human beings, there have been enormous strides in the toleration of difference, the different ways of being human, and in the recognition of human rights in general and sexual rights in particular. But to say that does not mean I believe change to be either automatic or inevitable. There are too many people who have given their all to the cause of human – including sexual and intimate – freedom to believe that the paths were easy to follow or the struggles cost-free.

Nor do I believe in the possibility of an unproblematic sexual libera-tion. As Michel Foucault (1979) pointed out more than a generation ago now, you cannot 'liberate' sexuality as if you were taking the lid off a cauldron. Sexuality is not a property that can be repressed or released, but a historically shaped series of possibilities, actions, behaviours, desires, risks, identities, norms and values that can be reconfigured and recombined but cannot be simply unleashed (see my arguments in Weeks 2003). The changes that have taken place have embraced all the elements that go to make up the sexual, from erotic practices to the reorganization of sexualized space, from the interactions of everyday life to religion, ethics and laws. But this is a qualitative shift in human relations, not a quantitative outpouring of more sex.

Finally, I am not assuming that the very idea of 'progress' is without its problems. How should we measure, say, the withdrawal of the state from the regulation of homosexuality, or the acceptance and promotion of birth control, or the outlawing of rape in marriage, or the recognition of widespread abuse of children (all of which has happened within the time frame of this book), against the commercial exploitation of children and women's bodies, the sleaziness of many parts of great metropolitan cities across the globe, the torrents of pornography on the internet, and what Bauman (2003, 2005) sees as the commodification of the erotic and the increasing fragility of human bonds? My own version will, I hope, become transparent in the coming pages. All I can say now is that I would not necessarily want to associate my views with all *soit disant* pro-gressives today, let alone the many dubious users of that term in the past. We have to weigh in the balance the gains and losses. Equally we need to understand what we mean by gains and losses. In the end that involves value judgements that we cannot avoid.

But whatever traps would be progressives may fall into they are as nothing compared with the next insidious trap. Trap number two is to see everything as a decline from a state of grace. Its characteristic tone is to lament the awful state of the present – the broken families, the high rate of divorce, the violence of young people, the incidence of mind-less sexual promiscuity, the commercialization of love, the incidence of homosexuality, the explicitness of sex education and the media, the decline of values, the collapse of social capital, the rise of sexual diseases – and to compare that with some golden age of faith, stability and family values (see, among others, Himmelfarb 1995; Phillips 1999; Davies 2006). Alas, it is highly unlikely that the past – whichever past it was – was ever quite that golden, and it is certain that the present can never be quite that awful. This is perhaps the mirror image of a mindless progressivism. If the progressive mindset assumes that sex in itself is a positive force for good, the socially conservative or declinist view assumes that it – or one of its variants, usually homosexuality – is not so much bad as dangerous unless framed in specific contexts – usually heterosexual marriage.

Characteristically, though not invariably, the declinist view is framed by a religious world outlook, whether Christian, Jewish or Islamic. It is a perspective that has had a powerful political impact in key parts of the world – from the United States to Iran – with major influence in many other cultures. In the West generally, I would hazard, it is a minority perspective; on a global scale it may well be on the rise. If, as I have argued elsewhere, we live in an age of great moral and cultural uncertainty (Weeks 1995), then a fundamentalist affirmation of the truth of the gendered body, heterosexual sex, the horrors of perversity and the sanctity of faith can seem an appealing antidote. That does not make it right or valid.

Trap number three is to believe that despite all the huffing and puffing nothing has really changed. There is a surprising head of steam behind this position, though from different starting points. There is, for example, a feminist subset of this position, which acknowledges superficial changes – a greater emphasis, for example, on the importance of female sexual autonomy, greater access to effective birth control, perhaps – but stresses the continuities, especially in terms of the relations of power. There may be equal pay legislation, but women on average still earn only about two-thirds of men. Women may be able to flaunt their sexual desires, but it is still for the sake of the male gaze. Men may now be willing to change a baby's napkins/diapers, but mothers still have prime responsibility for child care. Rape may now be better recognized as a crime against women, but sexual violence is widespread (see discussion in Holland *et al.* 2003). The arguments are familiar. Some might see them as part of the unfinished achievements of the long revolution. Others see them as reflecting the fundamental inequalities that persist between men and women.

A 'queer' subset of the trap again recognizes that there have been great changes in attitudes towards homosexuality and sexual diversity. Certainly Western societies have seen a cultural revolution, with affirmative LGBTQ (lesbian, gay, bisexual, transgendered, queer/querying) identities everywhere, carrying massive cultural weight, with gays in the vanguard of the new creative classes. But how much has really changed? Isn't a gay identity little more than a pseudo-ethnic identity that is easily accommodated by late capitalist societies, easily succumbing to the pink dollar or pound or euro? Isn't same-sex marriage simply an assimilation into heteronormative structures (see e.g. Warner 1993, 1999)?

Then there's a political economy subset of this trap. It takes elements of the previous two. It acknowledges the continuing exploitation of women on a global scale, economic as well as sexual. The structural readjustment policies of the World Bank trap millions in poverty that inhibits the development of sexual freedoms and intimate life. It recognizes the power of individualizing tendencies, but sees them as accommodating to the necessities of the latest phase of capitalist expansion. Indeed, the legal reforms and institutional achievements of LGBTQ people that many of us have welcomed as the signs of greater toleration (and the result of hard work) are seen as little more than the latest ruse of power, fully complicit with the strategic need of neo-liberalism (see e.g. the argument in Richardson (2004), and discussion below in Chapters 5 and 8).

I cannot deny that there are elements in all these positions which are at least plausible, and some of them I have absorbed into my own analysis. None, however, convince me fully. The progressive myth all too readily forgets the contingencies of history, the tangled roads that have brought us to the present. The declinist myth celebrates a history that never was, a world that was not so much lost as nostalgically reimagined to act as a counterpoint to the present. The continuists want to stress the recalcitrance of hidden structures, but in doing so forget the power of agency and of the macroscopic impact of subtle changes in individual lives that makes up the unfinished revolutions of our time.

Above all, in various ways they occlude what seems to me to be the inevitable reality: that the world we have won has made possible ways of life that represent an advance not a decline in human relationships, and that have broken through the coils of power to enhance individual autonomy, freedom of choice and more egalitarian patterns of relationships.

The unfinished revolutions

Before going any further let me try to offer some of the headlines of these changes that have remade the world of sexuality and intimacy, and which are discussed in greater detail as the book progresses. I offer, almost at random, the following.

The 'gender revolution'

This, the transformation of relationships between men and women, is surely the most powerful story of all. Millennia of male dominance over women have been fundamentally and almost certainly irreversibly undermined, even as on a global scale the impact is still uneven. The story is not so much that men and women are now equal, or treated equally. In many parts of the world that is manifestly not the case. The real achievement is that inequality has lost all its moral justification, and this has profoundly shifted the debate. Inequality now has to be justified in ways it never had to be before. The starting point has to be the full human equality of men and women, and from this flows all the other forms of equality. There may be genuine differences about what constitutes equality. Are women, for example, equal but different, as a variety of voices from some feminisms to evolutionary psychologists might argue? The content of equality may also be contested. For example, could the veil covering Muslim women be seen as a sign of patriarchal power, of religious marginalization, or of the empowerment of women, freed from the tyranny of the male gaze? But the fact that traditional differences now have to be rewritten in terms of equality is a measure of how far things have come (if also, at times, an index of how far there is still to go).

But there is more. The category of gender itself has been fundamentally challenged by the emergence of movements of transgendered
people to query the absoluteness of gender (Ekins and King 2006). That
there is a paradox in the whole experience – in seeking a real gender the
fixity of gender as a category must be fundamentally undermined – is
simply a powerful trope for the problematization of the traditional truths
about men and women in the contemporary world.

A 'transformation of intimacy'

The argument here is that the gender revolution underpins and is in turn
accelerated by a profound change in the ways in which men and women,
men and men, and women and women relate to each other (see Giddens
(1992) for a classical statement of this argument). Same-sex relationships
are seen as especially important to this transformation, as leading the
way to more egalitarian forms of relationships and creative life experiments, as much by force of circumstances as design (see discussion in
Weeks *et al*. 2001). The transformation is towards egalitarian, open
and disclosive relationships, marked by the 'pure relationship'. Again,
there are many critics of this position (see Jamieson 1998, 1999), and
I will explore the debates in later chapters. But the essence may be
summed up in the term 'democratization'. We are talking here about the
democratization of intimate life, a revolution in everyday life, which has
yet unrealized and unsettling implications for the relationship between
private passions and public life.

The pluralization of families

The 'crisis in the family' has become a totem for the radical shifts in
personal life. The apparent decline of the traditional family is frequently
seen as the marker, cause and consequence, of changes in sexual relationships, childbearing, the decline of marriage and so on. Its decay is
blamed for the weakening of social capital, those norms, values, networks
that are held to sustain social trust and stability (Fukuyama 1999). Yet
there is another, and to this writer a more plausible, story: of diversi-
fication of family forms caused by a weakening of patriarchal authority
over women and children, the emergence of a more complex and diverse
culture as a result of mass immigration, and the sheer pluralization
of household patterns and domestic arrangements: cohabitation and
the decline of (heterosexual) marriage, single parenthood, the growth of
people living on their own (approaching 40 per cent in the UK), the
emergence of serial monogamy as the dominant form of sexual partnering, the rise of non-heterosexual (and of heterosexual) 'families of choice',
the rise of the 'friendship ethic' (Lewis 2001, Weeks *et al*. 2001). All
these justify the claim that we should talk about families rather than
the family, that we should recognize and appreciate the varied ways of

doing family-like things, and that we need to celebrate the emergence of new and diverse forms of reciprocity – and of social capital – rather than lament the decline of the family.

The broadening of reproductive rights

There are many factors underlying the transformations of everyday life, but a key one is the dramatic changes in relationship to birth control. There was birth control before the Pill, and dramatic falls in the birth rate before the 1970s. Already by the 1950s we can see significant shifts in women's relationship to their bodies and fertility. But the Pill, as a female controlled and relatively reliable contraceptive, both helped to realize and symbolized a massive shift, a world-historic shift indeed: the separation of sex and reproduction (McLaren 1999, ch. 4; Cook 2005a). But as time has moved on it has become clear that the issue of reproductive rights has wider resonances: the right to have children as well as not, the right to terminate pregnancies in defined situations as well as to go ahead with them, the right to control fertility and to enhance it, and also fundamental questions of access to resources, of power and opportunity, on a global scale (Petchesky 2003).

The coming out of homosexuality

As the heterosexual nexus linking the gender order, family and sexual reproduction has crumbled, so homosexuality has come out of the shadows. Homosexuality always necessarily exists in symbiotic relationship, frequently as the threatening Other, with heterosexuality. The sharp binary schism between the two that has structured, defined and distorted our sexual régime for the past couple of centuries, and perhaps reached a peak with the final determined reassertion of what has been described as a 'heterosexual dictatorship' in the 1950s, is now profoundly undermined as millions of gays and lesbians, bisexuals and transgendered people have not so much subverted the established order as lived as if their sexual difference did not, in the end, matter (Adam et al. 1999a, 1999b; Altman 2001). Never underestimate the importance of being ordinary. Of course, it is simultaneously possible to acknowledge the transformed possibilities of living a non-heterosexual life, at least in most parts of the urban highly developed world, while recognizing the profound continuing weight of heteronormative values and structures. Nor is there yet agreement, as I have already suggested, about the ultimate implications of such innovations as same-sex marriage or civil partnerships. Can we see here the final stages in the domestication of homosexuality? Is this the ultimate incorporation of potentially transgressive and transformative eros into the dull rituals of heteronormative culture (Brandzel 2005)? Or if the closet is a product of the tyranny of binary thinking, then is its demise really a signal of powerful gusts of change that have transformed the meanings of sexuality – or have opened up the acknowledgement of the existence of a wide range of *sexualities* (Seidman 2002)?

The recognition of sexual diversity

Gayle Rubin (1984) famously spoke of the advance of the perverse sexualities out of the pages of Krafft-Ebing on to the stage of history. Today the very category of the perverse has all but disappeared. People proudly proclaim not only their gayness, bisexuality, sado-masochisms, transidentities, fetishisms and fantasies in all their infinite variety; they can satisfy them through the infinite possibilities of the world wide web. If your thing is eating someone alive then you can surely find other interested parties on the web. But so can you find the possibilities of more vanilla and caring interactions – no longer simply love on the dole or in a cold climate but love in virtual space. We dwell in a world of polymorphous non-perversities. But this is only a part of the radical diversity that characterizes contemporary life. There are different ways of life, shaped by 'race' and ethnicity, class and geography, age (dis)ability and so on. There are also, as Gilroy (2004) has argued, new forms of 'conviviality' which defy such simple categorizations and may be said to represent the fraying of difference if not yet the disappearence of divisions.

An explosion of sexual discourses, a proliferation of sexual stories

As this suggests, we can now tell our sexual stories in a huge variety of different ways. Michel Foucault (1979) wrote of the discursive explosion since the eighteenth century which produced sexual modernity. But that was defined by rules on who could speak, in what circumstances and on whose authority. The difference today is the democratization of sexual narratives. Now we can hear everyone who wants to speak, and can access means of speaking, speak their truths – from talk shows to home movies, from parliaments to the media, from the streets to personal blogs on the web. Through stories – of desire and love, of hope and mundane reality, of excitement and disappointment – told to willing listeners in communities of meaning, people imagine and reimagine who and what they are, what they want to become (Plummer 1995, 2003). Of course, all this does not mean that anything goes. It is noticeable that as some barriers to speaking are removed or redefined new ones are erected. Paedophilia began to speak its name in the 1970s, but has been redefined as child abuse and trebly execrated in the 2000s. Pornography was seen as a mark of liberation in the 1960s, as a major focus of women's oppression in the 1980s, as pretty much mainstream in the 1990s, and as a source of anxiety on the web in the 2000s. What is happening is that different voices are now speaking their truths in ever proliferating outlets, but there are no longer any universally accepted authorities who tell us what to say, when to say it, what to believe, what to be. Instead there are many would-be authorities competing cacophonously, especially in the anarchic democracy of cyber-space. By no means all of these voices are progressive by any definition of the word – there are evangelical Christian or radical Islamicist voices as loud as any liberal or libertarian voices. There are threats as well as opportunities in the hypermarket of speech. But we can no longer doubt the power of narratives. Through polyvocal story-telling we are remaking ourselves and reinventing the meanings of intimacy (Plummer 2003).

The recognition of sexual violence and abuse

The greater freedom to speak about what was for long covered in the ambiguous decencies of private life has led to a wider recognition of the risks attached to sexuality and intimate life. The silenced abuses of the intimate sphere, violent relationships, exploitation, wife battering, sexual and physical abuses of children (O'Connell Davidson 2005); and the public abuses, of rape, sexual harassment, intimidation, endemic fear (Bamforth 2005), have been opened up to view, to possible redress, but above all to public discourse, working from new benchmarks. It goes without saying that this is not enough, nor has it cured the disease. On the contrary, it is probable that there are perils to visibility. Queer bashing is a product of an out society. Date rape is a product of a knowing society – a society that is familiar with drugs and their effect on unsuspecting victims. Publicity about rape has encouraged more reporting of it but has not necessarily reduced its incidence. Violence remains wedded to the erotic like a dark shadow.

The expansion of sexual/intimate citizenship

Citizenship is about belonging, about being recognized, about reciprocal entitlements and responsibilities. Historically, it has been restricted – racially, xenophobically, by gender and by sexuality. We forget how recent has been the achievement of full citizenship rights for women, to what extent our prized welfare states have been built on assumptions about the right way to live, and the ways in which minorities and deviants have been excluded from the rights and obligations of full citizenship. Sexual or intimate citizenship is about the recognition of these exclusions and about moves to inclusion (Weeks 1998; Bell and Binnie 2000; Richardson 2000a, 2000b; Plummer 2003). The steps in the process have been erratic – giving access to resources for family planning, for removal of penal laws against sexual diversity, for equality before the law for homosexuals, for recognition of alternative ways of life, for enshrining that recognition in statute, for equal protection from risks, in health, in violence, in defamation – and in many jurisdictions, including the most wealthy and most powerful, not yet fully realized. Yet without the idea of full citizenship we cannot measure how far we have come; and without the ideal of equal citizenship we have no measure of how far we still have to go.

These are remarkable and unprecedented achievements. They are not the result of inexorable forces beyond our control, of the ruses of history working behind our backs. They are the results of myriad struggles, individual and collective, willed and unplanned, of many decisions made or not made, over a complex history. But in history, for every two steps forward there may be as many backward. In any measure of what has changed we need to mark the down sides. Here are some more headlines.

The instransigence of gendered differences

We may recognize the transformations in the position of women, but alongside these we must also place the resistances, both internal and external. What Connell has described as the gender order (Connell 1987, 1995, 2002) has been shaken, even destabilized, but its shape still looms before us. On all the markers – of education, employment opportunities, family roles, reproductive and sexual choice – there may have been major shifts, but their impact has been uneven. Caring remains a female concept even as some men have made substantial steps towards equal involvement in parental activities. Even the most self-confident women still hear the 'male in the head' (Holland et al. 1998) calling them back to sexual subordination. Even the most enlightened men find it difficult to cast off their privileges. We remain locked in relationships of superiority and subordination at various levels. Violence and abuse still police the boundaries. Power continues to ensnare our passions.

The continued institutionalization of heterosexuality

We now know that heterosexual is not only a preference; it is an institution, so embedded in the ways we think and act that it is almost invisible, unless you try to escape it. Homosexuality may have come out into the open, it may have made institutionalized heterosexuality porous, but even in the advanced cultures of the West it is still subjected to the minoritizing forces that excluded it in the first place. It remains the Other, even if its Otherness now for many has a warm and friendly face (Altman 2001; Weeks et al. 2001). In other parts of the world social obloquy, long imprisonment, even death (by stoning or beheading) remain the fate of many homosexual people (Bamforth 2005). For far too many that face of Otherness remains shrouded in mystery and fear, and the result is a terror that makes homosexuality as a way of life impossible.

The fear of difference, and the continued circulation of power around race and ethnicity, class, age

The continued reproduction of institutionalized heterosexuality, and the perpetuation of heteronormative values, remains a powerful constraint on sexual and intimate change, but those constraints in turn are locked into other hierarchical patterns that intersect with and shape our many sexual cultures. Sexual cultures are products of, and construct and constrain, many forms of difference, forms which are not neutral but are shaped by the various forms of power relationships that make up our late modernity. Sexual patterns are moulded by the intricacies of race and ethnicity, wealth and poverty, youth and age, mental and physical space (see contributions to Weeks *et al.* 2003). As these remain markers of division and exclusion, so sexuality and intimacy are scarred by their inequalities.

The commercialization of the erotic

Inevitably, as sexuality has emerged as a major focus of meaning and identity in the modern world, so it has become ever more entwined in the hyper-commercialization of the culture. The products are all around us, from the tawdry exploitation of the erotic to advertise and sell goods and services to the areas of every major city that survive on the sex industries to the global flows of the sex trades. Idealists in the 1960s hoped that a liberated sexuality would offer a form of resistance to global markets. Others pessimistically anticipated that advanced capitalism needed the controlled desublimation of sexuality to sell its products. The reality is a little more mundane. As global capitalism entered a new and astonishing phase of expansion from the 1980s, so it readily drew within its tentacles the newly visible worlds of sexuality, happily colonized them and transported their products universally. The erotic is inextricably entwined with market capitalism in all its forms (Hennessy 2000; Binnie 2004). At its most extreme we can see the vast expansion of the multi-billion-dollar flows of pornography, now complemented by the vast credit card culture of the internet. The triumph of world capitalism does not mean that every act of sex or love or intimacy is inevitably tainted by commercialization. But it does mean that the sexual and the intimate are never free from the threats as well as the opportunities provided by its giant presence.

The threat of sexual disease

If we can see the globalization of sexuality as a reordering of risk, then at the heart of the risks facing the world today is the inexorable presence and spread of the HIV/AIDS pandemic (Altman 2001). Twenty years ago it was possible to write about it largely as an appalling threat to the gay populations of North America, Europe and Australasia. The response to that was tardy enough, and deeply illustrative of the bigotry and prejudice that lay at the heart of public policy-making, the media and large parts of public opinion (especially in the USA and Britain). Today the wealthy countries have found ways of controlling the spread of the epidemic and of managing the progression of the virus. But globally the statistics, and behind them the realities of everyday life, are terrifying. Here sexuality has become intwined in the nexus of poverty, ignorance, fear and prejudice on a massive scale. The pandemic reveals as nothing else the impossibility of separating the sexual and the intimate from other social forces, and the inevitable flows, in an increasingly globalized world, of sexual experiences and tragedies from nation to nation, continent to continent. AIDS has become the symbol, if not the only example, of the risks of rapid sexual change in a world uncertain of its values and responses.

The rise of fundamentalisms, and the reality of culture wars

Fundamentalisms may be seen as a response to uncertainty, confronting the ambiguities and ambivalences of the world with an absolute certainty about truth, history and tradition (Ruthven 2004). As many have pointed out the various forms of fundamentalism, whether Islamic, Christian, Hindu or Jewish, are not really cultural throwbacks. They are very much products of late modernity, utilizing its technologies and global linkages brilliantly (Bhatt 1997). But they are against what they see as the deformations of late modern cultures, and at the heart of these are sexuality, gender and the body. The fundamentalisms of our time seek to restore demarcations between men and women, reaffirm heterosexual relationships and extirpate perversity. In the most extreme manifestations they enforce their will through the bullet, the knife and the hangman's noose. But though the tone and the tenor might be different, the religious and socially conservative movements of the USA, in their affirmation of traditional values and opposition to abortion, homosexuality, same-sex marriage, sex education, evolutionism and the like share some common assumptions with them: a belief that there is a truth to sexuality which they know the key to. Culture wars are the inevitable result.

As time goes by

These manifestations of gains and losses, achievements and failures that constitute our complex and mobile present are products of histories and tendencies that have deep roots. We will need to explore explanations in terms of the breakdown of tradition, secularization, individualization, globalization, the changing role of the state and the like. But our present has to be understood not only as the effect of large-scale shifts but also in terms of the contingencies of history, the accidents, the local circumstances, the unexpected events that modulate the configurations offered by the past. If we look back over the past sixty years, decade by decade, it is often difficult to see the patterns and shapes and narrative line that we like to construct to make sense of the apparent chaos of events. Each decade seems to be represented by a different motif. They are moments in a complex history. So before going forward from my starting point, 1945, I want to move back, through the seven decades of my story, to retrace our steps, taking the mid-point of each decade as my own point of orientation.

2005

This was the year – in December – when the Civil Partnership Act came into force. I have mentioned it several times already, and will examine its implications in more detail in Chapter 7. I want here, however, to see it as symbolic of other changes. It certainly represented a new benchmark for the acceptance of homosexuality. Although not formally marriage, and to that extent representing what some of its critics saw as an apartheid-type solution to the ancient problem of what to do about homosexuality – 'separate but equal' – it was undoubtedly immediately interpreted by the wider culture as identical with conventional marriage – and that tells us something about the changing meanings of marriage. Marriage had long ceased to be what it definitely was in 1945; the only gateway to status, respectable adult sexuality and parenthood. Progressively between the 1960s and 2000s the automatic unity between sexual activity and reproduction, between sex and marriage, and between marriage and parenting, had been severed. Marriage had become, for the majority of the population, a matter of choice, carrying rights and responsibilities certainly, but entered into voluntarily as and when the individuals decided largely as a sign of commitment. But until 2005 it still anchored a relationship between a man and a woman. After 2005, whatever the limitations of the Civil Partnership Act, and however long it takes to merge civil partnerships and traditional marriage, the automatic link between marriage and heterosexuality was also severed. This is a profoundly symbolic rupture. It is perhaps the most dramatic illustration of this new world we have made.

This 'de-heterosexualizing' of marriage, partial and limited as it may yet be across the world (and contentious as it especially is in the USA), represents a shift in the value systems of Western societies, the triumph not so much of a 'new class' as of a particular generation, the generation of 1945.

1995

In 1995 the American conservative writer and activist George Gilder, who was certainly not in favour of same-sex marriage, wrote:

> Bohemian values have come to prevail over bourgeois virtue in
> sexual morals and family roles, arts and letters, bureaucracies

and universities, popular culture and public life. As a result, culture and family life are widely in chaos, cities seethe with venereal plagues, schools and colleges fall to obscurantism and propaganda, the courts are a carnival of pettifoggery.

(quoted in Brooks 2000: 196)

Here is the authentic voice of moral conservatism seeing the triumph of liberalism in all he surveys, and he likes it not. In the mid-point of the 1990s, in a pre-millennial angst, conservative forces were mounting what they certainly intended should not be a last stand (and in the USA was an augury of a new wave of conservative energy in the 'culture wars' against sexual liberalism).

David Brooks, the author of *Bobos in Paradise: The New Upper Class and How They Got There*, writing at the end of the decade, is inclined to agree that what he describes as the 'bourgeois bohemians' – the creation, largely, of the generation of 1945, and liberal going on libertarian in their personal lifestyles – have indeed established a new hegemony, though he sees it in terms of a new synthesis, possibly leading to the ending of the culture wars. That now seems grossly optimistic. What I would stress, however, is less the triumph of liberalism as its apparent fragility in the middle of this decade. This was also the decade which in the USA saw the rushing into law of the Defense of Marriage Act, designed to block out any possibility of same-sex marriage. President Clinton faced inpeachment for unsavoury but undoubtedly consensual and private sexual relations with 'that woman, Ms Lewinsky'. And within a very few years a new president, largely brought to power by the cohesive backing of the religious Right, proved himself an ardent supporter of social conservatism, with the culture wars revving up again.

Britain, far from seeing the triumph of bohemian values, went through one of its fits of moral anxiety. The launch by the Prime Minister, John Major, of a 'back to basics' campaign seemed to presage a new tilt towards moral conservatism (Holden 2004: 267–309). In fact, it proved a disaster for him. Despite moves in a conservative direction on several fronts – efforts to achieve an equal age of consent for homosexuals were blocked largely by the Conservative Party in Parliament in 1994, while in the run-up to the 1997 general election various ministers renewed rhetorical attacks on one-parent families and on women who had children to get social housing and benefits – in practise the seriousness of the Conservative government was catastrophically undermined by the long string of minor sexual scandals among its ministers and MPs, not to say the tragicomic collapse of royal marriages, especially that of Charles and Diana. Nothing better illustrated the growing gap between moral posture and shifting realities.

1985

The late 1990s saw the widespread introduction of combination therapies for people living with HIV/AIDS, which revolutionized the possibilities of surviving the epidemic. Barely a decade earlier, however, we were in the belly of the beast. The HIV/AIDS crisis dominated the 1980s, and in retrospect, though eventually contained in the richer world, its impact globally has been as devastating as pessimists forecast. By the end of 2005 there were forty million cases across the globe; twenty-five million had died. In the 1980s the main impact was on the communities first exposed to the virus, especially the gay community. AIDS was to become the epidemic of the poor, the marginalized and the vulnerable. When it first appeared, however, at the start of the 1980s, it was widely seen as the disease of the already diseased, the result of sexual excess, the symbol of a sexual revolution that had gone too far. The confident gains of the 1970s for lesbian and gay visibility, space and rights, suffered a shuddering setback as those who seemed most vulnerable to the HIV virus were blamed for its appearance (see Weeks 2000: 142–62). Because it first manifested itself as an apparently gay epidemic, it suffered less than benign neglect from those in power. In the USA, the then epicentre of the epidemic, the administration presided over by President Reagan sat on its hands, until glamorous stars, such as Rock Hudson, fell victim to the epidemic, and the Surgeon-General issued dire warnings of the threat posed by it. In Britain, the Thatcher government did little more.

There was virtually no UK government response until 1984, when it intervened to protect the blood supply. Between 1984 and 1985 there were fifty-nine parliamentary questions on AIDS. Half of these were on the blood supply, followed by drugs. A minority related to the threat to the gay community, which housed the vast majority of the cases. Clearly, the unpopularity of homosexuality rather than health needs was dictating policy. The media panic about AIDS, largely fed by homophobia, far from galvanizing government, had terrorized it. Not until the end of 1986 was there any concerted governmental response. This ushered in a period of what has been described as 'wartime emergency' and the next few years did see a massive mobilization of public health interventions that largely controlled the epidemic (Berridge 1996). But despite its leading role in both being the focus of the epidemic and the main body agitating for more effective intervention, the gay community remained largely marginalized until the early 1990s. Opinion surveys showed a growing unpopularity of lesbians and gays throughout the decade. In 1983, 62 per cent censured homosexual relationships; in 1985, 69 per cent did so; and in 1987, the number was 74 per cent (Weeks 2000: 171). The period 1987 to 1988, indeed, saw the most significant attack on the lesbian and gay community for almost a hundred years, with the passing into law of what became known as 'section 28', banning the promotion of homosexuality by local authorities, and introducing a neologism, 'pretended family relationships', that was to echo through the next decade as a warning to the gay community: 'thus far and no further'. The Bishop of St Albans suggested that the Church of England could gain popularity 'by taking a firmer line' against homosexuality. The Chief Rabbi saw the pendulum beginning to swing back towards traditional values, and 'we ought to welcome and facilitate this' (Weeks 1989: 300).

And yet, under the surface of events, there were signs of decisive change. For perhaps the most dramatic result of the health crisis was the evidence of gay self-mobilization. The emergence of a large-scale, grass-roots adoption of 'safer sex' techniques throughout the 1980s led the way to effective prevention campaigns. The development of 'treatment activism' underlined that those most affected by the epidemic were prepared to intervene on a large scale not only in defining the issues but also in trying to find solutions. In medicine, research, campaigning, fund-raising, policy-making, caring, we can see that legitimization through disaster that Dennis Altman (1989) has described, a major portent for the future, and perhaps the greatest legacy of the emergence of gay liberation in the 1970s. Yet more significant still, people were, step by step, becoming more tolerant. The 1988 Gallup Poll while reporting that 60 per cent of those polled were not accepting of a gay lifestyle, also found that of those under 25, 50 per cent were accepting (Weeks 2000: 171). This was to be immensely significant for future trends.

1975

The 1970s may be best characterized as a decade of growing polarization. The decade opened with the immense burst of energy produced by the emergence of second-wave feminism and the gay liberation movement. Although separate in their histories, ultimate aims and trajectories, both may be seen as eruptions of new forms of activism around sexual issues which not so much changed laws or structures (though certainly in the long term that was the result) as values, attitudes and identities. Although the roots of both movements may be found in the 1950s and 1960s and earlier, and their specific politics, language and forms had been shaped by the experiences of the second half of the 1960s (the civil rights movement, student mobilization, anti-war campaigns, the counter-culture, the amorphous libertarian sexual politics of the baby boom generation), their impact in the early 1970s was dramatic because they shifted irreversibly the terms of the debates (Weeks 1989: 273–88). Here were subjugated knowledges bursting into speech. Here were new claims to personal autonomy and sexual freedoms. Here were bodies and pleasures entering into political discourse. And here were new forms of politics disrupting the exhausted forms of post-war social democracy. Above all, as a library of testimonies underlines, there were the transformations of thousands, perhaps millions of individual lives. The language of feminism may have faded in subsequent years, but every woman today lives under the spell cast by the women's liberation movement of the early 1970s. Similarly, it is impossible to think of ways of being non-heterosexual today which cannot trace their roots back to the emergence of gay liberation after 1969.

But already by the mid-1970s it was clear that the new social movements around sexuality were in turn shifting the elements of moral conservatism. In both the USA and Britain new forms of conservatism, broadly described as the New Right, were marrying a more dynamic economic individualism to various forms of social conservatism (Weeks 1985: 33–44). And many of the changes supported by feminists – such as access to abortion – became the subject of counter-mobilization, especially in the USA where abortion particularly became a touchstone issue. It is important not to exaggerate the impact of the general move to the Right on moral issues. In Britain the religious Right remained marginal to mainstream political discourse, and the Thatcher government was more concerned with economic restructuring than with moral reform (see Chapter 4). Her evocation of Victorian values was as ineffective as her successor John Major's later *démarche* on 'back to basics'. On many issues progressive reforms continued. Access to birth control was made free on the National Health Service and throughout the next fifteen years the indices of social change continued to move against traditional values. But what became really clear in the 1970s was that sexuality had become a focus of political as well as moral debate as never before. The culture wars began to accelerate in this decade. What above all became clear was that there was no longer an agreed moral framework within which dialogue could be conducted.

1965

So did it all begin in the 1960s? For the past four decades the 1960s have been hailed or condemned for their excesses, the fount and origin of the sexual revolution. For moral conservatives this was the decade in which a cultural revolution fatally undermined core values of family, marriage and sexual faithfulness. Already by the early years of the decade Professor Carstairs in his 1962 Reith Lectures was suggesting that 'Popular morality is now a waste land . . . The confusion is perhaps greatest over sexual morality' (quoted in Weeks 1989: 261). His suggestion, however, that charity might be more important than chastity, still managed to cause uproar, which suggested that traditional values had not yet abandoned their pulpits. The interesting point is that both progressives and traditionalists saw sexuality as the main battleground, the 'area in which the biggest breakdown in moral standards has occurred' according to Ernest Whitehouse, the husband of the supreme moral entrepreneur of the period, Mary Whitehouse (quoted in Weeks 1989: 279). And certainly there were dramatic changes in the 1960s. The eruption of highly sexualized popular music and culture symbolized this above all. The Pill became famously the new technological fix and liberating force for women. A recent historian, Hera Cook (2005a, 2005b), echoing contemporary assessments, has no doubt that this was the prime factor in the sexual revolution that followed. The decade also saw the greatest swathe of legislative reforms for a hundred years, with the partial decriminalization of abortion and male homosexuality, the easing of divorce laws, the abolition of theatre censorship and relaxation of the obscenity laws.

Yet these were not really effective until the latter part of the decade, or well into the next. For most of the decade, for most people, the revolution was going on elsewhere. It was not until 1965 that single women could obtain legitimate access to effective contraceptives. Male homosexuality remained illegal until 1967, and the number of prosecutions tripled after reform. A report on the age of majority in 1967 found that social attitudes differed little between adolescents and their parents (Weeks 1989: 253; see also Chapter 3, this volume). By the markers of later decades, indices of lax moral behaviour, such as numbers of partners, venereal disease, illegitimacy, breakdowns of marriages, remained surprisingly low, despite the growing moral panics they evoked. The harbingers of dramatic change were there. Only from the late 1960s did they really blaze. For most people this remained a revolution deferred.

1955

Ten years earlier and we are in the mid-1950s. For many ever since this has remained a byword for marital stability and domestic tranquility. Yet in many ways the patina of calm obscured painful stirrings. While family life seemed harmonious, anxious tensions lay barely beneath the surface. Two American movies of the year illustrate vividly the terrors that marched alongside the harmonious ideals of family life, in Britain as much as in the USA. In *Marty*, 'the love story of an unsung hero', Ernest Borgnine played an ordinary bloke, an unmarried butcher living with his mother, who spent his evenings cruising singles bars with his best friend Angie. But when he met and began courting Clara (played by Betsy Blair), Angie became bitterly jealous, while his mother developed nightmares about abandonment. Marty's struggle with his loneliness and needs, and his eventual pursuit of Clara, becomes a metaphor for the barely concealed neuroses of the period, and the individual struggle for happiness. The second film has become even more iconic: Nicholas Ray's *Rebel without a Cause*, starring James Dean. Dean's Jim Stark, yelling 'you're tearing me apart' at his rowing parents, became the voice of a generation who sought and failed to find guidance from elders as confused and unhappy as themselves. The search for kicks by Jim and his similarly alienated friends Plato (Sol Mineo) and Judy (Natalie Wood), and their attempts to find an alternative family in themselves, vividly illustrates the failure of the domestic ideals of the period, and the growing search for alternatives to isolation and alienation (Schneider 2005: 316, 320).

Britain was soon to experience its own outbursts of alienated 'anger', though the playwrights and novelists who earned this description were notably misogynist and homophobic (Sinfield 1989: 60–85; Sandbrook 2005). Homosexuality, or rather the fear of homosexuality, ran like a thread through the decade, belying the apparent apotheosis of marital morality in this decade. Anxieties about prostitution and homosexuality on the streets of the capital in the run-up to London's climactic burst of (fading) imperial glory, the Coronation in 1953, had created a climate of sexual scandal. The Montagu–Wildeblood trial became a symbolic focus, that in the short term re-evoked a characteristically British mixture of sex, class and hypocrisy, but in the medium term contributed to the setting up of the Wolfenden Committee to investigate prostitution and homosexuality (see Chapter 3). In 1955 this was sitting, and for the first time taking evidence from a small number of openly homosexual people. But reform of the law, which made all forms of male homosexuality illegal, was still more than a decade off, and Wilde's 'monstrous martyrdoms' were to continue for a while yet.

Terror lurked beneath the stability of family life in America and Britain. The first stirrings of fear about the baby boom generation were manifested in panics about latchkey children, rock 'n' roll, horror comics, identity crises. A new preoccupation with, and campaigns against, sexual perversity only underlined the terrors beneath the patina of normality.

1945

A decade before that we are in 1945, the first year, perhaps, of the modern era: when a new welfare world was dawning, and new principles of rights and belonging were being set out for the next fifty years – principles that enshrined civil, social and economic citizenship – as long as you were heterosexual (see Weeks 1998).

The settlement that followed the end of the Second World War, partial and limited as it was in many ways, has profoundly shaped this world we have made in the years since. That social settlement, which created the Welfare State, had its roots in earlier social reforms, and was inspired as much by liberal as by socialist ideals. It had implicit within it deeply conservative views on gender, sexuality and the family which provided the framework for legislation and moral temper for the next twenty years or so. And yet, in a nice irony of history, welfarism provided a crucial context for that transformation of sexuality and intimate life that is the subject of this book. The year 1945, with the end of the war and the election of a reforming Labour government, must be the crucial starting point. It was, among other things, the pivotal year of the baby boom, which produced a generation that was to shape the world in unexpected and unanticipated ways.

In an important analysis of the 'myth of decline', George L. Bernstein (2004) argues strongly that what actually happened after 1945 was not a fall but the 'rise of Britain'. First, even in areas where it has occurred, he argues, decline has been exaggerated. Second, Britain has done a 'pretty good job' of adapting to the radical changes wrought by the twentieth century. Finally, in focusing on decline, people 'have ignored a radical transformation of Britain since 1945 that has, on balance, been for the better and so represents progress rather than decline' (Bernstein 2004: xv). Bernstein here is largely focusing on economic and social change, but his words seem to me to be apt for the issues of moral change that concern me in this book. There has been no decline, I believe, in Britain's moral climate, though radical change there certainly has been, accompanied by a reconfiguration of the ways we think about morality. And despite inevitable disruptions in everyday life, on the whole people have adapted extraordinarily well to this world we have remade.

My purpose in this book is to trace the processes which have made this complex present. But I shall begin in the place where I was born, and in the year when I was born, 1945.

Cultures of restraint

[I]t's a known fact that you didn't talk about sex at all [to her husband]. It just happened and that was it, just when you felt like it.

(Millie, a working-class woman interviewed in Fisher 2006: 100)

It was ironic in an epoch that held the script of nature to be sacred that 'what came naturally' was the cause of so much misery.

(Hawkes 2004: 144)

For those who remembered the years between the wars, the gradual climb back to prosperity was a long, dispiriting haul . . . For the wartime children it was different . . . The world opening up before us was not a pale imitation of one we had lost, but a lucky dip of extraordinary things we had never seen before.

(Susan Cooper, quoted in Hennessy 2006a: 309)

Another country

The Rhondda Valleys in South Wales were still in 1945 among the most famous coal-mining areas in the world. The string of terraced houses, small villages and townships that clung precariously to the rocky hill-sides made up a remarkably homogeneous, and still geographically fairly isolated, culture, even as its dependence on coal declined precipitously in the post-war world. Many of its men had fought all over the world in the recent war, while others stayed put to work in the pits, which had zoomed back into full production to power the war after a decade or more of disastrous underuse. Its women had tended the home front and toiled in war work, including in the famous munitions factory at Bridgend. But whatever the commonalities with other working-class parts of Britain, it had a distinctive ethos, part of a distinctive South Wales mining history where the valleys shared a common history of labour and struggle, yet managed to produce recognizably different ways of being.

I was the product of a wartime marriage, hastily arranged by my father on his last weekend of leave in April 1944, just prior to D Day. He was a petty officer on a minesweeper; my mother worked in the munitions factory in Bridgend. Both were children of miners. I was born some nineteen months later, safely after the end of the war, part of the baby boom generation that was to shape the next sixty years. This is not a personalized history of the world we have won, but it's worth reflecting a while, before we go on, what a child of 1945, and in my case a child of the South Wales valleys, carried with him. For the valleys not only had an iconic social, economic, cultural and political history. They also had a distinctive sexual and family history which was to shape me and my generation indelibly, even as we were swept up in wider historical shifts and moved into a wider world.

Historians and demographers have seen Britain's family and fertility patterns as belonging to a long-entrenched Northwest Europe model, one characterized by deferred marriage, separate conjugal households, low and stable rates of illegitimacy, sexual constraint and, from the first decades of the twentieth century, rapidly falling fertility (see Szreter 2002). This is the broad picture, with suitable caveats, that Laslett (1965) powerfully portrays in *The World We Have Lost*. The history of the sixty years after 1945 is centrally about the gradual decline and then rapid supercession of this model in Britain as a whole. But that history, which is the main theme of the book, masks separate histories, different traditions, a variety of sexual and family cultures. The Rhondda pattern had long differed from the dominant model prevalent in much of England and the Scottish Lowlands. In many ways, despite its physical isolation and overwhelmingly working-class culture, it was closer to a surprisingly different pattern. The Welsh, says Szreter (1999: 163), 'appear to have behaved more like the French, the antithesis of the English model'. Couples married younger and had more children, and as fertility began to decline from the 1920s, they showed even more enthusiasm for nuptiality. There was a marked and highly gendered division of labour, with few opportunities for women's employment outside the home except in domestic service and shop work. Women's identities were overwhelmingly bound up with their domestic roles, while male culture was distinctly patriarchal and separate. Even many decades later, while showing quite dramatic changes in sexual and family patterns, South Wales remained different from England and Wales as a whole. In the 1990s people still married younger, were more likely to marry as teenagers, and gender segregation continued to be more extreme than elsewhere: a legacy of a long history (Betts 1994; Rees 1994).

The Rhondda of the 1940s was still recognizably a product of its formative experiences at the end of the nineteenth century as the twin valleys (Rhondda Fach and Rhondda Fawr, the little valley and the big valley) became for a while the most important coal-mining area in the world, a vast 'black Klondyke' in E.D. Lewis' famous words (Lewis 1980). By 1913 there were fifty-three large collieries in the two winding valleys that made up the Rhondda, with coal pouring down the Rhondda and Taff valleys to the ports of Cardiff and Barry. But after the First World War and the short-lived boom that followed, the bonanza years ended. Thereafter, a long-term, and in the end irreversible, decline began. The Rhondda, like other primary producing areas, suffered grievously in the interwar depression. Despite the renewed wartime demand from 1939 and the reconstruction that followed, by 1947 the number of mines was reduced to twelve, and the story of the Rhondda for the next half-century was the struggle to survive as a viable community while freeing itself from coal. Only after the last great miners' strike in 1984 to 1985 did the history of coal-mining come to an end in the Rhondda.

But coal, for good or ill, made the Rhondda community, and shaped its everyday life. Coal gave the place its identity, especially its sense of itself as a community, a good place to live despite its hardships. 'Community', as a dense network of kin, neighbours, friends and community organizations, had a long resonance in the Rhondda, an essential part of its political and moral imaginary (Charles and Aull Davies 2005: 672–90). It was fundamentally locally rooted in family and place, the dusty soil of the valleys, but it was also diasporic. 'When are you coming home?' was a question echoing in the ears of many a migrant (exile?) from the valleys down the years. But the Rhondda as it developed in the late nineteenth century and became known in the twentieth century was a product of the huge expansion of mining and of mass migration into the area in a very short period. By 1913, on the eve of war, this rapid expansion was coming to an end, and the community was stabilizing, and with it its values and family patterns. The real story of the Rhondda, wrote E.D. Lewis (1980: 110), is 'how large masses of people from all parts of Wales and England were adventitiously thrown together to achieve, in spite of all kinds of difficulties, a quality of personal living which was probably unsurpassed among the ordinary folk of that time'. It was, throughout all the fluctuations of the economic cycle, and the fantastic rise and painfully prolonged fall of an industry, a warm, vibrant, rugged, close-knit place. Community was bred in the hard labour and mutual dependencies of the pit, the union, the club, the chapel, the neighbourhood and the home. In many ways, said K.S. Hopkins (a noted educationalist and, as it happens, my former English teacher), 'we are of a village society. The school, the club, the chapel never more than just around the next corner' (Hopkins 1980: xi). It was, Dai Smith has written, a tragically deprived area in many ways, but it 'overcompensated by an incomparably full, close community life, in which the spirit of competition and acquisitiveness had been shoved under a stone by a population which had nothing to acquire by competition except envy and frustration' (Smith 1980: 53).

This was a community of intense family life, overlapping with a strong sense of neighbourhood so that family and locality often merged. Like in many working-class and minority communities elsewhere, blood and neighbourliness overlapped, so that neighbours and friends were known as honorary kin, elder members called promiscuously uncle and aunt, so that for a young child it was often confusing who was blood and who was not. Whatever the blood, marital or friendship links, however, the family was based on a rigid division of labour which seemed a law of nature. Men were the breadwinners, women looked after the home and offspring. The origins of these patterns lay in the dependence on work in the mines, seen overwhelmingly as a man's job, and the lack of work outside the home for women. Being able to maintain your family properly was a matter of male pride. Failure to do so was deeply shaming, in effect a de-manning. In 1935 the Rhondda MP, W.H. Mainwaring, put the position with stark clarity in the context of protests against unemployment and the hated means' test: 'They wanted security for their homes, sustenance for their wives. If they were not prepared to strike a blow for these things then they were not fit to be called men' (quoted in O'Leary 2004: 265).

Welsh women into the 1930s had much lower work participation rates in paid employment than elsewhere in the UK, and a higher percentage of those who did work were in domestic labour (Beddoe 1991). Domestic service did provide one route of relative independence, or at least adventure, for young girls, who regularly migrated to London and the South East in search of pay and a little more glamour than the valleys offered. 'Away' offered opportunities but also threats, especially of sexual exploitation, but young women would also frequently go south in search of work with local friends, and were diligent in sending home a substantial part of their wages to keep the family economy afloat (Beddoe 1991: 197–8; 2000: 80–1). They would often then return home to 'settle down'.

Women and men married young, often in their late teens, and set up home, perhaps at first in lodgings but then in one of the small terraced houses near their parents' similar home. Birth rates remained high by national standards, and even by the standards of other working-class communities, such as textile workers. There was a rigid segregation in many aspects of life – the pub and club were men's domains. Even in the 1960s it was seen as a bit shocking to see a woman in a pub on her own, and women were excluded from working men's clubs except on special occasions when their husbands could sign them in. But home was different. Presiding over it was the mythical figure of the Welsh mam; stern defender of their daughters' chastity and their sons' sensitivities and needs; self-sacrificial pivot of the household; the 'tidy' wife who held the family together through thick and thin. As Pilcher (1994) has shown in her interviews with three generation of South Wales women in the early 1990s, older women, in their seventies still saw their identities as intimately bound up with traditionalist views. Men could help out in the household, or even step in in an emergency, but the home remained the essence of a women's competency. Even for their daughters, in their forties, the baby boom generation, mostly now working outside the home, neo-traditionalist views were dominant: yes, men should play a part, but only generally as a back-up. Only in their daughters' generation, young women in their twenties, were expectations higher of egalitarian patterns in general; but there was still no great confidence that equality would be achieved.

These segregated patterns were common throughout the mining communities of Britain. A well-known study of the 1950s (though in England), *Coal is Our Life*, described sharply gender-divided and embittered communities, with men and wives leading essentially 'secret lives' from one another (Dennis *et al.* 1956/1969). This may, as Szreter (2002: 575) suggests, be simply a reflection of a hardening of gender divisions in the difficult conditions of the 1950s. There is no doubt that casual violence by men and patriarchal values often belied the sense of mutuality and community that was supposed to be the hallmark of the mining community, and this was as true in the South Wales valleys as elsewhere. It is noticeable that one of the most successful products of the 1970s women's movement in Wales was Women's Aid, which sought to provide refuge and support for women and children escaping male violence (Charles 1994: 48–60). But I have a distinct memory that Dennis *et al.*'s portrait of a coal-mining community was heavily criticized as unfair and inaccurate even at the time in South Wales, and Philip Dodd, brought up in the area of Yorkshire described in *Coal is Our Life*, has argued that it turned 'into a collective singular what were "varying forms of life"' (Dodd 2006: 36). These were complex societies, where the relations between men and women, though highly gendered, were not always or straightforwardly power struggles. (On the complexities of Welsh masculinities see O'Leary 2004.) As Fisher (2006: 226) remarks, men and women tried to please each other and work together, and love and generosity were as common as disputes.

But there can be no doubt of the difficulties of women's position well into the twentieth century. 'The quiet, strong woman selflessly working for the good of the family, holding the purse strings, holding the family together and keeping a meticulously clean and tidy home. This representation of Welsh women bears little relation to the reality of women's lives', argues Charles (1994: 48). The myth often obscured the unremitting hard labour that caring for the home involved with large families, poor domestic conditions, overcrowding and a constant battle against grime and coal dust. The scoured doorsteps and blackleaded grates were a daily miracle. In the earlier part of the century mortality rates for women in the Rhondda were higher than those of their menfolk (Jones 1991: 109), while infant mortality rates were much higher than the national average. Behind the myths was a history not only of relentless work but also of repression – including sexual repression (John 1991; Charles 1994).

Feminist historians have seen the sexual repression of women as a product of English middle-class moral colonization in the nineteenth century. The Education Report of 1847, the Blue Books, had condemned the immorality of Welsh women, and traditional forms of courtship such as 'bundling' (premarital, fully clothed courtship in bed) and produced a long-lasting backlash, led by nonconformist leaders and women themselves. The burden for refuting the charges fell largely on women (John 1991: 7). But sheer economic survival also dictated strict control of behaviour. Female chastity was strongly enforced on girls by mothers, reinforced by the messages of the chapels (Fisher 1999: 221). Throughout much of the twentieth century illegitimacy remained low – even in the 1990s, in a different world, illegitimacy remained below the UK average. Although large numbers of children were conceived outside marriage, community pressures ensured that the young couple did marry before the child's birth. When births outside marriage did happen children might be informally adopted by grandparents or elder sisters of the mother. I discovered at my grandmother's funeral, when the presiding minister referred to her four daughters rather than the three who I knew of, that her youngest 'sister' was actually her daughter, my mother's half-sister. Well into her old age, this family secret remained a shameful one.

The tidy wife was above all 'respectable', and sexual restraint was an essential element of this. Respectability provided the essential ballast for women's position. 'Respectability', Bev Skeggs has argued, 'has always been a marker and a burden of class, a standard to which to aspire' (Skeggs 1997: 3), for men as well as women. It underpinned men's struggle for a family wage, which would allow them to keep their family in a decent manner (Lewis 2001: 45). But it has a special resonance for women, where sexual indiscretion could so easily lead to public shame and private disaster. Respectability underlined women's guardianship of the home, which set patterns in the Edwardian period that survived throughout the twentieth century.

> Dress suits for male-voice choirs, Sunday-best outfits, China-dogs on the mantle piece over a fire-grate blackleaded daily, the front room and tea service kept, like museum pieces, for special occasions or visitors . . . This desire for respectability, for things in the local parlance, 'tidy', could exert an almost immovable hegemony over individual behaviour and family ambition' – especially for women.
>
> (Smith 1980: 40)

Under the surface, inevitably, there were other currents. As the evidence of premarital sex suggests, and the evidence of Rhondda-set novels by the likes of Rhys Davies and Gwyn Thomas confirms, neither the strictures of nonconformist ministers nor the fierce guardianship of the Welsh mother inhibited the young from dalliance in the back lanes or up the mountain sides. But there was a strong awareness of the communal constraints on behaviour, and the economic exigencies that reinforced caution. In addition, there was a basic shyness about, amounting often to ignorance of, sex in general, and birth control in particular.

From the 1920s, after the miners' defeats in 1920 and the 1926 strike and lockout, and the collapse of the coal market after 1924, there is evidence of a long-term decline in family size as miners adopted birth control – though usually by restraint than by mechanical means. Birth control was overwhelmingly seen as a male responsibility, and it remained important for women's sense of respectability that they accepted this. But leaving it to the man had its problems. Leslie, a miner from Pontypridd, never used condoms because he was too inhibited to go into a chemist's shop: 'always three-parts of time there were all women behind the counter, and [I] was too shy to ask for them.' The pressures on women were yet more constraining, as Ida, who attended the Rhondda Birth Control Clinic in the 1930s attested: 'when you were outside you did feel a bit self-conscious – going in without a baby – it was obvious what you were there for.' As this indicates, a birth control clinic had been set up in the Rhondda in the 1930s by the pioneer Marie Stopes, and in 1936, 183 women attended, largely free. But the results were not always satisfactory. One Rhondda woman who was offered a cap found using it a 'messy process' (Fisher 2006: 147, 124, 166). Perhaps not surprisingly, three-quarters of South Wales men who were interviewed by Fisher and her colleagues used withdrawal as their prime means of limiting births (Fisher 2006: 129).

Abortion remained the dominant female method of birth control. Attitudes were remarkably pragmatic, which tended to horrify the pioneering birth control clinics. Many ordinary chemists in the Rhondda sold slipper elm bark, widely used as an abortifacient, for which, according to the Birkett report on abortion, there was no other legitimate use (Fisher 1999: 215). Despite the power of the chapel, there does not seem to have been any strong religious hostility to abortion (and this was at one with evidence for other parts of the UK), and very little moralism. 'Bringing on a period' was in any case not seen in stark terms. Women were also only dimly aware of the illegality of abortion. Instead there was a pragmatic acceptance of its necessity, especially when women's health was concerned. Fisher (1999: 214) reports a general perception that abortion was on the increase in the 1930s.

From the 1940s onwards there was probably greater use of mechanical birth control, though less formal methods remained common. The couples who married in the 1940s, the parents of the babyboomers, were less restricted by nonconformist values than were their predecessors, and were more open to the alternative visions opened up by the cinema, the radio and from the early 1950s by television, and gradually greater freedom of travel in the dawning age of affluence. The valleys were opening up, and older values were weakening. By the 1950s chapels were closing in every village in the Rhondda. Yet the core values and mores remained socially conservative. And it was difficult, especially, to think outside of the heterosexual mould.

Homosexuality existed, but never as a distinctive way of life. It was subtly crafted into the heterosexual dynamic. Leo Abse, the Labour MP for a South Wales seat and one of the authors of the Sexual Offences Act which partially decriminalized male homosexuality in 1967, saw in the gender order one of the likely 'causes' of homosexuality in the areas, which he thought endemic. The dominance of 'mam' in the family, he once told me, deploying a rather crude Freudian model, produced a large number of homosexuals in the valleys, 'mammy's boys'. He wrote elsewhere that 'excessive attachment to the mother can be evoked and encouraged by too much tenderness on the part of the mother herself and can be significantly reinforced by the small part played by the father during the boy's childhood' (Abse 1973: 155).

Although his explanation is theoretically dubious, and it is now too late to substantiate his belief that there were substantial numbers of covert homosexual men in the valleys of South Wales (though personal experience certainly does not bear out the theory that there were hordes of homosexual men in the Rhondda when I was growing up), there is no doubt that their public presence was limited and their space for self-identification was narrow. The obvious candidates for suspect homosexuality conformed to a pattern common in highly gender-segregated societies, of effeminate men and butch women. The effeminate man would in all likelihood be called a 'proper bopa' (aunty) and tolerated as an anomaly, as long as he respected the gender order. Two women living together down the street might be acceptable as close friends, with a wink or two. But for the boy engaging over-feebly with the bracing atmosphere of school and sport, a mocked sissyhood remained the only fate, though tomboyish behaviour among girls was more warmly tolerated. Homosexuality was lived in the secret byways (see the stories of two Welshmen, Fred and Trevor, in Weeks and Porter (1998: 15–27, 70–90)), or in exile.

The story of Rhys Davies, the Rhondda-born novelist, is instructive. Born in 1901 in Clydych Vale in the Rhondda, he was of lower middle class (a shopkeeper's son) rather than mining stock, and that probably distanced him a little from the local community, but it is clear now that his developing homosexuality pushed him into a lifelong exile, mainly in London. He published his first novel in 1927, and was later befriended by D.H. and Freda Lawrence. His work had echoes of Lawrence's preoccupations with a puritanically repressed sexuality, and the contradictory pressures of a narrow nonconformity and cloying warmth undoubtedly constricted his sense of growing difference. He had to leave to be. Yet like many an exile, he never escaped fully the Rhondda, writing about it throughout his career. Nor did exile mean he ever felt able to be open about his homosexuality. He never writes explicitly about it, and one needs to be a subtle reader of the codes to see any reference to it in his autobiography, *Print of a Hare's Foot* (1969). He died in 1978, just as much younger people from the Rhondda as elsewhere were beginning to feel freer to talk about their gayness. For Rhys Davies, as for the vast majority of his generation, silence remained the necessary condition of his sexuality (Davies 1969; Stephens 2001).

The hegemony of a respectable ideology, however pragmatically applied, meant a fear of difference. Anyone growing up in the 1940s and 1950s in the Rhondda can remember the subtle distinctions made about people even in a culture that was overwhelmingly manual working class: the comments about rough families who lived in disreputable areas ('What do you expect. They come from . . .'), of loose girls who went to the pub, or went wild at Christmas parties in local factories, of young married men who 'fancied themselves' a bit too much, and were known to betray their wives. This was part of the local enforcement of standards. But it could go further for strangers. Newcomers to the street, even after thirty years or more, could be treated as outsiders. It was, as T. Alban Davies, a long-time nonconformist minister in the Rhondda, commented, 'a community in which it was a heresy to think differently' (Davies 1980: 11) – or be different.

The Rhondda, especially as the mainstay of its economy declined, built for itself a conservative, defensive culture: conservative in terms of its gender, family and sexual values, resistant to criticisms. It was ironic that it presented itself to the world as a politically radical society with a strong commitment to trade unionism and socialism, but these commitments rarely challenged the patterns of everyday life. Nor did the community welcome criticism. A writer like Gwyn Thomas, who was born in and loved the Rhondda and its peoples, was bitterly condemned as much as praised for his witty and sharp-eyed if often black-humoured commentary in fiction and in the media which seemed to do down the valleys. It was read as a betrayal, especially as he became famously well known as a dark and mischievous wit on television in the 1960s (Parnell 1997).

Like much of Labour culture in 1945 and for decades thereafter the Rhondda did not seek cultural change. Nor, it has to be said, did many of the theorists of the working-class movement who saw in the Welsh working class a model of solidarity. The fictions of the great Welsh academic, critic and writer Raymond Williams, especially *Border Country*, *Second Generation* and *The Fight for Manod*, though not about the Rhondda, evoke movingly the culture of the Welsh working class, and his identification with their history and struggles. I wept with identification when I first read *Border Country* (Williams 2006). As it did for Dai Smith (2006: ix), the book 'crackled with the excitement of a discovery I had somehow known all along'. His evocation of community and individuality, of the pains of exile and the sense of home, is intense and convincing – until you realize it is held together by the solidarities of work and socialist politics, and virtually excludes women (and, it barely needs saying, sexual dissidents). As Gwyneth Roberts has harshly but perceptively argued, 'Williams's definition of communal life as being advantageous for all its members does not apply to the women who appear in his own novels' (Roberts 1994: 214).

In many ways the close and intense sense of community is proof of strong social capital that sustained an area constantly battered by economic and physical hardship. Social capital has been broadly defined as follows:

> the values that people hold and the resources they can access, which both result in, and are the result of, collective and socially negotiated ties and relationships. The focus is on networks, norms and trust, and resources, and the relationship between them.
>
> (Edwards 2004: 2)

In the networks formed by the pits, the miners' lodges, the local Labour and Communist Party branches, the cooperative movement, the chapels, the brass bands, the rugby clubs, the male voiced choirs, the neighbourhoods and friendships and extended kin, as well as the contingent solidarities of the strike and lockouts and soup kitchens, we can find those resources and links that sustained a viable and supportive life. But it was, in the terms used by theorists of social capital, bonding social capital, which sustained strong ties, that held people together in intense but sometimes narrow solidarities. It bred intense local trust but also a distrust of a wider world. There were few signs of bridging social capital that could establish perhaps weaker but culturally broadening links beyond the valleys, that could open up new possibilities and, in the terms used by Williams, new resources of hope. This was especially true for women. Men had the wider solidarities of work, trade unionism, travel to war and in search of work. Women might travel to domestic service, and gain an experience of the wider world, but their destiny remained marriage and family, usually back at home, and that remained the overwhelming reality of their lives. In a valuable study of valleys' women seeking employment in the 1970s Callender found that despite the fact that most women now sought work outside the home they were still constrained by the conditions of their lives and the narrowness of their networks. 'Their networks were closed, restricted, home centred, and female centred' (Callender 1987: 47). As a result their employment opportunities and the types of jobs they could get were limited, typically, to what was perceived of as 'women's work'.

Despite, or maybe because, of the overwhelmingly collectivist political and social culture of the Rhondda, escape attempts often had to be individual, especially if like Rhys Davies and many others you felt sexually exiled. Characteristically, especially from the 1940s, with the establishment of universal secondary education, this was through education, and the mass export in particular of teachers of one sort or another. As K.S. Hopkins observed: 'To be top of the Rhondda in the "scholarship" was to bring honour to the family, the street and the village. To wear the Porth County green blazer was to become one of the chosen few' (Hopkins 1980: xiii).

Porth County was the school attended by Rhys Davies, Gwyn Thomas and numerous others, including myself, who went to seek their fortunes – or more realistically their identities – in the wider world. But even in the 1950s and 1960s it was a highly selective system that risked breaking the ties which bonded you to family and friends, risked losing the virtues of community for another world: 'It was a bitter irony that economic necessity should have forced a socialist community to such an elitist system, but it was inevitable. Survival had a higher priority than equality' (ibid.).

The education system in the Rhondda, which gave many, including myself, a route to leave, and to explore their needs and desires in a different way, in a different space, in a different world, was a product of the 1944 Butler Education Act. It was an early sign of the wave of social reforms that were to transform Britain, and the Rhondda with it, over the next generation. That major feat of social engineering under the Labour government of 1945 to 1951 was profoundly valuable, but deeply socially conservative, like most of the constituencies, not least in Labour Rhondda, which supported it (see Weeks 2004b). Yet beneath the surface of events, in the many spaces where individuals and families made millions of apparently private and unrelated decisions, fundamental changes were stirring. It is time now to see the experiences of the Rhondda in this wider context, where the world of sexuality was being remade.

Reproduction and restraint

In 1949 the British opinion organization, Mass-Observation, conducted the first large-scale sex survey in Britain, a mixture of a national random survey and qualitative interviews. In the wake of the publication of Alfred's Kinsey's far better known study of American male sexual behaviour published in 1948, it became known as the 'Little Kinsey'. Although used in part in a number of studies (see Weeks 1989: 238), its findings were not published in full until the 1990s, when Liz Stanley brought out a contextualized edition (Stanley 1995). But despite its 'lost' status, it provides, in Stanley's words, 'an unparalleled insight into British sexual mores'. The survey looked back and looked forward, providing generalizations about change but also showing the variability and complexity of change. Moral standards, the report argued, 'vary not only from one group to another, but also even within one group will be different on different occasions' (Stanley 1995: 186).

This sense of differentiated, overlapping sexual cultures is important, as my brief history of my particular birth culture suggests. But it is equally important to have a sense of overall tendencies, of wider and dominating structures, and of underlying shifts. At different paces, at different times, British sexual behaviours and mores were changing, and at the centre of these changes were profound shifts in attitudes to family size and birth control, which were manifest in the Rhondda by the 1930s, but which had begun earlier in other parts of British society. Whatever the specific circumstances and local histories, there was in the course of the twentieth century a fundamental trend towards declining fertility, and by the end of the Second World War this was generally seen as a fundamental change – so fundamental that it was perceived by many progressives as well as conservatives as offering a threat to the future of Britain. Mass-Observation, which saw itself as a radical social research organization, was pessimistic about Britain's demographic future in its 1945 report on the birth rate, which saw real dangers that the British population could no longer reproduce itself. It lined up, it said, with those 'who do not want the English people to disappear', and saw the birth rate as the 'coming problem for Western civilisation' (Weeks 1989: 232). A few years later, the Royal Commission on Population was even more alarmist about the implications of the population trend. It feared for the future of the Commonwealth and for the possible dilution of the British popu- lation itself. The United Kingdom, it thought, had a limited capacity to absorb immigrants of alien stock and religion, and like Mass-Observation it worried about the future influence of the West (Thane 1999: 122). But though official society was pessimistic, Mass-Observation's Little Kinsey confirmed something rather different: evidence that men and women were trying to reorder their family and sexual lives in ways that were more satisfactory to them rather than subservient to notions of national or imperial policy. The endeavour produced varying degrees of success in the 1940s and 1950s, and had a hugely differential effect on women as compared to men, homosexuals as compared to heterosexuals. But it signalled a potential rupture in a deeply rooted culture of sexual anxiety and restraint. And central to this was the transformation of the fertility politics of Britain, and in the conditions of human reproduction.

'Reproduction' was in a very real sense at the heart of concerns in 1945, at the birth of the Welfare State (Weeks 1989: ch. 12). In its widest sense of socially reproducing a healthy population as a critical step towards equal citizenship, the notion may be seen as at the heart of wel- fare philosophy. In the more specific sense of physically reproducing the population, in the wake of a painful war and the almost overwhelming problems of post-war reconstruction, and in the light of evidence of a long- term decline in fertility, the task seemed yet more urgent. At the start of the twentieth century (1901–05) the average crude birth rate per 1000 of the population was 28.2; by 1931 it had fallen to 15.0. The average number of legitimate births per 1000 married women dropped from 230.5 in 1901 to 1905 to 115.2 in 1931 and 105.4 in the Second World War. The fertility rate had dropped by more than a half in less than sixty years (Weeks 1989: 202). By 1933 the birth rate had reached a low level not to be replicated until 1976 in a completely different sexual world, where 80 per cent of couples were using effective methods of birth control (Cook 2005a: 108).

The result was a dramatic drop in the size of families. The average number of live births of those married between 1900 and 1909 was 3.37; for those married between 1920 and 1924 it had fallen to 2.38; and for those marrying between 1925 and 1929 it was 2.19. The family size of this cohort was 60 per cent lower than the mid-Victorian average; and by 1930, 81 per cent of all families consisted of three or less children. The

Rhondda, a little belatedly, was following a nation-wide tranformation in procreative decision-making. This decline was a cross-class phenomenon. In 1911, the least fertile part of the population had been members of the professions (doctors, lawyers) who had been increasingly limiting family size since the latter part of the nineteenth century. By 1931 the lowest fertility was among clerical workers, with one of the lowest birth rates in the world. During the previous decade the fastest decline had been among semi-skilled and agricultural workers. The size of manual workers' families was still on average higher than that of non-manual families, though the differences were narrowing. The trend towards smaller families was more marked in the relatively prosperous south of England than in the North or in Wales. But the direction was clear, and affected all parts of the population.

Behind these statistics are many different, complex histories. Szreter (2002: 537, 540) has argued that 'Changing fertility should be related . . . to the local politics and social divisions within specific communities' and has offered a picture 'of fundamental cultural and socio-demographic diversity'. The South Wales valleys represent one such pattern. The textile towns of Lancashire and Yorkshire represent another. Despite their early start in the process of limiting the number of children, there was no diffusion downwards from upper to lower classes in either philosophy or techniques, but complex local patterns as communities and regions and industrial sectors shaped individual and collective decision-making, dependent on the balance of economic opportunity and risk. Local sexual cultures mattered. What is striking, however, is that fundamental change was in process without being willed or directed, and indeed as the jeremiads of liberals and conservatives alike demonstrate, without the support of most of the political élite. This was a grass-roots movement to reshape family life and individual sexual behaviour.

In the long term these changes shifted the possibilities for individual self-fulfilment and for fundamental changes in intimate life, but they were born less out of the desire for sexual pleasure than out of social and economic circumstances and sexual restraint. England and parts of Scotland had, as we have seen, a unique marriage system, largely confined to Northwest Europe, with deep roots in the past. The key to this was 'prudential' marriage, sustained by strong community values. Most people married comparatively late, around 26 to 27 for men, 23 to 24 for women, when they felt able to establish a household of their own. A large proportion of the population, around 10 to 15 per cent, never married at all. Divorce was difficult and costly, and although many marriages did break up, many equally were never formally dissolved. Individual prudence was backed up by strong community sanctions, which regulated premarital sex. The stigma against illegitimacy was high at the level of local personal and family shame and was open to wider sanctions. Since the 1830s the Poor Law had sought to control and punitively limit bastardy. Notoriously, the Mental Deficiency Act of 1913 allowed the incarceration of unmarried mothers in workhouses or mental hospitals

(Humphries 1988: 63–4; Rose 1999: 139; Cook 2005a: 179, fn. 37). Even women who had been sexually assaulted were likely to face punitive attitudes. The economic sanctions were equally severe. Few women could earn enough to bring up children on their own. Poverty was the destiny of single mothers, whether that situation was caused by bereavement, separation or unmarried motherhood. Women, consequently, were likely to be reluctant to enter into sexual intercourse unless they could be sure that their partner would not abandon them. Illegitimacy rates remained relatively low – in the 1930s they averaged 4 to 5 per cent a year, which had barely changed since the 1890s (Hall 2000: 122). They increased dramatically during the war, due mainly to marriages that were planned but did not take place because of wartime disruption, conscription and death (Lewis 2001: 31). There was a relative degree of female autonomy in choice of partner, and couples were generally of similar ages and social background. In this context, premarital sex certainly went on, especially as a part of courtship, but pregnancy was usually the signal for marriage. The Registrar-General noted in his report for 1938 to 1939 that nearly 30 per cent of mothers were pregnant on getting married (cited in Weeks 1989: 208) – which confirms that premarital sexual restraint was far from absolute, but most sexual activity probably took place among couples anticipating marriage, and local pressures to ensure marriage were strong.

Marriage was institutionalized as the gateway to adulthood and to adult sexual relations, and its role in society had if anything strengthened since the nineteenth century as working-class weddings became as formalized and celebratory as middle- and upper-class marriage. As late as the 1990s, Clark and Haldane (1990), after several decades of fundamental change, described the British as still 'wedlocked' and only from the second half of the twentieth century do we see any real erosion of this. There were, as the South Wales example illustrates, sharp regional *variations* in age of marriage, and distinctive class patterns, and with them different structuring of gender relations. Certainly upper-class and bohemian attitudes and behaviour varied enormously from middle- and working-class populations. The well-documented promiscuity and complex emotional entanglements of aristocrats (including members of the Royal Family), the political élite, including well-known Nonconformist politicians such as Lloyd George, and intellectuals like the Bloomsbury Group, have been well documented in innumerable biographies. But all lived within cultural parameters that enforced marriage, disapproved of illegitimacy, frowned on divorce, excoriated sexual perversity, and generally limited sexual knowledge and experience. This impacted particularly on women, for this was also a deeply patriarchal society. Whatever their unhappiness in marriage, and terror of frequent and potentially dangerous pregnancies, marriage meant public acceptability, a division of labour which ensured women's survival, and legitimate children. It was, ultimately, women's sexuality that lay at the heart of the culture and its values and patterns of regulation.

Yet despite the overwhelming preoccupation with sexuality throughout the culture, a large part of its policing was through a selective but
powerful sexual silence, or at least severe injunctions about what could
be said and not said, both in public and private. In public the modes
of enforcement appear ludicrous from a contemporary perspective. The
Secretary of the Society for the Prevention of Venereal Disease noted
in 1940 that bank managers had expressly desired that cheques sent
to him should not mention VD 'for the sake of the "purity of the clerks"'
(Hall 2000: 134). The very fact of the existence of such a society of course
suggests more complex sexual behaviour than the strict codes would
indicate. But as Millie, quoted at the head of this chapter, vividly illustrates, sexual silences, secrets and lies, pervaded intimate life also.
Despite numerous publications that circulated, sometimes surrepti-
tiously, about sexual practices, birth control and the like there was a gap
between knowledge and practice (Porter and Teich 1994; Porter and Hall
1995). Shyness, inhibitions and often willed ignorance were common,
among men as well as women, as the letters to Marie Stopes illustrate
(Weeks 1989: 210–11; Hall 1991). Sometimes professed lack of knowledge proved a strategic necessity, especially for women. Ignorance could
be a necessary part of knowledge, an essential aspect of an acceptable
gendered identity, for 'Ignorance implied moral purity, innocence and
respectability' (Fisher 2006: 27).

Despite, or rather perhaps because of, limits on what could be said
in specific circumstances, the repressed often returned, especially in
the form of a widespread bawdiness in popular entertainment, seaside
comic postcards and everyday humour, in working-class communities
especially. Mass-Observation's observation of working-class women at
play on holiday in Blackpool in the late 1930s focused on this popular
vulgarity and sexual innuendo, blithely portraying a female culture
of sexual looseness. For middle-class observers, displaying a mixture of
disgust and desire, and oblivious to the irony and play of such behaviour,
this was confirmation that working-class women were perhaps, like
children, more sexual, closer to nature, than their socially more elevated
sisters. But the reality of this sexualized environment was 'anti-climax'
(Stanley 1995: 31). There might be an exuberant demonstration of erotic
display in public, but few were prepared to 'go the whole way'. As Gurney
suggests (1997: 272–3), 'Young workers, especially women, might drink,
flirt, and tell dirty stories, but they were generally loath to engage in
full sexual intercourse outside of a secure relationship – for economic
reasons as much as anything else'.

This is not to deny the existence of sexual pleasure or of marital satisfaction on many levels. The ideal of sexual harmony within marriage,
often as the basis of the spirituality of sexual love, had a long history,
and since the 1920s had had passionate advocates. The birth control
pioneer Marie Stopes looked forward to a 'glorious unfolding' in marital
love, and propagandists from Havelock Ellis to Bertrand Russell to Van
de Velde stressed the importance of sexual pleasure as a crucial element

in the development of 'companionate marriage' (Weeks 1989: 199ff.). On an everyday level many married couples had satisfactory emotional, and sexual, lives, but the passion of the advocacy for more relaxed sexual codes itself signalled the nature of the expected opposition in the culture as a whole. Sexual codes remained extremely conservative, based on restraint and abstinence. Cook suggests that from the 1900s to the 1940s no more than 15 per cent of the population could be regarded as exceptions to the general cultural norms: artists, bohemians, some wealthy businessmen, sexual radicals, sailors, and the non-respectable sections of the working class. 'None of the sources suggest that extensive sexual experience was usual or acceptable to conventional, respectable people before the 1950s' (Cook 2005a: 179). And there is plentiful evidence of real sexual misery among men and women.

The decline in fertility in the years up to the mid-twentieth century was therefore largely a product of the culture of restraint rather than of any challenge to it. Birth control advanced in Britain largely through abstinence or caution, especially through wide use of withdrawal, rather than mechanical methods. By the 1930s the birth control movement had achieved notable advances, and artificial methods were becoming more widely available. But these real achievements made little impact on most people's lives. Even in the 1940s only in suburban areas of Britain was there a significant shift towards appliance methods (Fisher 2006). Marie Stopes' blithe instructions about how women might insert the cervical cap paid little heed to the reality of the lives and constrained physical circumstances of most working-class wives. It was not just the Welsh wife quoted earlier who found it all a bit 'messy'. Whatever the caution and inhibitions required by traditional means, they still retained a sense of being more spontaneous and 'natural' than the newer, manufactured methods.

As important, perhaps, was a growing perception that working-class families could do something for themselves, even if this meant some degree of self-sacrifice, and potential conflict. In large part, Cook has argued, the demand for control of births was driven by women, not men, while most effective mechanical as well as physical means of control of births were male. The extent of the problem had been signalled by Marie Stopes' publication of 180 letters from working-class women, the 'dumb class', in *Mother England* (1929; see Geppert 1998). Most of the letters concerned birth control. Women's unhappiness with unrestricted births echoes through all accounts of the period, and from the late nineteenth century women had positive reasons for restricting family size. But women had limited means of restricting their fertility – apart from blank refusal of sexual favours, which was difficult and likely to inflame family relations rather than help – until their men were prepared to participate. Cook (2005a: 26) has observed that it was crucial that gender interests coincided before significant change occurred. Birth rates did not fall 'until changes in the family economy led to husbands' interests coinciding with their wives''. This happened at different rates in different sexual cultures in different parts of the country, but as we have seen, by the early 1930s it was clear that a radical limitation of family size was taking place. However, whatever the central interest of women in controlling family size, it was mainly men who had to take the lead. Some scholars have challenged this. Cook (1995a: 108), for example, sees in women's sexual abstinence a form of resistance to male demands, and a means of empowerment. By the 1940s, she argues, a crucial staging post had been reached in the 'long-drawn-out shift from communal, indirect control of fertility to effective, direct, female control of fertility' (Cook 2005a: 41). However, the direct evidence for this is limited. Fisher (2006) found little evidence in the oral history testimonies relating to the interwar years or later that there was much in the way of negotiation between men and women on limiting family size. As late as the 1970s the anthropologist Geoffrey Gorer concluded that there was a widespread, if inarticulate, belief among the working class that decisions on birth control remained a male prerogative (Gorer 1971; Fisher 2006: 100). Given the sexual silences that prevailed, it was often left to men to manage birth control. For many, across all classes, it became a duty and obligation to do this sensibly, as a basic element of their male identity.

They did so largely through the adaptation of long-established forms of sexual restraint and abstinence. Historians such as Szreter (2002) have recently argued that total abstinence was not needed for birth control to be effective. Reduction in the regularity of intercourse in itself would increase spacing and thus reduce the likelihood of conception. But whatever the methods, by the 1930s, as we have seen, smaller family sizes had become normalized among all sections of the population, including the working class, with a growing pathologization of large families, even in working-class communities. For the majority of the population, however, especially the working class, it was achieved still within the framework of relatively conservative sexual values, and mainly without benefit of artificial means of control. It was largely the result of working-class self-help in a context of sexual and moral restraint.

Changing sexual moralities

By the late 1940s there was a widespread sense that things were changing. Little Kinsey recorded this, though with nearly half of its survey population feeling that change was happening too fast or in the wrong direction, with morals going downhill – a lament that was to be echoed in every subsequent decade. As ever in such surveys it was the older people interviewed who lamented a decline in standards, while the younger, and the more middle-class, felt more optimistic (Stanley 1995: 166–7). Already by the early 1940s, in the midst of war, respondents to a Mass-Observation panel directive on venereal diseases were anxious to distance themselves from traditional moralistic attitudes, and wanted more knowledge and openness. Even the majority of the more traditionalist panellists were relatively liberal, and looked forward to better sex education as a long-term solution (Stanley 1995: 31). VD was on the way to being seen as a disease like any other. This is not perhaps surprising for a study conducted in the abnormal conditions of wartime, in a country fighting for survival. Many of the shibboleths of conventional morality were likely to be severely challenged by the huge population disruptions caused by military and industrial service. Accounts of wartime speak of a greater sexual freedom, more marriage breakups, fewer inhibitions concerning casual sex, and even more spaces for homosexuality. Rising real wages provided a greater sense of independence for many women. The British population had always preferred pragmatism to moralism in sexual affairs, and wartime conditions dictated a more pronounced pragmatism than ever before, which continued into the postwar world. The various Mass-Observation studies of sexual behaviour, especially on VD, the birth rate and Little Kinsey, look forward in many ways to changes that were to reach fruition in the 1960s and 1970s – better sex education, support for divorce for incompatibility, the separation of heterosexual sex from procreation through better birth control, and continued control of family size. Ideals of family life were changing significantly, largely because of the reduction in births, but also because of the dissemination of more democratic values on intimate life. They also suggested that, despite the continuing formal moral conservatism, a great deal of sex went on, in public places as well as private, and that much of this was sanctioned and legitimized, especially among young people, as long as the broader moral framework remained fairly intact. Little Kinsey, in fact, picked up a breakaway from absolutist standards of sexual morality, with individuals increasingly left to develop standards for themselves. It lamented the haphazard nature of much individual thinking, a 'half-aware accumulation of often conflicting tenets, rather than concise decision making', with values eclectically picked up from pulpit, surgery, birth control clinic, novels, the confessional, street corners, films, the psychiatrist's couch and so on, governed as much by feeling as by reason (Stanley 1995: 166).

A rather more nuanced way of seeing the same shifts, however, is to respect the solid pragmatism of large parts of the population, rooted in an awareness that sexual behaviour varied a great deal in different situations, and that what was deemed appropriate in one situation was not necessarily appropriate in another. This pragmatism was reflected above all in attitudes to marriage. Most people, Little Kinsey reported, 'have a more or less realistic and mundane view of marriage' (Stanley 1995: 120), largely devoid equally of spirituality, romanticism or yet cynicism. Marriage might be indispensable for most people, especially as the guarantee of respectable sexual relations, but there were few illusions. While 82 per cent of men said they were satisfied with marital intercourse, only 61 per cent of women felt the same – hardly a ringing endorsement of married bliss. Both Little Kinsey and Mass-Observation's earlier research pick up a strong sense of dissatisfaction among women, sometimes amounting, it has been suggested, to an unhappiness with heterosexuality itself (Stanley 1995: 6). Despite all the qualifications that can be made, and the reality that men and women often made strenuous efforts to make it work, marriage all too often brought drudgery and unwanted sex, endured rather than enjoyed, for women. Now alternatives were dimly visible, and these became critical to any sense that a new future could be won.

The war had brought new freedoms for women, and the welfare settlement after 1945 sought to recognize the changing role of women. A large element of this reflected a widespread desire to improve the conditions of motherhood, and to realize the ideal of the family wage, whereby the man in the family would at last earn enough to keep his wife and (smaller) family in a decent condition. The male breadwinner/female housewife model family was a potent ideal, even if it only ever applied to a proportion of the population (Lewis 2001: 45), but it aimed to improve rather than transform everyday life. The birth rate increased substantially between 1943 and 1948, but this baby boom was a result of the war and post-war catching up rather than a fundamental change. As peacetime conditions prevailed, many women left paid employment. Many experts concerned with the threat of population decline, and still influenced by a social-democratic version of eugenics, wanted the government to adopt pro-natalist policies, but there is every sign that government policy was highly contradictory in this regard. Family allowances introduced during the war were seen by some as a bribe for motherhood, but the rate of five shillings a week was not much of a bribe, and they were introduced more to alleviate poverty and manage the economy than to endow motherhood. Similarly, the closure of nurseries after the war has been seen as part of a policy to drive women back into their homes and to 'reconstruct the family', but the reality was more complex, with different government departments adopting contradictory positions (Weeks 1989: 232–4).

There was no concerted effort to develop a population policy based on exclusion of women from the factory floor. The Royal Commission on Population had been established due to widespread alarm at population trends, but its report recognized, however reluctantly, the changes in women's position. Despite fear of population decline and of a drop in intelligence levels of the population due to the continuing disproportion in the birth rate between working-class and 'higher income groups', the report stated that there could be no turning back of the clock (Weeks 1989: 234; Thane 1999: 128). Population trends, it noted with some alarm, 'now depend increasingly on the decisions of individual men and women about the number of children they will have' (Thane 1999: 120). In particular, population decline was happening because of women's rejection of excessive childbearing and the Commission saw this as an aspect of women's emancipation. In the same way they recognized that there was an increasing need for women in the workforce. By the late 1940s it was apparent that while children remained central to women's idea of marriage, couples, whether tacitly or explicitly, were making deliberate decisions about the number of children they would have, for a mixture of reasons – money, health, wanting to give children the best possible chance in life. But above all there was a new emphasis on women redefining the opportunities open to them. This was not without tension, as Pat Thane has noted (1999: 133), between the widespread zeal for social planning of the 1940s, and the role of the experts in shaping better ways of life, and a desire for individual autonomy by women and men alike, especially for resisting prescriptions on the desirable levels of the population and the right size of family from among the right people. Working-class women, Thane argues, 'were developing new conceptions of social selfhood', but on behalf of their children rather than for themselves (1999: 131). Some of their daughters, of course, were to provide the feminists of the baby boom generation, who were to seek to redefine fundamentally the condition of women.

There was an opening up of new possibilities but within a conservative framework. The power of the modernized male breadwinner family model into the 1950s and 1960s was that while it improved the lot of many women, it continued to marginalize and often pathologized those who fell outside its frame: people 'living in sin', unmarried mothers, homosexuals, and the burgeoning numbers of black and other immigrants from the old colonies with their apparently more lax sexual manners (Williams 2004: 34). Another Royal Commission, this time on Marriage and Divorce, sat between 1951 and 1955 and worried ineffectually over changes in the status of marriage (see discussion in Holden 2004: 44–50). The percentage of marriages ending in divorce had increased from 1.6 in 1937 to 7.1 in 1950, dropping slightly to 6.7 in 1954, and commentators were concerned that an increasing emphasis on sex in the media and the greater availability of contraception was fuelling, as Rowntree and Lavers put it in their *English Life and Leisure* in 1951 (cited in Finch and Summerfield 1991: 13), 'illicit sexual relations' at the expense of more conventional relationships. But the reality was rather different. Divorce still carried a social taboo. Sir Anthony Eden, the Foreign Secretary, received an unpleasant reaction when he remarried after a divorce in the early 1950s, while Princess Margaret was virtually forced to put 'duty', and her Royal position and benefits, before her love for a divorced man. 'Divorcee' remained a potent insult way into the 1970s and beyond. In reality, in the 1950s, marriage, far from declining, became more popular than ever. Because of the reduction of the death rate as a result of welfare reforms and near full employment, it had probably never been as long-lasting as in the 1950s. It was, Michael Anderson has suggested, a period of marital stability without historical precedent (Cook 2005a: 321; see also Szreter 2002: 576–7).

It was accompanied by the official burial (though the bones took a long time to stop rattling) of the patriarchal domestic ideology which had dominated the earlier part of the century. Partnership in marriage was the new ideal of the 1940s and the 1950s, and the model of a 'companionate marriage' as theorized in different ways by Edward Carpenter, Havelock Ellis, Marie Stopes, Bertrand Russell, and van de Velde became the goal to be achieved. What Collins (2003) has called 'mutualism' had a variety of roots, not all (or many) of which were radical. Advocates of 'free love', trial marriages, easy divorce, non-cohabitation and the like were easily dwarfed by supporters of a modernized marriage in which men and women were more ostensibly equal if still positively different. Such an approach was widely encouraged by experts, even as it potentially conflicted with other ideals of the period, such as that of the family wage and the emphasis on maternity. The Population Commission had looked for policies which would enable women to combine work outside the home with the care of the home and motherhood. The reformer Eva Hubback believed that domestic tasks should still absorb the main energies of women, while the educationalist John Newsom went further, linking lack of interest in motherhood with abnormality. Motherhood, he said, 'is the essentially feminine function in society', and those who did not agree with this were 'normally deficient in the quality of womanliness and the particular physical and mental attributes of their sex'. This was reinforced in the 1950s by new prescriptions about motherhood, such as those of the attachment theorist John Bowlby (Weeks 1989: 236, 237). The companionate marriage was not in the end a truly egalitarian marriage. It was a partnership, Finch and Summerfield (1991) have pointed out, in which women had sharply differentiated, if supposedly complementary, roles, with motherhood to the fore.

This revised model of relationships, however, was more openly a sexualized one, with a growing emphasis on the importance of sexual harmony in marriage. By 1948, David Mace, a leading member of the Marriage Guidance Movement, could argue that 'A good sex adjustment for husband and wife means satisfying orgasms for both – simultaneous orgasm is a desirable ideal' (Weeks 1989: 237). The Marriage Guidance Council, as a response to a widespread demand from married couples after the war, had published its first booklet *How to Treat a Young Wife*. This had suggested that it was an obligation of the man to develop the sexual potentialities of his wife. Revised as *Sex in Marriage*, this had sold over half a million copies by the late 1960s. Sexual pleasure was being recognized but strictly within a marital framework. Sexual pleasure could indeed be harnessed to strengthen marital harmony and stability.

The emphasis on the importance of sex alongside the promotion of marriage produced a variety of contradictions, especially regarding extra-marital sex. The emphasis on 'petting' in the literature of the period, making this perhaps the golden age of foreplay, indicates some of the tensions: a recognition of the need to sanction some form of sexual outlet while continuing to taboo unmarrieds 'going too far'. Many saw early marriage as an antidote to this, but premarital sex became an increasingly hot topic as the 1950s progressed, especially as the baby boom generation came of age. But on the whole, British sexual habits remained restrained. Geoffrey Gorer's anthropological study of English character in the early 1950s noted the exceptional chastity and fidelity of the English when compared to other peoples (Weeks 1989: 238). Half of his sample had had no sexual relationships either before or after marriage with anyone but their spouse, though the figures were higher for the working classes than for the middle class. A general respect for marriage went across classes, though for characteristically pragmatic reasons.

It is perhaps not surprising that for later conservative commentators the 1950s seemed to be a golden age of marital harmony. But this apparent harmony was born at a price. As a journalist on the (Conservative) *Daily Telegraph* observed in 1956, 'The welfare state is based on the drudgery of women', with women 'wanting to escape the Nest as men were climbing back into it') (Wilson 1980: 30, 69). For Hera Cook the period saw a reassertion of heterosexual male dominance of sexual activity: 'The outcome of the 1950s and 1960s was a sexual culture more conservative and rigid in gender terms, but less abstinent sexually' (Cook 2005a: 185). This ideological framework was reflected in what at the time was widely regarded as a radical eruption in the novel and drama. Sinfield (1989) has spoken strongly of the 'repellent misogyny of much Movement and Angry writing' as reflected in the work of John Osborne, John Wain, John Braine and the like. This generation of writers were openly in rebellion against what they regarded as an effete liberal establishment, so there was also a strong undercurrent of what later came to be known as homophobia, and a celebration of 'manly' values. As the critic Leslie Fiedler observed, every young British writer 'is able to define himself against the class he replaces' (quoted in Sinfield 1989: 80), but the harsh reality was that this was a refinement of rather than a fundamental challenge to the gender order (see Sandbrook 2005: 138–66).

The lessening of male and female sexual restraint, however desirable for many, was potentially costly to women, as rising rates of illegal abortion, illegitimate babies and painful adoptions attests. Dot Clancy, born in Newcastle-on-Tyne in 1932, became a trainee nurse in London in the early 1950s. At Christmas 1951, lonely in London, she caught the eye of a consultant and 'gave my all' in the back of his car 'under the stars of chronic delusion'. She became pregnant, and ended up in the ascetic ambience of a mothers' and babies' home to give birth. 'The home was full. It was always full. It seemed there were a lot of good girls around.' When she gave birth, the home tried to persuade her to have her son adopted. She resisted and kept her child. 'The rest was long and hard, not the fifties you see with your rosy nostalgia. At five he died of leukaemia' (quoted from Beddoe 2003: 195–200). A decade later a similar story unfolded. In 1961 Eirlys Ogwen Ellis, born in North Wales in 1937, gave birth to a mixed-race son David, again in a mothers' and babies' home. She decided to keep her son, and he was subsequently looked after by Eirlys' sister. Eirlys herself had a successful career until a breakdown, but she was told never to mention that she was an unmarried mother or her career would be wrecked (Beddoe 2003: 200–5). The story of Margaret Smith who was born in 1938 had a yet more painful outcome. Her illegitimate son eventually rejected her, unable to forgive her for his status (ibid.: 206–15). But if there was pain in keeping a child, and carrying the stigma of having an illegitimate child, there was the alternative agony of giving your baby up for adoption – vividly dramatized much later in Mike Leigh's film *Secrets and Lies* (Schneider 2005: 864). Here the pain and shame were linked with a permanent sense of loss.

The conventional mask of order that now shrouds the 1950s, and makes it a totemic decade for those nostalgic for that ever-elusive age of stability and civility, masked real tensions and contradictions not far below the surface, and a massive amount of suffering. From the perspective of the present the 1950s, Hall has suggested, 'looks like a period of instability rather than unthinking smug conventionality' (Hall 2000: 166). The moral anxieties about premarital sex among young people, working wives, latchkey children, horror comics, rock 'n' roll, Teddy Boys, street prostitutes (whose numbers on the streets of London, it was estimated, had risen from an annual average of 2000 in the early years of the war to over 10,000 by 1952) and homosexuality, all suggest a deep-seated fear of change, and of anything which suggested sexual unorthodoxy or dissidence. By the end of the 1950s all this was compounded by a growing sense among the cultural élite that the new 'age of affluence' was also an age of tatty commercialization, with solid traditional moral values being corrupted by consumerism and commodification.

Another profound change was also underway which was to challenge patterns of family and sexual life. In the 1950s, Britain was well set on the path to becoming a multiracial and multi-ethnic society, with new settler populations from West Africa and the Caribbean. In the census of 1951 some 15,000 Caribbean people were living in Britain. Ten years later it was approaching 172,000. A society which over 1000 years had witnessed many peoples settling, Normans, Jews, Huguenots and Irish as well as numbers of black and Asian peoples, yet never in large numbers, was now to experience mass immigration for the first time. There was a deep ambivalence in the response to this hugely significant change in the make-up of the population, despite the riots that erupted in Notting Hill in 1958. It was, for instance, barely noticed by the many social commentators on the family and intimate life of the 1950s, despite the popular stereotypes of the hypersexuality of the (largely male) early settlers, and the tabloid press's obsessions with hustlers and pimps (not to mention drugs) drawn from the new populations (Finch and Summerfield 1991: 23). Caryl Phillips has similarly pointed out the dramatic absence of any consideration of the black population in the (white) radical writing of the time: 'The "colour problem" was debated in parliament, on television, in newspapers, magazines, on the radio. It was the big story of the 50s. Yet where is it represented in the literature?' (Phillips 2004: 4). As Phillips goes on to say, neither John Braine, Kingsley Amis, John Osborne, Arnold Wesker nor Keith Waterhouse, all celebrated documenters of the *Zeitgeist*, feature the new black presence. It had barely touched the cultural horizons of these writers. Yet it had the potential to transform the sexual imaginary, as the two white writers who did explore interracial dynamics reveal.

In three novels written in the 1950s, *City of Spades* (1957), *Absolute Beginners* (1959) and *Mr Love and Justice* (1960), Colin MacInnes explores the grass-roots social, cultural and sexual changes that were making a new world, and in particular imagines himself into the world of the 'dark strangers' who were both of, and not of, the country, and whose sexuality clearly fascinated him (Phillips 2004: 5). In *City of Spades* particularly, MacInnes confronts the sexual anxieties that these newcomers aroused among the established populations. As Phillips points out, 'Much of the antipathy towards outsiders of all kinds in Britain had been framed in terms of purity and pollution', and here were young male newcomers in their thousands, without wives or girlfriends, who could readily be portrayed as sexual threats. MacInnes himself, despite his sympathy and identification with the newcomers, could barely himself escape associating black men with the classic stereotype of a natural, spontaneous sexuality, which was both desirable in comparison with the stiff formalities of England, and also challenging to settled, even frozen ways (see Sinfield 1989: 126ff.). In an essay in 1956, MacInnes spoke of the new Britons' 'wonderful instinct for the pursuit and capture of joy', which went with 'a certain fecklessness. They aren't responsible in the way so many Englishmen are' (Collins 2005: 184). The same ambiguous mixture of envy and infantilization was true of another well-known work of the period, the young dramatist Shelagh Delaney's play *A Taste of Honey* (1958), also later made into a film. This opens with the relationship between the teenage Jo and a black sailor, called 'Boy' in the stage directions, but Jimmie in the play itself. Far from being a newcomer, however, he comes from Cardiff. The black population had roots. He impregnates Jo and then unknowingly departs back to sea. When the mixed-race child arrives, she decides to bring him up herself, helped by a young homosexual friend. On one level this is a brave and certainly powerful exploration of the new cultural realities of interracial relationships, teenage pregnancy and non-heterosexual lives. But, to quote Phillips (2004: 6) again, 'even Delaney found it difficult to see her black character as much more than an irresponsible, though admittedly charming, sexual outlaw'. Ethnocentric assumptions about sexuality were deeply rooted, and even those drawn to the excitement of living in a more plural and diverse culture found it difficult to escape them. An ethno-sexual Otherness was beginning to haunt the British imagination in new ways, but in the 1950s few in the white population found the language to respond to it without fear, paternalism or simply passing by on the other side.

Chasing the perverse

The major changes we have traced in the 1950s amounted to a hetero-sexualization of mainstream culture. The family was reaffirmed as the privileged site of sexual normality. Marriage was confirmed as the gateway to respectable adulthood. The sexual division of labour was modernized, but not in such a way that traditional roles were challenged. And the mutualism expressed in ideals of partnership between men and women was more explicitly sexualized, so that (hetero)sexual intimacy was now being promoted as the glue of successful relationships and marital stability. All this was accompanied in the 1950s by the sharper definition of the divide between heterosexuality and homosexuality in public discourse. Homosexuality became the explicit Other, whose shameful existence reinforced the accepted norms, and strengthened the heterosexual assumption.

In 1952 the *Sunday Pictorial* newspaper published a series of articles on homosexuality entitled 'Evil Men', described as a serious attempt to get to the root of 'a spreading fungus' (Weeks 1990: 162–3). Its editor later saw this as 'breaking the conspiracy of silence' on the subject. But if there had been a public taboo on speaking about the subject for decades, except when punctuated by scandals and spectacular court cases, there could be no doubt of its threatening presence, not least because the law was drawing attention to it. The number of indictable male homosexual offences increased substantially from the late 1930s. In 1938 there were 134 cases of sodomy and bestiality known to the police in England and Wales. In 1952 the number was 670, rising to 1043 in 1954. Other figures showed a similar trajectory. Indecent assaults increased from 822 cases in 1938 to 3305 in 1953, while for 'gross indecency', the offence for which Oscar Wilde had gone down in 1895, the increase was from 316 in 1938 to 2322 in 1955 (Weeks 1989: 239–40). There is nothing to suggest that the number of illegal activities was actually increasing, though it is likely that the war and post-war social developments had encouraged a certain degree of openness; the Wolfenden Committee itself was extremely sceptical about this. The real reason for the rise in prosecutions was increased police zeal in hunting out miscreants, especially in key metro-politan areas such as London. This, of course, was a male phenomenon, because it was male homosexuality that was illegal in public or in private. It was men who posed the real nuisance and danger. Behind this was the growth of official concern and a generalized public anxiety which must surely be related to the more general trends emphasizing the importance of marital sex. In such a climate homosexuality looked ever more deviant. Mass-Observation's Little Kinsey had shown 'a more genuine feeling of disgust towards homosexuality . . . than towards any other subject tackled' (Stanley 1995: 241).

Official announcements did nothing to moderate popular prejudice. The Home Secretary, Sir David Maxwell-Fyfe, opined that 'homosexuals in general are exhibitionists and proselytisers and a danger to others, especially the young' (Weeks 1990: 241; David 1997). Anxieties were fed by a series of scandals and panics. Contemporary historians are less inclined than earlier ones to see this as a concerted anti-homosexual purge, regarding it as more a return to pre-war preoccupations and methods after wartime emergency, and an attempt to develop a more coherent national approach rather than relying on local responses and policies (Houlbrook 2005: 33–6). Similarly, contemporary writers are more sceptical of attempts to account for this in the climate generated by the flight of the (homosexual or bisexual) spies Burgess and Maclean in 1951 and a generalized McCarthyite reaction (see argument in Weeks 1990: 159–60; Higgins 1996; Houlbrook 2005) – though as Povinelli and Chauncey argue (1999: 443) there is still a need to account for what was a transnational anti-homosexual discourse in the post-war world.

Even if there is no real evidence of a concerted politically led purge of homosexuals, there was certainly a heightened sense of anxiety in the homosexual world by the mid-1950s, fed by several high-profile criminal cases, most notoriously the prosecution of Peter Wildeblood and Lord Montagu for gross indecency (Weeks 1990: 161–2). John Alcock, a young man at the time, recalls:

> I personally became very frightened during the time of the Peter Wildeblood trial in the fifties. I thought that every policeman coming up to me in the street was going to arrest me . . . The temperature of the time was quite unpleasant. We thought we were all going to be arrested and there was going to be a big swoop.
>
> (Hall Carpenter Archives 1989a: 52)

The case itself revealed a cat's cauldron of class and sexual prejudices, which in turn were magnified in the popular press. Even here it was difficult to prove any signs of the corruption that the Home Secretary was concerned with. There was no suggestion that the 'offences' were anything but consensual and in private, and the only evidence against the two prime accused was the evidence of participants in the acts. But what these cases did above all was to reveal the uneven responses to homosexuality across the country. Lesbians were rarely prosecuted, if at all. Although the possibility of prosecutions against lesbianism had technically existed since a 1930s case which had confirmed that the law on indecent assault was applicable to sex between women, in practice prosecutions remained very rare, despite sex between women being increasingly cited in divorce cases and libel actions (Waites 2005a: 96; for a general overview see Hamer 1996). At the same time, police responses to male activities remained haphazard. Other victims of police zeal, such as the actor Sir John Gielgud, had a sympathetic response to their alleged crimes (Higgins 1996). The truth was that most of these cases were 'victimless crimes', and pointed to the problems of a legal regulation of homosexuality that was simultaneously moralistic and contradictory. Liberal opinion in particular was stirred. Another young homosexual in the 1950s, Dudley Cave, thought that 'if anything the Montagu trials were favourable to us', because the accused had been treated very badly (Hall Carpenter Archives 1989a: 36). The law was a mess, and in 1954 an interdepartmental committee under the Chair of Sir John Wolfenden was set up to pick a delicate way through the tangled thickets of 'vice' (Weeks 1990: 164–7). As had been the case for a hundred years, homosexuality was seen in tandem with prostitution, and both were to be the subject of investigation.

A number of recent writers have noted the ways in which Wolfenden focused on the metropolitan experience of 'vice' (see e.g. Mort 1999; Houlbrook 2005). This is not surprising given the way in which, in Henning Bech's vivid words, 'the city is invariably and ubiquitously, inherently and inevitably, fundamentally and thoroughly sexualised . . . modern sexuality is thoroughly urbanised' (Bech 1998: 215). And it was the city, with its intoxicating blend of closeness and anonymity, that above all provided the spaces for sexual diversity and perversity to flourish, and the incentive and pressure for sexual regulation. For here could be found the sexual migrants who had fled the tightness and intimacy of country, the village and small town, the one-industry towns and mining areas. Here could be found the density of people to trawl the sexual markets and experiment with different life patterns. Here male homosexuality and prostitution lived side by side, often in symbiotic relationship. There were similar urban features in the small lesbian groupings: 'In the interwar years, lesbians occupied liminal spaces alongside prostitutes, criminals and male homosexuals in the enter- tainment culture of the West End' (Jennings 2006: 225). Post-war, a more organized lesbian subculture emerged, typified by the Gateways Club in West London (Gardiner 2003; Jennings 2004, 2006). But it was the male subculture that seeped into a wider public consciousness.

Street prostitution and male homosexuality had long been inter- twined in the official and popular imaginaries. Since the nineteenth century both had been policed by the same or related legislation – on solicitation, vagrancy and most notably the Criminal Law Amendment Act of 1885. It was an amendment attached to this law largely on prostitution and raising the female age of consent to 16 (the Labouchere Amendment) that had invented the offence of gross indecency and more effectively criminalized all forms of male homosexual activity whether in public or in private. Such legislation had not, of course, extirpated homosexuality. On the contrary: there is a strong argument that punitive legislation produced a positive incentive for the development of distinct sexual identities (Weeks 1990). It was in London above all, with its dense network of meeting places, its flamboyance, transgression and decadence, that unorthodox sexual contacts and identities could flourish.

Homosexuality, and male homosexuality especially, was intricately woven into the fabric of London's culture (Cook 2003: 39). Homosexuality was not confined to a distinct area. It could be found in the streets, parks, tube stations, public lavatories, theatres, music halls, Lyons Corner

Houses, squares, Turkish baths, cafés, gentlemen's clubs, hotels, shops, barracks, churches, embankments and boarding-houses. It lived in the interstices of a vibrant, bursting, anonymous urban life, and this had been true since at least the eighteenth century (Trumbach 1999, 2003). In turn London was part of an international informal network of cosmopolitan cities – Paris, Rome, Berlin, New York – where same-sex passions and interactions flourished (see e.g. Chauncey 1994). Nor could homosexuality be limited to a particular type. The figure of 'the (male) homosexual' overlapped with familiar urban types, the dandy, the bachelor, the bohemian, the theatre goer, the actor, the guardsman, the telegraph boy, the clubman. The sexological texts that began to emerge in the late nineteenth century recognized this exotic diversity and tried to make sense of it. Complex categorizations were invented, distinguishing the invert from the pervert, the congenital from the amateur, the queer from the normal (Weeks 1990: 23–33; 1985). But within this diversity there was the delineation of the homosexual person, a particular type of being with his or her distinct desires, ways of being and identity, which by the 1960s was becoming the generally accepted notion.

The 'homosexual' had been invented in a long and complex history, in a process of definition and self-definition (Weeks 1990). However, it is also fair to acknowledge that the impact of the idea of the homosexual as a distinct person was partial and uneven in its impact, common among the intelligentsia and the emerging middle-class homosexual, but perhaps incomprehensible to many others. The oral histories of self-identified homosexuals living in the early part of the century are very clear about the importance of sexual identification, and of relationships (see Weeks and Porter 1998). But at the same time the boundaries between the normal and the unorthodox remained problematical, unstable and easily breached. Matt Houlbrook (2005), in his evocative portrait of *Queer London* from the 1920s to the 1950s, vividly shows the complexity of queer life. He focuses on three distinct types: the effeminate 'quean', the working-class man who might have sex with both men and women, and the middle-class and would-be respectable homosexual. Of these, as Houlbrook observes, the most unfamiliar to contemporary eyes are the working men. They echo through the history of same-sex eroticisms, from Wilde's 'feasting with panthers' to the policemen who were partners of key members of the intelligentsia such as E.M. Forster or William Plomer, or the guardsmen who pleasured men like Joe Ackerley. They were the 'rough trade' of many a fantasy, especially of respectable middle-class men who dreamt of relations with a 'real' man (Weeks 1990).

The world of homosexuality was still dominated in the 1950s by ideas that remained firmly within gendered categories. Male homosexuality was most clearly associated with effeminacy, and lesbianism with masculinity, and the mincing queen and the butch dyke remained the most transparent stereotypes in popular representation. Diana Chapman, born in 1928, recalls her reading of Radclyffe Hall's *The Well of Loneliness* in the late 1940s:

I was shattered. I thought, 'This is me'; this is what it's all about
. . . But of course it also sold me the idea that all lesbians were
masculine and tall and handsome and Stephenish and, of course,
I should have looked at myself and realized I wasn't any of those
things. I didn't think of lesbians as being ordinary women.
                                    (Hall Carpenter Archives 1989b: 49)

Sam, born in 1910, identified as camp, and related especially to heterosexual men, 'real men':

I got to the pitch where I found I couldn't have any gay person.
All my lovers were either bisexual or married or had gone out
with girls and had done them. I couldn't have sex with anyone
who was camp. That was most peculiar.
                                        (Weeks and Porter 1998: 133)

It was noticeable that in the press's coverage of the Wildeblood case,
photographs were touched up to suggest the effeminacy – and degeneracy
– of the defendants (Weeks 1990: 162). This was ironic because Wildeblood
was himself anxious to distinguish himself sharply from his fellow
queers. In his presentation to the Wolfenden Committee, Wildeblood
offered himself as the spokesman for the 'good' homosexual. In his influential book *Against the Law* he distanced himself from what he called
pederasts and pansies, who 'form a quite separate group from men like
myself'. Instead he painted a picture of the respectable homosexual
man, one of many hidden in the population who 'do our best to look like
everyone else, and we usually succeed'. So he did not make a case for all
queers, 'Not the corrupters of youth, not even the effeminate creatures
who love to make an exhibition of themselves'. His plea for toleration was
for the respectable homosexual (Wildeblood 1957; Higgins 1996: 247–8).
Wildeblood's presentation of this position may be seen as a distinctly new
way of articulating a homosexual self, normal in all but his homosexual
proclivities (Waters 1999: 134–5). From being a liberal hero and victim
of an intolerant society in the 1950s and 1960s, Wildeblood has been
attacked for his illiberalism in recent years, for drawing lines between
the respectable and unrespectable homosexual. This is understandable
in the light of a post-gay liberation consciousness and contemporary
queer consciousness which looks back nostalgically to a more amorphous
way of life. In terms of his own contemporary experience we might wish
to be rather more generous. He had, after all, as a result of his trial and
conviction, lost his job as Diplomatic Editor of the *Daily Mail*, his privacy,
and had been imprisoned for his homosexuality. He was anxious that
there should be no further 'monstrous martyrdoms'. Nor were such
arguments new. From the early sex reformers onward we find similar
attempts to distinguish respectable homosexuals from the outrageous.
But critics like Waters and Houlbrook have an important point.
Wildeblood is representative of a new generation of homosexuals who

were prepared to argue for a distinctive homosexual identity, which looks forward to more radical changes in the 1970s and beyond. Ironically, many of his generation were to be highly disapproving of the more flamboyant gay consciousness of the succeeding generation. But what we see in Wildeblood is that greater articulation of the heterosexual–homosexual divide, an important move in the 1950s from a culture where queerness inhabited the world of heterosexuality to one where homosexuality was clearly distinct from heterosexuality. Alongside that is the emergence of a case for justice based on difference, even if it is articulated in painfully self-loathing language. Wildeblood's brave call for toleration was of toleration for a 'tragic disability' (Higgins 1996: 248). Whether this was evidence of a genuine self-hatred or a more tactical way of adjusting to the mores of the time it is difficult to say; certainly similar language may be found in the writings of other liberals during the period, including discreet pioneering homosexual researchers such as Gordon Westwood (a pseudonym: better known as Michael Schofield) and D.J. West (Westwood 1952; West 1955).

What perhaps we can best see in such language is a muted modernity. The earlier pioneers of sex reform such as Havelock Ellis had by the 1950s achieved a certain degree of respect, though their actual, largely biologistic theories of sexual development already seemed a little old-fashioned. Modern writers preferred to speculate in sub-Freudian terms about a form of arrested development as an explanation for homosexuality. The Public Morality Council's arguments for law reform were on such grounds, while the National Vigilance Association believed by 1951 that the time was ripe for new approaches to a problem that 'might be regarded as much as a mental illness as a criminal act' (Weeks 1989: 242). Homosexuality required full investigation by experts 'in the light of the new knowledge now available'. In turn the discourse of experts could be taken up by the subjects of these discourses – in Water's terms it also influenced 'those who sought to articulate and defend new forms of selfhood' (Waters 1999: 151).

The call for the application of expert knowledge was a powerful one in the climate of the times, even as it had to confront a rising tabloidization of the issue in the popular press. But the most powerful influence was not a British modern expert at all, but an American, Alfred Kinsey, whose two tomes on *Sexual Behavior in the Human Male* and *Sexual Behavior in the Human Female* had been published in 1948 and 1953 respectively, to tremendous reactions. His long-term impact in disrupting orthodoxy was immense (Weeks 1985). Despite the shakiness of his statistical base, which was pointed out at the time, the fact that, based on 18,000 interviews, he could confidently detail the widespread nature of homosexuality (37 per cent of men had homosexual contact to orgasm) was shocking and stimulating. If homosexuality was a problem it was perhaps not such a tiny one. Just as important as his suggestion of the incidence of homosexuality in the long term was his attempt to see homosexuality as a simple biological fact, part of a spectrum of mammalian sexual activities, that was neutral in scientific terms. Ironically his 7-point scale (from 0 as exclusively heterosexual to 6 as exclusively homosexual with a range in between) did provide a basis for self-categorization ('is he a fiver or a sixer?'), but in the 1950s that mattered less than his massive reputation as a scientist with a fresh way of looking at homosexuality. Not surprisingly, the Wolfenden Committee was heavily impressed by his testimony to it (Mort 1999).

The establishment of the Wolfenden Committee was a compromise, between the desire among more conservative elements to do something to control homosexuality and rid the streets of overt displays of prostitution, and a wish on the part of liberals to find more modern forms of regulation than prison or the law. Its task therefore was to navigate between the two extremes while trying to come up with an acceptable framework. In doing this it took expert advice, and Mort argues convincingly that Kinsey's evidence was a key moment for the committee (Mort 1999). Kinsey's matter-of-factness about homosexuality and his implicit moral neutrality pointed to a less punitive legislative framework. For the first time, also, openly homosexual citizens (two of impeccable professional standing, Patrick Trevor Roper and Carl Winter; the third the temporarily disgraced but clearly distinguished Peter Wildeblood) gave evidence to the Committee, as did perceived experts and a host of other interested parties. The result was not so much a compromise between conservative moralists and progressives as a bold new framework, offering the outlines of a new moral economy for the post-war world.

The Wolfenden proposals have been described as 'shockingly pragmatic' (Conekin et al. 1999: 16) and this is true in the sense that they came up with concrete proposals to deal with perceived social problems in practical and, as it turned out in the long run, widely acceptable ways. But there was a coherent framework behind the proposals published in 1957 which was to be enormously influential for the rest of the century, and not only in Britain (HMSO 1957). The recommendations were based on two axes: between private and public, and between legal moralism and utilitarianism. The philosopher of utilitarianism, Jeremy Bentham, had classed homosexuality as an 'imaginary offence' dependent on changing concepts of taste and morality. The greatest of his successors, John Stuart Mill, in On Liberty, had argued that the only justification for legal intervention in private life was to prevent harm to others. Wolfenden took up these arguments and agreed that the purpose of criminal law was to preserve public order and decency, and to protect the weak from exploitation. It was not to impose a particular moral view on individuals. So it followed, in the Wolfenden logic, that the law should at least partially retreat from the regulation of private behaviour, however distasteful the majority of the Committee (and the population) felt it to be, while at the same time the law must continue to intervene, more strongly if necessary, to sustain public standards. Just as prostitution in itself was not illegal as a private activity, there was no real logic in homosexuality conducted in private being illegal. Hence the thrust behind the two main recommendations. The report proposed that the law against street offences be tightened to eradicate the public nuisance of overt prostitution. But at the same time it proposed that male homosexuality conducted in private, between consenting adults, should be partially decriminalized, while penalties for public offences should be increased (Weeks 1990: 165–7; 1989: 242–4; Moran 1995: 3–28).

The report made a dramatic impact on publication, and its recommendations on prostitution became the basis of the Street Offences Act of 1959, which sought to eradicate street prostitution. It took another ten years before the recommendations on male homosexuality were translated in a modified form into law, in the 1967 Sexual Offences Act. We will look at the detailed implications of this later. At this stage we can draw three tentative conclusions.

First, the new legal and moral framework proposed was to prove immensely influential. The report generated an immediate debate, in the famous Hart–Devlin controversy. Lord Devlin in his Maccabean Lecture in 1959 firmly reasserted the absolutist view that 'Society cannot live without morals', and that it was fundamental to society that laws be based on morals, or at least on 'those standards of conduct which the reasonable man approves'. But the more pragmatic view endorsed by Wolfenden and H.L.A. Hart, effectively saying that the law's capacity to change private behaviour was limited, was the one that prevailed (Weeks 1989: 243–4). This was not after all a call to rip down all barriers. It was not in any sense a libertarian charter. For many subsequent critics the Wolfenden position put forward a more effective strategy for societal regulation than an outdated and distrusted moralistic legal framework. The recommendations themselves would have seen only a modest diminution of the prison population, while the Sexual Offences Act of 1967 actually did increase penalties for public displays of homosexuality, leading in the immediate aftermath of 1967 to an actual increase in prosecutions. The privatizing of homosexuality may be seen as a more effective way of controlling it. The same arguments may be made for other products of the Wolfenden strategy in the 1960s and beyond (Weeks 1989: 263–8).

The second point to note is that this new framework for regulation had differential impacts on men and women, and on heterosexual and homosexually inclined people. The Street Offences Act in 1959, a direct result of Wolfenden, drove women off the streets by increasing fines and imprisonment. But it led at the same time to a reorganization of prostitution, resulting in a huge expansion of massage parlours and call girl rackets under the control of men. As ever, legislation has unintended consequences.

Third, Wolfenden articulated a view of homosexuality that was to be immensely influential, both for women who were not the subjects that the report was mainly concerned with, as well as for men, who were. For in a real sense it brought the idea of a distinctive homosexual identity and way of life into the law for the first time. Prior to 1957, homosexuality as such had no presence within the law at all. It had hitherto been dealt with under legislation relating to 'unnatural offences', gross indecency, importuning and the like. In order to provide a more modern framework Wolfenden had to conjure the homosexual into being. As Moran (1995) argues, the Committee 'discovered', even invented, the meaning of homosexuality as sexual identity, sexual practices and forms of knowledge. A new form of sexual wrong was invented in order that it could be decriminalized. Although Wolfenden hardly endorsed homosexuality, it recognized that for many it was an irrevocable destiny. In tune with Peter Wildeblood's plea for recognition, it acknowledged a way of being in the world. As Waites (2005a: 105) has argued, behind Wolfenden's framing of the issues was a broad tendency away from ethical collectivism towards the individualization of decision-making, and a feeling that the autonomy and self-determination of individuals should be respected. The individualizing tendency that Mass-Observation had observed at the end of the 1940s, reflecting a decline in traditional values and institutions, was now expressed in the logic of an official report. Wolfenden, the classic restatement of legal liberalism in the 1950s, offered a framework for the expression of self-identities that pointed forward to the new opportunities of the 1960s and beyond. The dam may not have burst (Hennessy 2006b, ch. 11) but its foundations were beginning to shake.

3

The great transition 1
Democratization and autonomy

The best approach to this cultural revolution is . . . through
family and household, i.e. through the structure of relationships
between the sexes and generations. In most societies this had
been impressively resistant to sudden change, though this does
not mean that such structures were static . . . Yet in the second
half of the twentieth century these basic and long lasting
arrangements began to change with express speed.

(Hobsbawm 1994: 320–1)

The cultural and legislative shifts of the 1960s in much of the
metropolitan 'Western' world, at a time of full employment,
rising wages and increasing equality, really did transform the
sexual landscape, shifting the ways the world impinges on
our sexual lives.

(Segal 2004: 68)

Of all the revolutions sweeping the world today, political,
economic, social, scientific and moral, the last may prove to
be the most far-reaching, the most deep-going of all . . . a
thorough going change in the whole sexual economy. It could
more accurately be called the Erotic Revolution.

(Lawrence Lipton, author of *The Erotic Revolution*, 1965,
quoted in Escoffier 2003: 20)

Beckoning towards freedom

Between the 1960s and the 1990s Britain, like most other parts of the
Western world, underwent a historic transition in sexual beliefs and
intimate behaviour. There was no single cause (the Pill is most often
seen as the *deus ex machina*, but is only one spur), no regular pattern
across regions and countries, no common agenda for its main actors,
chiefly members of the baby boom generation. The process was messy,
contradictory and haphazard. But in the end it drew in and involved
millions of people, reimagining and remaking their lives in myriad
different ways. Its implications are still working their way through what
today is an almost unrecognizable world.

But the beginnings were ambiguous and uncertain. In her memoir of the 1960s, Sheila Rowbotham (2001), one of the founding mothers of second-wave feminism, has written powerfully and evocatively of the sense of being poised between two worlds as the decade opens. On the one hand was a world of petty hypocrisies and restrictions, of constraints and restraints, of tradition and hierarchy that was a long time dying. On the other was a world lusting to be born, a world that loomed especially bright for someone on the verge of adulthood, with a privileged education and a will to change the world – a classic baby boomer – but a world whose contours, possibilities, pleasures and dangers remained veiled in the mists: 'the promise of a dream':

> My generation was still being brought up as if ignorance was
> akin to innocence. Consequently a rebel minority found ourselves
> crossing from one extreme to the other over a chaos of unknowing
> . . . It was a kind of cusp in sexual attitudes; prohibition and
> permission were shifting but had yet to realign. There were no
> clear paths for us to take. On the other hand, the entrances
> towards sexual freedom had opened and were beckoning, not
> only among the young intelligentsia but in popular culture.
>   (Rowbotham 2001: 23)

The 'chaos of unknowing', before the Pill, before second-wave feminism, before sustained sex reform, now remains locked away in many individual memories as the decades pass. Individuals living through these times negotiated their own journeys, shaping and reshaping their own life stories, finding personal ways of dealing with collective processes of change. But there was a central motif, inchoate as it may often have seemed. It is that 'beckoning' towards sexual freedom which has coloured social and cultural memory of the 1960s ever since. It is indelibly stuck in the popular memory as the decade of the 'sexual revolution' and a long historical and ultimately political debate has raged about the significance of the decade. For some of those who lived their lives fully during the decade – 'if you can remember the sixties you weren't there' – it was never glad confident morning ever again. For many others it was but a prelude, and a difficult one at that, to the hope of better things in the graspable but still elusive future. For the young women giving birth to a child out of wedlock, and surrendering it straight away to adoption, there was still a heartbreaking contradiction between the hope of greater freedom and the economic and cultural pull of respectability and of sheer necessity. The young woman tentatively embracing a sexual career soon found that social taboos and practical means lagged well behind desire. While contraception was becoming more readily available all round, it was still officially unavailable for single women until halfway through the decade. The Brook Advisory Centres began providing contraceptive advice to unmarried women only in 1964, and it did not become available on the National Health Service until 1969. For a long time the fear of the consequences of incautious sexual practices continued to haunt indi-vidual activity. 'Of course,' Sheila Rowbotham remembers, 'I believed all the fuss about virginity was absurd. But what if anything happened? Not only were we all ignorant about contraception, but we had no idea who we could ask for advice' (2001: 48).

For the closeted queer, too, the promises opened up by Wolfenden and the more sex-positive mood of the early 1960s remained dreams largely deferred. Law reform beckoned distantly, and a few fashionable artists and hangers-on might for the first time offer alternative images of a more open homosexual lifestyle, but the fear of exposure, or the developing threat of aversion therapy, or what the soon-to-be-born gay liberation movement would label as 'internalized self-oppression', continued to haunt everyday life. None of the new rock 'n' roll stars came out as gay, nor did their impresarios (see Savage 2006: 66–74). And it is noticeable that those who sought a more open homosexual life – such as the poet Thom Gunn or the artist David Hockney – pursued the dream in the sun of California rather than the damper climate of old Britain. When in 1964 and 1965 the liberal journalist Brian Magee presented two television programmes on the 'One in Twenty' alleged to be homosexual (subsequently published as a book in 1966) the homosexual interviewees' faces remained shrouded in shadows. The same *Sunday Pictorial* that had discovered those 'evil men' in 1952 offered its readers advice on 'How to Spot a Homo' in 1963. It seemed to suggest that wearing sports jackets and wearing suede shoes and smoking pipes might offer some clues (Weeks 1990: 263). But the very humdrumness of such descriptions suggested the larger truth. 'Living in the shadows' was to remain the dominant metaphor for the homosexual, male or female, until the 1970s.

For many, then, the 1960s remained a decade of unfulfilled hopes. Yet within barely a generation, the old shadows had been dispersed, replaced by quite new shapes and configurations. In the early 1990s, following more than a decade of highly conservative government, the question of single parenthood became again the focus of political contro-versy and of cultural anxiety, but now one-parent families numbered approaching two million and could not easily be gainsaid, and the stigma of illegitimacy was disappearing from the statute book as well as from everyday life. Similarly, by the 1990s, in the wake of the AIDS epidemic, no one could have been in any doubt about who gay men were, and what they did after endless documentaries and media coverage of risky behaviour, and the increasing outness of prominent public figures, from actors and writers to politicians. In little more than thirty years, before the baby boomers had reached middle-age, the sexual world had been irretrievably transformed, and attitudes to marriage or non-marriage, to childbearing or non-parenting, to female sexuality, to family, to sexual unorthodoxy, all had changed fundamentally. Abortion and homo-sexuality had been at least partially decriminalized, and both had been followed by dramatic shifts in behaviour and attitudes. Divorce law had been modestly reformed but the results were dramatically immodest. The obscenity laws had been mildly reformulated but within a decade people were speaking alarmingly of floods of pornography. Theatre censorship by the archaic office of the Lord Chamberlain was abolished, contraception on the NHS made universal, lone-parent benefits were introduced, tax benefits for married couples had been drastically reduced, non-heterosexual families of choice were becoming commonplace, and same-sex parenting, adoption and marriage were appearing on the agenda. The 1960s, an arbitrary division of time, cannot be praised or blamed for all of this alone, despite the best efforts of moralists and moralistic politicians on both left and right. Many of the changes had a long gestation, and some were to take decades more to reach fruition. Other significant changes were not to appear until the 1970s, or in the case of other vectors of change such as HIV/AIDS and the internet, until the 1980s or beyond. But the 1960s were a crucial moment in the 'great transition'.

But agreement on that has been accompanied by profound disagreements about the real meanings and implications of the changes. For Francis Fukuyama (1999), the turmoils of the 1960s were at the epicentre of the 'great disruption' which broke the foundations of trust and social capital that sustained Western democracies, and explain the moral confusions and cultural divides that characterize the succeeding decades. Conservative thinkers as a body have generally concentrated on the 'cultural revolution' which fundamentally sapped the traditional values which had underpinned Western civilization, leading in the words of the conservative American critic, Gertrude Himmelfarb (1995), to the 'demoralization' of society. For the American sociologist Daniel Bell, this was the decade when the Puritan ethic was fatally undermined by an ideological tranformation which put hedonism and ultra-individualism and consumerism to the fore (Bell 1996). A flurry of British writers have followed this path. Christie Davies (2006) laments the fall of a once respectable, religious Britain from the 1960s into a violent and dishonest society, in which people and property were at risk, family breakdown was omnipresent and drug and alcohol abuse was rampant. In another jeremiad, the right-wing journalist Peter Hitchens denounces the 'abolition of Britain' as a result of the rot that set in during the 1960s.

There are, however, different, less embattled views. Sandbrook (2006) is inclined to wonder what all the fuss is about, and while acknowledging extraordinary changes sees a society caught between optimism for the future and fear of decline, leading at times to immobilism – terrified of heights, and fearful of falling, unable to get off the wall, British society reached a point and never quite turned. The historian Arthur Marwick (1998), on the other hand, in a magisterial survey of the decade across various Western countries, agrees that there was a decisive shift in attitudes and behaviour in the West, but sees its impact benignly. The cultural revolution of the 1960s, he writes, 'in effect established the enduring values and social behaviour for the rest of the century. . . There has been nothing quite like it; nothing would ever be the same again' (Marwick 1998: 806). Like conservative critics of the period he sees not a revolution that failed, as the most disillusioned witnesses fear, but a genuine transformation: in material conditions, lifestyles, family relationships and 'personal freedoms for the vast majority of ordinary people' – a genuine revolution in everyday life (1998: 15).

The evocation of the key term 'personal freedom' marks what is at stake in these debates: not so much the fact of genuine changes at many levels for which there can be no fundamental dispute, but the resonances, moral, cultural, political, of those changes. Did they represent the widening of the spaces for new personal freedoms and genuine individual choice, freeing people from authoritarian, 'traditional' values; or a decisive weakening of the moral conditions for a stable society, imprisoning individuals in an illusory 'liberation'? Both views, and a complexity of shades in between, have been regularly put forward ever since. But as Sheila Rowbotham (2001: xi) remarks, 'By wrenching aspects of experience out of context, this dichotomy inevitably distorts.'

The dichotomies and distortions have always been most acute in relation to sexuality. The domain of sexuality, always sensitive to shifts in wider social currents, has become the crucial battleground for conflicting and ultimately irreconcilable positions, and yet they often seem to refer back to one another. There are those who see the auguries of moral collapse in crucial aspects of the 'sexual revolution'. The philosopher Roger Scruton (as much a baby boomer as Rowbotham, with whom he shares a birth date but is a year younger, and a universe of values apart) had his own world view decisively changed by what he saw as the wanton collapse of values in the late 1960s. It was, he wrote in his autobiography, 'partly by reflecting on the disaster of sexual liberation, and the joyless world it seems to have produced around us' that led him to see the truths of traditional conservatism, and especially of Edmund Burke (Scruton 2005: 43). The 1960s' revolution, he argues, attempted to replace 'prejudice' – that set of beliefs and ideas which arise intuitively in social beings and reflect the deep experience of social life – with reason, which prioritized the pursuit of pleasure, leading to 'a breakdown in trust between the sexes' and 'a faltering in the reproductive process' (Scruton 2005: 42–4). The effect is a fatal undermining of the sexual puritanism which for him sustained a notion of Englishness:

Sexual puritanism is an attempt to safeguard possessions more valuable than pleasure. The good that it does outweighs the evil, and the English knew this. They were seriously repressed, largely because repression prevented them from carelessly throwing away those things – chastity, marriage and the family – which slip so easily from the grasp of people whose natural tendency is to keep each other at a distance.

(Scruton 2006: 51)

We must therefore, he wrote, 'silence those who teach the language that demeans these virtues' (cited in Weeks 1985: 225). From the other side of the political spectrum altogether, other philosophers have been equally pessimistic, and have seen the endless proliferation of speech about sexuality in the 1960s as masking the illusory nature of the freedoms on offer. Herbert Marcuse, who briefly became a radical icon of the decade, foresaw the danger of technological rationality working through the erotic to bind the individual to the status quo. Pleasure generated submission. The partial or 'repressive desublimation' offered by advanced consumer societies is a guarantor of the survival of oppression and exploitation. It is now the very form of sexual freedom on offer, not sexual restraint or denial, that binds people to their oppression (1969, 1972). As the German radical Reimut Reiche put it, 'Sexuality is given a little more rein and thus brought into the service of safeguarding the system' (Reiche 1979, cited in Weeks 1985: 167–8).

One of the problems with these positions is that despite the ostensible and ostentatious political dichotomies, they all rely on a particular model of sexuality, seeing sexuality as resembling a head of steam that could be either repressed or released. For Scruton, the erosion of prejudice opened up a spectre of diverse sexualities which threatened to erode the 'roots of innocence' that were essential to erotic love. For the Freudo-Marxists like Marcuse, it was advanced capitalism, with its heedless consumerism, which distorted human potentialities. But for far Left and far Right, it was the rationalism and technological rationality of modern culture which corrupted eros. What post-Kinsey sexual theorists like Gagnon and Simon (1974) have called the 'drive reduction' model of sexuality has long coloured both popular and élite writing about the uncontrollable nature of sex – 'if the bridle is removed, sexuality gallops', as a 1933 text put it (quoted in Wouters 2004: 154). But as contemporary sexual theory, itself a product of the upheavals of the 1960s and 1970s, affirms, sexuality should properly be seen as a social production, shaped, organized and regulated in complex social relationships (Foucault 1979; Weeks 1985, 1990, 2000). Rather than attempt to understand what happened in the 1960s to 1990s as 'liberation' or 'desublimation' or other variants of metaphors of repression and release, we need to be attentive to the shifts in the relationships within which sexual activity takes place. Between the 1960s and the 1990s we can trace a profound shift in the social relations of sexuality and intimacy, which we may list as follows:

- A shift in power between the generations
- A shift in power between men and women
- The separation of sex and reproduction
- The separation of sex and marriage
- The separation of marriage and parenting
- A redefinition of the relationship between 'normality' and 'abnormality'.

Together they led, over this period of the great transition from the 1960s to the 1990s, to the effective demise of the traditional model of sexual restraint and opened the way to a new moral economy – one that was more hedonistic, yes, more individualistic, indeed, more selfish, perhaps, but also one that was vastly more tolerant, experimental and open to diversity and choice in a way that had been inconceivable just a generation earlier.

In the rest of this chapter and in the next I want to explore these changes through a number of key vectors of change: an informalization and democratization of the social relations of sexuality; the process of individualization in relation to sexual choice; a rebalancing of the relations between public and private; and the reassertion of risk in relation to sex-linked disease. Through these approaches we can begin to excavate some of the foundations of the world we have won since the 1960s.

The informalization and democratization of sexual relations

A revolution democratized

Gertrude Himmelfarb (1995: 217–18) has made a pregnant comparison between the alleged 'sexual anarchy' of the nineteenth century *fin de siècle* and the 'sexual revolution' of the late twentieth century. 'A century ago,' she suggests, 'the "advanced souls" were just that, well in advance of the culture, whereas now they pervade the entire culture. This is the significance of our "sexual revolution": it is a revolution democratized and legitimized.'

Although Himmelfarb comes to condemn rather than praise this singular achievement (and as such has been enormously influential among British critics of the transformation, as well as among American neo-conservatives) there can be no doubt about the validity of her central argument. From the early 1960s we can see both an undermining of faith in the traditional élite, and the emergence of new voices – in popular music, the arts and literature, the media, in the emergence of the counter-culture and new social movements – which were seeking to articulate new experiences and possibilities. The erosion of public faith in the traditional élite was dramatized by the spate of sexual scandals which punctuated the last years of Conservative government in the early 1960s, especially the Profumo Affair and the Vassal spy scandal. The Profumo Affair seems relatively trivial in retrospect, but in 1963 the revelations of sexual high jinks in high places, involving a dubious list of characters ranging from promiscuous politicians and aristocrats to young call-girls, the Soviet military attaché, and fashionable osteopath cum informal pimp for his friends, grabbed the nation's prurient attention. More significant, perhaps, is that it demonstrated that sexual relations among the élite were no longer their private concern. They appeared to be politically combustible and exploitable remnants of a decaying order (Sandbrook 2005: 602–33). The revelations shortly before this of the arrest of a homosexual spy in the Admirality, John Vassall, evoked again the linkage of sexual unorthodoxy with betrayal of country which had been exposed by the Burgess and Maclean defections to the Soviet Union in the early 1950s. The rumours and gossip that surrounded this case also confirmed something more – that homosexuality was not confined to the social margins. It permeated the whole of society, and every walk of life, but in ways which were thoroughly hypocritical (Weeks 1990: 161–3; Sandbrook 2005: 596–8). Set against this, the raw sexuality of the Beatles, long hair among young men, the appearance of new fashion among young people generally, the greater explicitness on television, the rising tide in favour of a general 'modernization' of society, signalled the emergence of a more demotic culture, a more informal and democratic set of values. The results have been profound.

Over barely more than a couple of generations, for good or ill, there has been an extraordinary democratization of everyday life, gathering pace since the 1960s, seen everywhere across the old, hierarchy-bound countries of Europe as well as in the 'new worlds' of America and Australasia, and elsewhere in the world. Old hierarchies, of course, are always in danger of being replaced by new, and the creation of a global-ized élite, 'masters of the universe' with vast wealth and no national anchorage, may pose new dangers to egalitarian possibilities. We remem-ber the glittering stars, including the fallen stars of the 1960s, better than the quiet beneficiaries of greater individual freedom, hidden in the ordinariness and privacy of everyday life. But for many millions new spaces of possibility have emerged, and a crucial aspect of this process has been the enfeeblement of traditional sources of sexual authority and knowledge, and the proliferation of new voices and narratives.

Even the most resilient of hierarchies is not immune to the dissolving effect of democratized knowledge. Think of Princess Diana's resistance to the royal double standard in the name of a more feeling, emotionally literate relationships style (Burchill 1998; Campbell 1998; Steinberg and Kear 1999). Think of women's enhanced ability generally to escape imprisoning or abusive relationships – most divorces are instigated by women. For everyone, women as well as men, there has been a casualiza-tion of courtship and of erotic encounters. Think of TV reality shows like 'Big Brother' with their promiscuous intermingling of men and women, straight, gay and transgendered, black and white. Social relations generally are less hierarchical in the twenty-first century, and intimate relations in particular are more informal, more democratic. These changes are reflected in the proliferation of what Ken Plummer (1995, 2003) has described as sexual or intimate stories, not least in a host of confessional television shows in which private citizens appear to have no inhibitions in confessing their most secret wishes, desires and sexual deeds and misdeeds to millions of viewers in ways which they seem incapable of doing to their nearest and dearest in the intimacy of their homes.

Norbert Elias and his intellectual heirs have attempted to explain these changes in terms of a broad 'informalization' of social relations across the board in recent decades (Wouters 1986, 1998, 2004). 'Formalization', as theorized by Elias (2000) in his masterwork, *The Civilizing Process*, is an aspect of a sustained 'civilization process' through which codes of conduct and modes of behaviour sought to develop and sustain a more orderly and rule-driven way of life. It is a phase of increasing control over impulses with the development of a culture of self-control and restraint heavily based on internalized authoritarian conscience and values. It is essentially a disciplinary phase of social development, which projects wildness on to the other, to strangers, whether in the working class or in racial others. Unorthodox behaviour was seen as transgression or misbehaviour. What I have described as a culture of restraint throughout the first half of the twentieth century may be seen as an aspect of such a social configuration. That culture was punctuated by periods of relaxation, or informalization, as in the 1920s, and to some extent during the war, but the impact of these bursts was limited by class and other factors, and relatively brief.

Wouters (1998, 2004) among others has argued that gradually from the 1940s, but with a strong spurt forward in the 1960s, the process of informalization, a 'controlled decontrolling of emotion management' (2004: 9), became dominant in Western societies. Social conduct, especially as reflected in manners books, became increasingly less authoritarian, more differentiated and varied for a wider public, with an increasing variety of behavioural and emotional patterns of behaviour becoming socially acceptable. At the heart of this, it has been argued, is a tendency to greater self-control over behaviour, a process of responsibilization and self-regulation. Self-regulation, the argument continues, can only become dominant in societies with a high degree of interdependency and social integration. Only here can there be sufficient trust to allow a relaxation of well-established constraints on behaviour.

It is a little ironic that Wouters bases his argument on an increase in trust when the period from the 1960s on has been generally seen by conservative critics such as Fukuyama (1995, 1999) as one of declining trust as a result precisely of the breakdown of traditional values and restraints. It is also important to say that the sort of psychogenic and sociogenic explanations that underpin the historical explanations of Elias, Wouters and others are at the very least debatable. Giddens (1991, 1992), clearly in many ways influenced by the Elias approach, and certainly interested in psychological shifts, emphasizes other elements of the transformations of everyday life, particularly 'detraditionalization' and 'individualization' under the impact of profound economic and social change and globalization. But whatever the qualifications one might make, the thesis of informalization provides an important guide to what was happening. It suggests a period of rebalancing in social relations, of which two elements are particularly significant: between the generations, and between the sexes.

Inter-generational challenges

Young people of the baby boom generation were the focus of many jeremiads in the 1950s, and as they came to maturity in the 1960s their challenge loomed ever larger, as a series of anxieties and panics – about long hair, rock music, drugs, and above all sexual behaviour – began to shape the image of the decade. And young people genuinely had a new weight in the culture. By the beginning of the 1960s there were a million more unmarried young people aged between 15 and 24 than there had been a decade earlier, representing a potent bundle of emotional and erotic energies in an increasingly sexualized culture. And they had a new social weight. The first generation to be fully nurtured by the Welfare State, they were also beneficiaries of more inclusive educational opportunities, and more or less full employment. They were the children of a new affluence and of a new sense of security and opportunity. Real wages had increased by 25 per cent between 1938 and 1958, but those of young people by more than twice this rate. For the grammar school educated children of the working class, going to university in the early 1960s, though still a tiny minority of the population as a whole, new vistas of aspiration opened up. The disposable income of these young people, though only about 5 per cent of total consumer spending, was disproportionately powerful in certain key areas – records and record-players, clothes, toiletries and cosmetics, and so on (Weeks 1989: 252–3).

The impact of all this on sexual behaviour was complex. The overall age of marriage continued to decline, though of course this concealed regional variations. It fell from 27 for men and 24.5 for women in the late 1940s to 26 and 23.5 in the late 1960s (rising slightly again in the 1970s). But this was decreasingly the age of first sexual activity. The taboos against premarital sex were eroding, while the age of maturity continued to decline, largely as a result of growing prosperity. By the early 1960s, the average age of menarche had fallen to 13.5, compared to 16 to 17 a century earlier, while boys reached full growth and the peak of sexual potential by 17, compared to 23 at the beginning of the century (ibid.). Yet, at the same time as the social, economic and cultural potency of young people increased, a form of emotional dependency on their parents increased in many ways, a pattern that was to be continued and even accentuated to the end of the century and beyond.

At first, far from these shifts undermining marriage, there was an increase in the proportion of people marrying, and especially of women. In 1911 only 552 out of every 1000 women aged 21 to 39 were married, and in 1931, 572. By 1961, this had reached over 800. By the mid-1960s 95 per cent of men and 96 per cent of women were married by the age of 45. More people were also marrying younger. Whereas in 1921 less than 5 per cent of husbands and 15 per cent of wives married under the age of 21, by 1968 these figures had trebled (Weeks 1989: 257; see also Cook 2005a: 263). To put it crudely, it was likely that more people, and especially women, were having more sex in marriage than ever before;

there was also a growth in the proportion of women who became mothers, accompanying the decline of the proportion of couples who were childless. The effect of earlier marriages in a less sexually restrained culture combined with the absence of fully effective birth control was to fuel a new boom in the birth rate. The post-war bulge in the birth rate had levelled off in the early 1950s to the rate of the mid-1930s, about 15 per 1000 of the population. This began to rise again from 1956, reaching a peak of 18.7 in 1964. Thereafter it steadily declined. However, the increase fed into new anxieties in the 1960s over the population, this time aggravated by fear of the high birth rate of immigrant populations. But there was no obvious sign of a change back towards larger families. Much of the increase, it was suggested at the time, was caused by a move away from one child or childless marriages, and was most pronounced among young married couples. It was also, in many cases, probably a result of contraceptive failure. Within a decade, with better birth control freely available on the NHS the birth rate was to reach its lowest ever levels.

In the long term perhaps the most significant change was the incidence of premarital sex. The National Survey of Sexual Attitudes and Lifestyles (NATSAL) suggests that the median age of sexual initiation fell most markedly in the 1950s and early 1960s; that is, prior to the widespread use of the Pill, and preceding the sexual revolution (Wellings et al. 1994: 37–9; Szreter 2002: 573). This has been challenged by Cook (2005b), who has argued forcefully that it was the Pill that made the changes in behaviour possible. Certainly, on the surface, beliefs remained largely within a traditional framework, though Geoffrey Gorer (1955) was already suggesting in the mid-1950s that attitudes lagged behind actual behaviour. The Latey Committee on the age of majority in 1967 found that most adolescents differed little in social attitudes from their parents. Michael Schofield's study of the sexual behaviour of young people in the mid-1960s similarly found that attitudes were fairly conservative. Most young people wanted to marry, and expected faithfulness. Most boys felt that if they made a girl pregnant they should marry her, but they also wanted to marry a virgin – despite the fact that nearly half of boys and a quarter of girls were in favour of premarital sex. The rates of illegitimacy remained relatively low – increasing from 5 per cent of births in the mid-1950s to 8 per cent in 1967, possibly largely the result of a shift in timing, a move of illegitimacy and premarital sex to a younger age group, itself the result of earlier maturity. Rates of venereal disease also remained relatively low, despite the anxiety they aroused (Schofield 1973; Weeks 1989: 253–4).

At this stage, then, changes were apparently taking place largely within traditional frameworks of marriage or preparation for marriage rather than breaking them. Rates of premarital sex were increasing from the 1950s, as NATSAL (Wellings et al. 1994) has suggested, but among working-class women especially it was with men who they intended to marry. As in pre-war days a high percentage of young women who married were pregnant. The harbingers of change, Cook has argued (2005a: 339), were the relatively small numbers of largely middle-class women who had affairs, using birth control, detached completely from the idea that marriage would inevitably follow. This was the beginning of the separation of sex from marriage and automatic reproduction that was to be the real change over the next few decades.

Female sexualization

Women were being increasingly sexualized in the 1960s, but largely within conventional boundaries. Women were increasingly wooed by the new consumer industries, but at first largely in their roles as house-wives rather than as autonomous sexual beings. Even as their sexuality was brought into the frame of advertising it was generally in the context of their relationship to men – cosmetics, clothes and so on. Women's sexuality, especially young women's, was being reconstructed in terms of its possibilities for pleasure, for enjoyment, unencumbered by com-pulsory drudgery and endless childbearing. It is striking that while sex researchers found little change in attitudes to female sexuality in the population as a whole, among those born since 1945 there were significant changes (Weeks 1989: 258).

One of the keys to this was clearly more effective birth control. There had been a sixfold increase in birth control clinics over fifteen years, from sixty-five in 1948 to 400 in 1961. But still only a small minority had access to effective advice, and as we have seen it excluded unmarried women. It was estimated that of those married in the 1950s a quarter were likely never to have used formal birth control, with the figure rising to one-third in the manual working class. The abortion figures told a similar story. By 1961 there were around 2300 legal abortions, under highly restrictive conditions, on the NHS, rising to nearly 10,000 in 1967 on the eve of abortion law reform. It was the other figures which revealed the full story. There were about 10,000 private clinic abortions per annum, and an estimated 100,000 illegal or 'back-street' abortions per year (Weeks 1989: 259). When, in the early years of the next millen-nium, a film, *Vera Drake*, dramatized the peculiar mix of mundanity, anguish and hypocrisy that marked back-street abortions in the 1950s, the response was of incomprehension that such practices were necessary and relief at a world that was long lost. But until the advent of the Pill this remained the only method fully in female hands.

The demand for effective birth control was clearly present, and by the 1960s official opinion generally was coming around to a more accepting position on birth control. The Anglican Lambeth Conference of 1958 had endorsed birth control, declaring it to be 'a right and important factor in Christian family life' (Weeks 1989: 258). The Roman Catholic Church remained aloof from such liberalization, though until Pope Paul VI's encyclical *Humanae Vitae* in 1968 there was sufficient ambiguity in Church attitudes to encourage a degree of flexibility. But even after 1968, there is every sign that Catholic couples were following the trends of the rest of the population (Fisher 2006: 151). A key factor in changing attitudes was the general introduction of more effective and user-friendly contraception, represented above all by the Pill.

The Pill has achieved mythological status as the harbinger of women's liberation. A newspaper report of a survey of attitudes on what had most improved women's position in society, published in 2005, was headlined 'Women's lib owes it all to the pill' (D. Smith (2005), reporting on a study by Silvia Pezzini in the *Economic Journal*). Better birth control, including legal access to abortion, apparently trumped formal legal rights and employment rights in enhancing women's opportunities and increase in welfare. The veteran feminist writer Beatrix Campbell is quoted as saying that the results confirmed what she and others had always argued: for as long as women have been bearing children, they have been fighting for control over when and how they have children. Thus improved female control of fertility was vitally important. The use of the Pill, first available in 1961 was, in Hera Cook's view (2005a, 2005b), decisive in the further reduction of fertility, but more crucially in transforming the relationship between sexual activity and social behaviour, especially for women, by allowing them to gain control of their reproductive processes.

There could be no doubt of the enthusiasm with which women adopted the Pill. Barely a year after its introduction, 150,000 women were using it. Three years later, in 1964, the figure had risen to nearly half a million. By 1969, 48 per cent of all women aged 23 had used the Pill. Over 80 per cent of women born between 1950 and 1959 had done the same by 1989. The Pill was not, of course, risk-free. By the 1970s there was widespread discussion of the health risks to women, and a scare in 1977 led half a million to abandon the drug (Weeks 1989: 260). But what publicity of the Pill had successfully done was to stimulate a national conversation about effective birth control, and to increase use of other devices. By the end of the 1960s the vast majority of young married couples were using effective birth control.

A number of commentators since (including myself) have, nevertheless, been sceptical about the revolutionary implications of the Pill. Attention has been drawn to the fact that, though undoubtedly widely used, its incidence of use decreased down the social scale and in a movement from the southeast of England to the northwest (Weeks 1989: 260). Class and relative deprivation, as ever, shaped the impact of innovation. Moreover, the Pill was more likely to be used by the married and relatively secure than by the young, single and vulnerable. Despite its availability, and the Gillick ruling in 1986 which confirmed that doctors were permitted to prescribe contraception to under 16s (Weeks 1989: 297), teenage pregnancy remained far higher in the UK than in comparable European countries such as the Netherlands, and more like the US model where extremely poor sex education seemed to correlate with high teenage pregnancy. The Pill, and other contraceptive devices in and of themselves did not substitute for continuing inadequacies in sex education, conservatism in the medical profession, or above all traditionalism in many men. The possibility of women having greater control over their fertility often sat uneasily with the resistance of many men, especially working-class men, to the abandonment of male methods (Fisher 2006: 242). Finally, it has been all too tempting to see the widespread distribution of the Pill through the NHS as an aspect of continuing social regulation of women, particularly in a period of apparent population growth (Weeks 1989: 259–60).

But distance breeds more balanced perspectives. From the vantage point of forty years it is clear that the widespread use of more effective and mainly female controlled contraceptives, in the context of wider social changes, did have a crucial effect. For Cook (2005a: 339) the change since the late 1960s has not been primarily cultural but 'the transformation of conception and pregnancy from an uncontrollable risk to a freely chosen outcome of sexual intercourse', and in this the Pill has been materially decisive. What made the Pill so attractive was that it was not only a female birth control device – there had been various others – but that it was easy to use without the embarrassment of the earlier devices, and without fundamentally challenging the gendered order. It did not require complex negotiations, was less likely to provoke male shame or resistance, nor did it challenge the existing sexual practices of men or women. At the same time, it is difficult to see how better contraception, in women's hands, could have been so effective without an accompanying transformation in women's sense of their sexual freedom to choose, suggesting a wider change in the sexual culture, which involved a new assertiveness on the part of women around sexual issues (Fisher 2006: 239–40). Between the 1960s and 1990s the rebalancing of male–female relationships reflected a new sexual self-confidence among women, in which more effective contraception was a necessary if not sufficient factor.

Breaking the links: sex without reproduction, sex without marriage

When all the qualifications are made, the Pill symbolized highly significant shifts in the relationship between sexuality and society. As Cook argues, 'the dominant sexual culture in Britain is heterosexual, and use of the Pill enabled immense change to take place in this culture', and particularly in the position of women (2005a: 281). Not all women engage in heterosexual sex, but 100 per cent of heterosexual sex involves women. In the first place effective female control of fertility broke the link between sexual activity and reproduction, thus opening marriage and other sexual relations to seeing sex purely in terms of pleasure, and detaching it from economic and cultural consequences. One of the longer term effects of this was to weaken the tie between marriage and sexual activity. Over time it gradually ceased to be the privileged gateway to sanctioned and respectable sexuality, with marriage increasingly becoming a symbolic recognition of commitment rather than the key social institution that safeguarded society. The boundaries between married and single women became increasingly fuzzy. Single women could now be sexually active without a long-term commitment; and married women could remain voluntarily childless (Cook 2005b: 123). Marriage, relationships and parenting were also now potentially separable.

Most heterosexuals, however, still got married, and the majority still had children, though here again there were significant moves. The decreasing size of families from the late 1960s, and the compression of births into a relatively short period, meant that the traditional married relationship was no longer dominated by the fear of pregnancy, and could concentrate even more than in the past on childrearing. This fitted in with wider perceived shifts in family relationships. The companionate model espoused in the 1950s was, according to Young and Willmott (1973), being refined into what they described as the 'symmetrical relationship', made up of 'opposite but similar' partners, and this new model, which had originated in the more privileged classes, was now being diffused downwards (Young and Willmott 1973: 32–3). There were three major characteristics of this 'symmetrical family': the couple and children were more focused on the home; the nuclear nature of the family was becoming more pronounced than ever; and 'the roles of the sexes have become less segregated' (1973: 27–30). This was an ideal type, and the lived reality was more complex: the relationships within the household remained far from equal as feminist critics of the family were soon to point out. But what is important in retrospect is the degree to which the couple relationship remained normative, though from the 1970s it need no longer be a married couple relationship, nor did they necessarily feel the need to have children. Increasingly, cohabitation became an option, either as prelude to marriage or by the 1990s an alternative.

These changes took many years to work their way through the culture. Their impact has not been uniform and, in an increasingly diversified culture, in large part a result of large-scale migration into Britain, other patterns are discernible: of large families, arranged marriages, taboos against sexual unorthodoxy and so on. Not everything changed in this period of transition, but there can be no doubt about the general direction of change, nor of the impact on individual lives. As Wouters (1998: 189) argues, a process of 'trial and error' was going on among many millions of people, a 'collective learning process' to find the appropriate balance between the generations, between men and women, between reproduction and sexual pleasure, sex and relationships, and between relationships and parenting. Men and women, in reshaping in their everyday activities what Norbert Elias called the 'pleasure economy', and Wouters less romantically dubbed the 'lust balance', have had to ask themselves new questions: *'when and within what kinds of relationship(s) are (what kind of) eroticism and sexuality allowed and desired'* (Wouters 1998: 198; emphasis in original). In finding in their millions, and in different ways, responses to these questions, people were dissolving the old certainties, deinstitutionalizing and reconstructing the traditional life course, and working towards the democratization of intimate life.

Autonomy, agency and identity: the process of individualization

Autonomy

Democratization is a long-drawn-out process, involving many local battles as well as strategic shifts in the relationship between men and women, the heterosexual order and homosexuality, the state and individuals. At the heart of the process is the undermining of traditional sources of authority in order to achieve an ever growing sense of control over one's own life, of self-determination. This in turn involves resolving the complex relationships between individual autonomy, agency and personal and collective identities.

None of these issues was new, and we have seen how in the 1940s Mass-Observation was already picking up concern about the impact of changing mores on individual decision-making. The central dilemma was where, if faith in traditional authority and in religion-based morality was eroding, could notions of good or evil, right or wrong be found. The debates stimulated by the Wolfenden Report were, in effect, codifying where the only answer could be found: in consenting individuals in the context in which they found themselves, making pragmatic decisions about what was acceptable or not acceptable. In other words, the drift of debate, and increasingly of practice, was moving towards a full accept-ance of ethical individualism. This fitted in with wider transformations that were incipient in the 1960s, and most obvious from the 1980s onwards: an accentuated individualism in all aspects of social life, from economics to welfare. Forms of individualism had long been central to the organization of everyday life in Britain – a point made by Laslett (1965) in *The World We Have Lost*, and confirmed by many sociological accounts of family interactions (see Finch and Mason 1993; Lewis 2001), which have also stressed that it is not incompatible with responsibility to others – indeed, in some ways it is its precondition. I will discuss this in more detail in subsequent chapters. But what was becoming clear during the transition was a new emphasis on the importance of individual autonomy in relation to all matters relating to sexuality and intimate life.

It is important to see this in the context of what has come to be known as 'individualization'. For Beck and Beck-Gernsheim (2002), the best-known theorists of individualization, this is a *social* process in which individualism is institutionalized as the central aspect of the social structure, so that the institutions of modern society – from basic civil, political and social rights through to patterns of work and education – are geared to the individual not the group, with profound effects on family life (see e.g. Beck and Beck-Gernsheim 1995). It is quite simply the way in which late modern societies are organized, and is the product of profound restructuring of advanced industrial societies from the 1970s. Institutionalized individualism has to be distinguished from the neo-liberal concept of free-market individualism that became the ideological glue of the 1980s in both the USA and Britain. It does not celebrate the disembedding of individuals from old social structures, nor glorify the pursuit of self over others. It attempts to recognize, however, what the new configuration of contemporary societies actually is. Institutionalized individualism is not incompatible with what Beck and Beck-Gernsheim (2002: xxiii) call 'cooperative individualism'. On the contrary, it opens up the possibility of achieving it; but the precondition is that we fully understand the profound processes now at work.

In the 1960s and 1970s the wider transformations were only dimly presenting themselves, but the growing importance of the discourse of sexual freedom was central to the cultural ferment that was developing. At the heart of this was, again, the position of women. The question of female sexual autonomy had long been on the agenda, but until the early twentieth century it had been largely seen within a framework of risk and protection. Despite the efforts of more sexually radical feminists like Stella Browne and the *Freewoman* journal during the years leading up to the Great War, it was not until the interwar years that a positive discourse of female sexual autonomy and pleasure emerged, and this was limited in circulation until the late 1940s and 1950s (Lewis 1982; Weeks 1989: 160–7; Bland 2001; Szreter 2002: 567–73). For most women, as we saw in the previous chapter, individual aspirations were overwhelmingly shaped by and coincided with the needs of their families. Family and individual survival depended on the family sticking together. The introduction of the safety net provided by the Welfare State opened up other possibilities by reducing relative risk if women expanded their aspirations. The substantial decrease in women's reproductive labour from the 1940s, falling dramatically from the late 1960s, opened up new possibilities. As Pat Thane observes, daughters growing to maturity in the late 1950s and 1960s had 'more confident hopes than their mothers of their capacity to control their own lives' (Thane 1999: 131; see also Heron 1985). Carolyn Steedman (1986: 122), reflecting on the impact of the Welfare State while growing up in the 1950s, writes:

> I think I would be a very different person now if orange juice and
> milk and dinners hadn't told me, in a covert way, that I had a
> right to exist, was worth something. My inheritance from those
> years is the belief (maintained always with some difficulty) that
> I do have a right to the earth.

Women continued to be defined within their familial commitments, and indeed within their specifically class contexts. But something was changing. There was a clear weakening of female deference in relation to sexuality, and an assertion not only of reproductive rights but also of female sexual freedoms. Part of this can be related to wider structural shifts that were transforming relationships: the weakening of the family, the decline of patriarchal authority, the ever increasing inclusion of women in the workforce, the transformation of the conditions of parenthood, the consumer revolution that was giving women a greater purchase on society, albeit within constricted patterns, and so on. All of this is important. But in stressing such structural factors it is all too easy to minimize individual and collective agency. Like Steedman, many were now thinking that they had 'a right to the earth'. There was an opening up of choice, even if choice was still sharply constrained by economic and cultural factors. Despite greater social mobility, most women found love and sex within their own social milieux. But at the same time, the legal framework which had limited women's freedoms were changing. From the mid-1960s to the late 1970s there was an unprecedented retreat of state and community controls over women: free contraception, more relaxed abortion laws, easier divorce, equal pay and sex discrimination legislation. Women were achieving greater freedom than ever before to claim their individuality and remake their biographies.

The increasing agency of women was the key to other changes. In the first place, it was vital in the shifting relationships between men and women, to the rebalancing discussed earlier. But in reshaping heterosexual relationships it also opened up new possibilities, including non-heterosexual relationships, though in the 1960s these remained constrained by assumptions that homosexuality was at best an unfortunate condition. As Elizabeth Wilson remembered, speaking chiefly of the liberal intelligentsia, 'This then was our place in the permissive society – to make our friends feel liberated and progressive by "accepting" us, without their having to feel any challenge to their own sexual identity' (Wilson 1974: 114). But in the interstices of a liberalizing culture, a more explicit lesbian subculture in places such as London and Brighton provided the space for the negotiation of identity and community (Brighton Ourstory Project 1992; Gardiner 2003; Jennings 2004, 2006). Yet more promising was the rebirth of what came increasingly to be known as *sexual* politics, after Wilhelm Reich and more immediately the American feminist Kate Millett (see Weeks 1985). Here was a domain of agency that conventional politics had ignored. The new possibilities were dramatized and propelled by the emergence of the two movements that were to transform the meanings of agency in relation to the gender/ sexuality nexus: women's liberation and gay liberation.

Agency and social change

From the perspective of the twenty-first century it is less the 'movement' that seems important than an amorphous sense of individual empowerment. For those who proclaimed they were post-feminist or post-gay in the new millennium lifestyle improvements seemed more relevant than emancipatory claims (see discussion in Walter 1999). Yet as Segal forcefully asserts, 'Women's Liberation in its heyday was *a theory and practice of social transformation*' aiming at no less than 'increasing the power and self determination of women everywhere' (Segal 1999: 15, 27). In the same way, early gay liberation identified closely with other emancipatory movements, broadly allied itself with the radical Left, in Britain at least, and asserted that fundamental change was necessary to achieve sexual freedom (Weeks 1990: 185–206; Power 1995). The new sexual movements focused attention on the structural factors that inhibited individual autonomy and around which power, and relations of domination, subordination and Othering circulated. 'The family' for both second-wave feminism and gay liberation became the material and symbolic forcing house of inequality (see the arguments of Barrett and McIntosh 1982). The new movements were the forms of collective agency which could challenge this. For women it meant a fundamental challenge to the structures of male/patriarchal/heterosexist (the language varied) power. The ending of the binary divide between heterosexuality and homosexuality was an equally profound challenge. Looking forward to the 'end of the homosexual' as a distinct minority being demanded the 'end of the heterosexual' as the normative figure (Altman 1993).

The two movements had emerged first of all in the United States, but had come to Britain by 1969 (in the case of the women's movement) and 1970 (in the case of gay liberation). In each case there had been precursors, most famously in first-wave feminism, but also in the form of small-scale and often covert organizations for sexual reform, particularly the decriminalization of homosexuality, since the late nineteenth century. The two streams were often intricately, if often uneasily, entangled. Leading sexual theorists like Havelock Ellis or sexual radicals like Edward Carpenter were strong advocates, within the discourses of the time, of female emancipation as well as of homosexual rights and reform of archaic divorce laws, campaigners for birth control and so on. Other feminists were more cautious in associating themselves too closely with radical sex reform for fear of stymieing more immediate changes, such as suffrage reforms. Yet other feminists concentrated on attacking the double standard in men, which often resulted in legislation that had unintended consequences (Weeks 1989: 160–75; Bland 2001). Most famously, the Criminal Law Amendment Act of 1885, the culmination of a campaign against the double standard that had uneasily united moral feminists, working-class campaigners against sexual exploitation of their daughters and the popular press, not only sought to protect young girls by raising their age of consent from 13 to 16 and clamping down on brothels, but also led to the effective outlawing of all forms of male homosexual activity, whether in public or in private (Weeks 1990: 102; Waites 2005a).

On the other hand, campaigners for birth control played down their feminism. Marie Stopes was careful to wrap her passionate advocacy of releasing women from the toils of unwanted pregnancy and discovering the pleasures of sexuality within a conservative familial morality that eschewed feminism (Weeks 1989: 188–9). This, ironically, was in tune with the broad trajectory of women's campaigning. The early women's movement had pushed the case for women's suffrage and equal rights from the 1860s, and had a less overt but still influential afterlife in the women's organizations of the interwars, especially those pressing for support for better maternity and childcare facilities and family allowances (Lewis 1980). On the whole, its sexual politics had been morally conservative, concerned to protect women from the double standard and sexual exploitation rather than proclaim women's right to sexual pleasure (Bland 2001). Neither had it fundamentally challenged the sexual division of labour. But in this form it had fed into sustaining women's resistance to male predatoriness and had been a strong element in the construction of a culture of sexual restraint in the absence of effective contraception. Lesbianism may have been a quiet undercurrent in feminist circles but it played no part in mainstream women's activism. However unfairly, it is not surprising that, by the early 1960s, for a new generation of radical women, feminism seemed a conservative force when compared to the excitements of leftist and grass-roots politics (Rowbotham 2001). In the case of homosexual politics, there was no history of mass politics, but instead of cautious, pragmatic pressure group politics, especially associated with the Homosexual Law Reform Society founded in 1958 to campaign for the Wolfenden proposals (Weeks 1990: 128–43, 168–72).

Agency: the women's movement

Yet beneath the surface, in what Beck (1994) called the 'sub-political' world, profound stirrings were making themselves felt, which were to explode in the new radicalism from the late 1960s. Part of the energy, and a large part of the rhetoric, came from the counter-culture which had resisted 'straight society' and proclaimed a new age of hedonism and resistance to corporate culture. The political prehistories of the new activists were in CND, student politics, civil rights or anti-apartheid movements. Gradually young women were putting together the pieces of a coherent new philosophy and politics. For Sheila Rowbotham, too romantic to fall for the flip cynicism of Helen Gurley Brown's best-selling *Sex and the Single Girl*, *ad hoc* inspiration came from Simone de Beauvoir's *The Second Sex*, Juliette Greco singing 'Je suis comme je suise', Edith Piaf's 'Non, je regrette rien' and Bessy Smith's earthy blues (2001: 10). If the elements of a new female assertiveness were in the air, the unifying factor was the sense of contradiction between the promises opened up by the 1960s and the realities of most women's lives: working-class women continuing to face low pay, and male conservatism in the workforce; aspirant middle-class women frustrated by male indifference or outright opposition, especially in would-be progressive organizations.

As Lynne Segal sharply noted,

> I was one of so many student activists of the 1960s who
> discovered, all of a sudden, *after* working with our 'brothers'
> to oppose the evils of the Vietnam war, *after* being there to
> support students in 1968, *after* supporting workers in struggle
> in an era of trade union militancy, *after*, above all, seeing
> ourselves the hip chicks of the 60s sexual liberation, facing
> ever cruder sexist pin-ups and porn in the underground press,
> confronting the sexism of our comrades – after all this, many
> women glimpsed that we needed as bit of liberation of our own.
> And that was the birth of women's liberation. We danced into
> our own liberation. I know no-one who has looked back.
>
> (Segal 2006: 18)

This was part of a problem that was still finding its name, exploring the different languages through which to articulate new perceptions. Rowbotham again expresses this graphically. She speaks of

> a turmoil of confusion and a collision of assumptions (between
> young women and men) which many young women like us
> were facing all over the country. Determined not to follow the
> patterns set by our mothers in being women, we wanted to
> relate differently to men, but there were no received assumptions
> about how this might be.
>
> (Rowbotham 2001: 10)

The different elements that eventually came together may be symbolized by the early publications. On the one hand there was the radical individualism of Germaine Greer's *The Female Eunuch* (1970), the beginning of a writer's erratic journey that was later to see a move from attacks on female entrapment in maternity to passionate endorsement of its necessity, passionate advocacy of sexual pleasure to ardent advocacy of celibacy. On the other was the exploratory construction of the links between feminism and the new politics (Rowbotham 1973) or the links between Marxism and feminism (Mitchell 1973), or the beginnings of a vast outpouring of personal experiences, the stories of the new feminism (e.g. Wandor 1972; Feminist Anthology Collective 1981; Wilson 1982; Rowbotham 2001).

But despite the heady hopes and genuine reshaping of many lives, the new consciousness brought with it turmoil and conflict as well. Elizabeth Wilson's first novel *Prisons of Glass* (1986) captures this well. She explores the impact of the women's liberation movement on a group of young women. The central character Crystal feels liberated in the heady atmosphere of the 1960s, but only when she encounters the women's movement does she realize the limitations of the sort of liberalism she has so far encountered. She experiences to the full the promise of the new movement but also soon learns of the difficulty of breaking out of the glass prison. Through the 1970s into the 1980s Crystal and her friends discover how difficult it is to change. Aspirations for freedom of choice are balanced by a sense of guilt, self-criticism and alienation as many hopes and dreams crumble. New types of sexual experience bring pains as well as pleasures, and as time passes so hopes of early solutions fade, in a harsher social and political climate.

What they were seeking to put into words and action was the central dilemma. New spaces and opportunities were opening up for women as never before, in education, the workplace, in sexual freedoms, but in ways that often confirmed rather than fundamentally challenged the gender and sexual order: women's sexuality was often commercialized and trivialized even as autonomy was celebrated; even the most sympathetic of men could trap women by their needs, while women's caring responsibilities were resilient to change; the heterosexual hegemony remained unchallenged, while lesbianism remained marginalized. Above all, despite all the celebrated advances of women, they remained subordinate, largely due to the obduracy of male structures, but sometimes because of deeply embedded resistance to change in women themselves – what Rosalind Coward (1992) later called women's 'treacherous hearts', and the myriad bonds, conscious and unconscious, that tied women to the authority and power of men. The early demands of the new movement, despite its revolutionary rhetoric, had attempted to sum up the common agenda of all women in a list that was ostensibly modest: equal pay and full legal independence, free twenty-four-hour nursery provision, free access to birth control and abortion on demand, and sexual autonomy and the ending of the oppression of lesbians (Wandor 1972: 2; the final demand was subsequently added). Shorn of later analysis and rhetoric which introduced concepts such as (hetero)sexism and patriarchy, these basic demands nevertheless in principle posed a potent challenge to the structured inequalities which limited women's autonomy and agency. More than forty years later the majority of the demands remain, despite genuine progress in many spheres, unfulfilled in their entirety. They were not so modest after all.

From the start, as the basic demands vividly illustrate, questions of sexuality were at the heart of the new wave of feminism. The subordination of female sexuality was seen as central to women's inequality. As Beatrix Campbell wrote in 1972, 'We used to lie back and think of England. Now we lie back and think of the heavens . . . "it's the most beautiful thing that can happen to you", said one of my teachers. Precisely, it happens to you. You don't do it, it's done to you' (Campbell in Allen *et al.* 1974: 101). So, 'When we reclaim our sexuality we will have reclaimed our belief in ourselves as women' (Hamblin 1974: 96). Birth control, abortion, lesbianism, sexual pleasure, relationships to men, resistance to sexual violence, challenges to overt sexism as in the annual Miss World events, all raised questions about who should control women's bodies, about autonomy: 'Not the Church, not the state, women must control their fate', as a familiar slogan put it.

But saying this proved easier than living it. Sexuality, far from being the unifying element in women's struggle for emancipation, proved to be the most divisive. Part of it was the dilemma which had been at the heart of the first wave of feminism, between women's freedom and safety, between choice and security, between pleasure and danger (see essays in Vance 1984 and Snitow *et al.* 1984). Even the pleasures had their dangers and risks: of unwanted pregnancy, of potential disease, of continued subordination to men through emotional ties. For many, however, it was danger that increasingly defined women's situation: the danger of endemic violence against women, the violence, especially, of pornography, and more widely the dangers of heterosexuality. This tension between pleasure and danger was to prove particularly devastating in the American movement in the early 1980s, but had a dramatic impact in the UK also, and sums up a divide which in the end was to destroy the impact of women's liberation as a movement. By the end of the 1970s, the main trajectory of women's liberation had shifted from an emphasis on women's shared needs and struggles to end gender inequalities and social and cultural subordination, towards an exploration of difference, between men and women, and among women themselves, especially over race and ethnicity, and sexuality (Segal 1999: 5). In part this was a welcome development, particularly as it underlined the different experiences of women, and especially with regard to ethnic and racial diversity. The theoretical critique of the family in feminist discourse was widely seen by the 1980s as blighted by an ignorance of the role of the black family in resisting racism (see Mirza 1997). More widely, black feminists saw wider limitations in Euro-American feminism, which 'contributed to an improvement in the material situation of white middle-class women often at the expense of their black and working class "sisters"' (Amos *et al.* 1984; Amos and Parma 1984; Knowles and Mercer 1992; Segal 1999: 23). This potent evocation of raced and classed differences pointed to the difficulties of a unified feminism. Women, far from having naturally common interests, were positioned in different histories, different relationships to power and authority, and different relationships to the erotic. Feminism could no longer be readily seen as a philosophy for all women; it was a project to be constructed from difference and diversity. But what Segal (1999) called the 'allure of difference' led not to an easy acceptance of plural existences but to absolutist positionings, with sexuality as a major battleground.

At the heart of the divide was a fundamental clash over the relationship between gender and sexuality, and the possibilities of shifting the relations of power around the erotic. For an increasingly powerful and fundamentalist tendency, the cultural radical or revolutionary feminists, sex was the ultimate focus of women's oppression. According to the influential American cultural feminist Catherine MacKinnon (quoted in Segal 1999: 46), gender consolidates itself through emotional domination and submission: 'the social relation between the sexes is organized so that men may dominate and women must submit and this relation is sexual

– in fact, is sex.' This philosophy underpinned the highly emotional writings of the anti-porn campaigner Andrea Dworkin (1981, 1989), whose impassioned prose echoed the rhythms of frenzied, pornographic encounter, and which made a spectacular initial impact in Britain, and in turn produced a more nuanced and subtle, if no less forceful, analysis that refused the emotional blackmail (see e.g. essays in Rodgerson and Wilson 1991; Segal and McIntosh 1992). The same highly emotive rhetorical politics propelled the political lesbian current. For revolutionary feminists lesbianism was no longer simply and straightfowardly a sexual preference and identity that had been historically denied. It was more like the essence of essential womenhood, and a necessary form of resistance to hegemonic hetero-patriarchy. In the process lesbianism was desexualized, and heterosexual (and other forms of) feminism were effectively demonized (for a classic statement see Jeffreys 1993). The recognition that sexuality and power were inextricably bound together was common among all forms of feminism. For many, however, what was at stake in these increasingly fevered controversies was the rejection of a uni-dimensional analysis of women's oppression which attempted to reduce all forms of subordination to women's sexual victimization by men. The alternative was to recognize the diversity of female sexualities, from celibacy through chosen heterosexuality to lesbianism, including butch–femme relationships and sado-masochism (s/m). Female sexuality could be a domain of choice and identity.

Nevertheless, there were perhaps two important gains from this controversy. The first was the growing awareness of the complex and intricate coils of power that entwined women. Power was gendered. A major aspect of this was violence against women, a violence that could not be reduced to sex alone but had to be understood as part of a larger complex of forces that shaped masculinity and femininity. Few feminists dissented from this, but the meanings and implications of violence were contested (Wilson 1983). At the same time a more sophisticated analysis of the institution of heterosexuality began to emerge. The idea of 'compulsory heterosexuality' had been put forward by Adrienne Rich (1984) at the beginning of the 1980s, and in its emphasis on the lesbian continuum that bound together all women had been enormously influential on political lesbianism. But it pointed to a wider structural issue. Heterosexuality was not simply one possible choice among many in a pluralist world. It was the hegemonic form, institutionalized in all the major social organizations of the culture. Later analyses of what was variously described as the 'heterosexual matrix', the 'heterosexual panorama', the 'heterosexual assumption', 'heteronormativity' and the like, though differing substantially in detail, all pointed to the significance of the heterosexual–homosexual binaryism as a fundamental structural divide in Western cultures, which marginalized and subordinated non-heterosexual existence (see discussion in Weeks *et al.* 2001: 39–43).

Identity: the lesbian and gay agenda

As this suggests, same-sex relationships became a vital issue within second-wave feminism. But non-heterosexuality had its own intricate and vital history, and though the lesbian and gay movement was influenced by debates within feminism, it had its own central preoccupations (Weeks 1990; Adam *et al.* 1999a). The initial impulse of all homosexual politics since the nineteenth century had been the assertion of the validity of same-sex desire and love, and the shaping of a viable sense of self, of identity. This is a well-established process we can see at work with the earliest public attempts to articulate a sense of homosexual being, as reflected in the work of the Founding Fathers of sexology. Their theoretical attempts to explain homosexuality, far from simply being an imposition on the lives of the sexually unorthodox, developed in dialogue with their clients or patients or case histories, many of whom were attempting to affirm their ordinariness and normality in a culture which simply saw them as evil or sick or both. Physicians and sexologists such as Krafft-Ebing, Havelock Ellis, Magnus Hirschfeld and others were conceptualizing notions of 'inversion' on the basis of letters, interviews, cases coming before the court, but basically using the materials presenting themselves (a process vividly described in Oosterhuis 2000; see also Weeks 1985: 61–95). The invert in turn was developing a sense of self in dialogue with the great men. The impact of Kinsey at the end of the 1940s was even more dramatic. It is not so much a process of discovery or recovery as of formulation, creation, invention – invention not of the experience, or the desires, but of the meanings, discourses, categories, identities that are being forged in everyday life, and in the clinic, the court, the text. This was, perhaps, only a tiny part of the process of articulating a sense of self and of self-worth, but it symbolizes the long process which by the early 1970s was to lead to the explosion of gay politics.

The difference the gay liberation movement represented was that an individual process of the construction of the self now became a consciously collective process, a new form of agency through a social movement whose aims were radical. Central to this was the idea that the liberation of the homosexual, and homosexuality as a potential in everyone, could only be achieved by challenging and overcoming the roots of homosexual oppression: the normative family, deeply enmeshed in advanced capitalism, and the institutionalized nature of heterosexuality (London Gay Liberation Front 1971; Altman 1993). At its most cosmic, the purpose was to make the distinction between homosexuality and heterosexuality irrelevant, to free everyone from the tyranny of social categories. Behind this was an emerging theory about the 'social construction' of homosexuality and indeed, logically of heterosexuality (on homosexuality see Plummer 1975; McIntosh 1981; Weeks 1990; on heterosexuality see Katz 1995; Johnson 2004, 2005) which brought sexual identities within the framework of history rather than pre-ordained destiny.

McIntosh's brilliant insight, that 'the homosexual' was a social role, not a 'condition' or pathology, was first put forward in 1968, and initially downplayed by McIntosh herself because it might distract from the important goal of changing the law (McIntosh 1981: 44; Weeks 2000: 69–70). In the 1960s the idea that homosexuality was an affliction that needed treatment was more likely to influence liberal opinion than an argument that the heterosexual/homosexual divide was a product of culture rather than nature. Within the more radical context of the new social-sexual movements of the 1970s and 1980s, however, it proved a fertile ground for activist theorists to till. Because if the sexual categorizations that were taken for granted were actually human inventions, then they could be reinvented (Weeks 1990).

In practice, for most people this translated into a celebration of guilt-free same-sex activity, and the development of a meaningful sense of identity and community. The relationship between the two was not always straightforward. For men in particular *sexual* freedom was a high imperative, and remained so throughout the trauma of AIDS and beyond. This was in part about the possibilities of easy sex, and that became a leitmotif of the 1970s for gay men, though heavily criticized by many lesbians (Escoffier 2003). But more fundamentally it was also about questioning the social relations of sexuality: compulsory couple-dom, monogamy, marriage and the traditional family, which was as much of concern to lesbians as to gay men (Weeks 1985: 195–208). Keith Birch, a young gay man in the early 1970s involved in gay liberation, recalls that 'Like the Women's Movement, GLF [Gay Liberation Front] raised the question of power between the sexes and in sexual relationships. We opened up to scrutiny the conduct of personal relationships and everyday life' (Birch 1988: 53). Sexual freedom and critique of what subsequently became known as heteronormative institutions morphed into new forms of identity (see contributions to Cant and Hemmings 1988). The affirmation of valid identities, built around sexuality but not reducible to it, became the central element of the movement as it developed into the 1980s, sustained by a wider sense of belonging. The idea of 'community' became central to this (Weeks 2000: 181–93).

A sense of community, of wider belonging, was more than a pious aspiration. In a real sense it was a precondition of making new identities possible (Weeks 1995: 82–123). But as in women's liberation, the unity of the movement was at best, in Epstein's (1999: 30) happy phrase, a 'convenient fiction'. From the start, in Britain as in the USA and elsewhere, there was a proliferation of political beliefs, practices and organizations, often competing, or in sharp disagreement, with each other. Debates about identity and difference overlapped with debates about the organization of desire and with concerns about public policies and private practices. In each country and culture gay liberation took on local characteristics. In Canada it overlapped with Quebec secessionism; in France with republican ideals of universalism; in the Netherlands it was shaped by the heritage of 'pillarization', the belief in the coexistence of parallel but different patterns of life; in the USA it rapidly adopted a quasi-ethnic identity-based pattern (Epstein 1990); in South Africa it ultimately became part of a politics about the fundamental rights of non-discrimination (see essays in Adam *et al.* 1999b).

In Britain Gay Liberation was at first strongly associated with the political Left, and identified strongly with the trade union and labour movements. But as Plummer has pointed out, in the end, rather than see it in terms of its political positioning, it is more useful to see it as 'a broadly based overlapping cluster of arenas of collective activity lodged in social worlds in which change is accomplished' (Plummer 1999: 137). Like feminism, gay liberation was from the first largely a movement among radicalized, often university educated young people of the baby boom generation. It passed most of the lesbian and gay world, let alone the wider population, by during most of the 1970s. But what it did was to provide the cultural context for a mass coming out of homosexuality, and to provide a new and more positive context for the shaping of self in new collective worlds. This was, at the same time, an unintended effect of the initial radical impulse. As Epstein has written, with particular reference to America but with a resonance in Britain too, 'The irony of radical gay liberation is that its most profound effect was to promote the development of forms of identity, community, and politics that were antithetical to its liberationist visions' (1999: 42). Instead of 'the end of the homosexual', and of the heterosexual too, as proposed by Altman (1993), we see the embedding of strong lesbian and gay identities, and in their wake a proliferation of other sexualized identities, some acceptable, others soon to receive their own anathemas, based on gender (lesbian, gay male), sexual desire (sado-masochist, paedophile), ethnicity and race (black lesbian and gay identities, South Asian, Latino), faith (Gay Christians, Muslims, Jews), object choice (bisexual), the transcendence of biology (transgendered), and so on and potentially on (Weeks 1985, 1995). The coming-out narratives of the past couple of generations have ultimately been about finding the 'true' self, and of flaunting it: I am what I am, my own special creation (Plummer 1995).

There's a paradox in all this. The dominant narrative has been of discovering one's place in the binary divide, of realizing a truth previously hidden not only from others but from the self, of coming out as lesbian or gay. Identity, Giddens has suggested, 'is the creation of constancy over time' (1994: 80). The coming-out stories that are an overwhelming feature of the lesbian and gay movement, whether told in private to another person, or in consciousness-raising groups, or at demonstrations or carnivals, and increasingly in books, television and on the internet, have created common stories, common histories, communicative communities and a sense of belonging, anchoring people in time and place. But of course, the narrative suggests something more than a simple recounting of personal truths. What we are actually witnessing are stories of self-invention. Sexual identity, like gender identity, may be, in Butler's words, a 'stylized repetition of acts' (1990: 140). The acts of self-creation are not arbitrary or free, but structured: they follow certain possibilities, with an increasingly well-honed grammar and vocabulary. Yet the narrative of self-invention was very strong. This sense that identities can be not only made but constantly remade, that they are more fluid and flexible than many would want to acknowledge was, by the 1990s, to become the site of a fundamental challenge to apparently fixed and resonant identities: this was the space of 'queer'. If identity is arbitrary then why not query or queer them all (Warner 1993, 1999)? This new, more radical and transgressive stance had the nice merit of fitting in with broader theoretical efforts – mainly post-structuralist – to challenge the fixity of identities. Is it possible, Denise Riley asked in the late 1980s, to inhabit a gender without a feeling of horror (Riley 1988)? Similarly, could the constraints of identity categories really tell us all we need to know about the complexities and ambiguities of individual needs or desires (see Butler 1990)? But that, in practice, is easier said than done. Even the queer attempts to query identity end up reasserting it, for what else is the label 'queer' but a non-identity identity? For identities are, as I have argued elsewhere, deeply paradoxical. They tell us about what we have in common with some people and what differentiates us from others. They seem to be about us alone, and yet many people and traditions populate that 'we'. They seem absolutely fundamental to who and what we are, and yet the history clearly shows they are historically variable and contingent. They are 'fictions', stories told to and by us in an intricate and still unfolding history, but 'necessary fictions', in the sense that we do not seem able to do without them (Weeks 1995: 86–101).

In all societies, as Giddens (1994: 80) has argued, the maintenance of personal identity, and its links to wider social identities, is a prime requisite of ontological security, and creates a very strong emotional attachment. This was a crucial element in early gay liberation politics in fuelling political and cultural energy, and in stimulating the enormous growth of gay community institutions, from newspapers and journals to sex clubs, from faith groups to discos, from specialist sex shops to gay restaurants and hotels, from masseurs to gay lawyers, dentists and estate agents/realtors. This vast social and entrepreneurial space, evident in all the metropolitan areas of the West by the 1980s, represented a growing integration of dissident sexualities into the market economy. But it fed on, and in turn shaped, the spaces of identity through which individual lives were lived.

In retrospect we can see the women's and gay liberation movements as major forces in shaping what Giddens (1991) calls the 'reflexive project of the self', where we constantly write and rewrite the narratives of our lives in circumstances which seem free but have been handed down to us by complex, intersecting histories. Both movements were concerned with freeing individuals from the burdens of history, whether of tradition, patriarchy, homophobia or heteronormativity, and at their heart is the assumption of individual autonomy. Part of the legacy can no doubt be traced in the hyper-individualism that was to flourish in the 1980s, though the dominant moral tone of that decade was authoritarian rather than libertarian. A longer term legacy lay in the undermining of previous certainties about the nature of sexuality and the fixity of sexual identities.

4

The great transition 2
Regulation, risk and resistance

We are reaping what was sown in the sixties . . . fashionable
theories and permissive claptrap set the scene for a society in
which old values of discipline and restraint were denigrated.
(Margaret Thatcher in 1982, quoted in
Marwick 1998: 4)

A non-traditional culture dispenses with final authorities.
Increasingly we live in a world of multiple authorities.
(Giddens 1994: 87)

Private passions and public policies

Questions of the balance between private and public were inherent in the
new social movements, of which women's liberation and gay liberation
were probably the most successful. New social movements, their theorists
have argued, are located solidly in civil society, in the world of everyday
life (Castells 1983, 1997; Melucci 1989). They symbolically distance themselves from the state, and from the enmeshment in state policies that
characterizes the traditional great movements of labour. There was, at
least at first, a retreat from or rejection of conventional politics, but they
were of course highly political, both in broadening the definition of
what could come within the bounds of political practice, and in the basic
sense that they were concerned with power relations. They represented
that form of sub-politics which forces conventional institutions to
confront their limitations (Beck 1994: 20). But at the same time there
were new forms of creativity at the grass-roots level. In part this represented an 'inner migration' to new niches of activity and identity. Sheila
Rowbotham (2001) among others has seen this process as 'prefigurative',
which suggests that they preceded a bigger change to come. But in retrospect they *were* the change: this new politics was creating different ways
of being and relating in the here and now, not in some utopian future.
These were genuine 'life experiments' that were remaking identities and
what Bech (1997) calls 'ways of being in the world'.

Central to this was a crossing and blurring of the boundaries between
public and private. Feminist politics from the start had been concerned

with bringing into public debate the significance of private practice, with politicizing the personal. The media publicity given to some minor bra-burning in the early 1970s had nothing to do with its likely reality but with its symbolism. More significant and powerful were the ways in which women's experience, freely if painfully exchanged through consciousness-raising, set the agenda of issues, from mothering to sexual desire. Feminist theory soon followed, by demonstrating the ways in which historically women's oppression had been structured by the emergence of demarcations between the private spheres (the location of women's aspirations and duties) and the public (the domain of men). The historicization and politicization of this divide opened up the opportunity to shift the boundaries. There were several profound effects. In the first place it broadened the basis of politics. Abortion was an early entry into mainstream politics of what had previously been marginalized. In the USA from the 1970s it became a touchstone issue between progressives and conservatives, that was to consolidate the Christian Right and then the Republican Party base. In Britain it was always more of a cross-party issue that never became a transformative political issue (Weeks 1985: 33–9). By the turn of the millennium, however, a range of previously 'soft' or 'women's' issues became central to political re-ordering. Second, it produced a politics of paradox: where going public on an issue was seen as essential to achieving private gains. This was true, *par excellence*, of gay politics: the very idea of 'coming out' was to affirm the public validity of one's sexuality in order to safeguard one's private choices.

Already, before the emergence of the radical movements, by the late 1960s a coherent legal and moral framework had been put in place for dealing with sexual change. Across most of the Western world, although at different paces in different countries, the 1960s and 1970s saw a host of important legal changes which partially at least decriminalized homosexuality, abortion and pornography and promoted birth control and the like. In Britain, the so-called permissive legislation, enacted by the Labour government of 1964–1970, and steered by the reforming Home Secretary Roy Jenkins, was infused by the Wolfenden strategy as outlined in Sir John Wolfenden's report (HMSO 1957) which, as we saw in Chapter 2, relied on a critical distinction between public and private. The inherited moral framework had been draconian, if patchy in its implementation, and had assumed a moral purpose to law. The swathe of 1960s reforms piece by piece sought to dismantle this, and replace it by a more liberal and utilitarian framework, which sought to separate what the state could legitimately do on behalf of public order – basically sustain standards of agreed decency in public behaviour – and how it should intervene in private life. The Suicide Act of 1961 was the harbinger of change (Holden 2004: 4). Previously, suicide had been a criminal act; its failed perpetrators could wake up from an overdose and find themselves facing criminal charges with the prospect of prison (when I tell my students this they laugh in disbelief). As Hart put it,

'It is the first Act of Parliament for at least a century to remove altogether the penalties of the criminal law from a practice clearly condemned by conventional Christian morality and punishable by law' (Weeks 1989: 251).

This was a clear move from the traditional standards of public morality towards the centrality of individual consent about private actions. The separation of law and morality developed in the Wolfenden strategy, and reflected in the swathe of reform that was to follow, on censorship, abortion, homosexuality, divorce, birth control, marks a crucial stage in shifting the balance of decision-making from the public to the private sphere. This did not represent a positive endorsement of all the activities which were the subject of legislation. There was no full acceptance of obscenity, abortion, homosexuality or divorce in law. The main humanitarian thrust was more to remove archaic laws and to minimize suffering than to endorse alternative ways of life. The Obscene Publications Act of 1959, amended in 1964, sought to respond to changing tastes by introducing the test of 'literary merit' which led to the breakthrough *Lady Chatterley's Lover* case brought by Penguin Books, perhaps the most iconic moment of sexual change in the early 1960s (Sandbrook 2005: 421–2). It did not herald a flood of pornography. The Sexual Offences Act of 1967 modestly attempted to decriminalize male homosexuality in private rather than legalize homosexuality. The Abortion Act of the same year established social grounds for abortion but there was no abortion on demand. The Divorce Law reforms of 1969 modified the grounds for divorce to make it easier to exit failed marriages but did not fully legislate for divorce by consent. Even the National Health Service (Family Planning) Act of 1967 was concerned as much with tidying up the messy spread of family planning clinics by encouraging local authorities to provide facilities on social as well as narrowly medical grounds as with promoting the spread of birth control (Weeks 1989: 249–68).

At the same time there was no surrender to libertarianism and anything goes. Each piece of legislation maintained an element of control. Already in the wake of the Wolfenden Report, the rushing into law of the 1959 Street Offences Act, designed to sweep prostitution off the streets, to privatize it, demonstrated that reform could be restrictive as well as progressive. Decriminalization of male homosexuality in private was balanced by excluding the armed services and merchant navy, as well as Scotland and Northern Ireland, restricting the definition of private, and tightening the regulations on public indecency – which led to a threefold increase in offences in the next few years. Abortion reform required permission from two medically qualified people before an abortion could legally go ahead up to twenty-eight weeks. Divorce reform did not rid the law of the idea of a matrimonial offence. The free availability of contraception has in part been seen as propelled by an anxiety about population growth and, as has been argued, was as much about control of women's sexuality as a move towards greater freedom. Nor were all the legal shifts towards moral pragmatism. A renewed burst of prosecutions for obscenity in the 1960s and early 1970s saw attacks on other books, notoriously Hubert Selby's *Last Exit to Brooklyn*, and on alternative publications. Prosecution of the underground magazine *International Times* (*IT*) for publishing gay small ads, and of *Oz* for its Schools Kids edition, which unfortunately belied its claim that the law was a 'paper tiger', showed that legal moralism was not dead. But each case produced a furore, and gradually made prosecutors unwilling to risk bringing obscenity cases to court (Weeks 1989: 273–8).

What these legal shifts indicate is that efforts were being made to find a balance between consent and control, between private decision-making and public regulation. Jenkins had a notion of a more 'civilized society' but most of his more or less liberal supporters were concerned to modernize the law in accord with the rhetoric of the day, which in practice meant finding a pragmatic solution to problems posed by self-evident sexual and social change. Moreover, there were some areas where rebalancing public and private was absolutely necessary where reform proved slow to enter. This was clearest in relation to the privacies of the marital bed. In particular, the question of rape in marriage remained too delicate an issue for a further couple of decades. Under existing legis-lation the husband could not be guilty of rape because by the matrimonial contract the wife gave up consent to the husband. If a woman cannot consent she cannot be raped. The House of Lords only ruled against this interpretation in 1991, explicitly on the grounds that there had been significant changes in the nature of marriage and the status of women. This was given parliamentary endorsement in amendments to the Criminal Justice and Public Order Act 1994 (Cook 2005b: 127–8, n.73).

The liberal hour was limited, and brief. By the end of the 1960s, Jenkins' successor as Home Secretary, the embodiment of Labour social conservatism, James Callaghan, was signalling the end of the permissive revolution (Weeks 1989: 276). The Wolfenden strategy was nevertheless to provide an enduring framework for the rest of the century for moral reformers – for the unsuccessful proposals of the Williams Committee on obscenity and film censorship as well the successful proposals of the Warnock Committee on human embryology were clearly within the tradition (Holden 2004: 216–19, 258–63). And in many ways the settle-ment established in the 1960s was to endure, despite a new wave of moral conservatism in the 1970s and 1980s. Although there were many attempts, the abortion law was not restrictively amended. And even the most sustained attack on homosexual rights for a hundred years, the notorious section 28 of the 1988 Local Government Act, which banned the 'promotion' of homosexuality by education authorities, did not abro-gate the Wolfenden-inspired reforms of 1967. There was no attempt to make homosexuality illegal again. Rather, its obvious aim was to limit the advance of lesbian and gay entitlements. In effect it said 'thus far and no further' (Weeks 1991: 134–56).

But this was the problem for moral conservatives. From the point of view of the new radicals of the 1970s the reforms were timid in the

extreme. There was no positive endorsement of choice, no positive embracing of moral pluralism, no full acceptance of alternative sexualities. Many
homosexuals supported gay liberation because of the inadequacies of
the 1967 Act. Many feminists, in favour of 'a Woman's Right to Choose',
supported abortion on demand. In creating new sexual subjects, especially the ordinary, respectable homosexual, avoiding the pitfalls of
promiscuity, or the responsible woman, attending to appropriate birth
control, the reforms seemed designed to stem the tide of radical movements. As Lord Arran, the eccentric peer who had led in the House
of Lords on homosexual law reform, inimitably put it, 'I ask those who
have, as it were, been in bondage and for whom the prison doors are now
open to show their thanks by comporting themselves quietly and with
dignity' (Weeks 1989: 274). The lesbian and gay community disregarded
this advice spectacularly. Even so, apart from bringing Scotland and
Northern Ireland into line with the homosexual law reforms of 1967 (in
1980 and 1982), it was to be twenty-five years before the gay age of
consent was reduced from 21 to 18, the age of majority since the 1960s,
and a further five years before the age of consent was equalized at 16. By
then a new shift had taken place, with the emergence of a new discourse
of equality between heterosexuals and homosexuals that the change of
the 1960s had not even hinted at.

Despite this, the liberal reformers had achieved more than they
thought, perhaps more than they sought. For increasingly people acted
as if the reforms had opened up paths to greater freedoms. Over time
lesbians and gays acted as if they had been granted new rights which
needed defending and advancing. From the early 1970s there was a vast
expansion in the public presence of lesbian and gays, and of the lesbian
and gay community, that not even the AIDS crisis of the 1980s could
stem. At the same time, women acted as if they could obtain abortion on
demand. Abortions rose from 4 per cent of live births in 1968 to 17.6 per
cent in 1975. Over a million legal abortions had been carried out by 1980.
Similarly, divorce figures showed a dramatic upward move: between 1970
and 1979, the divorce rate trebled for those under 25, and doubled for
those over 25. By the end of the 1970s there was one divorce for every
three marriages, with women as the main instigators of divorce (Weeks
1989: 274–5; see also Lewis 2001). The reforms represented a major shift
in the mode of regulation of civil society, and this was to have incalculable
effects. In effect they attempted to put in place the autonomous consenting adult as the focus of moral decision-taking, with the law confined
to holding the ring and as the enforcer of acceptable standards of public
order. Its drive was towards individual responsibilization, in the interests
of creating that 'civilized society'. Individuals, Rose has argued, 'were
to become, as it were, entrepreneurs of themselves, shaping their own
lives through the choices they make among the forms of life available
to them' (1999: 230). Greater autonomization was itself potentially a form
of control, certainly if it led to the internalization of new norms. But the
symbolic importance of the legal reforms was enormous. They provided

the most concrete evidence for the dismantling of the authoritarian structures that had sustained the culture of restraint. A worried correspondent of the leading conservative moral entrepreneur, Mrs Mary Whitehouse, wrote to her after the passing of the 1967 reforms, 'The last session of Parliament has subjected us to the progressive moral disarmament of the nation BY LAW and there's worse to come' (Weeks 1989: 274). In the short term the correspondent was wrong. Reforming zeal was soon to be buried pro tem by economic and social crisis. But in the long term such pessimists were surely right. Things could never be quite the same again.

Shifting the boundaries

Perhaps the most important sense was that 'old Britain' was changing beyond recognition. The various dramatic events of the late 1960s and early 1970s – the student revolts, the mobilizations against the Vietnam War, industrial militancy, a sense of economic crisis – all fed into a generalized sense of crisis. More than this, the make-up of the British nation was visibly changing as a result of black and Asian migration into the UK, which in turn fed into new sexual anxieties and an exaggerated fear of crime and violence. Sir Gerald Nabarro, a maverick right-wing MP, had asked on a radio programme in 1963, 'How would you feel if your daughter wanted to marry a big buck nigger with the prospect of coffee-coloured grandchildren?' (quoted in Sandbrook 2006: 628). Such attitudes were by no means confined to deep-grained conservatives. Mick Jagger, the embodiment of the new rock establishment and ostensibly bursting with transgressive sexual challenge, told the *International Times*, the voice of the underground, in 1968 of his fears that immigration was going to 'break up British society', 'Because they just are different and they do act differently and they don't live the same, not even if they were born here they don't' (*International Times*, 17 May 1968, quoted in Sandbrook 2006:). The fear of radical difference was potently exploited the same year by the Conservative politician Enoch Powell, whose infamous 'rivers of blood' speech spoke to fears of an uncontrollable rise of black and Asian immigrant populations and the undermining of the British national identity (see Smith 1994: 129–82).

The facts were that, with the exception of the late 1950s and early 1960s when the anticipation of the restrictive Commonwealth Immigrants Act (1962) encouraged a surge of immigration, for most of the century Britain remained a net exporter of people. However, the composition of the population was clearly changing, especially in London and increasingly in the older industrial northern towns where the new immigrants were moving into factory jobs. By 1971 there were 650,000 new Britons from the Caribbean and the Indian subcontinent, ten times their numbers twenty years earlier. And the gender balance was changing significantly, which added to the perceived sexual threat. The 1971 census revealed that there were now more Caribbean women immigrants than men in

London: young, single and fertile. Caribbean immigrants as a whole were widely associated with wild parties, drug-taking, loud music, strange food and sexual abandon. The sociologist Sheila Patterson made the essential links in 1963. A coloured skin, she wrote, 'especially when combined with Negroid features, is associated with alienness, and with the lowest social status. Primitiveness, savagery, violence, sexuality, general lack of control, sloth, irresponsibility – all these are part of the image' (quoted in Sandbrook 2005: 309).

The new populations were in reality far from homogeneous, either in sexual or family traditions (see Chapter 6). When they first arrived they had seen themselves more in terms of the particular areas they had come from: the distinctive islands of the Caribbean, the faith or ethnic communities of India and Pakistan – Sikhs, Hindus, different Muslim groups, different language groups and so on. The experience of the racism in Britain forced a new identification. As Tryphena Anderson, who had come to Britain in 1952 and subsequently trained as a nurse, found, 'you weren't a person, you were a darkie' (quoted in Sandbrook 2005: 307). The immigrants who previously did not see colour as a badge were now forced to think of themselves as black, and were perceived more than ever as a sexual threat to the indigenous population.

It was this sense of fundamental change in the cultural foundations of Britain that fuelled a new mobilization on the moral Right. Just as the new sexual radicals saw sexual change as both a harbinger and focus for wider social transformation, so conservatives saw sexual change as symbolic of a wider breakdown in social order. The sands of the culture were shifting radically, and with them the settled imagery of a moral Britain. It was in this context that the emergence of Mrs Whitehouse, an ordinary teacher and housewife who had become concerned about violence and sex on television, was so important. In her desire for a refounded Christian moral order, in her sense of the damaging invasion of the privacy of the home and the marital bed by the modern media, with its explicitness and agnosticism, she evoked a more innocent past, but also forecast a more polarized future. The enemy was a secular humanism that seemed in danger of capturing the highest echelons of the state, from the BBC to Parliament and the executive itself. Sexuality was a key battleground, because it was here that secularism had been most successful: 'To accept the biological imperative, to acknowledge the importance within human behaviour of gratification, to indulge in practices long forbidden, is to rid sex of its sacred connotations' (Weeks 1989: 279). Sex should be heterosexual and monogamous, the necessary cement of marriage. The undermining of marriage in turn was destabilizing the family. It was the breakdown of the traditional family, with its demarcated sexual roles, its hierarchical relationships between adults and children, its social role as the glue of relationships and the focus of acceptable sexuality that was at the centre of social transformation. Its defence was therefore critical to restoring social and moral order.

Mrs Whitehouse was one among many who by the 1970s were attempting to mobilize a counter-movement to sexual radicalism in its diverse forms – a *galere* drawn from the churches, literature, the media and politics, as well as grass-roots movements such as her own National Viewers and Listeners Association, and the National Festival of Light, which targeted pornography. Initially, these campaigns were aimed at moral revival rather than moral censorship, and concentrated on letter-writing and raising petitions, culminating in a Nationwide Petition for Public Decency in 1972, which followed the quashing of the conviction against *Oz* magazine. The aim was to mobilize the masses behind strong moral leadership: 'All history has been shaped by a tiny minority. The "misty millions" go where they are led' (Weeks 1989: 281). But as the great unwashed failed to respond in sufficient numbers, the ardent minority changed their tactics. They took increasing recourse to the law, first by deploying the existing law, against obscenity, and most notoriously against blasphemy; then by attempting to change the law. The prosecution of *Gay News*, the new voice of the gay community, for blasphemy was the high watermark of the first approach. The magazine had published a poem entitled 'The Love that Dares to Speak its Name', in which a centurion expressed his fantasies about the crucified Christ. Here for Mrs Whitehouse and her followers was a highly symbolic issue, for which homosexuality emerged as the very definition of the irreligious, the embodiment of the would-be triumphant secular humanism that was destroying the gender order and the family. In the short term the move was successful. But in the longer term it proved counter-productive for the conservative cause. It set the terms of the debate and mobilized the lesbian and gay community, and behind it liberal opinion. It also made a martyr of the editor of *Gay News*, Denis Lemon, and gave vast publicity to the gay paper. The same was broadly true of the other prosecutions, whether of the *Little Red Schoolbook*, *Oz*, *International Times*, or the Swedish film, *More about the Language of Love*. Despite setbacks for liberal freedoms of speech, the clock was not turned back far. With regard to legislative change the most successful effort in the 1970s was the panic passing of a Protection of Children Bill in 1978, which by attempting to place limits on the use of children in pornography set an agenda which ran on for the following three decades. But this was an exception (Weeks 1989: 280).

There is no doubt that as the 1970s faded into the 1980s the political climate apparently became more accommodating to moral conservatism. Sir Keith Joseph, the intellectual stimulant to the new conservatism, what came to be known as Thatcherism, that was increasingly dominating the political landscape by the late 1970s, called Mrs Whitehouse a 'remarkable woman' and sought consciously to link the new economic conservatism to social and moral conservatism. Margaret Thatcher wove the same strands during the next decade or so in power, not least by evoking the idea of a return to 'Victorian values'. The 1980s did, indeed, see a significant closing of space, especially as the onset of the AIDS epidemic seemed at first to threaten an apocalypse (Weeks 2000: 163–76).

The rhetorical bias was towards the centrality of the family, the importance of bolstering marriage, a strong support of traditional moral standards, and apparent hostility towards single parenthood, and despite Thatcher's own success as a working woman, little support for women breaking away from inherited roles, and the 1980s saw a distinct backlash against feminism. Section 28, introduced at the high watermark of Thatcherism following the third electoral victory in 1986, was widely seen as an attack on all the advances of the previous twenty years. It sought to ban the 'promotion' by schools and their local authority funders of homosexuality as 'a pretended family relationship', thus introducing a neologism which was to resonate widely. David Wilshire, the right-wing MP who introduced the amendment of the Local Government Bill into the House of Commons, evoked the powerful traditional complaint against sex reform: that it was introducing change at the taxpayers' expense (a complaint previously used against free contraception). 'Homosexuality is being promoted . . .', he pronounced, 'and the traditional family as we know it is under attack' (letter to the *Guardian*, 12 December 1987, quoted in Weeks 1989: 296; see also Holden 2004: 249–56; Smith 1994: 183–239). Here we have a strong nexus of issues: the family under threat; an assault on the sexual purity of children; the pernicious nature of sex education; proselytizing homosexuals; all funded by the local government tax, the rates.

The agenda seemed ominously close to the New Right moral agenda in the USA which had targeted sex education as a crucial 'bridge' issue that could mobilize a wide range of disparate constituencies around a coherent conservative moral project (Weeks 1985: 33–53; Irvine 2002). Lesbian and gay and liberal opinion generally was outraged, but to little immediate effect. Conservative triumphalism held sway. And to a certain extent section 28 was successful. For almost two decades, though no prosecutions were brought under the new law, it undoubtedly inhibited any local government initiatives to advance lesbian and gay rights, and sex education in schools was more tightly wrapped into parental control (with the assumption that this would lead to more conservative policies). In other ways, however, the impact was totally counter-productive. For what it did above all was to mobilize a lesbian and gay community that had been badly battered by the HIV/AIDS crisis. It is from this date that a new energy for coming out, community-building and working towards legitimization, fuelled by anger at the neglect of lesbian and gay issues in the early epidemic, came to the fore, with incalculable effects (Weeks 2000: 149). It also rescued the reputation of the offending local authorities. The rather haphazard efforts by a number of left-wing controlled local governments to introduce equal rights policies were floundering under the weight of media attacks and financial crises. Suddenly these were legitimized, and a certain nostalgia arose for their courage, if not political good sense (Cooper 1994).

The New Right discourse, in Britain as in the USA, sought to link cultural change, racial diversity and challenges to hegemonic sexuality into a coherent political project, built on opposition to what Smith (1994) has called 'radical difference'. Certainly the 1980s saw an accentuation of racism and of official homophobia. And yet, despite all these efforts, the success of moral conservatism was very limited (Durham 1991). There were certainly pressure groups and think-tanks on the Conservative side of politics who believed that social and moral conservatism went hand in hand with the economic liberalism that the Thatcher government was pursuing. But this was never a logical connection. Economic individualism, which lay at the heart of the Thatcher project, could be readily allied with a form of libertarianism, for example, of sexual choice and abolition of laws controlling drugs, and some of the next generation of New Right Conservatives certainly attempted such a linkage, much to the concern of their elders. Margaret Thatcher herself, as the charismatic leader who had constructed a dynamic conservative coalition, embodied many of its carefully concealed contradictions. She espoused a religious morality but herself was not a deep Christian, moving easily from the Methodism of her youth to the Anglicanism of the Tory mainstream. Although an ardent defender of marriage, she herself was married to a divorced man, and was famously a working wife whose children had been nannied and safely ensconced in private boarding-schools. She was also apparently relaxed about the sexual behaviour of her closest supporters (her Parliamentary Private Secretary towards the end of her tenure was well known to be homosexual), and supportive when they encountered problems. More crucially, she did not herself have a straight-down-the-middle conservative moral agenda. She had, for instance, supported abortion law reform and voted against attempts to restrict it (see Durham 1991). Like the trail blazer of the new conservatism of the 1980s, Enoch Powell, who was opposed to the death penalty and had supported homosexual law reform, the leader herself – like many of her followers – was more contradictory than many at the time liked to imagine.

But there were wider reasons why a moral backlash had a limited impact in Britain. Although there were strong links with the New Right and Christian fundamentalism in the United States, and the rhetoric and intellectual underpinnings were similar – especially around sex education, the family, hostility to single mothers and lesbian and gays – the social and cultural context turned out to be dramatically different. Above all, apart from obvious exceptions such as Northern Ireland, Britain lacked the religious evangelicalism and the powerful fundamentalist constituencies that were firing the moral conservatism of the USA (on which see Herman 1997). By the 1980s Britain was an overwhelmingly secular society, and in this it was following strong European trends. Britain was close to the Western European average in its attitudes in the mid-1980s: more morally censorious than the Danes, Dutch and French, the first two of whom had become notorious for their liberalism; more relaxed than the Irish, Italians and Spaniards (Harding 1988: 35). As such figures suggest, secularism did not necessarily equate with rank libertarianism, and there were important cross-currents that did not sit easily with conventional political positions. The British Social Attitudes Survey of 1988 (Jowell *et al.* 1988), for example, showed that on a spectrum of 'libertarian' to 'authoritarian' Labour Party members were more likely to be libertarian, and Conservatives authoritarian. Even so, 24 per cent of Labour were authoritarian, compared to 49 per cent of Conservatives. This Labour moral conservatism was deeply rooted in the party and proved to be an explosive element in its political travails in the 1980s (Weeks 2004b). But the real point is that there was no morally conservative mass movement in Britain that could parallel the influence of the Christian Right in the United States, and threaten to realign traditional allegiances. Economics and class, despite all the changes that were taking place, including the rise of new social movements around peace, the environment as well as sexuality and gender, remained the prime predictors of political mobilization.

The 1970s and 1980s saw the rise of fundamentalist movements across the globe, and Britain was not immune from its influence if fundamentalism is seen in broad terms as a form of absolutism. We can talk, as Giddens argues (1994: 190), of many fundamentalisms if we see it not as a retreat to the past but more as a defence of the threatened familiar. There are ethnic, national and political fundamentalisms which defend a reinvented tradition, as well as the more familiar religious fundamentalisms, whether Christian, Islamic, Judaic or Hindu (Bhatt 1997). But what is most significant is the way in which gender, sexuality and the body feature prominently in all forms of fundamentalist thought and practice. If fundamentalism is a defence against doubt and uncertainty, a cry against the radical contingency that has become the hallmark of late modern societies, then we can see how the gendered and sexed body can become the symbolic focus of anxiety. Women who reject traditional notions of femininity or women and men who reject traditional notions of normal and aberrant sexuality, who blur the boundaries between men and women and in doing so undermine the traditional family as the guarantee of social order and reproduction, may be seen to threaten the whole culture and inherited ways of life. Perhaps even more crucially, they were potential threats to the emotional investment that embattled individuals had in the traditional order: 'Threats to the integrity of traditions are very often if by no means invariably expressed as threats to the integrity of the self' (Giddens 1994: 80). So we see the familiar characteristic of fundamentalist movements: an assertion of the truth of assumed tradition, and an absolutism in defence of this embattled truth. Fundamentalism may be seen from this perspective as an assertion of truth without regard to the consequences (Giddens 1994: 104); it is a refusal of dialogue.

Britain did not lack emerging fundamentalist tendencies. When the British Chief Rabbi, Lord Jakobovits, welcomed the supposed discovery of a gay gene because it might lead to the elimination at birth of those carrying it (Rose 1996: 63) we can see a dangerous, if perhaps unthinking absolutism, in which homosexuality was easily demonized. Later, in the 1990s and early 2000s strong Islamic fundamentalist movements emerged in the UK which sought to impose highly conservative views of gender and sexuality on their followers. But what was lacking in Britain was a focus for the rise of a mass social movement that was morally fundamentalist. Even the greatest challenge to the new sexual order that was emerging, the HIV/AIDS crisis from the early 1980s, did not produce such a reaction – though at times for those in the front line of the crisis it seemed that it would.

Risk and sexuality: the HIV/AIDS crisis

The HIV/AIDS epidemic broke on an unsuspecting world in the early 1980s, but was instantaneously burdened with many histories. Histories of past epidemics, including epidemics of sexually transmitted diseases such as syphilis, and how they were responded to; histories of scientific investigation, and of medical intervention (especially the long medicalisation of sexual difference, homosexuality in particular); histories of politics and social policy, which determine what priorities to assign to disease, especially illnesses which affected the marginal and marginalized; histories of prejudice and oppression, of racism and heterosexism: all these histories were evoked and powerful in shaping responses to the set of unexplained illnesses which appeared among gay men in American cities in 1980 to 1981, and soon grew to epidemic proportions, at first within the gay communities of the West, then increasingly in minority communities across America, until within a decade it had become a global pandemic (Weeks 1993: 17). But at the heart of any attempt to understand the impact of HIV/AIDS in the 1980s and since must be the history, or rather histories, of sexuality.

At the most basic level this is because HIV proved to be efficiently transmissible through sexual activity, especially penetrative practices, whether anal or vaginal. It also appeared during a period of unprecedented sexual change, at the turning point of the great transition, where sexual mores were in flux, old social disciplines were declining, and literally millions of young people were in movement and willing and eager to experiment with their sexual behaviour. Above all, what coloured the response to the epidemic from the start was that it first manifested itself among gay men, an increasingly assertive, but still marginalized and politically unpopular community that was already experiencing an element of backlash against the gains of the 1970s. It soon became obvious that this was a syndrome of diseases, and a potentially disastrous epidemic, that was not going to be confined to one group. Its appearance among Haitians, people with haemophilia, drug-users, early suggested various roots of transmission (through blood transfusions of contaminated blood, through sharing dirty needles, as well as sex), which pointed to a potentially unstoppable spread. But it was its association with a still execrated sexual minority that coloured the initial response, and the language and terminology that framed its early history, such as the 'gay cancer', 'GRID' (Gay Related Immune Deficiency), or more generally the 'gay plague', vividly dramatized the link.

The lesbian and gay communities of the USA and Britain were in an ambiguous position when the epidemic broke. There had been huge advances in social organization and public affirmation, and a highly sexualized (if largely male) culture had developed. But there were signs of attempted backlash in both countries, and the political climate had turned distinctly chilly under the New Right dominated Reagan and Thatcher administrations (Weeks 1985: 44–52). At the same time the New Right ideology-led policy climate, with threatened cutbacks to health and other entitlements on the grounds of cost-cutting and pushing back the state, was hardly conducive to vast new expenditure on health care which an unprecedented epidemic would require. In both countries public policy responses were tardy, effectively delayed until the mid-1980s, when the epidemic seemed likely to spread into the heterosexual world. In Britain until 1986, government response had largely been limited to attempts to protect the blood supply. When in 1986 the government was mobilized into action in conditions, according to the historian of the British response, akin to a wartime emergency, the epidemic was already well entrenched in the gay male population (Berridge 1996). The governmental response, however, was to produce a generalized policy that seemed to assume the whole population was at risk. The epidemic, as gay activists quickly pointed out, was not an 'equal opportunity' disease – it affected some groups disproportionately – but it was effectively 'de-gayed' (King 1993: 169–232; Watney 1994: 153–155; Weeks 2000: 194–211).

It was obvious at the time, but becomes even more so in historical context, that the HIV/AIDS crisis was a flashpoint that illuminated the sexual ecology in an unprecedented way. The moral panic around AIDS that broke in the media in the early 1980s suggested the deeply unsettled attitudes towards homosexuality which continued to shape public opinion, and almost certainly delimited any rational government policy until it was almost too late. The authoritarian and populist nature of the Thatcher government tied in well with the majority colour of both the tabloid and serious press at the time, which in turn was in the vanguard of the most virulent part of the new conservatism. The right-wing press had differing responses to the sexual revolution. The leading tabloid, *The Sun*, gloried in the sexualization of women, while the *Daily Mail* obsessed about the decline of the family, but in all cases homosexuality remained the despised Other (Watney 1987). For many other opinion-formers on the right, as the populist right-wing MP Sir Rhodes Boyson put it, 'AIDS is . . . a part of the fruits of the permissive society. The regular one-man, one-woman marriage would not put us at risk with this in any way' (quoted in Weeks 1991: 126).

The difficulty for the embattled gay community was that hedonistic sex had indeed become one of the binding elements of its culture, and the spread of HIV was in large part a result of multi-partnered unprotected sex among gay men. For many, gay identity without freedom of sexuality was like a denial of a newly affirmed sense of selfhood. For some, the epidemic seemed like a plot to return the community to the closet and to bring it once again under the surveillance of the medical profession (Weeks 1985: 50). Yet the historically remarkable feature of the gay response was its inventiveness and creativity. The elaboration of codes of safer sex (that is, sexual practices which limited the exchange of blood and bodily fluids) from the early 1980s, before the nature of HIV as a virus was proved, and in the absence of medical or other guidelines, was a pragmatic response to a perceived danger which proved remarkably successful (King 1993: 85ff.). By the late 1980s survey evidence suggested that a consistent two-thirds of the gay male population were using safer-sex techniques. In other ways, too, the lesbian and gay community was showing considerable maturity and sophistication. Until the major reversal of the governmental policy of less than benign neglect in 1986, the only coherent non-medical response came from largely gay community-based organizations, usually led by gay men, though with crucial support from lesbians and many individual heterosexuals. Gay-founded and led organizations such as the Terrence Higgins Trust, Body Positive, the Lighthouse and so on pioneered a range of responses, from fundraising to provision of services, from lobbying to the development of telephone help lines, 'buddying', and new régimes of care, personal as well as collective (Weeks *et al.* 1994; cf. Altman 1994). They also, crucially, developed effective alliances with doctors and public health officials.

The public health tradition in Britain had long advocated the importance of prevention of disease, and was clear about the need for pragmatic but coherent policies to halt the spread of HIV. Those struggling against the epidemic in the gay community similarly, in the absence of a 'magic bullet' to cure the infection, were anxious to limit its spread, but were aware of their limited pull outside their own community. An alliance between the two provided the entrée in policy debates that the community lacked (Berridge 1996). One consequence of this, however, was that the gay aspects of the disease were minimized. Yet as the rest of the decade was to demonstrate, HIV/AIDS remained in Britain overwhelmingly an epidemic that disproportionately affected minorities: gay men especially, but increasingly other minorities – drug-users and Africans, women as well as men (Richardson 1987; Strang and Stimson 1990; BHAN 1991; Gorna 1996; Weeks 2000: 196–8). It was not yet a heterosexual epidemic in the sense that the straight white population was seriously at risk *en masse*. That said something about the relative sexual conservatism of the majority population. Although numbers of lifetime partners were increasing, and serial rather than lifetime monogamy was becoming the norm, there was no great outburst of 'promiscuity' (see Chapter 6). Sexual experimentation was more likely in marginalized communities. It was above all still the gay community that was most seriously at risk.

This was one of the paradoxes of the 1980s response to the crisis. Although popularly seen as the gay disease, policy-makers, whether straight or gay, in the voluntary sector or in the state, made strenuous efforts after 1986 to play down its gay links (King 1993: 169ff.). The de-gaying was most acutely felt in the area of HIV prevention work. Gay men who had been involved in early community-based efforts to educate other gay men about safer sex practices began to experience serious difficulty in continuing this work in both voluntary and statutory organizations keen to spread the message that everyone was at risk. In 1992 a new grouping, Gay Men Fighting AIDS (GMFA), heavily influenced by gay liberation and nascent 'queer politics', was set up to right the balance. It identified the weakness of prevention work whose concern was less with the needs of gay men than in preventing the spread of HIV into the heterosexual population. Behind this it saw distinct elements of homophobia, and a real ignorance of the specific needs of the population most at risk. Against this was counter-posed a model of health promotion which prioritized community mobilization (Watney 1994: 134–52). The existence of a moral community in the early days of the epidemic had provided the basis for an initial resistance to the epidemic. Thus community-building, it was argued, was critical to the resistance to the continuing epidemic. As one volunteer said about the role of GMFA, 'it's there for the survival of the gay community. Without organisations like GMFA, the gay community will die out or be driven underground' (quoted in Weeks 2000: 202).

An organization like GMFA was influential – not least in the changing emphases of health promotion campaigns – because it tapped into an existing discourse of sexual politics. But it also signalled a shifting perception of risk. The official response to HIV had been shaped by a generalization of risk to the whole population. This reflected a sense that HIV could in theory affect the whole population: 'everyone is at risk', the early doom-laden advertising campaign intoned. But by the early 1990s it was clear that some people were more at risk than others (Watney 2000: 228–41). In a sense, early debates about whether risk groups or risk activities should be targeted were becoming irrelevant: there were populations as well as individuals who engaged in risky activities, and each group needed to be addressed in specific, community-based ways: whether women, black and minority ethnic communities, young people, or intravenous drug-users. Absolutist attitudes were less than useless in the face of an unpredictable epidemic. What was needed was a culturally sensitive response that engaged with local identities and needs.

This fitted in with a growing recognition of the tentative and fluid nature of sexualized identities. Perhaps what HIV/AIDS unsettled most of all was the assumption, which lesbian and gay politics had fostered since the early 1980s, that there was an easy fit between sexual desire, sexual practices and sexual identities. The epidemic revealed with dramatic clarity that this was a dangerous assumption. Men who had contracted HIV through sex with other men frequently denied a homo-sexual identity – and this was true among white men who had easy access to gay identities as well as to BME (Black and Minority Ethnic) peoples, whose cultural traditions might be extremely hostile to homo-sexuality. To cope with this, prevention workers invented a completely new social category, 'Men who have sex with men' – 'MSM' – which attempted to divorce identity and practice, but in fact ended up by becom-ing a description simply of men who did not identify as gay (see King 1993: 198–200). An obsession with exact description and categorizations was in danger of obscuring the diversity of sexual practices. Epstein has commented on the ways in which alliances between state and community organizations, however useful and vital they may be in mobilizing neces-sary resources, carry the danger of reifying and biomedicalizing sexual identities, of fixing them as if they were true and permanent (Epstein 2003: 135). That was a temptation behind all interventions into sexual communities, which tended to treat them as if they were fixed by nature. The actual history of AIDS told otherwise.

And yet, the lesbian and gay identities that had emerged from the 1970s proved critical in combating the epidemic in the 1980s and beyond. Without them there would have been no community mobilization, no community-based organizations, no discourse of safer sex rooted in every-day experience, and no intervention in shifting the biomedical discourse. One of the unique features of the whole early history of HIV/AIDS was the degree to which those most affected by it were involved in both defining the problem and intervening against it, not only socially and culturally, but medically. 'Treatment activism', especially, which sought to intervene in the identification, testing and provision of new drugs and therapies, helped transform the ways in which people with illnesses responded to their diagnosis – not with passivity but with individual and collective resistance and intervention (Watney 2000: 199–212).

People with HIV and AIDS proved to be harbingers of a profound shift in the relationship between medicine and society. They had been preceded by feminist health movements, and were succeeded by a host of other campaigns, but the essence of all of them was the mobiliza-tion of people who were themselves at risk to take some control of their treatment and care. This marked both a new reflexivity in relation to health issues, in the sense that individuals were involved directly in issues relating to their own bodies, and an attempt to democratize knowledge, to recognize science as 'impure', incomplete, partial, and new knowledges could come from below as well as from the traditional biomedical élite (see Epstein 1998, 2003). The sick and the vulnerable found that 'truth' could be contested, and new truths could emerge from their own experiences and struggles with illness. But this in turn repre-sented, I would argue, a major shift in the ways in which society was reacting to risk. Sexuality has always been associated with risk: the risks of unplanned pregnancy, the risks of pregnancy itself, the risks of disease, of violence, of moral condemnation. By the 1980s perception of these risks, many of which were in the crudest sense 'manufactured', that is man-made, had become generalized, and new risks were emerging (Giddens 1991; Beck 1992). The People worried about the effects of early sexual experience, of sex and cervical cancer, of the long-term impact of the Pill, of the increase in sexually tramsmitted infections, of the growth of teenage pregnancy, of single parenthood, of male violence. These were risks of different levels and status but they reflected the growth of what has come to be known as 'risk culture'. They reflect new uncertainties and fears. HIV/AIDS appeared at a critical moment in this development. It dramatized the new uncertainties over sexual behaviour. It demonstrated the growth and power of the new affirmative identities, but also showed their limits and contingency. Yet at the same time it also showed the potential power of new social forces to intervene and help shape the social.

The immediate impact of HIV/AIDS had seemed disastrous for new cultural forces and the gay community in particular. Surveys of public opinion in the 1980s are quite clear that there was a setback in the gradual tolerance and acceptance of homosexuality. In 1983 62 per cent of those polled had censured homosexual relationships; in 1985 the figure had risen to 69 per cent; and in 1987, 74 per cent, before gradually improving. However, there were straws in the wind which pointed to a more hopeful future. A Gallop Poll for the *Sunday Telegraph* in 1988 suggested that 60 per cent of the population disapproved of gay lifestyles; however, 50 per cent of those under 25 were more accepting, and this was the population that was to shape attitudes in the 1990s and beyond (Weeks 1993: 28–9). In part, changes in the next decade reflected the normalization of HIV/AIDS, which became less salient a part of the sexual landscape. The widespread introduction of new anti-viral drug therapies from the mid-1990s drastically reduced the risk of premature death, and offered new opportunities for fruitful lives for those infected with HIV disease. This was not the end of the epidemic. Its incidence continued to increase in Britain, and elsewhere in the world it became pandemic. But by the 1990s it was well on the way to becoming in many ways what early campaigners had seen as the best to be hoped for, a chronic manageable disease. It had become one of the risks of unprotected and unsafe sexual activity in a world of ever increasing risk.

The legacy

Margaret Thatcher was widely welcomed by moral conservatives as the champion of traditional values, and feared by progressives as the arch reactionary who would halt and push back the tide of sexual and moral change. Yet during the decade or more of her period in office, and continuing under her successor, all the indices showed an acceleration of change. About 7 per cent of single women were prepared to live openly with a man in 1970; by the 1980s the figure had risen to 50 per cent, more than triple what it had been just a decade earlier when Mrs Thatcher came to office. The proportion of children born outside marriage rose from 12 per cent in 1980, to over 25 per cent by the end of the decade. For women under 20, the figures were much higher: around 82 per cent in the north-west and north of England. By 1980 there were approaching two million single parents. The proportion of people getting married continued to decline during the 1980s, while the number of divorces rose. At 150,000 divorces a year Britain had one of the highest rates in Europe, with nearly one in four marriages contracted likely to end in divorce (Weeks 2000: 170).

There continued to be wide variations across Britain, shaped by class, ethnicity and geography. But the pattern was consistent. Sexuality, due to almost universal use of birth control by heterosexual couples, was increasingly uncoupled from reproduction. Cohabitation was increasingly separated from marriage. Marriage was no longer the *sine qua non* of family formation and parenting. Premarital sex had become normalized, and the stigma of bastardy was rapidly disappearing. And while the British population showed an admirable commitment to fidelity, remaining resolutely hostile to extra-marital sex, there were clear signs that serial rather than lifetime monogamy was becoming the norm. Individuals might hope for lifetime commitment but increasing numbers were prepared to exit dying relationships, dust themselves down and try again – and again and again if necessary. And what about the sexual Other, homosexuality? In the late 1980s many feared that AIDS would wipe out the gay male population within a generation. Many expected that section 28 was the beginning of a legal onslaught that would negate the social gains of the previous two decades. Neither happened. On the contrary, by the early 1990s, there were signs that the lesbian and gay community had emerged strengthened rather than weakened by its trials by fire in the 1980s. Altman (1989) had observed in the 1980s a 'legitimization by disaster' wrought by the AIDS crisis as openly lesbian and gay individuals and groups got drawn into the policy arena. By the end of the 1980s a number of public figures had come out (some, like the actor Ian McKellen, soon to be knighted, in the wake of section 28). At the same time, the lesbian and gay social scene was expanding as never before. In Manchester and Soho in London gay villages were providing new social and sexual opportunities. Mort (1996: 164–70) has seen the Soho of the late 1989s as a site for 'experiments in masculinity' underpinned by 'rituals of consumption'. Through the creation of a gay mass market, lesbians and gays were being tied by cords of silk into the pleasures of consumerism, ending the isolation and ghettoization of gay life. The ghetto was coming out.

None of this should be taken to suggest that the sexual revolution had yet conclusively won. Women's greater sexual freedom had been hard won, but as Janet Holland and her co-researchers were to show, based in interviews with young people in the late 1980s and early 1990s, women's own internalized fears, anxieties and gendered assumptions still inhibited equal relationships (Holland *et al.* 1998). Despite the much proclaimed emergence of the caring and sharing 'new man', caring remained overwhelmingly a female zone, and social policies in the 1980s had underlined this graphically. The women's movement itself had fragmented, with feminism a growing force in the academy but a diminishing force on the ground. Single mothers could all too readily, well into the 1990s, become the target of media panic and political opportunism. And progress on homosexual law reform remained deep-frozen. Efforts to achieve an equal age of consent in 1994 failed, as the Conservative majority supported reduction to 18 only (Waites 2005a). It was to take a new government, and a new decade, before meaningful reform was passed.

Yet the harbingers of change were there. The thirty-year transition had brought profound changes: in individual attitudes, in family life, in sexual behaviour, in sexual identities, in moral values, in cultural norms, and in social policy. The changes were uneven and often contradictory in their impact, affecting younger rather more than older people, the metropolitan population more than the surburban and rural, the affluent more than the poor, women more than men, the dominant white population more than many of the new minorities (on the geography of family and sexual diversity see Duncan and Smith 2006). Yet in the end, changes in substantial parts of the population were bound to affect the whole, whether through convergence and acceptance or divergence and rejection.

The motors of these changes were varied. Underlying all the changes were structural shifts in the political economy – especially the growth of affluence and of increasingly avid consumerism. The Welfare State of the early post-war years had provided a solid underpinning for change by providing a security which had hitherto been unknown for large segments of the population, a collective provision which made possible a new emphasis on individuality. The New Right politics of the 1980s undermined the old welfare settlement, but did not dismantle it. At the same time, the opening up of the economy and the celebration of a new, globalizing entrepreneurialism, accentuated the individualizing tendencies in the culture. 'People are condemned to individualization', Beck has argued (1994: 14); it becomes a 'compulsion'. The negative side of the tide of individualization was the elevation of economic man as the measure of all things. On the positive side was a new logic, towards greater individuation and personal freedom. As became apparent in the 1990s, it was difficult to confine the celebration of individual freedom only to the marketplace. Most people were more interested in personal freedom and choice in relation to their everyday lives.

Social developments were loosening up everyday life. They were also offering new possibilities of personal and collective agency. From the free availability of effective contraception to the rise of women's and gay liberation movements the opportunities and spaces for gaining greater control over personal life increased. There were limits and constraints, political and cultural setbacks. A growing recognition that Britain was becoming an ever more complex, open and diverse society was not yet accompanied by a widespread appreciation of the value of diversity, let alone an awareness of how to live with diversity. The divisive moral rhetoric that characterized so much of 1980s discourse – the initially punitive reaction to HIV/AIDS, the vindictiveness of section 28, the tendency to moral panic, the scapegoating of single parents – all suggested a society that was not yet able to look its changed nature in the face. But of the importance of that change there could be little doubt. By the 1990s Britain had conclusively moved from a society characterized by restraint to one characterized by moral pluralism and growing toleration. This was the achievement of the great transition.

5

Chaotic pleasures
Diversity and the new individualism

[Post Fordist men and women] are today integrated through
seduction rather than policing, advertising rather than
indoctrinating, need creation rather than normative regulation.

(Bauman 1998: 23)

Britain now has one of the most libertine societies in Europe.
Particularly among the younger Brits in urban areas, which is
where most Muslims live, we drink more alcohol faster, sleep
around more, live less in long-lasting, two parent families and
worship less than almost anywhere in the world. It's clear from
what young British Muslims themselves say that part of their
reaction is against this kind of secular, hedonistic, anomic
lifestyle. If women are reduced to sex-objects, young Muslim
women say, I would rather cover up. Theirs is almost a kind
of conservative feminism. Certainly, it's a socially conservative
critique of some aspects of British society, particularly visible in
their generation, in the urban neighbourhoods where they live.

(Garton Ash 2006: 25)

[T]here are other stories about 'race' and racism to be told
apart from the endless narrative of immigration as invasion
and the melancholic blend of guilt, denial, laughter, and
homogenizing violence that it has precipitated. Those
emancipatory interruptions can perhaps be defined by a
liberating sense of the banality of intermixture and the subversive
ordinariness of this country's convivial cultures in which 'race'
is stripped of meaning and racism, as it fades, becomes only
an after-effect of long-gone imperial history rather than a sign
of Europe's North American destiny.

(Gilroy 2004: 166)

Individuals should be free and equal in the determination of the
conditions of their own lives . . . as long as they do not deploy
this framework to negate the rights of others.

(Held 1987: 290)

Metaphors and meanings

Writers have delved deep into their imaginative prose to portray the age in which we live. Perhaps, as Hobsbawm (1994: 16) suggests, we are adrift on choppy waters where old maps and charts no longer help us to understand the landscape or find our way across the sea. Or maybe we are sailing in modernity's wake, splashing around behind those sleek modernist liners that signalled romance and elegance until utilitarian flight made them hopelessly uneconomic (Phillipson 1989). A little nearer land, perhaps we are, as Bauman has suggested (2005), 'learning to walk on quicksand'. He writes prolifically and evocatively about 'liquid times', 'liquid modernity', 'liquid love', suggesting the flux and insubstantiality of contemporary culture. If we venture too far inland, however, we are in danger of being overwhelmed by the juggernaut of modernity, going ever faster in this 'runaway world', as Giddens (1990) suggests. All these metaphorical excursions evoke speed, change, endings and beginnings, uncertainties, insecurities, high risks, producing anxieties, fears, anguish, sometimes an underlying sense of barely suppressed panic. A sense of an ending, I argued in an earlier book (Weeks 2000: 235–44), haunted sexuality in the run-up to the millennium, and now that we have safely negotiated that landmark (where very little affecting sexuality actually seemed to happen) the sense that something is afoot is signalled today by the proliferation of 'post' worlds: post patriarchal, post socialist, post liberal, post feminist, post gay, post AIDS, post sexual, post family . . . The list is potentially long. Just as long are the attempts to characterize more broadly the epoch we live in: postmodernity, late modernity, high modernity, post-Fordist, 'new times', a second modernity, reflexive modernity, risk society, the information age, network society, liquid modernity. All these are pointing to something new, even if we are not quite sure how new or where things are going, a coming after something that is definitely passing, with, as Bauman has argued, 'a succession of new beginnings' (Bauman 2005: 2) which are just as unsettling.

We may differ over meanings and interpretations, but they all try to put into language a sense of profound and irreversible change, and a world that is in constant and often baffling flux. The solid traditions that those in authority attempted to reaffirm and re-establish after the Second World War have melted away under the hurricanes of social change, and with them have gone the old moral certainties that governed sexual behaviour and beliefs. We are making a different world, a world of uncertainty perhaps, but one that is no less value-laden than the world that has gone before. In many ways, I would argue, the very uncertainty that surrounds us is the spur to re-evaluating our lives, to finding new resources and values, and moral communities, through which we can build valid ways of life. But what is inevitable is that the world we are making is a profoundly diversified world. We no longer all try to live in the same way, nor do we see everything in the same way. In a very useful exercise Plummer has attempted to balance the utopian and dystopian ways of seeing these changes: same facts and evidence, different perspectives. Widening disparities between rich and poor may be set against higher standards of living for most, if not all; social fragmentation may be read as a 'pluralization' of life chances; impersonality and loss of community may be set against a new sense of belonging in new sexual worlds; narcissism and selfishness must be measured against a proliferation of new individual freedoms; McDonaldization and standardization have to be seen against a proliferation of choices in the democracy of the marketplace; dumbing down is matched by a sophisticated self-awareness, an ironic reflexivity; moral decline may be countered by a definite moral effervescence and global citizenship; entrenched hierarchies of exclusion are met with the language of inclusion and belonging, and a deepening democratization of everyday life; uncertainty and risk are set against the possibilities of a new global order and global human rights (Plummer 2003: 10; I have freely adapted his list). A case may be made for each side of the balance, yet surely what is most striking is that these are often presented as stark polarities, either/or options which divide rather than complexities and contradictions with which we all have to live. Both sides of the dichotomies may be true. The reality is that this is a world that has lost the unifying myths, the grand story which linked gender, sexuality, family into a more or less coherent unity sanctified by church, state and community values. That world was never quite what it claimed to be, and in many ways was as fractured and divided as is our contemporary world (compare Plummer 2003: 18). Yet its unifying myths did provide a sort of glue that held the structures together. Today that glue has dissolved. The power of traditional authorities, of religion, family, conventional morality, even of ideology, has been battered by decades of challenge and change and eroded by the dissolving powers of global flows, economic modernization and cultural transformations, as well as by the will for change represented by the everyday choices of countless millions. Today, we live in a plural world, a world of irreducible diversity and multiple sources of authority, made especially challenging due to the existence of apparently irreconcilable divisions of religion, ethnicity and moral codes, and yet it is also a world that is productive of creative efforts at coexistence. To say that this is producing new opportunities, new aspirations, and new forms of eroticism, love and intimacy is not, I would argue, 'utopian'. For many it is an everyday reality.

Intersections

Sexuality, because it is shaped in and through history as a unique matrix of the private and the public, the personal and the social, the 'natural' and the human, has become a privileged site for the working through of contradictory and intersecting forces, and for the thinking through of the meanings of diversity. Sexuality is less a source of meanings as a site where diverse meanings are constructed and contested. I want to distinguish three dimensions of diversity which are central to contemporary understandings of sexuality and intimacy: diversity of lifestyles; diversity of ethnicity and faith; and life course diversity. These, of course, are overlapping forms. Frankenberg (1993: 10) has written of the 'simultaneity' of the impact of gender, class and race in shaping the lives of women. But we can use that concept more broadly to suggest the simultaneity of various intersections in contemporary societies: of age, physical ability or disability, geography, education, faith and so on, as well as the ones Frankenberg refers to, all of which impinge on and shape the sexual. Each of the dimensions of diversity are shaped at the intersection of complex and often contradictory elements.

Sexual lifestyles

The late Quentin Crisp (1998) once sought to tell his readers 'How to have a lifestyle'. In the contemporary world everyone has a sexual lifestyle, some more or less a traditional one, some very new. The idea that we need to think in terms of sexualities rather than a single sexuality, and sexual cultures rather than a dominant sexual culture, has been central to my arguments in this book. The separation of sex from reproduction and marriage has, however, created a new dimension to this. First of all, it potentially makes irrelevant the social and cultural emphasis on heterosexual reproduction in judging relationships. So, for example, heterosexual relationships can have no a priori privilege over non-heterosexual once we move away from the reproductive imperative. This points the way to an ethics based on quality of relationships rather than teleological assumptions about the nature of sexuality. But second, it shifts the emphasis to sexual practices, what you do in bed, and how you see your identity and placing in the world. Once reproduction ceases to be the only valid justification for sex, sex itself can become more varied and diverse without moral censure, more 'plastic' in the perhaps unfortunate term used by Giddens (1992). Sexuality can now mean many things, and become the focus of very different life choices and lifestyles.

The more traditional values lose their purchase, the more the global impacts on the local, the more individuals are forced to negotiate their lifestyle choices. There are standardizing influences at all levels, but because of the greater openness of social life, the pluralization of contexts and of authorities, lifestyle choices become increasingly central to the constitution of self-identity and daily activity. In the conditions of late modernity, Giddens (1991) has argued, we have no choice but to choose, and at the heart of the discourse of choice is the question 'how should we live?', with living and loving inextricably intertwined.

It has become increasingly possible to choose ways of life organized around sexual preference, and to live in social worlds where desire, identity, behaviour, consumption, patterns of intimate life, even wider social involvement and employment can be worked through in common with others like oneself (Binnie 2004). The pioneers in this were lesbian and gays from the 1970s onwards, creating a wider sense of community, which in turn embodied meeting places, clubs, social networks, work-places and neighbourhoods in most metropolitan centres across the world, and in countless smaller places as well (Adam *et al.* 1999a). By the early 2000s these were at the centre of an ever more culturally complex set of assumptions and values. Mark Blasius (1994) has written convincingly about the emergence of a distinctive 'gay ethos', based on a set of values which embraced egalitarian friendships and open attitudes to sexual practices and relationships as the basis for everyday life (see also Weeks *et al.* 2001). Increasingly, this 'gay' category was itself becoming both broader and more diverse, as the use of LGBT (Q) as a form of self-labelling suggests: Lesbian, Gay, Bisexual, Transgender and Questioning (or Querying or Queer) – a move from 'nowhere to everywhere' (compare Valentine (2000), though this refers specifically to lesbians). But of course none of these terms are obviously stable or uni-versal, and themselves embrace a variety of differences: male or female, vanilla or s/m, transvestite, transsexual or intersexed, with other identities proliferating based on ethnicity, age and disability to mention but the most obvious (Mercer 1994; Heaphy *et al.* 2003; Shakespeare 2003; Langdridge and Butt 2004). Some of these labels by now have decently long histories. Some represent the eruption of new voices, such as those represented by the movement of disabled people to affirm that 'people are disabled by society, and not by their bodies' (Shakespeare 2003: 143), and disabled people have sexual as well as civil rights. Others have recently changed their meanings, such as bisexuality which, despite its ancient lineage, is being redefined by bi-activists as a postmodern identity, a product of late twentieth century possibilities which funda-mentally challenge binary sexualities (Bi-Academic Intervention 1997; Storr 1999). Yet others represent a transformation in self-definitions and political analysis, seen in the development of transgendered voices (see Chapter 6, this volume). And these are just the broadly non-heterosexual parts of the spectrum.

Choices of sexual ways of life may start with desire or identification, but are bisected by many other sources of difference. Many of these have been made possible through the opportunities opened up by new forms of consumption. Superficially at least the idea of a lifestyle seems inextric-ably tied up with marketing, advertising and consumerism, and there have been significant shifts in the marketplace. A new emphasis in advertising in the 1980s pointed to the changes taking place, with tradi-tional status emulation and reliant social relationships being replaced by a new emphasis on lifestyle choices, focusing particularly on new styles of masculinity and overlapping with emergent gay lifestyles (Mort 1996: 97–8). As Mort stresses, 'Consumer rituals and a contemporary sexual lifestyle were understood to be inextricably linked' (ibid.: 188). This reminds us that economic inequalities and class differences inevitably shape lifestyle options. Broadly we can say that old class divisions in relationship to sexuality and family life have been diminishing, but some differences remain resilient. Similarly, geography, and all the assumptions of economic, cultural and class life behind that word, remains a strong influence. A sexual map of Britain at the beginning of the new century would have shown a changing pattern of behaviour superimposed upon the old (Duncan and Smith 2006). A poll for *The Observer* (2002) found that old puritanical Wales was now apparently the most promiscuous part of the UK, with the highest number of reported sexual partners (thirteen) – a very different world from the Wales of 1945! In parallel, the allegedly dour and puritanical Scottish were the most likely to cheat on their partners (with 34 per cent reporting they had done so), while people in cosmopolitan London, long seen as the epicentre of lax morals, the capital of sin, were the least likely to cheat (with 7 per cent reporting). But sophisticated London had among the highest proportion of lone parents, with inner city boroughs reaching nearly 50 per cent (ONS 2006: 27). London remained the most diverse part of the UK on almost all dimensions, and is by legend the most diverse city in the world. But NATSAL reported in 2001 (Johnson *et al.* 2001) that the greatest changes in reported change had taken place outside London since 1990. The rest of the country was, it seems, catching up. But the country was changing along well-hallowed old routes as well as new.

The post-structuralist theoretical revolution has stressed the multiplication, fluidity and dissolution of identities, emphasizing their invented and contingent nature (Weeks 1995: 83–123). We can talk of chosen plural identities, multiple identities, hybrid identities or even attempts to reject sexual identities altogether in a world of individual lifestyle choices. But it is important to remember that identities are also sedimented, rooted, difficult to escape, even as they change. Class assumptions around appropriate sexual and family behaviour continue to shape the lives of young working-class women in relation to parenting (Duncan and Edwards 1999). There is, for example, a strong continuing correlation between teenage pregnancy, class and disadvantage (Duncan 2005; Rowlingson and McKay 2005). Different ethnic, raced and faith groups reveal quite distinctive attitudes to sex, marriage and parenting (see Fenton *et al.* 2005: 1246–55). Families of Asian and Chinese ethnic origin, for example, were least likely to be lone parents; in 2001 85 per cent of Indian families with children were married. Single-parent families were most common among black Caribbean, African and mixed populations (ONS 2006: 27) – in the case of Caribbean families reflecting distinctive norms of mutual care and support paralleling those of their original homes (Goulbourne and Chamberlain 2001b: 7). Black African and black Caribbean men were more likely to engage in sexual risky behaviour (unprotected sex), with a higher likelihood of sexually transmitted infections, than white, Indian and Pakistani men. White women were more likely to engage in risky behaviour than other ethnic groups (Fenton *et al.* 2005). In the broadest sense all these groups also have sexual lifestyles, if not necessarily in Quentin Crisp's sense of the term: they are not necessarily chosen in the ways in which the lesbians and gays can choose their ways of life. For many, their identities and lifestyles are still fates, not opportunities, while more radically different, and transgressive, lifestyles remain largely confined to more liberal metropolitan areas (Duncan and Smith 2006).

And yet in this complex mixture, and often uneasy coexistence of communities of fate and communities of choice that characterize the contemporary world, there is a common thread. These are, all the evidence suggests, intensely moral communities, not in the sense that individuals struggle to adhere to an external moral code, but in the more profound sense that they try to make sense of their world, and live in it, through elaborating their own moral stories, embodying choices that are right by their standards. Plummer (1995) has shown the importance of sexual stories in shaping communities of knowledge and identity among the sexually marginalized, and in the emergence of new concepts of elective families, the friendship ethic and same-sex intimacies among non-heterosexual people (Weeks *et al.* 2001). In a similar way, Duncan (2005: 6) argues that stories told by teenage mothers belie the picture of irrationality portrayed in official reports and government policies. On the contrary, they show that 'becoming pregnant, and the decision to continue to become a mother, made moral sense in terms of the social worlds of family, community and locality which the mothers, and fathers, inhabited'. In the case of the Caribbean diaspora, the tradition of female-headed families has led to cultural stereotyping of dysfunctional relationships, and has obscured the continuing role of fathers, the strength of neighbourhood ties, and the strong transnational kin networks that sustain everyday life and mutual obligations and responsibilities (Goulbourne and Chamberlain 2001b: 7; Reynolds 2001: 133–54).

Each social world has its own particular moral rationality, which is, as Duncan and Edwards (1999) argue, highly gendered in the sense that men and women might inhabit overlapping but differentiated moral universes, particularly in relationship to intimate life. Moral decision-making, then, is not confined to social commentators or received authorities, whether of church or state. Instead we can see a multiplicity of sites of authority, each speaking its own truth. The challenge we face is how to distinguish between these voices, how to decide which are the moral stories that advance human well-being, and which damage the life chances of the individuals and groups concerned.

Race, ethnicity and religion

Racialized minority ethnic and faith communities are the sites where the tensions and ambiguities of different régimes of sexuality are most fiercely contested. Race and ethnicity are separable from religion, but in practice, in key areas, they have become intertwined in recent years as religion has become one marker among many for racialized and ethnic differences. I noted earlier (Chapter 3) the close affinity between some forms of fundamentalism and faith-based identities, where sexuality, gender and family become critical boundaries for demarcating community values. 'Women's bodies', Polly Toynbee (2006: 33) writes, 'have been the battle flag of religions, whether it's churching their uncleanness, the Pope forcing them to have babies, the Qur'an allowing wife-beating, Hindu suttee, Chinese foot-binding and all the rest.' Christian, Islamic or Hindu evangelicals cum fundamentalists have been in the vanguard in asserting neo-traditionalist hostility to women's sexual assertiveness, together with gay rights, sex education and abortion. The major Christian churches have been badly split over sexual change, with even the traditionalist Catholic Church, while continually resistant (despite the practice of its worshippers) to birth control, buckled under the stress of discovering multitudes of 'paedophile priests' in its ranks. But all faith groups have found it difficult to cope with the gay revolution. Gay priests and same-sex marriage split even the traditional broad church of Anglicanism. Attempts by self-identified Muslim gay men to articulate their sexual identities in their communities have been fraught with difficulty and deep hostility (Yip 2003, 2004b; Bates 2004a, 2004b).

Broadly, however, the trend towards a diminished influence of religion has continued, and provides a dramatic difference between Europe and the USA. A poll in 2004 suggested that only 2 per cent of all voters in the UK went to church more than weekly, compared with 63 per cent of George Bush voters in that year, and 33 per cent of John Kerry voters (Riddell 2004: 17). 'What we are now', the journalist Mary Anne Sieghart (2003: 22) has suggested in a nice phrase, 'is a nation of shoulder-shruggers'. People by and large prefer to mind their own religious business. While that might be true for the majority of people, however, it is clearly not the case for many minority communities who fundamentally challenge secularization (Kaufmann 2006).

The rise of Islamic radicalism from the 1990s, not only in traditional Muslim societies but in many Western cities, has particularly challenged easy notions of secularization, and dramatized a global conflict of values in which the female body has become a major symbolic and material focus. Controversies over the wearing of the headscarf or veil by young Muslim girls in schools have been a feature in several European countries since the 1980s (Weeks 1995: 150–2). France eventually banned the headscarf completely, seeing such apparent religious symbolism as a challenge to its tradition of secular education. In Britain there has been a more general acceptance, with 64 per cent of the population in early 2006, according to a survey, in favour, much higher than in any of the eight European countries surveyed (Woolcock 2006a: 32). The extent to which Muslim women should veil their bodies has, nevertheless, become a touchstone issue which has dramatized the dilemmas of diversity . This was brought to a head in October 2006 following mild comments about the difficulties for community relations posed by some Muslim women covering their faces made by the Leader of the House of Commons, and Blackburn MP Jack Straw (Browne 2006: 6; Wainwright et al. 2006: 4). The wearing of the hijab (headscarf) and even more the niqab (a veil covering the face) and the burqa (which covers everything from top to toe) is, as Amrit Wilson (2006: 22) has said, a topic that is 'brimming with politics'. It is historically a symbol of control of female bodies by men in traditional Muslim societies, especially in the Middle East, an enforced modesty. However, in Western societies, some argue, it can take on a different meaning: 'In a situation where women's bodies are endlessly and relentlessly sexualised, many Muslim women choose to wear the hijab to establish their own boundaries and their own space . . . but also the claiming of non-sexualised identity; carving out a space, and in this way not so much accepting patriarchal boundaries as establishing one's own in the face of the male gaze of British society' (Wilson 2006: 22). The irony of this position is that it involves deploying a feminist language of individual choice to adopt a deeply traditionalist, separatist and socially conservative stance stance towards the world, as Garton Ash (2006: 25) has pointed out. For the writer Saira Khan (2006: 21), herself of a Kashmiri Muslim background, this is unacceptable: 'The veil restricts women, it stops them achieving their full potential in all areas of their lives and it stops them communicating. It sends out a clear message: "I do not want to be part of your society"' (see also Toynbee 2006).

Other cultural traditions, including 'arranged marriages' among people of South Asian origin, have often conflicted with white European discourses on individual choice, and indeed been part of inter-generational conflicts within minority communities themselves (Gavron 1996; Hennink et al. 1999: 868–90; Durham 2004). On the other hand, shifts in the majority population, towards greater sexual explictness especially, have proved offensive to various minority communities – reinforcing claims by women as well as by men for the protection of female modesty. These issues divide, but only become sources of conflict where dominant values are imposed on minority views, or when notions of what constitutes cultural 'harm' are fiercely contested (Cooper 2004). Arranged marriages may be easily accepted when they are akin to similar arrangements traditionally made among the aristocracy, where alliances among great families were gently propelled along by moral pressure on the individuals concerned (the fate of Princess Diana may have been very different if her notions of romantic love did not so readily conflict with royal concepts of dynastic duty – Campbell 1998). They may be deemed totally unacceptable when imposed on a reluctant partner. The difficulty inevitably lies in the challenge of deciding what is freely chosen and what is imposed, whether subtly or not. But ultimately these issues become truly divisive and problematic when dress or marital traditions become the bearers of absolute cultural difference – and a rejection of your (our?) society. The dilemma, then, lies in the extent to which moral pluralism can accommodate a faith which is itself intolerant, and has absolutist and hegemonic claims, enforcing both collective standards and preventing individual voice and exit (Weeks 1995: 151). In the post 9/11 climate of fear and paranoia concerning Islamic radicalism it becomes all too easy to see acute cultural separatism as the encouragement of the 'enemy within' (see e.g.

Phillips 2006); and simultaneously for embattled religious radicals themselves to use the body – especially the female body – as the site where a
defiant difference may be asserted.

The development of extremist Islamic ideologies, though among
only a tiny minority of diasporic Muslim people, represents one notion
of radical diversity, an overflowing of Otherness (including sexual
Otherness) in which pluralism becomes a map of incommensurable differences. This is a danger that some believe they see in contemporary
multiculturalism (Schuster and Solomos 2004). Yet for many others from
minority communities sexuality may better be interpreted as a locus of
cultural hybridization, in which new identities and ways of life are being
forged (Durham 2004). The early migrants of the 1950s and 1960s, of
varied backgrounds and cultures, were homogenized into a feared racial
Other. But it was not the arrival of the incomers with their cultural
and sexual Otherness that posed the problem or caused a racist response.
As Gilroy (2004: 165–6) remarks, 'The racisms of Europe's colonial and
imperial past, preceded the appearance of migrants inside the European
citadel. It was racism and not diversity that made their arrival into
a problem', and racism dogged the making of new communities and
identities, and the reactions to their intimate behaviour. The ethnic
geography of what had long been an ostensibly homogeneous culture
has transparently been transformed. Between 1991 and 2001 the black
and minority ethnic (BME) populations grew from 3.1 million to 4.6
million, increasing as a proportion of the population from 5.6 per cent to
8.1 per cent (Connolly and White 2006: 1). But this population was itself
highly diverse, and so are its patterns of personal life.

Mass migration in the 1950s, 1960s and 1970s from New Commonwealth countries, particularly the Caribbean, India, Pakistan,
Bangladesh, Hong Kong and Africa, had been followed from the 1980s by
dramatic increases in numbers of asylum seekers, and from the 1990s
by large numbers of East Europeans. There are several important points
to note in relationship to the impact of these new populations on sexual
and family life. First, they tend to be concentrated in specific metropolitan areas. Although other cities have a higher proportion of BME
populations, London has by far the largest numbers: 45 per cent of the
BME population live in London (which has 10 per cent of the total British
population). That includes 78 per cent of African immigrants, and 61
per cent Caribbean. Second, related to this, a majority of births in some
British cities come from recent immigrants, rising to 70 per cent in some
London boroughs (Woolcock 2006a: 32). Nearly four-fifths of Bangladeshi
families have children compared to two-fifths of white, the smallest of any
ethnic group (ONS 2006: 25). Among all families, those headed by a non-
white are more likely than white families to have dependent children.
This can be partly explained by cultural or religious differences in
relation to birth control. A more significant reason is the age profile of the
populations concerned, with large numbers of women of childbearing age.
There is evidence that the longer the population has been settled in the

UK the more likely it is to approximate to national fertility tendencies, with African Caribbean patterns closest to white British. The historical evidence, as we know, suggests that fertility patterns will tend to approach each other over time, even as motivations for reduced births will reflect different cultural values.

Racial and ethnic diversity, such data suggest, is more obvious in major cities than elsewhere, with London especially displaying the plural populations and lifestyles one would expect in a genuine world city. The perceived size of the minority populations, nevertheless, has become a potential source of conflict, even for those who lived some distance from BME communities, but especially in those areas where a largely white working class felt displaced or in danger of losing their cultural identities. In their follow-up of Young and Willmott's *Family and Kinship in East London* (1957), which signally failed to mention racial and ethnic change, Dench *et al.* (2006) have traced the resentments of white working-class people at their sense of being bypassed and ignored in the transformation of their neighbourhoods, and the loss of trust in political authority that has followed. In a similar vein, Collins (2005: 224) has lamented the stereotyping of the white working class of South London as 'racist, xenophobic, reactionary', even though the reality has been that this is the very class that has been 'the melting pot of interracial relationships'. Neighbourhood, family, local identities have become the bearers of embattled values as the world changes around them. In parallel, for many members of minority communities, the family has been a site of support and resistance to racism, as much for black feminists or LGBT peoples as for the rest of their communities (Amos and Parma 1984; Frankenberg 1993: 8; Mirza 1997).

The point I want to make here is that the facts of diversity that can be readily assembled do not straightforwardly translate into an easy pluralism, based either on mutual acceptance of different ways of life or the more modest, and perhaps more attainable, ethos of live and let live. Ambivalances, ambiguities, tensions and contradictions are real, and often passionately felt. Moreover, complex processes of racialization of new minority populations continued to work around ideas of otherness, especially around sexuality. In a study of the process in relation to individuals of mixed Thai, and German or British origins, Jinthana Haritaworn (2005) has shown how people draw on half-conscious assumptions about the sexual availability of Thai women or the androgyny, passivity and potential homosexuality of Thai men, which in turn derives from a repertoire of sexual assumptions that have their roots in colonial times. Whatever the patina of liberal tolerance, whiteness remains the dominant, if unmarked, norm, a 'set of locations that are historically, socially, politically and culturally produced and, moreover, are intrinsically linked to unfolding relations of domination' (Frankenberg 1993: 2; cf. Dyer 1997).

Having said that it is also important to mark genuine changes. A survey in 2006 suggested that more than half of Britons felt that immigration had made the UK a better place to live in (Woolcock 2006a). By and large it seems that intercommunal relationships were better the longer different peoples lived close to one another, even if in contiguous rather than mingled communities. More hopefully, perhaps, many young British people were practically demonstrating their growing acceptance of diversity through establishing intimate relationships across the ethnic and racialized divides. Connolly and White (2006: 5) have noted the emergence of a new British-born ethnic group, comprising some 700,000 people in 2001, born of mixed parentage. This is scarcely one ethnic group because as the authors themselves point out there were distinct groups in England and Wales: those born of mixed white and African Caribbean parents, the largest group; those of mixed white and Asian origins; and a smaller group of mixed white and African. African Caribbeans were most likely to be involved in mixed relations, South Asians least. But of all the minority groups they list, the highest proportion of under 16s are from the mixed population, suggesting an increasing rate of intergroup relationships. The rates of inter-ethnic relations were higher in Britain than in any comparable country in Europe, and certainly higher than in the USA (see Alibhai-Brown and Montague 1992; Weeks 1995: 41). Whatever the hardening lines of division in many urban centres, towns in the north like Blackburn and Burnley, but also in Royal Windsor, or inner city boroughs in London, and whatever the continuing evidence of racism, white on black but also across other ethnic divisions (in a 1997 survey 32 per cent of Asians and 29 per cent of Jews claimed they would have a problem if a relative married an Afro-Caribbean compared to 13 per cent of white Britons – Collins 2005: 224), new forms of what Gilroy (2004) has called 'conviviality' have developed in many parts of Britain that look to a different future.

In his book *After Empire* (2004) Gilroy questions whether the emergence of essentialized racial and ethnic identities has contributed anything worthwhile to the struggle against racism, and sees the hope for genuine change more in the development of 'multiculturality', rather than the forms of multiculturalism – based on the reification of group identities – that have characterized official governmental responses to diversity. The multiculturality that Gilroy defends is based on the idea of conviviality, which refers to 'the process of cohabitation and interaction that have made multiculture an ordinary feature of social life in Britain's urban areas and in postcolonial cities elsewhere' (Gilroy 2004: xi). It is the very ordinariness, banality even, of everyday coexistence in family life, youth cultures, sexual interactions, music, that is the real answer to what he describes as a post-colonial melancholia which marks the anxieties and fears of multiculturalism expressed by many on the liberal Left, who despair of effective cohabitation. Both the absolutist affirmations of separate identities that underline the attitudes of socially conservative ethnic leaders and official policy, and their liberal critics who advocate a new push for integration and new cohesive definitions of Britishness are challenged in favour of a new project which is:

prepared to break with the notion that racial differences are a
self-evident, immutable fact of political life. It refuses the idea
that this order of difference is somehow necessary to the very
stability of our conflicted world. Instead, it suggests that the
reification of race must be challenged if effective work against
racism is to be accomplished. It seeks to turn the table on all
purity seekers, whoever they may be, to force them to account
for their phobia about otherness and their violent hostility in the
face of the clanging, self-evident sameness of suffering mankind.
The version of multiculturalism that takes place at this point is
not then a lifestyle option. Its dissident value is confirmed
everywhere in the chaotic pleasures of the convivial postcolonial
urban world.

(Gilroy 2004: 167)

The 'radical openness' that conviviality points to does not abrogate the
reality of racism (or of other forms of domination and subordination,
especially around gender and sexuality). On the contrary it points to
the importance of identifying the forces which inhibit and deny the
possibilities of more egalitarian and just lives. But it also suggests the
importance of valuing the everyday life experiments that very many are
already engaged in, and a radical humanism built around our 'ability
to live with alterity without becoming anxious, fearful, or violent' (Gilroy
2004: xi; see also essays in *Soundings* (2006), and further discussion of
radical humanism in Chapter 8, this volume).

The life course

If race, ethnicity and faith threaten to divide the culture vertically, age
threatens to divide it horizontally. That has certainly been an historical
pattern, and few would deny the generational clashes that marked the
great transition. But just as spontaneous conviviality weakens absolutist
identities around visible differences, so the cultural revolutions of our
time have undermined the 'seven ages of man'. A more pluralistic world
has profoundly undermined traditional assumptions of a natural life
cycle through which individuals pass in their progression from birth,
childhood, adolescence, early adulthood, marriage, children, to retire-
ment, old age and death. Instead, as a life course perspective emphasizes,
we need to understand the 'multiple temporal and social contexts' (Mabry
and Bengtson 2004), the differing historical and social circumstances
through which individuals negotiate their various journeys.

Significant demographic shifts have contributed to this. By 2004
there were 21 per cent fewer births than in 1971, 34 per cent fewer than
in 1901. There were 2.6 million fewer young people aged 16 in 2001 than
in 1971, while the number of people over 65 had increased by 2.2 million
(ONS 2006: 18). This heavy weighting of older people is destined to
increase as baby boomers reach their sixties. The population is being

skewed in new ways, with the weight falling on older people. Not surprisingly, well-established categorizations are crumbling. The key factor is that traditional concepts of childhood and adulthood, long under assault, have fragmented, raising difficult problems about the meanings of these terms, and of the transitions between them. Young people are having sex earlier; older people are maintaining active sexual lives longer (or at least more publicly), and even, due to the technological revolution around conception, having children and parenting at later ages, and different publics are deploying sexuality and intimacy in ever more diverse ways.

Britain, like all late modern societies, has long been familiar with different youth cultures, certainly since the Teddy Boys, and mods and rockers of the late 1950s and early 1960s, and sexual precocity added to the frequent sense of moral panic that these cultures generated. By the 1980s dystopic sociologists were fearing the emergence of irreconcilable tribes, inward-looking, self-obsessed, sexually precocious and potentially violent (Maffesoli 1995). In reality, contemporary young people seem to share many of their basic values with their parents, with nuances. At the same time there are distinctive 'value régimes' that are shaped by and relate to young people's preoccupations (Thomson 2004: 135) On the whole they appear to be more tolerant of sexual difference, and more supportive of lesbian and gay rights, than their parents' generation, though acceptance of homosexuality is frequently tempered by homophobic language and behaviour. By the turn of the millennium 'gay' had become a common term of abuse among young people: 'The word "gay" now means 'rubbish' in modern play-ground speak and need not be offensive to homosexuals, the BBC Board of Governors has ruled', though LGBT people themselves vehemently objected (Lusher 2006: 7; Sherwin 2006: 5). Whether this was any different from the marking of the boundaries of difference, betokening acceptance and outsiderdom, common in youth cultures for generations, is not clear. What is apparent is that there has been a subtle shift in the role of sexuality. Traditionally, the onset of sexual activity had been a marker of adulthood, but has usually been associated with the assumption of new responsibilities, as in marriage. Where material dependence is prolonged, as it increasingly is with extended education and larger numbers of young adults remaining at home into their late twenties, especially men, sexual agency in itself becomes an increasingly important marker of autonomy and grown-up status (Thomson 2004: 135). It becomes a rite of passage to adulthood otherwise denied them. There has been a striking shift. The *Observer* poll (2002) suggested that 23 per cent of young people had had first sex at age 14 to 15, with 32 per cent before they were 16. The average age of first sex has dropped to 16 for men, 17 for women. This compares with an average age of 19 for those over 55. There was also evidence to suggest that first sexual activity was often in confusing and fraught circumstances. Research conducted by the Trust for the Study of Adolescence found that eight out of ten teenagers lose their virginity when they are drunk, feeling pressurized into having sex, and are not using protectives against conception or disease (Campbell 2006b: 16).

Young parenting can also provide a status otherwise denied young women, especially those coming from deprived backgrounds, where motherhood provides a sense of identity and personal meaning (Duncan 2005). The teenage pregnancy rate in Britain, despite fluctuations since the 1980s, and intensive government pressure after 1997 to reduce it, remains one of the highest in Europe. In 2003 there were twenty-six live births per 1000 females aged between 15 and 19, amounting to nearly 100,000 conceptions, a proportion that was some 19 per cent higher than the next highest, Latvia. The lowest rates at six births per 1000 women were in Cyprus, Slovenia, Sweden and Denmark, a strange mix of cultures, ranging from the socially conservative to the most sexually liberal, suggesting the complex range of factors – and the very different cultural meanings – shaping teenage pregnancy rates (ONS 2006: 31). At the same time it is worth noting that fewer than one in ten of the conceptions were to girls under 16, the age of consent, with just over 300 of these to girls under 14. Although these conceptions (many of which ended in abortions) arouse peculiar media frenzy and government anxiety, they seemed rarely to be seen as shameful in the – overwhelmingly deprived – families in which they occurred. Class and local communal meanings and status mingled with diminished economic and cultural opportunities to sustain a culture of early motherhood (Duncan 2005).

Sexuality is clearly a central aspect of young people's agency, but produces a paradoxical response. The culture simultaneously sexualizes young people (in advertising, entertainment, through pop music, clothing) and fears the results, as recurrent panics about young people's sexual behaviour suggest. It is not surprising, therefore, that there is a profound confusion about transitions to adulthood, especially in policy terms. Young people move, in often very different ways, through the various, but intertwined transitions to recognized adulthood, in relation, for example, to employment rights and pay, educational opportunities and intimate involvements (Thomson 2004: 135). The age of criminal responsibility starts at 8, you can buy cigarettes, leave school, have legal sex and marry at 16, buy alcohol, have social security rights and vote at 18, but have to wait until you are 22 to be entitled to the minimum wage.

Confusion about youth and young adulthood is matched by a fragmentation or pluralization of adulthoods. In a sense we can see this as the story of this book, which has traced the development of different identities and lifestyles. Baby boomers have here, as in so many other areas, led the way. Their ambition to 'have it all' has led to a distinct delaying of ageing. Its onset may be delayed by new relationships, late parenting, originally a prerogative of men, but now, through IVF, of women as well, enhanced sexual activity (via Viagra and Cialis and the like: see Chapter 6), and the dominance of youthful and highly sexual values in specific cultures, such as in the gay community (Heaphy *et al.*

2003). *The Times* (19 July 2006: 5) captured a melancholic milestone in this shift under the headline '"Swinging" pensioners need sex education':

> Pensioners have been urged to practice safer sex after figures
> showed that the number of sexual diseases diagnosed among
> the over-50s has soared in the past five years . . . Ruth Holman,
> a consultant . . . said 'People are more frequently having
> relationships at older ages with more partners and more sexual
> experimentation'.

In a world of often bewildering change the stable boundaries are no longer fixed or immutable. Individuals are forced to negotiate their life courses with imagination, confronting their critical or fateful moments, 'phases in which things are wrenched out of joint, where a given state of affairs is suddenly altered by a few key events' (Giddens 1991:113; see also Thomson *et al*. 2002), with as much emotional skill and equanimity as they can muster. During such moments they are forced to re-evaluate and to reconstruct the narratives of their lives. These might be the impact of first relations or separation and divorce; coming out as lesbian or gay, or realizing your sexual fantasies; moving to a new city or even country; ageing or confronting major health problems. All these force individuals to face their pasts and confront their futures, to reassess their life course and reshape their biographical narratives, to fit the very changing circumstances in which they find themselves. Under such pressures generational attributes and identities are no longer pre-determined or stable.

The contemporary world is haunted by the spectres of difference and diversity, of which the three dimensions I have so far discussed are only aspects. Differences in terms of identities, politics, culture, taste, consumption, economic and social opportunity, reproduction patterns, health opportunities, education, erotic pleasure, family life, ability and disability, access to media, voice and exit: all have a high salience in our complex, pluralistic and fluid present, and all teeter on the verge of becoming the site of conflict, of division. There are controversies arising from diversity across the Western world, on everything from young people's sexuality to STIs, from the rights of lesbian and gay parents to gays in the military, from same-sex marriages to surrogacy, from the needs of lone mothers to the rights of transgendered people, from abortion and stem cell research to porn on the internet, from immigration rights to welfare entitlements, from the demands of faith communities and the rights of ethnic minorities to the claims of radical political sects. The list is potentially long, as overlapping communities and social movements make their claims. And it is not just social movements that assume a progressive lineage and agenda that make their claim to recognition. Even powerful fundamentalist or (in the literal sense) reactionary movements, such as anti-abortionists or fathers' rights organizations, claim their place in the pluralistic universe, presenting themselves as vulnerable victims of liberal intolerance and 'political correctness gone mad' (Cooper 2004: 6). In other parts of the world the concerns are often more basic: how to survive if your way of life, your sense of yourself, or your everyday sexual practices do not fit into traditional or neo-traditional patterns. Think of the fundamentalist preoccupations with the body, and with gender and sexual conformity. Think of the stoning to death of (women) adulterers and of homosexuals. Think of the still fearful response to HIV/AIDS even in countries like South Africa, where an ostensibly enlightened president follows myths peddled on the internet and for a long time blocked the adoption of sensible drug therapies (Bhatt 1997; Altman 2001).

To an unprecedented degree the question of how we live with sexual diversity has become a key issue about the ways we live today, and it causes enormous tensions. Diversity causes trouble. More positively it also produces, certainly in the highly developed societies of the global North, a host of new voices clamouring to be heard, a 'pluralization of the public spheres' (Plummer 2003: 73): of feminists, gays, traditionalists, fundamentalists, faith groups, environmentalists, sexual dissidents and subversives, moral conservatives, health professionals, patients, debating, shouting, reasoning, experimenting, preaching in multiple social worlds, social movements, on the streets, in newspapers and journals, via the web and the blogosphere, on television and radio. Old stories are being repeated, new stories of sexuality and intimacy are proliferating, speaking from and to specific constituencies, but ever enlarging the babel of voices that want to be listened to.

Recognizing the fact of diversity is not of course the same as valuing diversity as a good in itself. Many prefer to affirm the norm and castigate the abnormal. Nor should a recognition of sexual variation preclude debate about how to evaluate the myriad forms of diversity, demarcating the acceptable from the unacceptable, the harmful from the harmless. We may all easily agree that sexual activities involving force and coercion, and abuse of the young and vulnerable are wrong. But how do we evaluate consensual practices, embodying 'extreme' forms of erotic pleasure, that we might find ethically or aesthetically distasteful? How do we interpret 'harm' when one person's poison is another's delight? To what extent can we exclude the intricate coils of power from our evaluations and ethical judgements? Is it possible to forget gendered subjectivities or age differences, or different abilities when we look at erotic practices? As Cooper has argued, there are two particularly troublesome forms of diversity: differences of power, especially those organized around gender, race and sexuality; and social and cultural practices perceived as harmful or undesirable (Cooper 2004: 190–1). The first are often underplayed, but frequently represent the critical intersection of forces and of inequalities that reinforce each other. The second have been the source of some of the most intractable battles in the 'sex wars'; for example, around s/m practices, pornography and intergenerational sex.

The problem here is that sexuality in itself embodies no obvious rights or wrongs. The days when it was possible to argue that such or such an act was 'unnatural' have long gone. We can no longer understand the sexual, despite the best efforts of some contemporary theorists influenced by the new genetics (see critiques in Lancaster 2003; Segal 2004), as a fundamental instinctive drive, wired into our genes, to which the social must react. Rather, we can see the erotic as highly socially malleable, shaped by permissions and inhibitions, interventions and non-interventions, definitions and self-definitions, which create sexual categories, hierarchies, meanings and subjectivities (Plummer 2004). To respond to these issues we must inevitably draw on ethical standards that are largely external to our perception of the erotic. Awareness of sexuality does not in and of itself tell us how we can intervene to promote the benign and prevent the perverse (both of which are themselves contested terms). There are of course those who offer a fundamentalist defence of 'traditional values' – usually, in practice, offering a reinvention of tradition – and we cannot underestimate their influence in some jurisdictions. There are others, on the Left as well as the Right, who believe that all such questions are complicit with forms of power or adjuncts of modern consumerism and neo-liberal economics, and surrender to a sense of cultural despair, as we will see shortly. More often than not such questions tend to get buried whenever moral panics sweep over us, as they all too frequently still do, suggesting we are still desperately uncertain in confronting the complexity of contemporary mores. But the fact that sexual issues are now transparently central to the political, social and cultural agenda, in ways they were not barely half a generation ago, underlines that profound shifts have taken place in our cultural landscape, and in our individual and collective priorities (Weeks 1995).

The new individualism and its critics

What does this all mean for the contemporary individual, hailed, addressed, 'interpellated' in and through these various discourses of diversity, shaped by the intersection of these multiple elements? The desiring, relating, actualizing self, Rose has suggested, 'is an invention of the second half of the twentieth century' (Rose 1999: xxi). We have seen the emergence of this sexual self, the individual conscious of his, and increasingly her, erotic needs, sexualized identity and cultural positioning, throughout the sixty years or so since 1945: the sexualizing couple and the respectable homosexual in the 1940s and 1950s, the sexually aggressive newly affluent but socially dissatisfied young male and the young woman emancipated by the Pill in the 1960s and 1970s, the women's liberationist and the out gay man and lesbian of the 1970s, the risk-takers and survivors of the 1980s and 1990s, the new would-be sexual citizens of the present. The contemporary self is shaped in a continuously sexualizing culture where the erotic becomes meaningful for a sense of who and what you are. And the meanings of the erotic are themselves in constant flux.

Plummer (2003) has listed some of the social flows in late modernity which influence for good or ill potential subjectivities, sexualities and intimacies. He names the media revolutions, the digitalization revolution, the technologizing of life, globalizing flows, individualization, trends towards disclosing intimacy, greater egalitarianism, the growth of insecurity, commodification, medicalization, culturally destablizating tendencies. Each of these produces new forms of subjectivity. There are mediated lives, digitalized lives, technologized lives, globalized lives, individuated lives, disclosing lives, egalitarian lives, insecure lives, commodified lives, medicalized lives, destabilized lives. There are many more. But they all suggest elements of self-making, of story-telling, of self-fashioning. We are here on the terrain of sexual biographies and the rise and rise of sexualized identities.

One of the most striking features of contemporary sexuality is the emphasis many put on self-invention, on the creation of a viable sense of self, which has become a key element of the individualizing process. What in the 1960s and 1970s was the aspiration of radical minorities has become a general cultural trope, though it remains fundamental to those still on the margins. 'Speaking from my generation', Greg, a 38-year-old gay man said, interviewed for our book *Same Sex Intimacies* (Weeks *et al.* 2001: 43) in the late 1990s, ' . . . discovering that I was homosexual meant having to invent myself because there was nothing there'. In a similar way, the late Tamsin Wilton (2004) has used the phrase 'self-fashioning' to describe the processes of transition of women she interviewed from heterosexual 'normality' to lesbianism. Implicit in such phrases is the idea of a process rather than an ending, a journey rather than a destination (King 2003). There are numerous accounts by LGBT people of their complex pathways to a viable identity around sexuality or gender. For many it is a realization of a true self, previously hidden by guilt, self-oppression, fear of exposure or the trappings of an alien body in a homophobic or transphobic world. But for many others it is an opportunity to reshape one's life, to engage in what theorists from John Stuart Mill in the nineteenth century to Anthony Giddens in the present have called 'life experiments' (see Giddens 1992: 135; Weeks 1995; cf. Reynolds 2002). For Paul, a 36-year-old gay man, it's 'constantly experimenting with just how far we want to go . . . trying to push the boundaries a bit' (Weeks *et al.* 2001: 50). Such reflexive comments may be more common among those who have had self-consciously to rewrite the story of their lives because of the need to affirm themselves against marginalization, but they are one aspect of a much wider social development. In the contemporary world, people are being forced to remake themselves constantly, to see their lives as a project that must be constantly attended to. The standard biography of earlier periods becomes a chosen biography, a do-it-yourself biography (Beck 1994: 14; Beck and Beck-Gernsheim 2002). Individualization means 'First, the disembedding and, second, the re-embedding of industrial society ways of life by new ones, in which the individual must produce, stage and cobble together their biographies themselves' (Beck 1994: 13).

Staging, cobbling together, designing, juggling – these are the evocative words Beck uses, and they resonate because they link with a radical shift in the language used to discuss sexuality in recent years. The most characteristic metaphors used in early sexological writings (and in 1960s liberatory writings) revolved around Manichean conflicts: between the sacred and the profane, sex and society, suppression and release, repression and liberation. They suggest that the social acts to repress the natural, that a titanic struggle is in process between two overwhelming forces, in which sexuality was either dangerous or life-enhancing, society was either repressive or libertarian, a 'never-ceasing duel' (Weeks 1985: 96–126). Today the most common metaphors in writing about sexuality and sexual identities are 'invention', 'construction', 'embodiment', 'social practices', 'fictions', 'narratives', 'roles', 'scripts', 'performances', 'performativity' – all emphasizing the ways in which sexual meanings, identities, enactments are cultural artefacts, in which self-creation is a critical element. These terms are not, of course, universally accepted. For some, sexuality still embodies moral absolutes. There is also a passionate flirtation among some with the 'truths' of the genes, which has led to a vogue for evolutionary psychology (cf. Segal 2004; see Chapter 6, this volume). But to my mind the most useful way of trying to understand sexuality today is as a set of practices which are shaped in a complex and changing network of social worlds, and are made meaningful through language (Weeks 2003, forthcoming). The languages of sexuality shape the way we see the body and its potentialities, and the ways we live our erotic lives. Among the most powerful terms are those associated with self-making and self-invention. We are talking again here of agency, and therefore of the individual and collective practices through which personal life is shaped and reshaped.

Reflexivity is a key feature of these new processes. It crucially involves the ability of individuals to reflect on their situation, to bring to bear their particular knowledges, their perception of risk to their everyday lives, and to act in the light of this. Reflexivity in this context means self-confrontation (Beck 1994: 5; see also Adkins 2002). This is individualization not as an abstract process, but as a key force in individual lives, a social process that imposes its imperatives on individuals, but within which individuals can fashion their lives, can choose. There is a massive paradox here. Most people may not feel they can choose their sexual desires, which seem to be theirs by instinct or wired into the genes. More crucially, this freedom to choose is always constrained and limited. Is it a genuine freedom when one is forced to be a free agent? The reality is that choice is always limited by the same social forces that have made it available. Nor is choice without its dangers – of violence, disease, anxiety, uncertainty. The choice biography is essentially a risk biography, as Beck (1994) has pointed out. Individuals are forced reflexively to organize and calculate the pros and cons of their future action, and that can bring a sense of isolation, the loneliness of moral choice. In that context sex can become a source of meaning, an anchor against drift. A review of attitudes in 2002 found a 'society in thrall to the flesh' (Adams 2002), which sums up one significant perception of what was at stake. Yet at the same time, especially compared to the restraints of earlier periods, individuals have unprecedented freedom to choose identities and lifestyles, and this can only be seen as a positive advance towards a more humane and tolerant culture.

The 'new individualism' has nevertheless been subject to searching critique (see Elliott and Lemert 2006). I want to look at four key arguments which have had powerful resonances in relationship to sexualities and intimacy.

Individualism and the manipulated self

The belief that capitalism distorts and damages human potential, creating a manipulated self, has had a long history, traceable to German theorists of the early twentieth century such as Simmel, and developed and carried through by the Frankfurt School in the interwar and post-war years (Robinson 1972; Jay 1973). They achieved a wider a currency through the work of Marcuse, whose *Eros and Civilization* and *One-dimensional Man*, as I discussed in Chapter 3, struck a chord with radicals in the 1960s and early 1970s (Marcuse 1969, 1972; see also Weeks 1985: ch. 7). The implication of this critique is that individuals are given the illusion of new freedoms, especially erotic, but are really under 'tutelage', colonized by consumer capitalism and the associated bureaucratization of everyday life, their intimate hopes and desires commodified. In the conditions of late modernity such arguments have been given a new edge.

Contemporary consumer society, Bauman (2005: 84) has argued, 'cannot but be a society of excess and profligacy – and so of redundancy and prodigal waste'. Gail Hawkes argues that a key feature of the twentieth century has been a 'commodification of sex and its pleasures in ways that connected the spheres of profitability and self identity' (2004: 147). What was once seen as special and mystical, even, has become mundane as the commercialization of sex has sucked it dry of any threatening or disruptive characteristics, establishing a series of playgrounds within which to simulate freedom. Tyler, following Habermas, argues that 'the contemporary management of sexuality constitutes a notable example of a managerial colonization of everyday life, signifying not only an intensification of "Fordist sexuality" and a "Taylorisation of sex", but also a corresponding threat to imagination and ingenuity' (Tyler 2004: 82). Eros is harnessed to the performance principle, and capitalist values have penetrated deep into intimate life, colonizing intersubjective processes and thus reshaping the sexual world. Examples of this include pre-nuptial and cohabitation agreements, where presumably a contract culture has invaded everyday life (compare Lewis 2001), and self-advertising to meet partners, which we have to assume is seen as the marketization of relational values. Arlie Hochschild (2003a, 2003b) sees this process as 'commercializing' all intimate life, stalling the hopes of early feminists for a more equal society, and corrupting ideals of care and altruism. Heath and Potter (2005) go further still, by arguing that the counter-culture of the 1960s, which of course heavily influenced the birth of second-wave feminism and gay liberation, was fully complicit with consumer capitalism. For as Bauman says, 'liquid life is consuming life' (2005: 9).

These are powerful critiques, and heavily influence a contemporary mood of sullen disillusion among many former radicals, and culturally conservative critics especially on the Left, but in strange parallel with the political right wing. In part, at least, we can see once again a harking back to not so much a lost society as a society that never quite existed. Sexuality has never existed outside the shaping influence of culture; there has never been a pure undefiled eros uncorrupted by capitalism. There was no 'beach beneath the paving stones', to echo one of the key phrases of Parisian radicals in 1968. Sexuality has always necessarily been shaped and moulded by the society that orders it, and invents and reinvents its significance. To that extent, it is scarcely surprising that contemporary sexuality, as an aspect of a highly commercialized culture, will be shaped by these influences – indeed it is a tautology. That does not, of course, mitigate the cultural impact of such a critique.

Individualism and the dissolution of human bonds

The process of individualization, it is argued, dissolves the human bond. The trends of contemporary culture involve, according to these critics, the replacement of authentic, reflective subjectivities with narcissistic, hedonistic values (Elliott and Lemert 2006: 60). In *The Minimal Self*, Christopher Lasch (1985) argues that the pluralist concept of freedom represents a surrender to consumerist values, and the celebration of a protean sense of self which accepts oxymorons like 'open marriage and 'non-binding commitments'. Bauman (2005) echoes this in lamenting the 'frailty' of human bonds. There are no fixed bonds that link people together as there were in old kinship patterns. People have to make bonds for themselves, but they are dependent now on their own skills, and none are guaranteed to last. In the modern world, 'loyalty is a cause of shame, not pride' (Bauman 2005: 9). He conjures up a picture of our contemporaries abandoned to their own wits, and feeling easily dis-posable, yearning for togetherness and a helping hand, desperate to relate, yet afraid of being related (ibid.: viii).

Instead of commitment we have enforced 'privatism' (Elliott and Lemert 2006), and again we can find a long tradition of moral critique. Sennett (1992) famously lamented 'the fall of public man', and the dominance of notions of self-fulfilment at the expense of social bonds. Lasch's 'minimal self' focuses on survival, one day at a time. Bauman

(2005) sees the invasions and colonization of 'communitas', the site of the moral economy, by market forces as constituting the most awesome of the dangers facing our human togetherness (see Rose (1999: 217–20) for a critique). Heath and Potter (2005), like Hochschild, see a 'cultural cooling' manifested in cool emotional strategies, such as those deployed in popular television series like *Sex in the City* and in the lifestyles of the new urban demographic, the 'metrosexual'. Cool is the new hot, and the passions of the 1970s social movements are displaced into the intricacies of private life. Private life is a source of comfort and pleasures. It is also a site of emotional isolation, where possessions are substituted for emotional links, and individuals compensate for their loneliness by 'maniacally' searching for illusory substitutes to fill the gaps in their lives (Elliott and Lemert 2006: 41), to rebuild their self-esteem.

Psychology has a special role to play in this emotional desert. It provides the discourse and practices that sustain the fiction of the autonomous subject. Individuals look to psychology, in its various forms, as a form of explanation and a 'restorative practice' that can heal, make one whole again, through counselling and therapy. But this is at best a regulatory fiction itself, and is no more liberating than the traditional ties and relationships it is replacing, leaving individuals even 'more stranded' (Walkerdine 2005: 48–9). We live, Furedi has argued, in a 'therapy culture', 'distracting people from engaging with the wider social issues in favour of an inward turn to the self' (Furedi 2004: 203). But this is a confessing self, part of a therapeutic culture in which everyone confesses to every other self, manifested in twelve-step therapy programmes, personal counselling, memory recovery work, addiction management, phone and cyber therapy, peer counselling, not to mention the confessional extravaganzas of television programmes like Oprah (Elliott and Lemert 2006: 130; cf. Plummer 1995, 2003), and other technologies opened up by the media revolution.

Individualism and neo-liberalism

The problem with the arguments put forward so far is that they all assume that the individual is forced to live the illusion of freedom while actually being wrapped in the gilded cords of late capitalism. We may imagine we can do what we want, the argument seductively goes, but in reality that is an illusion. Such arguments are not a million miles from the idea that we are all suffering from false consciousness, trapped in our hopeless pleasures, imprisoned by ideological blinkers in a system that manipulates, isolates and privatizes, making impossible the most important and precious human bonds. Such arguments have many difficulties, but not the least of them is that they all tend to assume that some people are better placed than others to see through the murky clouds of ideology in order to glimpse the truth of our real nature. As I have argued throughout the book, there are problems both with this idea of truth and with the notion of a pure, uncorrupted nature. A related argument, which avoids these dangers (while unfortunately generating other problems), has recently achieved a significant purchase. Central to this is the proposal that ideas of individual autonomy and self-responsibilization are not so much illusory or deceptive as the very forms of regulation which can be most effectively articulated with the current form of capitalist, and by extension social and cultural, organization: neo-liberalism. Neo-liberalism has since the 1990s become the bugbear of progressive polemics, and the focus of hostile international mobilization, for example, through the European Social Forum and the anti-globalization movement. It has also been used as a convenient target for a more mainstream politics, in both rapidly industrializing countries of the global South, and by major European countries such as France in articulating their hostility towards Anglo-Saxon economic and welfare policies. It has been portrayed especially as the ideological face of globalizing forces, undermining welfare policies that protect the individual against the depradations of international capital (see Chapter 8).

However, the critiques of neo-liberalism as they apply to sexuality and intimate life owe most to a particular reading of the work of Michel Foucault (for a different reading see Watney 1994; Weeks 1995, 2005a). This stresses the discursive construction of subjectivities within specific régimes of power. From this perspective, neo-liberalism may be seen as the latest configuration of power, a new form of governance through which the individual is, in Rose's phrase, 'forced to be free' (1999), to manage him or herself. These tendencies, the argument goes, have been implicit in sexual-social policy since Wolfenden, but have become dominant in this period of late modernity and risk society. Under neo-liberal imperatives, individuals become 'entrepreneurs of themselves, shaping their own lives through the choices they make among the forms of life available to them' (Rose 1999: 230). This elaborate and sophisticated form of subjectivity/subjectification does not, however, lead to the abandonment of governance; rather it substitutes self-governance as the principal form of social regulation. So, for example, Rose argues that the shift in family policy from the 1980s to family rights and privacy did not represent an abandonment of the efforts of the past 150 years to socialize and regulate the family. It is its culmination in that the family now becomes the 'responsible autonomous family'. The modern family remains intensely governed, not by mechanisms of social control but through the promotion of subjectivities attuned to the needs of neo-liberal forms of governance.

Similarly, recent liberalizing sex reforms may be seen as heading in a similar direction. Critics of same-sex marriage have seen it as a move towards creating the respectable gay as opposed to the transgressive, disruptive, and challenging queer (see Chapter 7). Respectability would involve a voluntary regulation of the sexual self in the interests of full acceptance and citizenship (Richardson 2004: 393). Some have seen this process working its way through the management of HIV in the 'post-crisis' world (in the West at least). A surveillance medicine, based on a risk rationality, replaces hospital medicine, with the aim of creating self-reflexive, self-managing subjects. People with HIV learn to calculate and manage risk, using their knowledge of their HIV status, their T cell count and blood viral load count, and the likelihood of infection to negotiate sexual partnerships (Adkins 2002: 108ff.; Davis 2005: 251).

From this position the self-reflexive person is the ideal subject of neo-liberal discourse, and 'reflexivity is constitutive of new forms of classification, hierarchies, divisions, struggle and forms of contestation' (Adkins 2002: 123). As Foucault argued a generation ago, modern forms of power work through normalization of particular forms of behaviour rather than overt state direction (Foucault 1979; see also Weeks 2005a). An emphasis on individual freedom and rights, and the importance of self-surveillance and regulation for the individual who has internalized the norms and goals of liberal forms of governance, is central to the new society (Richardson 2004: 393). This form of governance, it must be stressed, is not the product of a singular direction of normalizing power. The new subjectivities that constitute self-governing citizens are the result of complex processes, 'the confluence of a whole variety of different shifts in practices with no single point of origin or principle of unification' (Rose 1999: xvii). But in the contemporary world they are all the more potent for seeming to be so dispersed, underplayed and voluntarily chosen.

For some there is little to feed even a tincture of optimism in this bold new world. A leading progressive social thinker such as Zygmunt Bauman (2005: 129) has no compunction about stating baldly that 'we live in what . . . can properly be called "dark times"'. This sounds ominously like ringing the tocsins for something akin to the fall of the Roman Empire, which since the eighteenth century has been a potent metaphor for societal collapse. Dark times bring with them decadence and barbarism, if not plague and pestilence, where frail human bonds are being frayed beyond survival in a world of rampant and selfish individualism and glittering consumerism, a new dark age indeed. This, it should be noted, comes from a man of the liberal Left, not from a Christian fundamentalist. Echoing this profound cultural pessimism, yet more liberal sociologists Elliott and Lemert (2006) see their proclaimed 'new individuals', the avatars of globalizing culture, as dystopic inhabitants of this dark new world, dwelling in a 'plastic culture', with 'hollowed out' identities, seduced by instant makeovers, bodily fascism and worship of an evanescent celebrity, suffering a demeaned public language, an enforced privatism, and displaying acute signs of narcissism and emotionalism. The culture of advanced individualism, these authors argue, has generated a world of individual risk-taking, experimentation and self-expression, which is underpinned by new forms of apprehension, anguish and anxiety stemming from the perils of globalization. The emotional costs of globalization, neo-liberalism and compulsive consumption are high, and we are all forced to pay the price. Our striving for individuality and autonomy are illusory, 'tragically self-defeating'.

Individualism and democratic autonomy

It often seems impossible to counter these torrents of pessimism and despair coming from leading liberal theorists. If they think like this, imagine what real conservatives must imagine is happening to us. Yet others see in this new world something more hopeful. A world of uncertainty and contingency, perhaps, and of threats and fears But also a world of new freedoms, positive identities, genuine choices, a world we are striving to make for ourselves, a world of challenges and opportunities, dangers and pleasures. This is a world view broadly endorsed by theorists such as Anthony Giddens (1992), and I include myself among them. What are the markers of this?

Surely the most obvious factor is that we have become a more tolerant culture, more able and willing to live with difference. All the evidence suggests that we have become more accepting of non-marital sex, of divorce, birth control, of sexual explicitness, of erotic variety, and of different forms of intimacy. To say this is not to ignore the intransigence of attitudes among many groups, especially those whose faith and cultural traditions make them turn their back on sexual change, or the continuing undercurrent of violence and phobic prejudice that affects women and those who are sexually or gender nonconformist in particular. But the context has changed radically. A MORI opinion poll early in 2006 suggested that a 'quiet revolution' was taking place in the UK, in which 'Britons have become strikingly liberal over a range of key issues' (Campbell 2006a: 16–17). This echoed many polls during the early part of the new century which indicated an accelerating change in private mores. In 2001 the National Survey of Sexual Attitudes and Lifestyles noted that 'Changes in reported behaviour have occurred across all demographic groups' (Johnson *et al.* 2001: 9), and these were broadly in the direction of less restrictive behaviour, increasing coalescence in male and female behaviour, and greater acceptance of different life patterns. At the same time, the law was continuing its retreat from the bedroom, at least in its traditional form, and many churches – certainly the Christian churches – by and large preached and pontificated but most people ceased to listen. The best example of this remained the dramatic decline of fertility among observing Catholics, despite the continuing strictures of the Roman Catholic Church against abortion and artificial birth control (Neale 1998). Even on homosexuality, where many traditionalist churches tortured themselves over whether to accept the sin as well as love the sinner, there were notable advances in everyday practices. Similar patterns may be observed across the Western world. Even in the United States, where the moral right was closely allied to the governing régime and abortion and gay rights and same sex marriage remained highly divisive touchstone issues, there was evidence of increasing toleration of homosexuality (see Chapter 6). In Europe, as in Britain, there was a dramatic erosion of traditional sources of authority over sexual matters (Scott 1998, 1999), but commentators were noting that Britain was becoming the most sexually tolerant country in Europe, with some of the most liberal laws: a huge shift from the 1950s where, as we have seen, Britain still had some of the most draconian laws on sexuality in any part of the industrialized world (Charter 2006: 22; for comparative detail see Wellings *et al.* 2006).

But toleration is only one aspect of a good society. A society can tolerate the crass, the corrupt, subtle forms of violence and total self-regard. What ultimately matters is the quality of relationships within which the new forms of individualism are embodied. I will argue in the next two chapters that there is plentiful evidence of new forms of reciprocity and care that challenge our cultural pessimists. I want, however, to make a slightly different point to conclude this chapter. The late modern period is marked by a general scepticism about grand narratives of sexual progress, as of other forms of social advance, and perhaps Jackson and Scott (2004a: 234–5) are right to note a 'persistent unease' about the erotic that sits aside an acceptance of greater sexual freedom and diversity. That unease is itself an aspect of that air of uncertainty which characterizes an era that has largely rejected old forms of authority, and throws us back on a multiplicity of authorities, and in the last resort on ourselves (Weeks 1995). But it is important once again to assert, against the torrents of pessimism, that the new individualism is about more than doing your own thing. It is about developing forms of autonomy that are also profoundly social. As Heller and Feher (1988: 36) argued, 'If the end of the individual is self-determination, then the higher purpose to which the individual is committed is likely to be the self-determination of others'.

If individualization is a profound social process that is reshaping the world, and individualism is an ambiguous philosophy that embraces everything from the pursuit of civil rights to neo-liberal economics, then what David Held (1987: 290) has called 'democratic autonomy' is perhaps more about the pursuit of individuality, the expansion of individual freedoms and the broadening of life chances in full awareness of the opportunities that promote and the limits that restrict (see Beck 1999: 10–11). This is a relative form of autonomy in the sense that it is individuality in and through our relations with others (Weeks 1995: 66). This is fully in line with the agenda of the social movements of the 1970s, such as feminism and gay liberation (Ryan 2001). It is also, I believe, as much a truth about contemporary culture, in its multiple and chaotic forms of conviviality, as the evidence put forward in the anguished lamentations of the critics of the new individualism.

6

The contradictions of contemporary sexuality

Look in one direction and the dreams of the sixties have come to pass. No Briton, it might seem, in our promiscuous culture, should have any excuse for not having the sex life they undoubtedly feel they deserve. No corner of our public life is asexual . . . Not only that, but there is a democracy of desire: no man or woman, young or old, should be excluded from it. There is a sex-shop on every high street, a vibrator in one in three bed side drawers. The great god Viagra and its attendant chemical fixes have ushered in a gloriously priapic future for the hungriest of libidos. Little is proscribed . . . you have never – particularly if you live in Wales – had it so good (or at least so often). Look in another direction, though, and we are more screwed up by sex than ever before.

(Adams 2002: 4)

A morality that only sanctioned sex within marriage has been largely replaced by one that sanctions sex among consenting adults in loving relationships regardless of marriage, and for some regardless of heterosexuality.

(Jamieson 2004: 36)

One gay young man, a business consultant, participating in a coming out group, described how he had used a PowerPoint demonstration in helping his parents to understand both what it meant to be gay and what changes this disclosure would have on their relationship and on their roles as parents of a gay son in a committed relationship with another man.

(Cohler 2005: 70)

Seen through one lens, virtual reality is a new space for undermining old social relations, a place of freedom and liberation from conventional gender roles. Cyberfeminists have coffee in cyber-cafes, surf the internet, and imagine a gender-free future in cyberspace . . . Seen through another lens, the Internet is marked by its military origins and the white male hacker world that spawned it.

(Wajcman 2004: 3–4)

A precarious freedom?

Whatever our hopes for the future, as we ride the roller-coaster of sexual change, we are inevitably prone to bouts of anxiety. Have we really come this far? Why have we stopped at this dangerous point? How do we manage this acute sense of vertigo? Can this last? Will we fall?

In a 'world risk society', Beck has suggested, we live a 'precarious freedom'. On the one hand there is the script of self-fulfilment that drives an individualizing culture, and has done so increasingly since the 1960s. But on the other is the new political economy of uncertainty and risk in a globalizing, deregulating, economically frenetic, dramatically changing world. In this 'second modernity' the structures of identity are losing their 'ontological cement'. 'Endemic uncertainty', he writes, 'is what will mark the lifeworld and the basic existence of most people – including the apparently affluent middle classes – in the years that lie ahead' (Beck 1999: 12).

If a sense of uncertainty does indeed mark the contours of our intimate lives, as I myself have argued (Weeks 1995), it is not surprising that some of the most acute commentators of our sexual world express a certain ambiguity and hesitation about the way things are going. Here is the sociologist Ken Plummer:

> I am personally caught in ambivalence: with the good news of
> a possible democratic sexuality and open dialogical intimate
> citizenship on one side. And a painful world of growing intimate
> inequalities and tribal sexual clashes on the other. We do not
> live in easy times.
>
> (Plummer 2004: 60)

And now the feminist psychologist Lynne Segal:

> The more things change, the more it seems fresh obstructions or
> incitements arise to trouble the joys or consolations we might seek
> in intimacies with others . . . Massively popular with its readers
> and audiences, portrayals of the pains of sex and relationships are
> evidently eagerly consumed.
>
> (Segal 2004: 65)

Greater autonomy, openness, democratic intimacies, broader citizenship on one side against unease, uncertainty, pain and anguish on the other. Greater sexual freedom has brought immense gains but it has its costs. In this chapter I want to explore the 'antinomies' (Jackson and Scott 2004a) of sexual and intimate transformations, balancing the real achievements against the downsides, the breakthroughs against the new battlegrounds, the new pleasures set against the new insecurities. Are we, as the quotation at the head of this chapter poses, moving towards a genuine democracy of desire or are we yet again in danger of getting all screwed up about sex? Big ideas, like choice in sexual relationships, the transformation of gender relations, the emergence of new subjectivities, inter-generational anxieties, the technologization of the body, and sexual citizenship, which are the main themes of this chapter, open up these dilemmas acutely.

The choice relationship

The model late modern relationship is supposedly based on choice and equality: choice of partners, of whether to get married, cohabit or love together separately; egalitarianism between partners, and greater informality between adults and children. This is what Giddens (1992) has described as the 'pure relationship', or what Jamieson (1998, 1999) calls 'disclosing intimacy', based on an openness to the other, and on 'confluent love', an active, contingent love which presumes equality in emotional give and take. Pure or disclosing relationships, the argument goes, are sought and entered into for what the relationship can bring to the individuals concerned. They are mediated through a host of socio-economic and gender factors. They survive often through inertia, habit and dependency. But ultimately the relationship is based on mutual trust between partners, which is in turn related to the achievement of the desired degree of intimacy, and the forms of love which develop. If trust breaks down so in the end does the relationship. As the divorce figures and the rates of breakdown of cohabiting relationships suggest, this can lead to a high degree of instability in personal relationships. But at the same time, the emphasis on personal commitment and trust as the key to emotional satisfaction has radical implications.

Chosen commitment, freely entered into, implies the involvement of consenting individuals, with equal rights and responsibilities. It assumes open communication and dialogue and a willingness to negotiate. Trust has to be worked at and not taken for granted. The relationship must be free of arbitrary unbalances of power coercion and violence. Because it is freely chosen it has the possibility of enduring, and of being stronger due to the personal investment in it. This egalitarian relationship underlines the democratizing impulse in intimate relationships: the stress on individual autonomy and freedom of choice provides a radicalizing dynamic that is transforming personal life (Weeks 1995: 37). In particular, women are leading the way, both in seeking more equal relations and in ending old ones. For the first time, Beck and Beck-Gernsheim (1995: 62) suggest, 'two people falling in love find themselves both subject to the opportunities and hindrances of a biography designed by themselves'.

This has been an influential argument, but has provoked a major debate. While Giddens (1992) has seen in these changes evidence of growing agency among men and, especially, women, for Beck and Beck-Gernsheim (1995) the new forms of love appear to be a balm for the emptiness opened up by the breakdown of traditional familial patterns, a functional response to the decline of old meanings and religion.

Individuals are less like newly empowered agents than automatons, forced to be free (Smart and Neale 1999: 15–16). For others the 'hindrances' referred to by Beck and Beck-Gernsheim have been more obvious than the opportunities. With Bauman it is the very contingency and 'frailty' of contemporary relationships that is the essential problem. He cites as evidence of our cynical disregard for others a man into computer dating who says bluntly, 'you can always press "delete"' if you want to get out of a commitment (Bauman 2003: xii). It suggests the disposable culture made up of 'semi-detached couples' that he so deprecates (Bauman 2003: 36).

But more fundamental than theological arguments about the merits of the pure relationship and confluent love is the question of the degree to which the egalitarian couple of choice is indeed the norm. Jamieson (1999) has pointed to the difficulties in realizing fully disclosing relations. Jackson and Scott (2004a: 240) have agreed that there is a greater degree of egalitarianism in heterosexual relationships than in the past, but point to the persistent asymmetries between men and women. Holland et al. (1998) have shown the survival of female psychic subordination to men in sexual behaviour, the 'male in the head'. Even lesbian and gay relationships, which Giddens (1992) and others have argued are more likely to approximate to the pure relationship due to the absence of structural inequalities, have been criticized for the persistence of power imbalances (Weeks et al. 2001: 114–18). Yet having acknowledged some truth in all these points, it is equally true that the nature of relationships is changing, though not always in the direction suspected.

For conservative commentators the decline of marriage is the most serious indicator of social decline. Patricia Morgan (2006: 7, 1995) laments that marriage is now so disparaged by the state that the very term is vanishing from official use in favour of 'relationships' and 'partnerships', and in turn fuelling 'our feckless society'. Is it 'farewell to the family?' she asks rhetorically (1995), and we may be sure she knows the answer. Unfortunately all this clouds the real trends. While it is true that the number of marriages fell to its lowest figure for over a hundred years in 2001, with few signs of significant recovery thereafter, it remains the case that in 2005, 70 per cent of families were still headed by married couples (Yeoman and Bannerman 2006: 35). The same percentage of couples with children marry. Among many BME people, the percentage was still higher, especially people whose origins were in South Asia. While it is undoubtedly true that non-marriage relationships were more likely to break up than married relationships, for many others these relationships resembled marriage in their stability. Most children born outside formal marriage were registered by both parents.

Of course, there are instabilities in relationships. The divorce rate is one obvious indicator of the fragility of some relationships. As a result of the Divorce Reform Act of 1969 which instituted a single ground for divorce, namely irretrievable breakdown of marriage (via adultery, desertion, separation or unreasonable behaviour), divorce doubled between 1969 and 1972, peaking in 1995, since when it has fluctuated at around 160,000 a year. The separation figures are much larger for unmarried couples. Whereas about 8 per cent of marriages break up before the child is 5, 62 per cent of cohabiting parents split up at the same stage. Marriage is obviously one marker of involvement (Lewis 2001). But it is dangerous to assume from this that the state of marriage is itself a guarantee of stability. Most people now enter marriage as a mark of commitment, when they are ready for it, can afford the (ever growing) cost, and are prepared to accept the mixture of rights and obligations that entails. Others prefer to opt out. The reality is that for many women in particular, and not just those influenced by 1970s feminism, marriage is still an institution carrying weighty implications about gendered power and heterosexual normality which are seen as hindering individual autonomy.

Many people choose to live on their own. The number of single households rose to 29 per cent of total households by 2001, amounting to some seven million people, mainly men. Men were most likely to live with their parents into their twenties – 57 per cent of men aged 20 to 24 did so – and thereafter were most likely to live alone in their thirties (ONS 2006; see also Hall *et al.* 1999). However, it would be quite wrong to assume that these seven million, whether heterosexual or homosexual, were not involved in sexual relationships. LATs – living apart together – have become a significant new demographic in the new century, although not a unified group. Roseneil (2006) has described three types of LATs: those who live apart regretfully; those who live apart gladly; and those who live apart undecidedly. Whatever their motivations, they are in essence another example of the pluralization of life patterns that is redefining relationships.

Whether cohabiting or distant, sexual pleasure in relationships remains both the spark for intense relationships and a major factor in cementing them and making them meaningful. If sex goes wrong it can undermine the harmony and break the trust. Its importance may be seen in the torrent of self-help books increasingly directed at women. The belief in the specialness of sex and the urge to successful performance, however, gives it a weight it often cannot bear. Therapeutic texts aimed at women portray love as a narcotic, an intoxication or addiction that can 'literally kill' (cited in Hazleden 2004: 204). There is evidence that for many companionship is a more important element in building trust (Jamieson 2004: 36), but monogamy remains an important value, and this is true across regions, cultures and nations (Wellings *et al.* 2006). Around 80 per cent of those questioned in surveys believe affairs to be always wrong. People make subtle distinctions between casual sex and affairs. One husband cited by Duncombe and Marsden (2004a: 143) states baldly: 'If my wife had a quick screw it wouldn't upset me, but an affair would'; while a wife made a similar comment: 'I don't mind if he *fucks* them, as long as he doesn't *talk* to them.' *Affair* no longer refers exclusively to a threat to marriage. It has come to refer to any breach of monogamy and exclusivity in couple relations (Duncombe *et al*. 2004: xi). There appears to be a gradual convergence of male and female patterns, though women still tend to deplore unfaithfulness more than men, and men are more likely than women to have had concurrent relationships than women. There is evidence from both men and women, however, that individuals put the couple before individual autonomy. Affairs may be epiphanies, fateful moments, life-changing, but they are also secretive, guilt-ridden and anxiety-making. The exception is when attempts are made to negotiate non-monogamy, sustaining the emotional stability while attempting sexual autonomy. This involves drawing on a complex repertoire to balance the areas of stability and instability.

Among lesbians and gays *affair* originally had a different meaning, standing in for the relationship itself ('my affair'). As gay relationships have matured, however, the term itself has largely dropped out of use. But the concept is a crucial one as negotiated non-monogamy is a common feature of same-sex relationships. Dialogical openness is also a common feature of such relations. Equally, being in a dialogically closed relationship is a relatively consistent feature of narratives of infidelity and betrayal. A common feature, however, is the downplaying of sexual fidelity as the marker of commitment and fidelity. Emotional faithfulness tends to be valued much more highly than sexual (Weeks *et al*. 2001: 148–52; Heaphy *et al*. 2004: 81).

Another variant is the polyamorous relationship, which advocates see as 'responsible non-monogamy' (Bettinger 2005: 98; see also essays in *Sexualities* 2006b). The NATSAL report in 2001 estimated that 14.6 per cent of men and 9 per cent of women had concurrent relationships, though these tended to decline with age (Johnson *et al*. 2001: 4). For advocates of polyamory, these relationships are a matter of principle, representing a refusal to be trapped within traditional concepts of monogamy. 'For some, like ourselves,' write Jackson and Scott (2004b: 151), 'the critique of monogamy remains central to living as heterosexual feminists while challenging the institutionalization of heterosexuality.' Among non-heterosexuals polyamory may similarly be seen as a way of escaping the heteronormative, though Adam (2006: 24) suggests it may be more of a lesbian than a male gay preoccupation. The editors of a volume on lesbian polyamory suggest that it 'compels us to question traditional definitions of fidelity, family and intimacy' (Munson and Stelboum 1999: 2), and includes many different forms of multiple intimate relationships (see also Klesse 2005: 445–64). This is an arena of complex distinctions. Bettinger makes a distinction between emotionally monogamous (if sexually non-monogamous) relationships and those engaged in several emotionally committed relationships, and constructs a series of models. The unifying ideal, however, is that 'polyamory frees up each partnership from having to meet all the needs of the other' (Bettinger 2005: 104).

For most cases, however, it is the couple that remains the norm. 'Sex with many partners?', asked *The Times* (1 November 2006), and answered 'No thanks, we're British' over its report of the most recent

NATSAL survey (Rose 2006: 29; Wellings *et al.* 2006), though this is in fact not a British phenomenon alone. What has changed is the growing practice of serial rather than lifelong monogamy. Egalitarian relationships have to be negotiated in this changing context. Whatever the ideal, equal relationships will fail unless the conditions for trust, equality and disclosure are there. The prime conditions, Ryan argues, are equalizing resources, shared decision-making and making sure the process continues (Ryan 2001: 96). These are the basis for the mutuality which she argues must be at the core of women's claim to sexual freedom. So how near are we to achieving this goal?

Gendering sexualities

There have been remarkable changes in the organization of gender over the past generation. This is not simply an ideological shift, but also reflects a shift in the whole economic and social basis of gender. In most Western countries, women have been increasingly incorporated into the workforce, and legislation has formally recognized the equality of men and women. This in turn has influenced ongoing debates in non-industrialized and recently industrialized societies. So was women's advance at the expense of men? The biologist Steve Jones has written wittily that from an evolutionary standpoint 'males are wilting away' and their current status is precarious. From sperm counts to social status, from fertilization to death, there has been a relative decline of men and an advance of women. 'From middle age onwards it is a woman's world' (Jones 2002: 243). For many men, no doubt, it has felt like that. Behind the claim by some militant men that they have been unjustly cut off from parenting their children following acrimonious divorces, because all the privileges now belong to women, is a real sense of loss. Some sociologists see a genuine social crisis in the weakening role of men in families (Dennis and Erdos 1993; Dench 1996). Melanie Phillips (1999) writes of the 'Neutered Male', a disturbing story, as she polemicizes in *The Sex-change Society*, of the attempt to feminize the state, to reverse the roles of men and women, and to run masculinity out of town. 'As marriage becomes ever more meaningless and men ever more marginalized, the door was pushed wide open for extreme "gender" feminism which maintained that marriage was a patriarchal plot to keep women oppressed by men' (1999: xv). In effect this is the image of the castrating feminist, who since the 1970s has effectively reversed the normal order of things, and under the New Labour government after 1997 became entrenched within the state apparatus itself. 'Hard line feminists', says Patricia Morgan (2006: 7), have moved into positions of power, promoting their friends 'like Angela Mason from a homosexual pressure group' to head up the government's Woman and Equality Unit, and proceed to undermine marriage (and promote homosexuality presumably) and destroy the balance between the sexes – with fathers the unexpected victims. On the other hand, the undoubted success of these victims of the feminist revolution in gaining vast media coverage, and the undoubted popular support they gathered, hardly suggested an effortless triumph of egalitarian ideals. Despite a pervasive sense of crisis about masculinity that some, from pro-feminist men to unreconstructed masculinists and socially conservative moralists, detect (Weeks 2005b), it is difficult to see the crumbling of masculine hegemony in early twenty-first century culture.

But what is also increasingly clear is that whatever the moves towards formal equality, and whatever the local successes of both long-term economic and social shifts and ideological transformations, the traditional assumptions about the social meanings of masculinity and femininity remain deeply embedded in everyday practices and in the psychic and emotional relationships between men and women. Individualizing processes may have changed intimate relationships for the better but women remain the caring gender (Holmes 2004: 197). The undoubted trend towards greater sexualization of female bodies still has to struggle against persistent gendered notions of respectability and sexual decency, which are highly classed (Skeggs 1997). The development of a common language of female autonomy, sexual desire and female pleasure has been uneven and haphazard, celebrated by assertive female pop groups but not easily lived in the fevered circumstances of young people's lives, or in the intricacies of family life, where sexual coercion and violence persist (Jackson and Scott 2004a: 240). Among the women whom she interviewed, Wilton found low expectation of men, of heterosexuality and of marriage. 'For many, the fact that a man is neither violent nor a drunk is good enough reason to marry him' (Wilton 2004: 99). Many of these feelings echo those of married women in the 1940s. What has changed is the possibility of escape, whatever the emotional and economic uncertainties:

> I divorced my husband four years ago after a long marriage – 23 years of misery. Two young children, fitting in with society, doing the right thing. And then I thought, no, I just couldn't bear it any longer. I just couldn't see myself doing this until I was in my 50s and 60s and retiring with this man. No, I am not doing it any more . . . as soon as I was able to financially support myself, and my children were much older, I called it a day.
>
> (Wilton 2004: 163)

Calling it a day has become much more possible because of the shift represented by feminism and the recognition of female autonomy. The fact that the majority of divorces are instigated by women suggests that they are no longer willing to endure entirely unsatisfactory relationships. But economic opportunities to escape remain precarious for many. Despite equal opportunities and equal pay legislation and a generation of pressure, women's pay on average remains about one-fifth less than men's, and the expansion of women's jobs in the long post-1980s boom was largely in the part-time insecure sectors of employment. On the one hand we can see vital gains in the formal equality of women; on the other intransigent inequities remained.

Whatever the blockages to full autonomy, changes in patterns of fertility continue to shift the life patterns of women. Women are delaying childbirth, or avoiding it altogether, to an unprecedented extent with an all-time low point in births in 2001. By 2005, the average age of women giving birth was 29.5, with most births in the 30- to 34-year-old group. Twenty-two per cent of women aged 35 are still childless (Hinsliff and Martin 2006: 8–9). Lone mothers, on the other hand, tend to be considerably younger (Boseley 2006a: 5; ONS 2006: 29). These trends, as in earlier years, have aroused many, even on the liberal left, to worry about the impact on the population's make-up, as it tended to be professionals who limited their fertility most obviously, with the poor and immigrant groups most fertile. A report from the Institute of Public Policy Research suggested that women and men felt forced to put their careers before family life (Hinsliffe and Martin 2006: 8–9). Anxiety about fertility was a wider European phenomenon. In countries in Southern and Eastern Europe it was well below replacement rate, below 1.3 births per couple. In Northwest Europe, especially in those Scandinavian countries with good childcare and maternity and paternity leave provision, it was recovering (*The Economist* 2006a: 46). In Britain, exceptionally, the population was projected to increase substantially, but through better life expectancy and immigration rather than improvements in the fertility rate.

Women are still overwhelmingly responsible for childcare, though by the early twenty-first century men were doing about one-third compared with a mere 13 per cent in 1971. In 1972 the average father of a child under five spent fewer than fifteen minutes a day in child-related activity. This has risen by a factor of eight. It is probable that fathers see more of their children in the new century than they did a generation ago, the optimists argue (Sieghardt 2005: 2). There is less talk of the 'new man', but things are changing. As Segal wisely suggests, 'it is an understanding of the differences between men which is central to the struggle for change' (1990: x). But perhaps the most profound change of all is not so much in the reality of male power as in the legitimization of that power. As Connell has argued, 'In all public forums, and increasingly in private forums, it is now the denial of equality for women and the maintenance of homophobia that demand justification' (1995: 226). There is a new horizon of intelligibility and possibility around gender relations that pervades the culture, and with this comes an inevitable sense of the historicity and contingency of gender itself. Even the most traditionalist defender of male privilege, the most morally uptight believer, like Phillips and Morgan, in moral decline, has little alternative but to recognize that the gender order changes, that gender relationships are social practices that can shift, or in some cases be fundamentally reinvented. If, as Butler has famously argued, 'gender is an identity tenuously constituted in time, instituted in an exterior space through a stylised repetition of acts' (1990: 141); that is, it is not so much expressive of a deep nature but is performative, defined by its reiterations, then how gender changes matters.

Transgendering

Transgendered experiences illustrate this most vividly, for cross-dressing and cross-living are practices that parody the very notion that there is an original true nature (Rubin 1999: 184). This is not, however, quite how it is generally seen or necessarily lived. Transgender contains within it both a move towards the essentializing of traditional gender and a profound unsettling of gender categories. It is the first move that has attracted the most vitriolic challenges, especially from some feminists who see both cross-dressing and transsexuality as a surrender to the most stereotyping of gender imagery (most famously Raymond 1979), an all too easy acceptance that there is a true gender that trans people want to live. It is also, ironically, a critical and necessary stance for many preoperative trans people who have to convince the medical authorities before they can receive medical support not only that they passionately believe that they are currently living in the wrong gender, but also that they can live in the other gender. The acceptance of the idea that transsexuals can claim certain new rights, for example, to medical treatment and to change their birth designation, is based on the assumption that they have been trapped within the wrong body, and have now transitioned to a new self. The UK Gender Recognition Act of 2004 (Department of Constitutional Affairs 2004) gives legal recognition to those who have taken 'decisive steps' to live fully and permanently in their 'acquired gender'. The text carefully avoids mentioning a true gender, but it is clear that the campaign to change the law, which gives the right to change the birth certificate, was the result of a long campaign, fought through European courts, for the justice of recognition and respect for private life, which would not have happened without an essentializing discourse that proclaimed the new gender was the true gender. This, Morgan (1999: 234) has suggested, is the 'transsexual dilemma':

> They are trapped between the desire to explore the possibilities of the performative gender bending and the need to fight for basic rights . . . for which they need to present a coherent, essentialist identity without ambiguity.

But the reality is that the emergence of transgender as a central motif in the struggles over gender since the 1990s does reflect a significant shift in the politics of gender and sexuality, that may be seen as an aspect of the queer moment which has challenged fixed categorization. Gender fucking had been a key element in gay liberation since its stormy birth at the mythic Stonewall riots in New York in 1970 (Playdon 2004). But it had also, simultaneously, aroused a strong feminist opposition. The subversive and transgressive emphasis of the contemporary trans-gender moment thus represents a significant shift, a juncture of various elements. As More and Whittle (1999) argue, 'transgender' becomes an umbrella for all cross-living and cross-dwelling people, a whole gamut of 'gender-complex' people. The transgendered person has become an iconic figure for boundary crossing, for challenging fixity, and trans-genderism has 'increasingly come to be seen as a privileged vantage point from which it is possible to observe how sexed and gendered bodies are conceived and enacted in everyday life' (Kulick 1998: 259). Drag queens, drag kings, transmen, transwomen, bigender persons, cross-dressers, gender queers, gender ambiguous and gender fluid – all suggest that the gender constellation is not binary but multi-polar, polyvocal and sub-versive (*GLQ* 1998; Halberstam 1998, 2005; *Journal of Homosexuality* 2002, 2004). 'Tales of transgendering', as Ekins and King (2006: xiv) remark, 'take many forms.'

Yet the queer celebration of transgression can obliterate the ordinari-ness of transition, and erase crucial distinctions, for example, between the butch queer lesbian and a trans person, or the specific experiences of pre- and post-operative transsexuals (Rubin 1999: 189). Prosser has spoken of transition as a journey not an event, but a journey that has its own specifications and location, not a postmodern celebration of mobility (1999: 91, 110). This is well put. Journeys across boundaries, migrations, are a common feature of the contemporary world. They are not mythic adventures; they are not necessarily transgressive. They are part of a lifelong process of negotiating identity, difference, marginality, the right of exit and the right to voice. The concept of gender migration, as King puts it, 'focuses attention on what is happening socially – the movement from one social position to another – and it provides a framework within which we can examine the ways in which gender borders are policed and gender citizenship is granted or denied' (King 2003: 190). It also asks us to map out the hazards on the journey, to see things from the point of view of the traveller, to see how far we have come, and how long we have to go.

Subjectivities, subversion and sexual pleasures

In his book on lesbian and gay migrations, *Invented Moralities?*, Bob Cant writes that the stories he tells are 'about self-discovery and about relationships; they are about love and sex; they are about consciousness-raising groups and the difficulties of traditional radicalism; they are about isolation and belonging' (1997: 13). The trajectory of these migra-tions is from one form of belonging, the home in which you were born and brought up, where you may have received warm love but also experienced a sense of unbelonging as a young lesbian or gay, to a new home, a chosen home, where your sexuality is at one with your identity. A young lesbian

Jackie, recalled, 'I went to London and then life changed completely ... I suddenly realised these were different people and I could talk to them – and I'd never talked to anybody on that level in my whole life.' A gay man recalls: 'I came away to college and that was it – I just went completely mad ... I was up and away' (quotations from Weeks *et al* 2001: 82).

The migration, the journey, was frequently to a large urban space where communities, networks, private and public spaces could be marked out, where desires met and identities were reinvented. When for the first time the UK census made a tentative effort to check the numbers of lesbians and gays in the population in 2001 it found that a mere 78,522 people identified as lesbian and gay (by indicating the nature of their relationships). But what was more interesting than these unfeasibly small figures was where they were. Brighton was the gayest city, followed by certain London boroughs (Lambeth, City, Islington), Blackpool, Manchester, Bournemouth. These were also more or less the same areas where five years later the first civil partnership ceremonies were held. The straightest parts of England, on the other hand, were equally predictable: Essex and the northeast (Ford and Frearn 2004: 3; see also Duncan and Smith 2006). Migration was reshaping the social geography of the major conurbations of Britain as it had cities in North America, Europe and Australasia. Many lesbian and gay stories are 'tales of the city', which is no doubt why the novels of that title by Armistead Maupin were in 2006 found to be the most popular gay novels of all. By the new millennium these cities were also the happening places in a variety of different ways. Florida (2004) argued that those cities where diversity was most welcomed, and gays most tolerated, were also the most creative and upward moving, 'plug and play communities', where somebody could come into and put together a life straight away, in an environment where creativity, individuality and difference were a merit. In the regency ambience of Brighton, or the old Victorian terraces of London or the lofts of Manchester, lesbians and gays were now an intimate and welcomed part of the urban scene (see Whittle 1994). The migration was moving people from the margins to the heart of the city.

This is not, of course, the whole story, perhaps not yet the majority story. The LGBT world is increasingly diverse and complex, and there are many different stories that could be told, many still of prejudice, homophobia and the continuing weight of the heterosexual assumption – the quiet but iron belief that if you are not openly gay then you must be straight, that annihilation by blandness that can kill the soul. But it illustrates a significant staging post in the journey, and one it is important to signal before we explore the other stories. In a variety of different ways lesbians and gays have reached a new public profile. In the arts, theatre, politics, trade unions, academia, business, television, journalism, the police – in 2006 a policman won the Mr Gay UK title – there are now openly lesbian and gay people in prominent places (see Summerskill 2006). Beneath the froth of public life something yet more important was happening. Thousand of LGBT people were quietly building their lives as if they were fully equal citizens, assuming rights and responsibilities often in advance of the law, but creating facts on the ground to which the law ultimately had to respond.

Despite a slow start, largely because the House of Lords blocked reforming legislation, the post-1997 Labour government – prompted in part by European court decisions – moved to equalize the law and treatment of LGBT people: immigration rights, equal adoption and fostering rights, an equal age of consent at 16, repeal of the infamous section 28 of the Local Government Act, abolition of the specifically gay offence of gross indecency in the Sexual Offences Act, protection against discrimination in the provision of goods and services, employment protection, the Gender Recognition Act, and the passing of the Civil Partnership Act (Bainham and Brooks-Gordon 2004; Weeks 2004a, 2004b; Waites 2005a, 2005b). There was no positive crusade to promote LGBT rights by the government, and some of the legislation was passed following back-bench amendments to wider legislation rather than the government leading from the front (though it did use the Parliament Act in an unprecedented way to ensure passing of the equal age of consent). This was liberalism by stealth, helped along by the quiet but forceful lobbying of Stonewall. But the result was a remarkable modernization of the law, historically unprecedented and one of the most important batches of reforms introduced by the Blair government (and characteristically ignored in most attempts to assess the successes and failures of that government). When the Royal Navy, which until 2000 was sacking around 200 sailors a year for their homosexuality, announced it was working with Stonewall to recruit lesbian and gay sailors (Hellen 2005), or when the Metropolitan Police sponsored Lesbian and Gay History Week for 2006, something remarkable has happened to traditionalist Britain.

The direction of change was unmistakable, but its meanings were more contested. Seidman *et al.* (1999) wrote about the gradual ending of the closet in America during the 1990s, and it is important to understand what he means by this. The concept of the closet, he argues, has unique socio-historical conditions: the prioritizing of sexual identity and a systematic mobilization of social and cultural forces to enforce the heterosexual norm (Seidman 1999: 10). Central to it is the idea of a double life and strategies of everyday management that sustain that life. The aim is to create a protected space which allows individuals to fashion a gay life and the creation of gay social worlds. The closet, from this point of view, was 'a strategy of accommodation and resistance' which simultaneously reproduces the binary divide between homosexuality and heterosexuality and contests it. From this point of view the development of the post-1970s lesbian and gay world was a contradictory movement, both deploring the closet, but also strengthening it in some ways through the development of distinctive communities and ways of life. The question that Seidman stimulates, for Britain as much as for the United States, is the degree to which this comfortable 'ghettoization' of homosexuality is dissolving under the impact of broadening liberalization. For some the very idea of the homosexual is dissolving as formal equality erases the distinctiveness of the gay world (Bech 1999). Others point to the minoritizing logic implicit in even the apparently most radical of reforms: civil partnerships for same-sex couples (Waites 2005b). But it is undoubtedly the case that in Britain as in the USA, many lesbians and gays are increasingly 'normalizing' and 'routinizing' their homosexuality, so that a double life is less and less a defining aspect of their lives, with sexuality one part rather than the core of their identities. At the same time one can see not the dissolution of identity but the multiplication of possible subject positions and ways of life, in which a strong sense of self, embedded in relationships and distinctive social worlds, remains the key to personal meaning (Cooper 2006).

A sense of difference is continually reinforced by the continuing strength of the heterosexual assumption (Weeks *et al.* 2001). Despite really significant transformations, in many quarters homophobia remains rampant, from vicious queer bashing to school bullying, from heterosexist jokes to the minstrelization of openly gay television personalities. A continuous undercurrent of unease remains pervasive (see Summerskill 2006). The gay lobby group GALOP has claimed that 83 per cent of young gay people have experienced verbal abuse, and 47 per cent anti-gay violence (Webb 2002: 49–53; see forum dedicated to homophobic violence on www.gaytimes,co.uk; Adam 1998). Reality television shows such as *Big Brother* may show the easy coexistence of a group of multicultural multi-sexual young people trapped in a house together, but on the streets young gay people may still be murdered just because of their sexuality:

> A tart corrective to the idea popular among some liberal
> intelligentsia that Britain has completely changed for the better
> as far as 'gay stuff' goes was the killing of Jody Dobrowski on
> south London's Clapham Common in October 2005. Still too
> shy and embarrassed even to visit a gay bar, the 24-year-old
> was kicked to a slow death to reported chants of homophobic
> abuse.
>
> (Summerskill 2006: 3)

In a heteronormative culture homophobic violence can be routine, commonplace, performed by ordinary people as part of the routine of everyday living, which is why it is so often invisible (Moran and Skeggs 2004: 27). The new visibility of lesbians and gays since the 1970s in gay spaces such as Soho or Manchester's gay village has had a double edge: they are sites of safety, underpinned by consumerism, but also potential sites of contestation, which could lead to random violence (Binnie and Skeggs 2004: 39–64). Space is not neutral, and in practice is heavily heterosexed, to the extent that heterosexuality is taken for granted, so that any entry into the space by those deemed immoral or just different is potentially destabilizing (Hubbard 2001). But the 'reterritoralization' of space by LGBT people (and others on the sexual margins) through bars, coffee shops, restaurants, Pride, Mardi Gras, gay villages, parks and so on has been a crucial stage in the evolution of safe lifestyles. More crucial still has been the creation of private space at home, which is inevitably shaped and controlled by resources and opportunities. Concepts of home and belonging have become crucial to the LGBT experience (Weeks *et al.* 2001: 77–103).

So how subversive or transgressive is lesbian and gay sex today? Some commentators have detected a double turn, with a partial domestication of gay male sexuality being matched by a sexualization of lesbian identities. Certainly the excesses of the 'political lesbianism' of the 1980s, which stressed political identification at the expense of sexual being, has faded, though Wilton (2004: 26–7) perhaps speaks for many when she says firmly: 'I continue to believe that *lesbian* is the only site from which to carry out a sufficiently radical demolition job on the hegemonic apparatus of my time.' A queerer position is that advocated by Eves (2004), who emphasizes the potential in the development of 'lesbian genders', especially the negotiation of butch–femme subject positions, to subvert traditional discourses of female sexuality and lesbian asexuality: 'Butches and femmes use specific interpretive and aesthetic repertoires in a variety of ways to create lesbian space and make their desire visible' (Eves 2004: 495). Pat, who was interviewed for *Same Sex Intimacies* (Weeks *et al.* 2001: 133), saw the significance of sex in these terms: 'there's something about having sex and feeling attractive . . . Or not feeling as fulfilled or a sexual being . . . if you're not having sex, there's something missing.' Similarly for Niamh, 'I like feeling desire and I like being desired' (ibid.: 134).

Gay men have not lacked spaces to make *their* desires visible (see Higgs 1999; Turner 2003), but the impact of the AIDS crisis has crucially modified their relationship to sex, and especially casual sex. There was early evidence that the AIDS crisis was leading many gay men to modify their behaviour, with the widespread adoption of safer sex techniques achieving considerable success in avoiding infection with HIV. Before 1996 only around fifty cases of heterosexual infection were diagnosed in the UK. But for the first five years of the 2000s there were more heterosexual than homosexual diagnoses, with a record 2000 new cases in 2004, of which only 28 per cent were gay . However, AIDS remained overwhelmingly a syndrome for minorities and for gay men. More than 75 per cent of heterosexual cases diagnosed in the UK were infected abroad or by a partner infected abroad, 68 per cent of these in Africa. Black Africans in the UK were around 1 per cent of the population, and 42 per cent of new HIV diagnoses (Scott-Clark and Levy 2005: 24–43). 'HIV in the UK is black and it is gay' (ibid.: 24). Because of the new combination therapies there has been a dramatic reduction in the numbers of deaths of gay men from AIDS, but since the mid-1990s the number of gay men living with HIV has doubled. Many gay men have abandoned safer sex and are engaging in high-risk activities. This is partly the result of exhaustion, partly the changing age distribution of the gay male population, with younger people less familiar with threat as witnessed in the 1980s, partly a result of negotiated safety.

Mark Davis (2005) has argued that post crisis, AIDS has disappeared as a collective problem for the gay community, and has become a privatized experience, where the individual is engaged in self-surveillance and self-management of risks, balancing responsibility and individual need, in line with neo-liberal tendencies in the culture. In the broader European context, the UK now lags in AIDS awareness among the general population, with only the famously relaxed Netherlands having a more laid-back attitude (Charter 2006: 22). The more individualistic and casual attitudes to sex generally are reflected to a certain extent in gay attitudes. The gay men's sex survey suggests that more than half of HIV-positive gay men had had unprotected anal sex ('barebacking') with at least one other man; one-fifth had barebacked with an HIV-positive man (Scott-Clark and Levy 2005: 33). Barebacking was an international phenomenon (see Carballo-Dieguez and Bauermeister 2004), and had multiple possible meanings. For many gay men it had a deep symbolic significance concerning intimacy and identity. As sex had defined gay men it was difficult for some gay men to identify without that sex (Yep *et al.* 2002: 1–14). But it also carried other legacies. Ridge (2004: 274) questions the value of negotiated safety and suggests that it is men's own meanings (anger, fear of rejection, power, need, masculinity, letting go, intimacy) and the circumstances of sex encounters themselves that determine the degree of safer sex. We can relate this to the widespread acceptance of sexual non-exclusivity within the gay male world (Heaphy *et al.* 2004: 167). Yet at the same time, more gay men entered civil partnerships than lesbians following its legalization in December 2005 (see Chapter 7). Clearly, here as elsewhere, forms of commitment are being negotiated which do not rely straightforwardly on notions of sexual monogamy.

How queer is this? 'Queer means to fuck with gender. There are straight queers, bi queers, tranny queers, lez queers, gay queers, sm queers, fisting queers in every single street of this apathetic country of ours' (leaflet quoted in Whittle 2002: 61). Unfortunately, this does not seem to be quite how non-heterosexual people see themselves. Of 16,000 men who responded in 2004 to the annual gay men's sex survey (Weatherburn *et al.* 2005: 6) 81.6 per cent defined themselves as gay, 12.3 per cent as bisexual. Of the 0.6 per cent who ticked 'Other' (ninety-two men), only eighteen defined themselves as queer, one 'queer as fuck', and the rest as open-minded, open to offers, confused, straight, transgendered, transsexual, anything, batty boy, bent, bloke who likes having sex with men, experimental and so on. Farquhar found a similar reluctance among her female interviewees to use the term *queer*, most preferring *lesbian* or *dyke*: 'Dyke is a more powerful word, because we named ourselves that'; 'It's in your face. "I'm a dyke", it's really in your face' (Farquhar 2000: 224). Queer theory developed in universities, especially among the literary intelligentsia, where it stressed the transgressive nature of playing with sexuality and gender (Sullivan 2003; Schlichter 2004), and unfortunately largely ignored earlier lesbian and gay studies (Halperin 2003). Despite an activist flirtation with queer, in Britain queer theory has largely remained confined to the academy, at best appealing to a new urban middle class and ignoring other lesbians and gays (Adkins 2002: 22; Schlichter 2004). Queer theory, like LGBT theory generally, theorists such as Judith Butler, Teresa de Lauretis and Leo Bersani as much as overt gay conservatives, displayed a general tendency towards liberal individualism according to Blasius (1998: 672): 'all take individual "consciousness" and self-transformation as the starting and ending point for LGBT theory and politics.' The 'queer wars' that Robinson (2005; see also Warner 1999; Goldstein 2003) chart in the US had limited purchase in Britain, though the issues raised are similar: the role of sexuality, especially non-exclusivity, the link between sexual freedom and wider social change, the meanings of integration, and the merits of legalizing same-sex partnerships. It has become clear that support of civil partnerships has no necessary links with sexual conservatism. Sexual transgression has no necessary links with political liberalism. The overarching question is the degree to which the new toleration of homosexuality in a live and let live/love atmosphere fundamentally undermines the social relationships which continue to reproduce heteronormativity and the heterosexual assumption. Here the file remains open.

Intergenerational tensions

One of the most difficult areas in the progress of lesbian and gay acceptance has been relations with children. The hallowed, if largely unfounded, association of gay men particularly, with sex with minors, has long overshadowed discussion of the age of consent (see Waites 2005a), and represented perhaps the last great taboo in the full integration of LGBT people. It was noticeable that as European countries moved towards legalization of same-sex partnerships and marriage, rights to adoption were at first excluded (see Green and West 1997; Wintermute and Andenaes 2001). But just as this prejudice began to fade – in the UK equality in relation to adoption and fostering actually preceded civil partnerships – so anxiety about general adult relations with children has assumed a new significance.

As Beck and Beck-Gernsheim remind us, children have become increasingly a focus of meaning in family life (1995: 15–18). In the climate of uncertainty produced by heightened individualism and the tentativeness of the pure relationship, children, O'Connell Davidson (2005: 18) suggests, 'are the "gift" that couples can give to each other in order to secure their own relationship as well as to establish social links with each other's kin'. To achieve this, children need to be different from us adults, to be in a morally bounded and protected realm where they are absolutely dependent on us. Yet the boundaries between adults and children have never been so contested. The dialectic of agency and dependency on the part of young people, and duty and anxiety on the part of adults, makes for a potent brew of tensions and anxieties in which the fear of sex abuse assumes sometimes catastrophic levels.

The earlier sexualization of young people combined with their increasing dependency raises issues about agency, responsibility and authority that play their way through family and communal relation-ships, with the spectre of the paedophile focusing particular anxieties. There is enormous anxiety about preserving childhood sexual innocence, as tensions over sex education underline – with every evidence that it is of variable quality, and probably weakest where it is most needed, namely among vulnerable young people (Jackson and Scott 2004a: 235). The age of consent nominally polices the boundary between adult and child sexuality, but in practice it 'confuses' the young, according to research carried out by Kaye Wellings (2005, reported in Frearn 2005: 34), or is 'ridiculed' according to Rachel Thomson's research among young people (2004: 138; more generally see Waites 2005a). Sexual agency is seen by young people as a private realm, in which they do not expect the state or parents to intervene. Consequently, it is a very difficult law to implement. 'It's sort of like in law, but it's not sort of there, is it', as one of Thomson's young interviewees put it. On the other hand, few of the young people interviewed were against an age of consent – some even thought it should be higher, up to 18. It is seen as useful when young people feel under pressure.

However, legitimacy for sexual activity comes not from the law, let alone the long distant days when marriage legitimized sexual activity, but from a sense that it should happen only when the young individual is ready, that it is a product of agency, choice and control mediated by time (Thomson 2004: 142). A 16-year-old schoolgirl, interviewed in a newspaper, commented: 'Most people I know haven't had sex yet and didn't have sex before turning 16. I don't think they care about breaking the law as they think no one will find out . . . My friends are pretty responsible' (Campbell 2006b: 16). But this sense of balance and agency has to be set against increasing anxiety about the pressures on young people, boys from their peers, and girls from their partners. A Trust for the Study of Adolescence report showed a high degree of ignorance about sexual behaviour and indulgence in high-risk behaviour, with significant differences among different ethnic groupings. Many from minority communities knew little about how to prevent and identify sexually transmitted infections, and young African Caribbean men were more likely than others to engage in risky sex.

Sexual behaviour among young people is as structured by class and ethnic group as that of adults. As we have seen, teenage pregnancy is viewed as a problem of the disadvantaged which requires targeted government intervention – though rates are much lower than they were in the 1950s and early 1960s, and the absolute numbers are less than half what they were in the early 1970s (Duncan 2005: 1). But race and ethnicity have complicated the picture. Black girls are now the major target of efforts to reduce the incidence of young parenthood – though ironically it is the affluent suburbs which show the fastest rise in teen motherhood (Frearn 2006b: 4; Sherman and Bennett 2006: 14). Above all, the sexual behaviour of young people remains ordered by institutionalized heterosexuality (Jackson and Scott 2004a: 237). As Thomson argues, different discourses provide different ways of talking and thinking about sex, providing a range of possible identities and locations to capture and use:

> Yet these different ways of talking and thinking about sex do not offer freedom to young people to create unique individual identities and desires. Rather they are underpinned by power and enduring asymmetries that are effectively enforced and policed within young people's own moral communities.
>
> (Thomson 2004: 146)

But public anxiety is not simply about the sexual behaviour of young people. It is also about adults' own behaviour: 'Today's fears emanate from the sexual desire of the parents, not of the children' (Bauman 1998: 29). The age of consent may be an ambiguous barrier for young people themselves but it is a fraught one for many adults, usually men. The age of consent itself is constructed in terms of protection of young girls, and it assumes male agency (Waites 2005a). But the growing awareness of the extent of child sex abuse poses wider questions about the power relations between adults and children (see Reavey and Warner 2003; O'Connell Davidson 2005). The government has responded to widespread anxieties about breach of trust on the part of adults by attempting to write into law notions of protection that should operate in certain types of adult child relationships, such as teaching (Bainham and Brooks-Gordon 2004; Epstein *et al.* 2004). These have the habit of all attempts at redrawing boundaries of becoming fiery touchstone issues, as the Secretary of State for Education and Skills, Ruth Kelly, found out in early 2006. The discovery by the press that there were teachers in schools who had previously been accused of abusing children threatened to engulf her and end her career, though she could realistically have had very little knowledge of how her civil servants operated the register of offenders (Doward 2006a: 8–9; see also Aaronovitch 2006: 21). Behaviours which were once regarded as natural and even healthy (childhood nudity, for example) have become fraught with menace, as parents and carers have discovered when their holiday photographs of naked children playing on the beach have been processed, and police summoned.

Many of these anxieties had been brought to the surface following the murder of the 8-year-old Sarah Payne in summer 2000. The *News of the World*'s campaign, in response to this, of naming and shaming alleged paedophiles, in turn stimulated a local vigilante campaign led by mothers on the Paulsgrove housing estate in Hampshire (Bell 2003: 108–28). This raised in turn a number of crucial issues: the role of the press in stirring up moral panic, the role of class in configuring the response to the working-class mothers' action, the role of women in confronting an alleged lack of communication from the state, and the role of the state itself in responding to acute anxiety, ignorance and fear. But as important was the shift in the perception of sexual risk and the management of risk that was taking place. As Rose (1999: 206) points out, outrage at the neglect of abuse emerged most strongly from the very group in society that was once deemed most likely to abuse children – the working class itself. And in practice, of course, the vast majority of cases of abuse take place within families or are by someone known to the child. Yet the anger focused on the dangerous stranger, the paedophile, bearer of a particular psychopathology and history, completely detached from the family. A similar process has been at work in relation to so-called paedophile priests in the Roman Catholic Church. A scandal that the church had long hidden, it raised crucial questions about the religious calling, church discipline, priestly celibacy and simple trust. Yet in the church's eyes it became less about abuse than about Catholic attitudes towards homosexuality, gay priests and the like. When in 2006 a new Pope sought to ban gays from taking up the priesthood, it was widely seen as a response to the paedophile scandal (Loseka 2003: 13). Anxiety has become individualized, thus expunging the most dangerous sites for the production of abuse, the home, the local community, and it appears the Catholic church, from the story.

The technological fix and the lure of science

With the decline of traditional sources of legitimization, and the multiplication of sites of authority, who can now speak the truth of sexualities? From the early sexologists of the late nineteenth century to the evolutionary psychologists of the late twentieth century, there have always been 'experts' who have sought to define and redefine the rules of the game, to bring the chaotic, fluid and ever changing world of sexuality within the bounds of scientific understanding (Weeks 1985). At times, the search for scientific certainty, or for a technological fix, has become like a religious quest, or a substitute for religion. For a leading scientist like Richard Dawkins, author of widely read popularizations of socio-biology *The Selfish Gene* and *The Blind Watchmaker*, science does indeed become religion-like in its certainties. For over a hundred years, many, including pioneering feminists, have been arguing that science has been aching to become the new church. The problem for those who seek a scientific answer to the question of sexuality is that it becomes ever more difficult to assert a single truth in this protean field (Lancaster 2003).

The reality is that advances in science often serve to compound the general air of uncertainty about sexuality (Johnson 2004; Segal 2004).

What are the implications of the genetic revolution? How should we react to the possibilities opened up by embryological research? What are the implications for sexual values and ethics of the internet revolution? In this late modern world, if it is difficult to see how there can ever be agreement on a fixed set of values, or a categorical list of rights and responsibilities to which everyone can readily adhere, then claims for the hegemony of science have a slightly hollow ring.

The elusive gene

That does not, however, stop people trying, and there is a huge popular audience for explanations rooted in biology. The rise of evolutionary psychology, following on from the socio-biology that was popular in the more conservative 1980s, speaks to an audience that wants to locate itself firmly in time and an intractable history. How much easier to understand the continued differences between men and women as rooted in repro-ductive capacities, and a primate division of labour on the African Savannah 500,000 years ago, than to grapple with finding means to tackle structural inequalities in the here and now (Segal 1999: 78–115; see also essays in Rose *et al.* 2001). It is so much easier to explain away homosexuality as an evolutionary quirk, fixed in the gay brain or in a gay brain ('born gay'), than to try to understand the infinitely complex ways in which sexuality and subjectivities are shaped at the interface of bodily potentialities, psychological make up and cultural forces (Rose 1996; cf. Wilson and Rahman 2005). A headline in *The Times* sums up an easily popularized story: 'So it is down to mother: gay gene survives because it boosts fertility' (Henderson 2004: 5). The theory is that the same gene which triggers homosexuality in men also promotes fertility in women, thus apparently disproving social constructionism. For these scientists, who see differences of gender or sexuality as a result of adaptive patterns laid down in the course of human evolution (Lancaster 2003), the challenge is to find social space for the biologically determined differences between men and women to flourish. All these positions, however, ultimately reflect an essentially conservative philosophy, despite its endorsement by large parts of the liberal intelligentsia (as in the pages of *Prospect* magazine – see Ridley (2003) and critique by Walter (2005: 34–9)), belied by the flourishing of difference on grounds quite different from those of biology. Segal sees 'the cultural fluidities of sexual and gender identity celebrated in recent post-structuralist and queer feminist readings mocked by the return of a Darwinian funda-mentalism and the rise of genetic determinism in popular culture and much of the social sciences' (Segal 1999: 6), and it is difficult not to agree with her. Ultimately, whatever the apparent scientific neutrality of evolutionary theory, it can all too readily justify inequalities.

Reproductive technologies

However, in disregarding the pseudo-scientific certainties offered by evolutionary psychology, we cannot ignore the revolution in reproductive technologies that the genetic revolution has sparked off. When the early second-wave feminist Shulamith Firestone (1971) looked forward to conception without heterosexual copulation, few thought this was little more than a radical feminist fantasy. Barely a generation later its reality is beginning to restructure reproductive possibilities. There is a deep paradox here, because at the same time as women are delaying, and concentrating childbirth, or avoiding it altogether, and abortion is commonplace, if highly contested, the new reproductive technologies are in high demand. Whether through infertility, the hopes of lesbians and gay men to parent, or the choice of older women, even into their sixties, to conceive, new possibilities have produced a vast new medical industry, and in the case of grass-roots self-insemination, a sort of flourishing cottage industry (Saffron 1994). What started through IVF as a medical aid to help the infertile has become a multi-billion dollar industry chasing a huge demand for different ways of making a baby. A report in *The Economist* (2006b: 73) estimated in early 2006 that there were one million customers and $36 billion revenue in the United States alone, with top-quality eggs, from highly educated women, costing around $50,000, and surrogate mothers charging up to $59,000. It is hardly surprising that this has quickly become a global market. Guatemala generates around $50 million per annum by exporting babies at around $25,000 a time. Denmark has become the world's largest exporter of sperm. And if this should ever run out, now artificial sperm has been produced to fertilize mouse eggs, and promises to eventually end male infertility (Henderson 2006: 3).

The United States is the global centre for fertility treatment because there the industry is largely unregulated. Britain has anguished over the implications of this revolution probably longer than any other society, and following the report of the Warnock Commission has established ethical standards and acceptable practices through the Human Fertility and Embryology Authority. But the explosion of technological possibilities is in danger of outstripping the cautious utilitarianism of the Warnock approach. What rights does a woman have to use the frozen sperm of a long dead husband? How can you regulate gay men fathering children with a surrogate mother outside the UK? How do you control women over 60 using fertility treatment and conceiving? What priority should the National Health Service give to satisfying an exponentially growing demand for fertility treatment when there are abandoned babies in their millions across the globe? How, on the other hand, do you control the traffic in eggs and sperm as well as babies? Is there not a new spermatic economy developing where women are reduced to little more than wombs? Could the new technologies lead to fresh violence against women and even gynocide? (Plummer 2003: 41–2). Above all there is the spectre of human cloning, and the possibility of breeding out not only harmful genes but also 'unwanted' types in a new form of eugenics (the baby with inherited genetic disabilities, the offspring of the 'underclass' or ethnic minorities, those feared to have the 'gay gene'). New dilemmas arise all the time, some of them all too painfully real, but all creating new potentialities of regulation and difficult decisions, by the state, by courts and by individuals. The Pill helped separate sex and reproduction. The new technologies go further, splitting reproduction from blood kinship. A simple example, though complex in its implications, occurred in 2005, when new regulations sought to ensure that the offspring of donated sperm should have the right to know the identity of their biological parents. This followed a growing interest in the legitimacy of blood relationship, which the genetic revolution has encouraged. It is certainly fascinating for a Welshman to learn that his chromosomes are almost identical with those of men from the Basque country, and via Siberian tribal people to native Americans. Blood can tell an important historical story (Jones 2002: 191). On a less cosmic scale we similarly want to know our family story, as the popularity of 'searching for your ancestors' attests. But in the case of the example here, the inevitable result was a drop in the number of men volunteering to donate.

A chemical fix

If science has promised to free us from reproductive inadequacy, it also promises us freedom from sexual inadequacy. Sex may no longer be necessary to reproduction, and reproduction no longer the sole goal of sex, but this has only served to ensure that the pleasure principle has become inextricably part of the performance principle. If eros is now seen as fundamental to the pure relationship, the greatest failing is likely to be inadequate sexual performance, and increasingly this has been tech-nologized. If the Pill was the technological fix of the 1960s, Viagra and its kin chemicals has become the fix for the early twenty-first century. Sex in America, says Meika Loe, author of *The Rise of Viagra*, 'will never be the same again' (2004: 5). But this is not just an American story. Since Viagra was launched by the Pfizer pharmaceutical company in 1998, it has become a global boom story. The little blue pill that 'changed sex in America' has now been joined by others, Cialis and Levitra, that compete for a multi-billion-dollar market, and the search is on for 'a female Viagra'. At the time of writing PT-141, a nasal inhaler for women that would enhance excitement and performance, was expected within three years (Dibbell 2006). The demand is apparently insatiable. When the British Health Secretary authorized the distribution of Viagra via the National Health Service in the late 1990s, it was to be supplied only to those with serious erectile problems. Since then the criteria have been progressively loosened. But not only are they distributed through the NHS. The wonder pills are now freely available illicitly through the web, and anyone opening their email of a morning is likely to be deluged with spam offering instant happiness at the click of a mouse. A quarter of all spam is allegedly linked to Viagra and similar pills. These have ceased to be mere medical alleviators of genuine problems. They have become happiness pills offering an instant fix. Governments may fulminate against illegal substances from cannabis to cocaine but they are apparently happy to license Viagra and its siblings, and to tolerate a vast grey market that has little now to do with erectile dysfunction (ED) as a certified male medical problem of a minority, and everything to do with enhanced performance by the majority, including women. The 'big O' has become a key definition of sexual satisfaction. Men are apparently willing to risk premature heart problems, even blindness, to satisfy their desires.

In the process, there is an acute danger that anything less than a hyper performance will be pathologized. The American therapist, and author of *Sex is not an Unnatural Act* (1995), Leonore Tiefer, has powerfully argued that 'Sex is about the culture, and the brain. They are talking about the McDonaldisation, the idea that it should be exactly the same wherever you go' (quoted in Cooke 2002: 31; see also Tiefer 2006: 273–94). All the science is just window dressing for an industry, she argues, and the most dangerous aspect of this is the invention of a new medical problem for women, for which the female Viagra may be the solution: 'female sexual dysfunction' (FSD) (compare Henderson 2006). Allegedly 43 per cent of women 'suffer' from this new condition, for which there is negligible evidence. Pharmaceuticals have nevertheless become a major player in this redefining of sexual normality, and the search for a fix (see essays in *Sexualities* (2006a), and especially Tiefer (2006)).

Cybersex

If drugs provide one sort of erotic performance, cybersex provides multiple forms of erotic excitement, enticement and entanglement at the click of a button. We now have cybersex, cyber-stalking, cyber-rape, cyber-victims, cyber-porn, cyber-voyeurism, compu-sex, sex chat rooms, sex news groups, sex bulletin boards, camcorder sex, virtual sex, cyborgs, blogs, MySpace, YouTube . . . A 'cybersexual smorgasbord' in Plummer's evocative phrase. The list is potentially limitless as the power and use of the internet expands and our erotic imagination finds new virtual nooks and crannies (Plummer 2003: 9–12). The internet is a site for sexual pick-up, courtship, chat, confession, self-affirmation, experiment, fantasy, masturbation, friendship, networking, virtual community (Wakeford 2002) – and for potential exploitation, violence and threat. Most optimistically, the internet, Sherry Turkle argued as far back as 1995 in *Life on the Screen* (1995; see also 2004), is where people create virtual realities in the hope of transforming inherited realities about sexuality, identities, relationships and the wider culture. As such it is a site of feminist and queer spaces and possibilities (Wolmark 1999; Wakeford 2002), as well as their fundamentalist opponents. In theory, you can remake yourself and explore your wildest fantasies and desires. Ruth (quoted in Elliott and Lemert 2006: 112), whose humdrum marriage is enlivened by cybersexual encounters, says:

> [T]he anonymity of chat rooms was such an eye opener, just marvellous . . . I've got to find out all sorts of things – about people and exciting ideas, but above all about myself. My on-line experience, particularly when the discussions concern more explicitly sexual things, has taken me far beyond what I knew about my identity.

The internet provides a new form of intimacy where anything seems possible, with fewer of the risks than traditional forms of contact. It gives you, as the journalist Alexandra Frearn (2006a: 6) has written, a 'Chance to pick and choose and still remain in control'. She sees the rise of online contacts as a form of 'technological Darwinism': as old forms of interactivity have died out – such as the church, the extended family, the local community, the factory floor or the office, the ball or the dance-hall or party circuit – websites have sprung forth providing pragmatic and highly efficient alternatives. Electronic intimacy offers an apparent degree of control over one's environment that people no longer expect to get from face-to-face encounters. And they are already immensely popular. A survey by Parship.co.uk, a British subsidiary of Europe's largest dating service, with 1.5 million members, says that 3.6 million British subscribers used online services in 2005, which they claimed to be 65 per cent of those actively looking for a relationship (Hoyle 2006: 6). The internet has removed the stigma against dating services. Online contacts offer privacy, you can do it from home, you don't need to dress up for it, you don't have to go through a middleman, and you can see a picture of the contacts and converse with them via email before you risk a meeting. You do not even have to meet them if an intense online emotional relationship is what you want. As one married man, emotion-ally entangled with another woman largely via email communication, has written:

> Soon I became dependent on her daily thoughts: on what made her laugh, the music and books she liked. I kept telling myself we were only discussing CDs and books, so where was the harm? . . . I spent a lot of time on the office phone and lap top: two or three hours a day. The deadly immediacy of e-mail makes unguarded, flirty comments all too easy, so we moved fast . . . I must have hurt Julie, ending the whole thing. I e-mailed her, told her about the showdown [with his wife] and said that was it. Her e-mail came back quickly, terse and cold. And that was the last I heard of her.
>
> (Jackman 2006: 5)

Casually started, passionately pursued, instantly ended. Whether people get smitten or not, hurt or not, by 2005 there were over a hundred online dating agencies in Britain, with a market estimated at £12 million, expected to rise to £47 million by 2008. And this was just the polite side of the business. There were many other sexual worlds. By 2005 the internet had become the prime site for gay male cruising as websites such as Gaydar became the focus of gay pick-ups (Elford 2002: 1–3; O'Riordan 2005: 28–32). Business in gay bars and clubs was reportedly well down, and they were shifting their emphasis, away from the site of casual encounters towards either social arenas or explicitly sexual action places. At the same time sites were proliferating online for every conceivable taste. On the specialist s/m scenes you may specify down to the smallest detail your particular tastes. Paedophile sites have exploded, despite sustained police attempts to hunt down the users. Websites providing information on 'dogging', heterosexual open-air public sex usually conducted in secluded places, have promoted it exponentially. Once in the right place bluetooth and other digital technologies are used to ensure physical contact (Bell 2006). The most esoteric desires could be catered for, even down to sexualized cannibalism. Notoriously, a German man, Armin Meiwes, murdered a man whom he met through the internet and ate his sexual organs. 'His cannibal fantasies became a reality when he started to surf internet chat rooms and discovered Bernd Jurgen Brande, a computer software specialist from Berlin, who declared himself ready to be eaten.' On his appeal against conviction Meiwes argued that 'I don't need to do it anymore – but I do believe everyone should be able to decide what he wants to do with his own body' (Boyes 2006: 3). Here we have notions of sexual autonomy and self-determination taken to an extreme point where it effectively contradicts itself by destroying another autonomous person.

Cybersex opens up questions of autonomy and choice, and points to new forms of exploitation, not least because it is big money. Already by 2001, internet users were spending an estimated £2 billion on online pornography (Hammersley 2002). In the process a massive shift in the wider pornography market is taking place. There is a noticeable decline in the use of the Obscene Publications Act in relation to printed work, opening up the corner shop market to harder stuff, and shifting the nature of control of pornography (Wilkinson 2002: 37). But expenditure on other electronic media is also expanding vastly. A 2005 survey by ChildWise, a market research agency specializing in young people, found that in England 13 per cent of 5.6-year-olds and 24 per cent of 7.8-year-olds already had mobile phones, rising to 58 per cent at age 10 and 95 per cent at 15-plus. A young teenager is reported (in Buonfino and Mulgan 2006: 1) as saying, 'if an hour goes by without a [text] message I start to feel a bit anxious'. Sixty per cent of children aged 12 to 15 use the internet, with girls leading the way (Elliott and Lemert 2006: 25; Gibson 2006: 3). We are producing a generation of 'techno-kids', brought up with new electronic media, genuine offspring of the 'Information Age', with incalculable implications for our notions of identity, intimacy, individuality and the erotic (for a pessimistic view see Elliott and Lemert 2006: 25–6).

Conflict of values

This extraordinary globalizing, pluralistic, diverse, individualistic, technologized, digitalized and informationalized world is inevitably subject to unavoidable conflicts of value that can neither be wished away nor easily resolved, either by a resort to absolute standards, science, history, tradition, or to the assumed moral righteousness of our own positions, whatever they may be. This is why questions of values cannot be left to the social conservatives who have most openly espoused a values agenda. We live and die by values, and as, I believe, there can be no return to 'traditional values', so there is no alternative but for us to engage in a continuing conversation – however difficult dialogue may be – about what the most appropriate values should be (Weeks 1995). In a world that is simultaneously globalized and challenged by emergent differences and new fundamentalisms, questions of values and ethics inevitably come to the fore, and sexuality is inevitably at the heart of them, is the litmus test for them. Controversies that seemed intrinsically about private life have become public, a 'public discourse on the personal life' (Plummer 2003: 68). Debates about who and what we are, what we need and desire, how we should live, are to a striking degree also debates about sexuality. It is not surprising, therefore, that debates over sexuality display anxiety and uncertainty. The fear aroused by the HIV/AIDS epidemic was more than simply concern about a new and possibly incurable disease; it also underlined our uncertainty both about contemporary moral stances and the impact of actual sexual practices. The frequent waves of fear about the prevalence of the abuse of children reflects uncertainty about the relations between adults and children, about the nature of commitment, responsibility, the demarcation of roles and the policing of appropriate behaviour, the erosion of traditional sources of authority, and the problems of combating exploitation and protecting the vulnerable. Controversies over the scientific and technological recasting of sexuality and desire – test-tube babies, stem cell research, sex-enhancing pharmaceuticals, the opportunities and threats of cybersex – challenge us to ask what are the limits of scientific discourse, and who can decide. And pervading all is the challenge provided by an ever more frantically accelerating consumerism: What is the irreducible core of humanity that must stay free of commodification?

The language of human rights and of sexual or intimate citizenship has come to the fore in recent years precisely as a way of focusing these value controversies within a viable, and to some extent recognizable, moral and political framework (Plummer 1995, 2003; Petchesky 2000; McGhee 2005). A rights discourse has a long history in Western traditions (though a more erratic history in Britain), and the feminist and gay politics since the 1970s have allowed us to clearly identify the lacunae – especially with regard to gender, sexual identity and relationship choices. The Welfare State settlement after 1945 was based very much on a particular, restrictive view of citizenships, rights and entitlements, largely confined to civic and social rights predicated on the heterosexual family (Marshall 1950; Weeks 1998; see also Chapter 2, this volume). Talking about citizenship and rights in the contemporary context provides a discursive form through which the necessary debates can be carried on in working out what is and is not possible and desirable. It offers the opportunity to incorporate new claims, new realities in intimate relationships, and provides an iterative framework through which we can try to agree the minimum standards we need to attain to recognize simultaneously each other's differences and common humanity. As Plummer puts it, the deployment of the concept of what he calls intimate citizenship 'flags a proliferation of debates about how to live a personal life in a late modern world' (2003: 68).

The erotic offers a space of possibility for exploring and positively affirming the different ways of being human. But these possibilities, I argued in an earlier work, must be tempered by two fundamental principles that constitute a minimum universal standard: the right to life and the right to liberty. These principles require in turn that we reject actions which involve domination, coercion, force and violence (Weeks 1995: 63–4). What follows from this, I suggest, is a recognition of the need to delineate the factors that make for autonomy and choice, and I have suggested three basic 'rights of everyday life' which can help guarantee that: the right to difference, the right to space, and the rights of exit and of voice (Weeks 1995: 142–54).

I do not pretend that that these in and of themselves answer our dilemmas. They provide at best guidelines to rethink the ways we live our sexual lives today. I refer to them here to illustrate my main point: that in order to make use of the emerging discourse on sexuality and rights, both citizenship rights and human rights (on which see Chapter 8), we need to clarify our values, to say where we are coming from, and to say where we stand. In doing so we should not claim that these are the only values, the necessary starting points, the settled truth. On the contrary, we live in a world of many and conflicting truths. We can only move forward, towards creating agreed minimum standards dialogically with those who might disagree with us, if we know where we stand, which are our truths. That is the best response to the accusations of relativism frequently thrown at those who espouse the value of sexual diversity.

What is clear, to me at least, is that debates about sexual rights and wrongs (Weeks 2004a) must in the end be debates about relationships, about intimacy, about the ways we care for, and show responsibility, for one another – and I will explore this further in the next chapter. Despite the best efforts of prophets of the internet and of cybersex, sexuality is always ultimately about interaction with flesh-and-blood others. It is through this interaction that the meanings of sexuality are shaped, and what we know as sexuality is produced. In the process we are also producing new stories about the types of relationships we want, narrative frameworks which articulate and configure emerging values (Plummer 1995, 2003).

The emergence of an explicit and increasingly mainstream political and cultural discourse around personal life since the 1960s is no accident. It is a product of the disruption of settled patterns of sexual life under the impact of profound social change on a global scale. Traditionalists aspire in vain to a restoration of stability. New voices articulate the aspiration for recognition of new identities and new ways of being. A cacophony of sexual narratives, of old and new 'sexual stories' (Plummer 1995), compete to be heard – about families, partnerships, sexual pleasures and pains, identities and differences, faith and unbelief, freedom and imprisonment, adults and children, parenting and childlessness, health and illness, living together and living apart, living and dying well, individuality and collective belongings. The growing 'sequestration' or privatization of sexual life that Giddens (1991) noted as a characteristic of modern Western erotic experience has been balanced by an explosion of discourses about intimate life, which have profoundly redefined what we understand as sexuality on a global scale.

There is a growing number of stories about citizenship, rights and belonging. But as might be expected in this diverse, pluralistic world there is no necessary agreement about which way citizenship should go. While many of us, as I have indicated, see citizenship as one necessary focus for thinking about what it means to bear rights and to belong, for others it carries the danger of accommodation to the traditional (vigorously argued in Brandzel 2005). Same-sex marriage and the wish for gays to serve in the military may be seen as little more than an abject surrender to heteronormativity (Bell and Binnie 2000, 2002; cf. McGhee 2001). Concepts of citizenship are not only heterosexualized, but are criss-crossed by assumptions about gender, race and nationality – the ultimate limit of what belonging means (Anthias and Yuval-Davis 1992; Yuval-Davis 2005) . Perhaps it is indeed a fantasy to think that we can escape those iron determinants.

Yet it is important to remember that the ways in which we talk about sexuality and intimate life help to shape them. 'The telling of stories bridges different worlds and can . . . connect the moral, the aesthetic, and the political', Plummer argues (2003: 101). Stories of grounded moralities, he goes on, provide shared stories through which we can learn of moral and ethical dilemmas which people experience, and begin the necessary dialogue (2003: 108). People may work through their problems in their own ways, following their own values and guidelights, telling their own moral tales. But it is through sharing these stories that people can begin to reflect upon their lives in reflexive ways. What makes people moral agents, Smart and Neale suggest (1999: 114), 'is not whether they always make the right decision, but whether they reflect upon the decisions they take and weigh up the consequences of their actions'. Reflexivity becomes the hallmark of ethical action as, in Foucault's terms, 'practices of the self' begin to shape ethical lives (Foucault 1988; see also discussion in Watney 1994; Weeks 1995). But these practices are not isolated actions but always situated, ultimately based on norms and values of reciprocity. As Sennett (2003: 219) puts it, 'Reciprocity is the foundation of mutual respect'.

Respect for human dignity through a multiplicity of social worlds is the basis of a grounded morality by which people can live with uncertainty and ambivalence. Relying on a fixed moral content is giving way to new ways of thinking, new processes of interaction; the search for absolutes is being replaced by pragmatic decision-making. Abstract principles are surrendering to actual life stories. General rules, universal principles, are countered by situated, grounded, local responses (Plummer 2003). Principles dictated by authorities are faced by struggles with the self. We are here on the terrain of what Inglehart (1997) has called 'post-materialist' values. In a survey of forty-three countries, 70 per cent of the world population and over a time span of twenty-six years, he sees a post-scarcity society emerging, where economic motivations weaken and values become post-materialist, emphasizing self-actualization, esteem, social belongingness and love.

The challenge of late modern ethics is precisely to encourage these post-materialist values into dialogue as part of what has been variously described as 'life politics' (Giddens 1992), a politics of 'living well' (Rutherford 2005), a political ethic of care (Williams 2004: 28), 'dialogic citizenship' (Plummer 2003) or a 'love ethic' (Weeks 1995). These come from different starting points, but cohere around a series of concerns with intimate relationships: how to have and raise children, how to relate to others as gendered beings, how to honour the body, how to be erotic. The weakening or absence of a foundational ethic does not lead straight-forwardly into a moral swamp, as many critics propose. Instead we can see the development of a postmodern ethics based on a recognition of ambivalence, conflict and constraints, which is particularist and con-textual, but which strives for a minimum or thin universalism (Weeks 1995). Plummer (2003: ch. 7) suggests several key elements of such an ethics, which are broad enough to allow the debate to continue:

1   to acknowledge minimum human functional capabilities;
2   recognition of others;
3   to promote daily caring for others, which assumes the core values of attentiveness, responsibility, competence and responsiveness;
4   an ethic of love based on trust, reciprocity, altruism, commitment, sacrifice, tolerance, understanding, concern, solidarity and inter-dependence.

Most people are not especially interested in politics in general, or the politics of family and sexuality in particular. They do not have grand visions of new ways of living, even as at an everyday level they do necessarily engage in 'experiments in living' (Giddens 1992; Weeks *et al.* 2001). There is both a pragmatism in the adaptation to changes in everyday life and a new contingency, as people have, in a real sense, to create ethical standards for themselves. Their liberalism may well be limited to a form of live-and-let-live morality or 'shoulder-shrugging'. There is often no positive endorsement of different ways of life. Yet there are very few households in Britain which are not touched by the transformations of sexual life. Most people know single parents. Most people know a member of their family who may be lesbian or gay, or a member of an interracial partnership. Most households have experienced divorce, remarriage cohabitation, broken families, reconstituted families. We all now have to live with the consequences and implications of dramatic changes in our personal lives, and the evidence surely is that most people adapt extremely well.

These changes have not been led by the political élite, but by the grass-roots shifts described in this and the previous chapter. Governments, of course, have to respond, but they inevitably do so in a variety of different ways, depending on political traditions, the prevailing balance of cultural forces, the nature of the political institutions, the day-to-day crises which force some issues to the fore, and the pressure from below, whether from conservative or fundamentalist resistance to change, or from radical social movements. By and large, legislators prefer to follow trends in public opinion, and in a changing social geography, rather than lead them.

There is, inevitably, a wider argument to be had over whether these tentative, ambivalent, usually reactive responses from governments are enough, especially if they rely on popular, essentialized differences, such as the belief that gays and straights are akin to two separate species (see Waites 2005b). I suspect that in most cases they do reflect a public mood that generally seems to be saying 'let well alone' unless some spectacular abuses or contradictions come to light. The contradictory elements revealed in the Sexual Offences Act in 2003 (Bainham and Brooks-Gordon 2004) – on the one hand expressing a discourse of equality by getting rid of anachronistic laws which penalized male homosexuals in particular, on the other seeking, without any clearly defined principles, to define new areas of sexual harm – perhaps reflect a public opinion which is simultaneously more tolerant of homosexuality and increasingly intolerant of anything which may be described as abuse or sexual harm, especially of young people. In the process new restrictions may emerge. Kulick (2005) has provided a vivid example, showing how attempts by the social democratic élite in Sweden to follow a feminist agenda concerning prostitution have led to the categorization of men who use them as a new type of deviant: 'Four hundred thousand Swedish Perverts.' Some see in the recognition of same-sex relationships a new drawing of boundaries, new forms of control, and an underlying adaptation to neo-liberal exigencies (see Chapter 7). New definitions of normality and abnormality, of what is acceptable and unacceptable, are emerging which pose new challenges – opportunities and threats. Societies will continue to address individuals in complex and contradictory ways. The free subject will in turn find forms of resistance, individual and collective, creating new possibilities on the ground. Respect for private choices and the urge for protection vie for hegemony in a changing world of sexuality.

The reality, nevertheless, is that across the world many thousands are making choices about how they want to live on a day-to-day basis. Most of them are not particularly preoccupied by theoretical disputes. They are concerned, however, that they can live their chosen lives with openness and legitimacy, that indeed they have the full freedom to choose, that they can live their lives with a sense of mutual care, responsibility, respect and transparency – and all the other values that Plummer has outlined. Through the vicissitudes of everyday, intimate life, new ways of living are being legitimized by a grass-roots morality that we are making for ourselves.

7

Moments of intimacy
Norms, values and everyday commitments

The 'facts' of family change are real and hard to exaggerate.
In one generation, the numbers marrying have halved, the
numbers divorcing have trebled and the proportion of children
born outside marriage has quadrupled.

> (Lewis 2001: 4)

Every family has a secret and the secret is that it is not like other
families.

> (Bennett 2000: 38)

Anyone who lives with a lover chooses the comforts of repetition
over the dangers of adventure.

> (White 1980: 80)

[in the late modern world] Love will become more important than
ever and equally impossible.

> (Beck and Beck-Gernsheim 1995: 2)

I'm delighted that you are no longer an outlaw and now you're my
in-law.

> (Father to his 42-year-old son's new civil partner)

There's queer. Whatever next?

> (85-year-old mother on being told by her 60-year-old
> son that he was about to enter a civil partnership
> with his long term male lover)

A centuries-old celebration of marriage is preparing to welcome
gay couples. Organisers of the Dunmow Flitch trials in Essex,
which since 1104 has given couples who have not had a cross
word for a year a reward of a side of bacon, are considering the
change to stay in line with civil partnerships legislation.

> (*The Times*, 11 November 2006: 4)

The trouble with marriage

John Boswell, an openly gay and avowedly Roman Catholic historian, famous as a pioneering chronicler of 'gay' life in early Christian history, and of same-sex unions apparently sanctified by the church, offered a slightly disenchanted view of traditional marriage. He compared marriage in pre-modern Europe with marriage in the modern West. In the earlier period, he argues, marriage began conventionally as a property arrangement, in its middle it was chiefly about raising children, and ended about love. Western marriage, on the other hand, begins about love, in its middle is still largely about raising children, and often ends about property – 'by which point love is absent or a distant memory' (Boswell 1994: xxi, xxii).

We can perhaps forgive Boswell his cynicism. Traditional heterosexual marriage was not quite what it seemed, and never was what its most ardent defenders wanted it to be. Marriage, the pillar, ostensibly, of Western societies, has had a convoluted history, but as it enters into a more problematic and contested period, where same-sex marriage has become the flashpoint for debates about the future of marriage, so its past aura grows. Perhaps this is not surprising, since the pinnacle of its popularity and social significance was not in the dim and distant past, but coincided with that very 'sexual revolution' which conservative critics have thought was destroying it. It was practically universal marriage in the 1950s and 1960s that fostered dissidence, especially for baby boomers (see Chapter 3). During the first half of the twentieth century the proportion of women who were or had been married never fell below 60 per cent, and reached 75 per cent in 1951, and almost 80 per cent in 1971. Since then, despite a modest recovery in the early years of the twenty-first century, it has fallen back to 1950s levels – still quite high by historic standards, but clearly on a declining path. First marriage rates have fallen precipitously, and are lower than at the beginning of the twentieth century (Lewis 2001: 29). For our cultural conservatives marriage, as the corner-stone of a stable and moral society, the guarantor of couple commitment and of proper care of children, is in possibly terminal crisis (Morgan 1995). Yet at the same time as politicians, religious leaders, moralists and journalists (insofar as they can be distinguished) lament the putative collapse of this key social institution, the very same people are often in the vanguard of the opposition to same-sex marriage, which in the early twenty-first century has become the single most important issue for LGBT activists, among whom clearly the demand for marriage is very much on the rise.

As gay conservatives, such as the Anglo-American journalist Andrew Sullivan (1995, 1997), have pointed out, one would expect cultural conservatives generally to favour the extension of marriage rights to same-sex couples as a way of 'taming' their wayward sexuality and anchoring them to traditional institutions. On the contrary, particularly in the United States, and echoed by conservative régimes elsewhere, same-sex marriage has become a touchstone issue for moral and cultural conservatives, a so-called 'wedge' issue that may be deployed to strengthen the conservative base against the threats of rampant liberalism, a liberalism that in the 1960s and 1970s had been denounced by radicals as a sophisticated form of fence-sitting, and was now too revolutionary to be even mildly tolerated (see Cahill 2005). When President George W. Bush faced political melt-down in the mid-term elections in 2006 he (re)affirmed his support for a constitutional amendment to ban same-sex marriages, just as he had done in his re-election campaign two years earlier: this could get the religious and socially conservative base mobilized, it seemed, in fervent opposition to this example of moral decline, better than any other issue. In the event the Christian conservatives seemed less impressed than might have been anticipated (Lexington 2006: 66), and the November 2006 elections saw a political collapse for Bush, with a substantial number of evangelicals putting their hostility to war, political corruption and incompetence higher than their hostility to same-sex marriage.

Yet, in an illuminating paradox of our time, at the same time as American conservatives find same-sex marriage an intolerable threat, queer radicals apparently see same-sex marriage as not enough of a threat, and an unacceptable surrender to heteronormativity. The fervour of their opposition is sometimes as sharp as that of conservatives, often directed less at conventional religious or cultural conservatives than at mainstream LGBT activists and more specifically at those deemed to be gay conservatives in the so-called 'queer wars' (Warner 1999; Yep *et al.* 2003; Robinson 2005). We have the interesting and sometimes perplexing situation that for conservatives, same-sex marriage is seen as an ultimate threat to the centrality of heterosexuality as underpinned by traditional marriage, whereas for queer radicals same-sex marriage is unacceptable because it represents a surrender to heterosexual values. Marriage law, argues Brandzel (2005: 177), is 'a primary site for the production of normative citizenship' and a key mechanism by which the nation-state produces a properly heterosexual, gendered and racialized citizenry. Marriage matters because it promotes and naturalizes heterosexuality as the norm, and thus by definition excludes non-heterosexual people. This was an argument that had its roots deep in the moment of gay liberation in the early 1970s, and has influenced LGBT discourse ever since.

Despite all the fervour of this clash of cultures and norms, however, in practice in Britain the population seems to have adapted very well to the apparent downgrading of marriage, and with relative indifference to the legalization of civil partnerships for same-sex couples. Since the 1970s marriage and divorce have increasingly come to be seen as issues of a couple's own making and unmaking rather than subject to higher moral codes (Williams 2004: 30). What has increasingly come under scrutiny by governments of various political colours is less the relationship of husband and wife and more their roles as fathers and mothers, and hence the welfare of their children. A series of acts, from the Divorce Reform Act of 1969, through the Family Law Act of 1987 to the Children's Act of 1989 have progressively uncoupled marriage from parenthood. While marriage has become less an issue of public regulation, and cohabitation both before and instead of marriage has become commonplace, parenting, previously largely a private matter, has become increasingly a matter of public concern. Marriage and relationships might end, but child responsibilities go on and on. With this has gone a recognition of previously excluded parents or partners (Williams 2004: 26). From this perspective, equality for same-sex couples with heterosexual couples with regard to parenting as well as other spousal rights and obligations (as in the Adoption and Children Act of 2002 and the Civil Partnership Act of 2004) is less a rupture with long-term developments than a logical next step, and part of a fretwork of family practices.

There is no 'standard British family', as research by Simon Duncan and Darren Smith confirms (2006; see also Williams 2004: 62; Wellings *et al*. 2006). Using national statistical datasets, they map the variety of family forms and practices of parenting, and confirm the continuation of a wide variability across the UK. At the same time, they question the extreme form of the individualization thesis. They see less a pattern of individualization as a detraditionalizing of inherited patterns, with people shaping family ties in changed circumstances. People work out their family lives with reference to everyday contexts and networks rather than follow normative ideas that operate at the national level, but they are clearly deploying values of reciprocity and care that are rooted in their specific social and moral worlds.

At the same time it would be wrong to see the different cultures as frozen in time and history, scarcely talking to one another. It is precisely one of the most crucial features of late modernity that apparently incommensurate ways of life are now in dialogue, especially given the absence of overarching moralities. Duncan and Smith's (2006) work might demonstrate the enduring significance of regional and class divides, but it remains true that new forms are continuously jostling with old in a changing social geography. Alongside the reworking of old norms and values we may also see the emergence of new norms involving a reordering of the meanings of commitment, to partners, significant others and dependants. And a broad conclusion is incontestable. Across the board, far from exhibiting signs of amorality or irresponsibility, most people are living lives of extraordinary ethical intensity, creating a relational ethics in which individual needs and desires are balanced by commitment to the other.

These commitments are not so much obligatory as negotiated, driven by concern about 'the right thing to do' rather than a sense of duty – except in the case of dependants, where a sense of duty remains absolute. Yet the sense of mutual responsibility provides a steady guide to action, precisely because responsibilities seem freely chosen, and are neither predetermined nor contractual (Finch 1989; Finch and Mason 1993;

Weeks *et al.* 2001). Beck and Beck-Gernsheim (1995: 98) argued that freed of all outer constraints about whom you can like, and can marry, it paradoxically turns out that you may need new kinds of mutual control, for example, through pre-nuptial contracts that may regulate everything from property rights to who does the washing up, or through the vogue for self-help books. But Lewis (2001: 182) in her study of marriage found little support among her interviewees for purely contractual views of marriage. Even those in the minority who were in favour of a more contractual model were not clear what it would be about. Instead, people have increasingly to make it up as they go along, adapting traditional patterns or shaping new ones. At stake are decreasingly the binary cultures of heterosexuality and homosexuality which traditional marriage set in stone, but rather the forms of mutuality appropriate to the conditions in which we find ourselves. Marriage, civil partnerships, various forms of cohabitation, or non-cohabitation as in the case of LATs, and commitment to friendships and personal communities have increasingly become choices not moral imperatives. These choices are not always absolutely free choices precisely due to the web of relationships within which they must be exercised, but they signal the different ways of committing oneself in relationships of reciprocity and care. In this chapter I want to explore the key values of reciprocity and care that underpin different patterns of relations. I will then look at the 'friendship ethic' that has been central to LGBT experiences of mutuality, but has become a more general feature of late modern society. Finally, I look at same-sex marriage as an issue that crystallizes debate on commitment, which symbolizes all that has changed, and which also underlines what has remained the same.

Reciprocity, care and cultures of intimacy

Moral conservatives and prophets of moral decline regularly see in all these changes in personal relationships signs of systematic collapse, and in particular the breakdown of the social capital that sustains an ordered society, and that ensures civility, stable family life, proper sexual socialization and mutual respect (Fukuyama 1999; Putnam 2001). At its most extreme, the situation is portrayed as scarcely less than catastrophic. Here is the conservative sociologist Christie Davies (2006: 1): 'Britain at the beginning of the twenty-first century is characterized by levels of dishonesty, violence, illegitimacy, and drug and alcohol abuse that would should shock an imaginary time traveller projected forward from 1910 or 1925 or even 1955.'

There are real problems in many parts of contemporary society – the very problems that give rise to the jeremiads which Christie Davies and many like him deplore. Many of these do stem from precisely the collapse of traditional communities and the tight bonding relationships that enforced norms of sexual restraint and family obligations – though largely as a result of economic collapse and deprivation rather than of moral dissolution. The Rhondda that I grew up in has experienced the most dramatic deindustrialization, high levels of poverty and, like many other post-industrial communities, now experiences difficulties that would have been unimaginable half a century ago – serious drug problems, for example (for a vivid fictional portrait of the Rhondda today see the brilliant stories in Tresize (2006a, 2006b)). The moral restraints that kept even poor people 'respectable' have loosened. The breakdown of family life is frequently believed to be at the heart of this disaster. For most theorists of social capital the family and the norms of community which sustain them are crucial to social integration and individual advancement (Edwards 2004; Furstenberg and Kaplan 2004). In the context of the family, social capital in particular inheres in the relationship between parents and children which gives the child access to parental resources, whether intellectual, material or emotional (Lewis 2001: 6) and, from this perspective, looking back to the brave new postwar world of 1945, on the surface at least a great deal has happened to support a declinist vision. Although less pessimistic, some critics of social capital theories can readily end up in the same boat, weighing in the balance the changes in gendered relationships and finding a huge deficit. While declinists might regret the erosion of the gendered division of labour, feminist critics and others can readily criticize its continued entrenchment. While one is concerned with breakdown and demoralization, the other laments enduring power relationships that inhibit social coherence and social justice. But a consistent underlying concern is with what is perceived as the excesses of individualism (Edwards 2004: 3; see also Holland *et al.* 2003). For those, however, who, while recognizing the continuing inequities, nevertheless want also to recognize the importance of growing individual autonomy and democratization, the picture is more nuanced, with the greys, whites and blacks illumined by brilliant flashes of vibrancy and new life. For far from declining, new forms of social capital – associations, networks, emotional and cultural resources – are surely emerging. The social movements and communities of the 1970s onward offer prime examples: seed-beds of new values and norms. We can see the same in the community-based struggles for recognition of the rights of lesbian families from the 1970s, in the struggle against HIV/AIDS in the 1980s, and in the development of same-sex unions and marriage. But even more important, I suggest, we can see both the embeddedness of forms of social capital as well as the emergence of new forms of social networking, resources and support in the grassroots, everyday life experiences of many different types of people. The challenge lies in finding an appropriate balance between family bonds and individual autonomy.

The work of the Families and Social Capital ESRC Research Group, of which I have been a member, has offered critical insights into these processes (Edwards *et al.* 2003, 2007). The research team has found that despite all the changes that have taken place, families in the broadest sense remain extremely important for those involved, and family bonds continue to generate emotional and social capital across class, regional and ethnic differences, though not necessarily in the forms that theorists of social capital tend to emphasize (Edwards 2004). Despite a prevalent pessimism, research into parenting has found little evidence for social capital deficits, the social capital lost narrative (Edwards and Gillies 2004). Parents themselves do not lament a golden age of support: they are too busy making use of the resources to hand. They have not become helpless in the face of the decline of traditional structures, and have not become 'dependency junkies'. They still look to their families as well as their friends for support in parenting, and not to external agencies. They work within their own moral rationalities, which lay down the balance of mothering and fathering activities, attitudes to work and so on, and these tend to reflect continuing class and ethnic differences (Duncan and Edwards 1999). But generally, parents, and working-class parents in particular, tend to reject what they see as the top-down parenting classes offered by government parenting policy. 'Experts' have a role to play only in relation to more institutionalized aspects of children's lives and welfare, such as education and health. Instead, they find resources and support closer to hand, in their families, friends and neighbourhoods. The processes of parenting, however, remain highly gendered. Mothers, especially, are the generators of social capital, embedded in family and community, while fathers tend to pursue more individualized routes (Edwards and Gillies 2004). This has been a continuous thread in the history of intimate life, as we can see by reflecting back on the experience of sexual and family life discussed in Chapter 2.

Young people themselves, often portrayed as the victims of a collapse of social capital, on the contrary show the strength of their ties with others, especially in sibling relationships (Edwards *et al.* 2006). Brothers and sisters attach profound meaning to their relationships. Sibling ties are widely viewed as a source of protection, support, obligation and company. They provide children and young people with a sense of emotional security, even where they do not get on with their siblings, and they see these relationships as more resilient and dependable than friendships. This is not to say that there are no conflicts between siblings, and this is characterized by relational power struggles around recognition of status and sense of self, for example, as the oldest or more feminine. There are also distinctive classed patterns. Generally, working-class children and young people see themselves as part of a sibling group, whereas middle-class brothers and sisters are more likely to see themselves as individuals who also happened to be a sibling.

Far from seeing a collapse of values in this changed world, the social worlds of young people are intensely moral (Smart 2006). A study of youth transitions based on interviews with young people aged 11 to 18 found that young people follow a route to moral competence strewn with complicated domestic, social, structural and cultural factors, and they develop strategies for dealing with the complexity and diversity with which they are confronted. They can be flexible and reflexive, drawing on available cultural and personal discourses and resources. They can pursue the autonomous, independent subject in identity construction, while valuing above all connectedness, relationship, reciprocity and trust. Their families may take many forms, may fragment and reform, but they draw strongly on the family, parents and particularly mothers, while also questioning traditional authority. They are immersed in both the local (family, school, community) and the global (media carried youth and general culture) from which they draw support, but which they also question. The young people's narratives reflect intensely the effects of class, gender and community on their values and life chances, and the physical, material, social and discursive resources upon which they can draw as a result of that positioning (Holland *et al*. 2000; see also Thomson and Holland 2004).

Subsequent findings indicate a similar approach to adulthood (Thomson *et al*. 2004; Henderson *et al*. 2007). In examining young people's understanding of adulthood two major themes may be identified. The first is a 'relational' understanding of adulthood, which is associated with taking care and responsibility for others, locating oneself in sets of interlocking relationships in the different areas of one's activities. The clearest expression of this arose when the young people interviewed were thinking about parenthood and are encapsulated in the view that 'you have to think of someone else now'. This relational perspective contrasts with an 'individualized' notion of adulthood, whereby young people stress individual and internal aspects of feeling and acting in a mature way. Adulthood is associated with a process of increasing choice and autonomy and decreasing dependence. This version could be consistent with practices associated with an extended youth – socializing, drinking, clubbing, having sexual relationships – and could be enjoyed here and now. Here we have neatly encapsulated the differing pulls of late modernity, the individualized and the relational – but there is no suggestion that they are decisively incompatible. Young people strive to find a balance, tipping in one direction or another depending on the social worlds they inhabit, which are powerfully shaped by class and ethnicity.

Class differences remain significant, though these cannot be reduced to judgements about depleted social capital in working-class communities, which many commentators tend to concentrate on, especially in the context of theories of an 'underclass' beyond repair or redemption. Gillies (2005) argues that the stereotypes of indifferent, irresponsible, and particularly working-class, parents purveyed by official bodies ignore the high levels of emotional investment evident in her interviews. Working-class parents care deeply about their children, and generate significant levels of emotional capital. She argues too that parental involvement in education is an emotional investment that makes considerably more sense to middle-class parents, paying off in terms of academic success and future prospects for their children. Middle-class parents deploy their social and cultural capital to transmit advantage, while working-class parents are more concerned to ensure that their children have the skills and strength to be able to cope with the instability, injustice and hardship that might characterize their lives (Gillies 2005: 842).

This is backed up by other research. Young middle-class people, interviewed for the youth transitions project, tend to be better networked than working-class children, with both themselves and their families exhibiting some of the fluidity of identity associated with late modernity. They also tend to be flexible and their networks span different age groups and communities – local, family, educational, work, leisure – and a wide range of activities. They are often well resourced by their family. Although some of the working-class young people interviewed are also well networked, keen to be socially mobile upward, often through education, and are resourced by their families, many of them have networks that tend to link them into family, community and locality, rather than providing broader opportunities for contacts, education and work (Thomson *et al.* 2004). As was true in the Rhondda in the 1950s and 1960s, working-class young people often still have to adopt individualist strategies in pursuing educational advantage (see Chapter 2).

If theorists have tended to emphasize the weakening of working-class solidarities as one index of the decline in social capital, they have also stressed the significance of racial and ethnic differences. The strengths of Asian families, for example, have been favourably compared with the weakness of social capital in African Caribbean communities (Reynolds 2004), though more recently the tight bonding and 'separatism' of Muslim communities has been portrayed, as described in Chapter 5, as a barrier to integration and the social benefits that might derive from this. The familial values of Asian families, it is argued, generate mutual obligations and cooperation, which is reflected in economic and professional success and educational attainment among many Asians while providing sanctions for individuals who do not follow group norms. The downside of this, however, is a major burden on family members to provide the necessary resources, and the social conservatism based on entrenched notions of honour and shame that often enforces restrictions on sexual diversity and intermarriage. Against this, Caribbean communities have been stigmatized as having weak social capital and little upward mobility precisely due to weak family ties, the prevalence of single-mother-headed families and male individualism (Dench 1996; Berthoud 1999). But as Goulbourne and Chamberlain have stressed (2001b: 7), concentration on family structures obscures the strength of family meanings and bonds: the emphasis on personal values of care, affection and mutual support, the richness of family-type rituals and customs, the importance of wider kin, including diasporic links, the powerful sense of neighbourhood, with a wealth of community organizations, and the opening up to other communities and identities represented by multi-ethnic sexual and partnership links. The narratives of the Anglo-Caribbean experience, Mary Chamberlain (2005) has argued in her book of that title, are about *Family Love in the Diaspora*. The ties of blood are seen by the community as stronger and more enduring than marriage, and responsibility, connectedness and commitment within and across generations remain primary values. What it illustrates above all is the flexibility and resilience of Caribbean kin relationships through diaspora and the experience of deprivation, racism and discrimination. This is a very different picture from that painted by social capital deficit theories.

My purpose here is not to establish hierarchies to measure one set of experiences against another, but rather to emphasize that separate communities have found often different ways of sustaining networks, values and resources – what broadly theorists mean by social capital – related to their specific histories. In a more diverse, multi-ethnic and multi-faith culture this can give rise to tensions and conflicts in finding the right balance between group identity and cultural and political integration, individual autonomy and communal values, bonding and bridging relationships. There are indeed many problems among young people, manifest in poor educational attainment among both black and white working-class males, and norms of violence and what has come to be called 'antisocial behaviour'. But despite the pessimists, there is at the same time clear evidence for the strength and resilience of norms of reciprocity and care across a wide range of social worlds.

What is also striking, however, is the extent to which women still bear the major role in sustaining these norms. A good example of this is again provided by the African Caribbean community in the UK. Although Reynolds emphasizes, against the stereotype, the importance of fathers in Caribbean families, she, in line with other research findings, also sees mothers, and women in general, as principally responsible for maintaining the norms of reciprocity and care (Reynolds 2001, 2005). This is in line with plentiful evidence that women continue to be central to caring in all its forms. Feminist theorists have developed conceptions of autonomy that emphasize mutuality, relatedness and recognition of the needs of the other, a relational ontology encapsulated in an 'ethic of care' (Gilligan 1982; Benhabib 1987; Sevehuijsen 1998). These are not necessarily gendered practices, as I have discussed elsewhere (Weeks 1995: 177–9). But it is women who still disproportionately do the caring in contemporary culture. While the male breadwinner/housewife-carer way of arranging matters within the household is now of negligible importance, it still exercises influence in the division of unpaid work among heterosexual couples (Lewis 2001: 64), though it is subject to much more negotiation and equality in non-heterosexual households (Dunne 1997, 1999; Heaphy *et al.* 1999). The emotional division of labour among heterosexual couples remains, in Duncombe and Marsden's (1999) term, 'asymmetrical'. This is especially true of childcare, which despite increasing family diversity, and growing involvement of fathers, remains primarily the mother's task. Ribbens McCarthy *et al.* (2003: 11) found that over 80 per cent of children in step-families live with their mother and a stepfather, with the mother as the main carer. Even when couples live apart (usually for career purposes), there may well be a greater sense of autonomy among women, but there are still highly gendered demands on them, and feelings of guilt (especially around children) and isolation, which for Holmes (2004: 189) suggests an 'incomplete extension of individualization processes to women'.

All this confirms that while individualizing trends are strong, people, and especially women, do remain firmly committed to relational values. Mason's (2004) study of narratives about residential moves in the North of England found a strong sense of relational rather than individualized identities. People's narratives were built through relationships they had or connections they made with other people, usually but not invariably those who they saw as family and kin. Practices and identities were embedded in webs of relationships, and 'to understand these we need to be able to keep the *processes of relating* in focus just as much as, if not more than, the individual or the self' (2004: 177). It is not simply selves in relation, which Mason sees as the focus of Gidden's family democracy, but 'relational selves' that are at the heart of people's narratives. This does not mean that all relational identities and practices are positive. Relational narratives may speak of warm and supportive connections with others, but also of constraint, conflict, claustrophobia and isolation (2004: 167). Another point, made by Ribbens McCarthy *et al.* (2003: 37), reminds us that there are in any case structural limits to democracy in the family. Families are made up of individuals who are differentiated rather than equivalent, that children especially have special needs and adults particular duties, and this is usually taken for granted. Mason's aim, however, is not to elevate morally one form of individualism over another, but rather to recognize the 'connectivity of social relations, identity and agency' (Mason 2004: 178).

This is in tune with the wider findings of the CAVA research group at Leeds University. This broadly found that people are energetic moral actors, embedded in webs of personal relationships, working to sustain the commitments that matter to them (Williams 2004: 41). People may lack grand ethical schemes but they live by highly contextualized values and ethics, based on a weighing of the odds, a balancing of possibilities, not so much what people ought to do but how can we deal with this, what is the appropriate thing to do (cf. Plummer 2003). Thus the operative principles are not so much prescriptive as practical, based on ideas of fairness, attentiveness to the needs of others, mutual respect, trust, reparation, being non-judgemental, adaptability to new identities and circumstances, being prepared to be accommodating, and being open to communication (Williams 2004: 74).

This is an ethic based on interdependence, in which care is an essential and defining element. Autonomy, in the sense of the capacity for self-determination rather than individual self-sufficiency, is a critical component of an everyday morality, but it is inevitably exercised in and through a variety of commitments and responsibilities, and in cases involving children particularly an acute sense of obligation. For Ribbens McCarthy *et al.* (2003: 140), 'When it comes to parenting and step-parenting . . . we still appear to be living in a modernist, morally absolute society. The moral imperative that children's needs take precedence may be one of the few remaining unquestionable moral assertions', though once again in strongly gendered ways. People tell gendered moral tales, with men still seeing themselves as the providers, moral decision-makers with responsibility for their children, and women prepared to put their own happiness second to that of their children (Ribbens McCarthy 2003: 59–61). These are very old stories, and extend even into new family patterns. Interestingly, even in lesbian families studied by Gabb (2004: 168; 2005), none of the same-sex couples shared childcare roles equally, and birth mothers often jealously guarded mother–child time.

As Williams (2005) strongly argues, the jeremiads of Left and Right which see moral decline as the hallmark of the present too readily collapse the moral economy of capitalism with the moral agency that people exercise in their close relationships, and underestimate the nature and extent of people's resistance and resilience as they struggle with the dilemmas in their everyday lives. They confront these dilemmas in ways which remain highly gendered, and which are shaped by diverse circumstances and influences, and relational practices. But the crucial point it is worth underlining again is that despite the multiplicity of social worlds and cultural patterns, the variety of relationships and different types of family, a common normative consensus does exist around the importance of the values of reciprocity, care and mutual responsibility.

Friendships, new families and beyond

In this chapter thus far I have sought to emphasize the importance of informal, local, contextualized relationships in underpinning the emergent norms of a diverse society. These are sustained by what Spencer and Pahl (2006) have called the 'hidden solidarities' that are a major source of social capital in the contemporary world. I want now to look in a little more detail at a crucial aspect of this, the significance of friendship, and its links with changing family forms. This link has been most evident in the developing culture of the non-heterosexual world (Weston 1991; Weeks *et al*. 2001), but as various writers have indicated (e.g. Pahl 2000; Roseneil 2004; Roseneil and Budgeon 2004; Vernon 2005) it has profound implications for wider personal relationships, challenging narrow interpretations of what constitutes family and intimate life.

I do not want to exaggerate the cultural significance of television series such as *Friends*, *Sex in the City* or *This Life*, which have concentrated on young attached (and usually highly attractive) people living or interacting with one another in intense, often family-like and sexually relaxed contexts, but they are popular because they echo new realities about the importance of friendships. Research commissioned by the food manufacturer Dolmio and published in 2006 has found that increasingly the boundaries of friendships and families are dissolving for young people, who often spend more time with friends than with family.

Apparently, 67 per cent of Britons now feel their best friend is part of their family, and whereas twenty-five years earlier half the population sought to keep friends and family apart, in 2006 only 15 per cent sought to do so. This has given rise to the rather ghastly neologism of 'framilies', which people feel happy to identify with. Here is 32-year-old Kirsten:

> My relatives live in Australia, which makes my friends all the
> more important. My framily and I eat together once a week, and
> I speak to most of them everyday. These people understand me
> and I understand them. We all feel comfortable around each
> other and I don't have to make too much of an effort. I don't
> see my framily as a replacment for my blood family. They're an
> addition to my family.
>
> (Mowbray 2006: 19)

What is interesting about this quotation is that it echoes much of the language used about lesbian and gay friendships. The non-heterosexual world, I have argued elsewhere, is sustained by the intricately woven but durable strands of a 'friendship ethic' (Weeks *et al.* 2001: ch. 3). Of all our relationships, claims Sullivan (1998: 176), 'Friendship is the most common and most natural. In its universality it even trumps family.' Peter Nardi (1999), reflecting on the significance of gay male friend-ships, describes them as the basis for 'invincible communities'. They provide the strength for gays to develop fully creative lives, and the protection against a potentially hostile world. Even more strongly, Michel Foucault saw in gay friendships the really subversive outcome of the gay revolution since the 1970s. 'Society and the institutions that frame it have limited the possibility of relationships [to marriage] because a rich relational world would be very complex to manage' (quoted in Vernon 2005: 134). Gay friendships open up new possibilities of loving, befriend-ing and relating which challenge the narrow solidarities of traditional families, and contribute to the development of Blasius' (1994) distinctive 'gay ethos'. Lesbians and gay men who may feel excluded from the traditional nuclear family can ground their emotional security and daily needs in strong friendships, where the boundaries between friendships and sexual relationships are often blurred. Lovers can become friends, friends lovers, and significant others are not necessarily sexual partners in a 'queering' of conventional boundaries (Roseneil 2000, 2004; Roseneil and Budgeon 2004).

Friendships provide a web of support and security which is particu-larly important in times of rapid change. They flourish when broad identities are undermined or shattered in periods of rapid social change, or at turning points in people's lives, or when lives are lived at odds with social norms (Weeks 1995: 145–6; Weeks *et al.* 2001). Friendships are, like Paris, a 'movable feast', they can be sustained over time and place and distance, yet they can allow individuals who live at the margins to feel constantly affirmed and confirmed in who and what they are through evolving life experiences. They offer the possibility of developing new patterns of intimacy and commitment, based on choice (because friendship is by definition elective, not given) and some degree of equality (because friendships are peer relationships, tend to homogeneity, and can be escaped from if differences become divisions). All these features give a special meaning and intensity to friendship in the lives of those who live on the edge. Friends can provide emotional and material support, but also affirm identity and belonging.

But this is not simply an LGBT experience. Friendships, for example, have been widely portrayed as central to women's experiences, underpinned as they are by an ethic of reciprocity (see Harrison 2004). So in periods of social upheaval it is not surprising that heterosexuals and non-heterosexuals alike are giving a new emphasis to friendship. The 'bonding ties' of traditional families can be too restrictive, enclosed, protective and limiting for the post-traditional individual. The 'bridging ties' and flexibility provided by friendship, families of choice or 'personal communities' where friendships and families overlap provide flexible and effective ways of negotiating risk and uncertainty, and of providing care and support (Allan 1996; Pahl 2000; Roseneil 2004; Budgeon 2006; Spencer and Pahl 2006). Friendships provide the space for exploration of who or what you are, and what you want to become. This is true at all stages of the life cycle, from the first tentative stages of exploring sexuality and identity, through the pleasures and crises of relationships, to the problems of ageing and potential loneliness of old age – those fateful or critical moments (Giddens 1992; Thomson *et al.* 2002) in a life which force individuals to reassess who and what they are, and to find ways of adapting to new situations.

Friendships are more than crutches for those who society barely acknowledges or accepts. They offer the opportunity for alternatives. In our study of non-heterosexual families of choice, fluid network families composed of friends, lovers, ex-lovers, biological kin, and increasingly children (Weeks *et al.* 2001), we found a range of life experiments in which individuals sought to balance autonomy and relatedness, flexibility and responsibility, negotiation and commitment. The language of 'family' used by many lesbian and gay people may be seen as both a challenge to conventional definitions and an attempt to broaden these; as a hankering for legitimacy and an attempt to build something new; as an identification with existing patterns and a more or less conscious effort to subvert them. The new narratives that many non-heterosexual women and men tell about families of choice and intimate life are creating a new public space where old and new forms jostle for meaning, and where new patterns of relationships are being invented (for US comparisons cf. Weston 1991; Carrington 1999).

Everyone, an American gay writer has argued, has the right to shape family forms that fit his or her needs (Goss 1997: 19), and this is like a leitmotiv for the emergence of 'new families'. Many LGBT people, traditionally seen as excluded from the scope of conventional family life, are simultaneously rethinking the meaning of same-sex relationships, and developing new meanings of family. Even the most passionate theoretical advocates of the rights of non-heterosexual people to form their own 'families' are careful to emphasize the dimensions of difference. Goss writes: 'In fact, we are Queering the notion of family and creating families reflective of our life choices. Our expanded pluralist uses of family are politically destructive of the ethic of traditional family values' (Goss 1997: 12). Others are not so certain that it is not a surrender to heteronormativity (Roseneil and Budgeon 2004). But more crucially, the emergence of non-heterosexual families of choice has to be seen as part of the wider pluralization of forms of family life that has been a central theme of this world we have made. If there are indeed so many types of family, why should same-sex families be ignored (Stacey (1996: 15)? Non-heterosexual relationships and families of choice are part of a wider struggle over meaning, both participating in and reflecting a wider transformation of family relationships. If the future of marriage is a critical ground of contestation in the wider world, it is hardly surprising that lesbians and gays should focus their demands on it. If parenting is perceived as in major need of rethinking, then why should non-heterosexuals be excluded from the debate? If families get ever more complex as a result of divorce, remarriage, recombination, step-parenting, surrogacy and so on, why should the chosen families of lesbians and gays, including with increasing frequency children, be denied a voice (Weeks *et al.* 2001)?

As Morgan (1996, 1999) has suggested, it is more useful today to see family in terms of a set of social practices rather than a fixed institution to which we belong. From this perspective 'family' may be seen as less of a noun and more as an adjective or a verb. ' "Family" represents a constructed quality of human interaction or an active process rather than a thing-like object of social investigation', writes Morgan (1999: 16). This approach displaces the idea that the family is a fixed and timeless entity of which one is either a member, or excluded from. We may see it instead as a series of practical everyday activities which we live: through activities such as mutual care, the division of labour in the home, looking after dependants and 'relations', all of which practices LGBT people regularly engage in. 'Family' is about particular sorts of relational interactions rather than simply private activities in a privileged sphere. Instead of being an objective phenomenon, 'family' may be interpreted as a subjective set of activities whose meanings are made by those who participate in them. Family practices focus on everyday interactions with close and loved ones, and move away from fixed boundaries of co-residence, marriage, ethnicity and obligation that defined the male breadwinning family. It registers the ways in which our networks of care and affection are not simply given by virtue of blood and marriage, but are negotiated and shaped by us (Williams 2004: 17). From this perspective, it is less important whether we are *in* a family than whether we *do* family-type things. Following Judith Butler (1990) we can describe family practices as 'performative', with families constructed through their constant iterative enactment. We live family rather than dwell within it.

This allows us to recognize and begin to understand the fluidity of everyday life practices, and the way doing family is related to the ways we do or perform gender, sexuality, work, caring and the other activities that make up the totality of life experiences. Family life is a historically specific, contextualized set of activities, intimately linked with other social practices. From this perspective there is no theoretical reason to exclude non-heterosexual everyday practices – or anyone else's – from the pantheon of family and kin.

Having said that it is important at the same time to acknowledge that diversity in family forms does not necessarily mean diversity in family lifestyles or moral guidelines, as we saw in the previous section. The study of step-families by Ribbens McCarthy and her colleagues (2003) pin-points the continuing power of family discourse and ideals. Although family can be accepted as an accumulation of practices, people act as if it were a coherent unity, involving commitment, togetherness, putting the family first, mutual support and responsibility. The idea of the family as a loose, diffuse alliance or network across households was largely held by white, middle-class liberal interviewees, but others wanted a more closely defined boundaried unit. 'Being there for you' was a complex notion, but at the heart of it was a set of relationships that offered a sense of security, a unit in which children could be reared. Even step-families are communities of need rather than elective affinities, argue Ribbens McCarthy *et al.* (2003: 50–2). Gabb substantiates this to some extent in her study of lesbian parents in Yorkshire. She did not find any particular resonance of the friends as family model, and was critical of what she calls the 'community narrative' which normalizes it (2004: 168, 174). For her sample, 'blood was thicker than water'.

Again, we can see in this the complex coexistence of attitudes. On the one hand there is clearly an awareness of the fluidity and flexibility of intimate arrangements that are able to adapt not simply to non-heterosexuality but to key moments in heterosexual life – especially marriage breakup and remarriage, and the complexity of step-parenting arrangements that then emerge. On the other hand, there is a strong urge for what Giddens (1991) calls 'ontological security', based on a strong narrative of belonging and identity that can make sense of the past and present, and allow for planning for the future. A sense of family, embodying connectedness and belonging, provides that. But for some, as Ribbens McCarthy *et al.* and Gabb illustrate, this is necessarily embodied in the tight relationship of parent and child rather than the expansiveness of 'families we choose'.

We can draw a couple of useful observations from this. In the first place, while we can agree with those who argue that the shifting patterns of friendship represent a significant destabilization of the homosexual/ heterosexual binary insofar as friendships and 'families of choice' cut across the gay/straight divide (e.g. Roseneil 2000; Roseneil and Budgeon 2004), they do not necessarily lead to the dissolution of what are seen as core values of family life. Rather they are reformulated for new times. Second, as Henning Bech (1992, 1997) suggested some years ago, referring to the first, Danish, experiments with legalizing same-sex partnerships, it is a step towards the end of the homosexual – but of the heterosexual too. It begins to make meaningless the categorical distinctions of which marriage was a key marker. That puts into some perspective the debate over the significance of same-sex marriage.

Queer, how queer?

History of a sort was made on 5 December 2005 when *The Times* carried three short notices in its Court and Social Register (p. 55) announcing three forthcoming civil partnerships between same-sex couples. The fact that the traditional paper of record made the gesture speaks for several things: a marketing initiative (tapping a new market), a jolly piece of headline-catching of its own on the day civil partnerships became legal (the fact that *The Times* carried the listings was widely referred to in the media), and a logical extension of the paper's documentation of the rites of passage of the élite, now indelibly queered (even though a lieutenant-colonel was one of the fathers listed). But what is surely most striking is the normalization of same-sex relationships by *The Times* that it signalled.

Britain has been classically hesitant in proceeding down this route. While controversy raged in the USA about same-sex marriage from the 1980s (see essays in Estlund and Nussbaum 1997; Sullivan 1997), and other jurisdictions from Canada to Australia and most of Western Europe had more or less willingly implemented domestic partnership arrangements and eventually marriage (Wintermute and Andenaes 2001; Merin 2002), the UK had dragged its feet. Under Conservative administrations same-sex unions were too far away from a morally conservative agenda to be even contemplated. Under a new social democratic government after 1997 it seemed too radical a move. Two commentators on the debates around same-sex unions in the early part of the new century signally failed to notice that change was imminent (Bailey-Harris 2001; Merin 2002). But by 2004, legislation for civil partnerships that had once appeared so controversial had easily passed through Parliament. I will discuss some of the reasons for this below, but the point I want to make now is that by 2005, when civil partnerships were launched on the world with a flurry of media coverage and little hostility, it seemed an inevitable move in what has become the most secular and tolerant of countries – and the two aspects seem clearly linked. The first civil partnership ceremony actually took place in the least secular and tolerant part of the UK, Northern Ireland, and had to face the 'native Old Testament tendency' howling its dismay. But the couple, Shannon Sickels and Grainne Close, easily defied the bayings, and Ms Sickels said afterwards, 'This is about making a choice to have our civil rights acknowledged and protected, and we could not be here without the hard work of many queer activists and individuals from the queer community'. All this was true, but behind it was another truth: that the country itself had profoundly changed. Even here in Belfast, 'in this once dourly Presbyterian city, where playground swings used to be chained up on Sundays', the ice was cracking (Sharrock 2006: 14).

It is easy to dismiss civil partnerships as a minor shift affecting only a minority. But conservative critics of legal recognition of same-sex unions are surely right to see in that process something much more significant. Logic would usually suggest that de-heterosexualizing marriage by promoting same-sex unions/marriages is a potentially transgressive and subversive assault on its heteronormativity, an undermining of its cornerstone role, and a destabilizing of the hetero–homo binary that constitutes the gendered and sexual order. That is clearly what the conservative movements assume, and why they are so violently hostile to same-sex marriage. But the queer critiques of same-sex marriage in effect argue that marriage can never be freed of its heterosexual assumptions. Queer analysis, Brandzel (2005: 195) argues, suggests that 'marriage is a mechanism by which the state ensures and reproduces heteronormativity, and absorbing certain types of gay and lesbian relationships will only further this process'. Marriage, Warner (1999: 82) writes, 'sanctifies some couples at the expense of others. It is selective legitimacy'. Which is why social conservatives and queer theorists can both oppose it: conservatives because it confers legitimacy on the illegitimate, because it normalizes the abnormal; radicals because it elevates one type of same-sex relationship over others, it normalizes a particular type of couple relationship, not the subversive and transgressive possibilities that sexual radicalism implies (see discussion in Robinson 2005; Rothblum 2005).

Catherine Donovan, a British scholar far removed from the ideological divides of North America, expresses similar fears very clearly:

> I am against same-sex marriage (or any same-sex partnership
> legislation) for two main reasons. First, the place in UK
> society of marriage as a privileged legal and emotional contract
> reinforces inequalities between people depending on the way
> they organize and live their personal lives. Second, I believe
> that the model of love represented by marriage should not
> be held up unquestionably as the idea to which we should
> all aspire.
>
> (Donovan 2004: 25)

According to this argument, marriage is at the apex of a hierarchy which marginalizes single people, lesbians and gay men generally, and the complex forms of friendship and intimacy that have emerged in lesbian and gay communities. The potentiality for different types of relationships offered by the friendship ethic discussed in the previous section are

threatened by this apparent reversion to normalizing couple relationships. The formalization of same sex unions is based on an exclusive
notion of love, which is still locked into ideas of possession and wrapped
in violence. And it channels sexuality into forms of monogamy and lifetime commitment which the sexual transformations of the 1960s and
1970s sought to undermine. 'Marriage comes with a baggage that is
difficult to wrestle free from' (Donovan 2004: 27).

When Catherine Donovan, Brian Heaphy and myself were research-
ing for what became the book *Same Sex Intimacies* in the mid-1990s we
found that these sorts of sentiment were widely echoed, but they also
have to be seen in the context of rapidly evolving attitudes about care
and commitment and the legal framework needed to sustain them.
Many of those who we interviewed were sharply aware of the implications of the absence of legal recognition for their relationships as part
of a wider denial of rights. Two experiences particularly since the 1970s
had dramatized the disadvantages of their legal standing: the absence
of parenting rights, especially among lesbians who had formerly been
married heterosexually, which had led to a long-lasting and difficult
campaign for the rights of lesbian mothers; and the experience of the
HIV/AIDS epidemic among gay men, where there was a multitude of
personal experiences of partners of people living with AIDS being denied
anything remotely like spousal rights.

The first issue, of course, relates directly to the very issue that has
traditionally been at the heart of marriage: the question of parenting.
Even as early gay liberation doctrine challenged the idea of marriage and
the sanctity of the family, serious dilemmas for lesbian mothers were
apparent. The more open they were about their gayness, the more likely
they were to lose custody of their children – at one stage up to 90 per cent
of lesbian mothers were losing custody of their children in contested
divorce cases – and to face media caricature (Hanscombe and Foster
1983; Rights of Women Custody Group 1986; Allen and Harne 1988;
Harne 1997). But the issue was soon going beyond custody issues as new
technologies opened up new fronts. The growing use of self-insemination
and donor insemination from the late 1970s within lesbian relationships
posed new challenges to assumptions about heterosexual motherhood,
and during the 1980s and 1990s these became yet more controversial
in relation to access to new reproductive technologies and who could be
considered appropriate to foster and adopt (Saffron 1994). In both the
USA and Europe parenting was becoming a major issue, for lesbians
(Lewin 1984, 1993; Griffin and Mulholland 1997), and more widely for
the gay community as men also began to affirm their rights to parenthood (Bozett 1987; Benkov 1994; Ali 1996; Drucker 1998). The so-called
'gayby' boom from the 1990s involving both lesbians and gay men, often
in partnership. dramatically demonstrated the new centrality of parenting in LGBT lives (Weeks *et al.* 2001; 156–79; Stacey 2006). Yet rights
of gay parents, and of couples in particular, remained uncertain, for
example, in relationship to adoption, and in equal access of lesbians to

donor insemination and IVF, while anxieties about the impact of gay parents on the children themselves remained a fraught issue (Hicks 2005).

The HIV/AIDS crisis had illustrated the absence of legal recognition and partnership rights in a different way. Same-sex partners found themselves bypassed by medical authorities as their lovers fell ill or lay dying. Insurance companies refused cover for same-sex couples. Mortgage companies were reluctant to lend without intrusive medical tests. Surviving partners often lost their homes when their partners died, and were denied inheritance rights. In extreme cases they even found themselves excluded from funeral services by legal next of kin (Heaphy *et al.* 1999; Weeks *et al.* 2001: 17–19). These difficulties were often compounded for individuals who were not in a one-to-one relationship, as officials and families sometimes refused to recognize the role of friends in sustaining individuals who were sick and dying (Sullivan 1998). All this gave a dramatic impetus within the gay community itself to the acknowledgement of the importance of both a wider sense of community and of the sense of kin that close friendships can produce (Weston 1991: 183). Without that, individuals, especially the many who were exiled from families of origin by homophobic prejudice, might suffer illnesses and death alone. The epidemic revealed how vulnerable LGBT people were in the absence of full recognition of their significant commitments, without full citizenship (Watney 1994: 159–68).

Citizenship is about recognition and belonging, and about the rights and responsibilities which follow from that. It also raises questions of equality, about how far and in what ways a just society should accept different ways of life as equally valid and worthy of respect – and what sort of legal framework is needed to ensure full citizenship. But citizenship discourses need to go further if they are to be able to tackle the roots of inequality and social exclusion, especially those stemming from heteronormative values. Formal equality under the law will have limited impact unless it is accompanied by real efforts to address the inequalities of power that continue to structure everyday life (Jackson 1998; Cooper 2001). The claim to rights and entitlements by LGBT people without a wider recognition of sexual inequalities and without problematizing heterosexuality does not challenge the *status quo*: it is in danger of freezing it (Rahman 1998, 2000).

The interviewees portrayed in *Same Sex Intimacies* had an acute sense of this. They wanted their differences respected while claiming equal rights. So while there was a widespread belief that non-heterosexual people had as much right to marriage as did heterosexuals, and most people wanted some form of legal recognition for their relationships as a matter of right and justice, it did not necessarily mean that they themselves intended to seize the opportunity. Many were highly critical of traditional marriage and wanted nothing to do with it. Angela commented that 'marriage is all around property and ownership and roles', while David felt that tailoring heterosexual laws and understandings towards gay relationships is 'bound to fail'. Melanie felt that equal rights 'shouldn't be on a marriage model', while Warren stated that 'marriage in heterosexual terms is such an oppressive institution, and I wouldn't like to see lesbians or gay men simply kind of reflecting it'. Charles, more bluntly, said it was 'bullshit' for gay couples to get married (Weeks *et al.* 2001: 192–4). Yip's interview with lesbian and gay Christians echoed these sentiments: while the vast majority wanted recognition of their relationships, most were against same-sex marriage, seeing it again as a dysfunctional heterosexual institution (Yip 2004a: 175).

Behind such strong assertions was a clearly developing set of values about the nature of LGBT relationships which Donovan's views reflect. Most of the self-defined LGBT people who we interviewed believed that they had unique opportunities to lead more egalitarian lives than their heterosexual fellow citizens precisely because they were excluded from the gendered and hierarchical relationships that traditional marriage represented. They are, as Adam (2006: 6) puts it in his study of relationship innovation in male gay couples, 'condemned to freedom' in the absence of strong traditional guidelines about how to live partnerships. Nothing can be taken for granted, and the evolving norms, rooted in the necessity of living lives against the grain, are based on the assumption of equality, disclosure and negotiation. Differences and divisions do of course survive: there are inequalities of income, power, opportunity, even of class, age and ethnicity, but the ethos is based on relationships of autonomy and choice, unconstrained by external rules (Weeks *et al.* 2001: 109–13). For Giddens (1992), lesbian and gay relationships, based on confluent love and freed from traditional bonds, were models for the development of 'pure relationships', which he saw as the logic of late modern patterns of intimacy. What was *faute de mieux* in an era of oppressive legal codes and endemic prejudice, has become normative within the gay community itself in more liberal times.

Given this background, it is not surprising that LGBT people on the whole have been sceptical about the merits of same-sex marriage or legalized partnerships insofar as they replicate traditional marriage. The sort of conservative justification for same-sex marriage put forward by Sullivan (1995) and similar gay conservatives (discussed in Robinson 2005), that it will mark the full integration of lesbians and gays into conventional society, finds little favour among those who we interviewed, though there is some evidence of support for marriage on other grounds. An online survey of mainly LGBT people drawn from twenty-seven countries, reporting in 2006, found strong support for equal rights, and for same-sex marriage on these grounds (Harding and Peel 2006). A smaller qualitatative study at the same time, however, found attitudes towards marriage 'more messy' than the debates tend to assume (Clarke *et al.* 2006: 155). Instead we find an interesting duality. On the one hand there has been a conscious desire for formal equality with the heterosexual majority in the whole range of citizenship rights, from benefit entitlements to care responsibilities, up to and including marriage. On the other hand, there has been a widespread reluctance to simply 'mimic' straight society. 'We create our own lifestyles and . . . relationships that are different from heterosexual relationships' (Malika, quoted in Weeks *et al*. 2001: 191). Behind this was the wider issue of whether the ultimate purpose of gay activism was assimilation or difference, inclusion or dissidence, citizenship or transgression. As Pat put it,

> 'we should all be treated equally in the eyes of the law. But
> . . . I believe now that we are not the same as straight people;
> that we do have differences, that we are diverse, and that we
> are creative and we take a lot more risks around lots of things
> . . . We're almost like a tribe – I think we create things in society
> and we help people move forward'.
>
> (Weeks *et al*. 2001: 193)

If this is the case, then same sex marriage hardly seems to be the right way forward.

Yet although there had been little popular pressure for change (see Shipman and Smart 2007) when in December 2005 it finally became possible in Britain for same-sex couples to legally confirm their relationships under the Civil Partnership Act, LGBT people appeared to welcome it with aplomb, and there was an early rush to local registry offices. Although carefully not officially deemed same-sex marriage, the legislation was deliberately framed by the government in parallel terms to heterosexual marriage. The only significant differences, ironically given the obsessive cultural tradition of defining LGBT people solely by their sexuality, concerned sexuality: consummation was not required to complete the partnership, and adultery could not provide evidence for the dissolution of the union. Not surprisingly, many in the gay community decided to call it marriage right away, and took up the offer with enthusiasm.

The government had been cautious (possibly for financial reasons) in its estimation of the numbers likely to take up civil partnerships – between 11,000 and 22,000 by 2010. But numbers grew steadily. Within the first six weeks 3648 same-sex couples 'got married', and within the next three months the figure had reached 6500 (Curtis 2006: 14; Muir 2006: 7). By September 2006 over 15,500 civil partnerships had been contracted, involving 31,344 individuals (Ward 2006: 9). The busiest areas for civil partnerships were in the likeliest pro-gay places, largely in the south of Great Britain, including Brighton and Hove and West London, but even the most conservative, declining industrial areas showed some enthusiasm – Rochdale produced ten, and the Rhondda, that bastion of traditional values which we have visited several times already, eleven, within the first six weeks. In more conservative Britain, the surprise was not so much that numbers were relatively small, but that it happened at all. And perhaps most significant of all, disrupting all the stereotypes, at first twice as many men entered civil partnerships as women (Curtis 2006: 14), though over the course of the first year women began to equalize numbers (Ward 2006: 9). The legislation allowing civil partnerships, especially when linked to the changes in the adoption law, gave same-sex couples in Britain as many if not more rights and responsibilities as in most other countries in Europe, even though it still denied the title of marriage to same-sex couples.

The Civil Partnership Act was part of a radical swathe of legislative changes which on one level signified the formal move to homosexual equality. This goal had been signalled by Tony Blair as long ago as 1994, and was worked towards, if sometimes haphazardly, during the Labour government after 1997 (Weeks 2004b). The Civil Partnership Act, in the end, was significantly more radical than had been signalled in the earlier consultation, but ministers consistently reiterated that it was not endorsing same-sex marriage. In part this was obviously a way of avoiding the divisive debates in the United States, and which had threatened at one stage to block parliamentary progress in the UK. From this point of view, the introduction of civil partnerships may be seen as a typically pragmatic way of adjusting to changing social realities without abandoning traditional forms, and without as a nice consequence arousing too much political hostility – a very British compromise. Although conservative religious organizations and pro-family groups voiced strong opposition, they were by now very much minority voices, and the legislation had cross-party support as it went through Parliament. What especially diminished religious opposition was that what was on offer was a marriage-like arrangement separate from but parallel to civil marriage which had long existed. It was left to the churches themselves to decide whether they were prepared to add a religious element in the form of a blessing or fuller service (the majority of traditional churches of course at this stage declined to make such an offer).

From another perspective the introduction of civil partnerships may be seen as part of the Europeanization of British social legislation, and the anticipated outcome of the introduction of a European-style human rights act (see Waaldijk 2001a). The government had already been pressured by the European Court to concede various forms of equality, regarding spousal rights in housing, pensions and the like, and there was a clear logic in going further (Bell 1998). By 2004 most European Union countries had introduced some form of recognition of same-sex unions, starting with Denmark, which led the way in 1989 (Wintermute and Andenaes 2001; Merin 2002).

Each country took its own path, reflecting its own cultural bias. The Pacs legislation in France, for instance, followed classic republican traditions by refusing to recognize the separate cultural identities of lesbians and gays (Jackson 2006: 80). It was a contract which allowed civil partnership arrangements for heterosexuals and homosexuals alike, and was clearly distinguished from marriage, whose legal status was not affected: the partners remained individualized, no new legal entity was created, and no challenge was offered to the permanence of sexual difference. It was opposed by conservatives of Left and Right (Fassin 2001, 2005; see also Velu 1999; Borrillo 2001; Probert 2001; Borrillo and Lascoumes 2002). In the Netherlands radical changes came about through what Waaldijk (2001b: 440) called the 'law of small changes', an incrementalism which fitted in easily with the tradition of pillarization that assumed different rights claims, and was committed to recognizing them. From a more radical perspective what was delivered was a conservative sexual settlement that had a narrow definition of sex: 'the sexual liberalism of the Dutch', Hekma has polemicized, 'is a surface phenomenon only', which validates the monogamous couple, whether homosexual or heterosexual, at the expense of more radical possibilities (2005: 220).

One area of consistent conservatism across Europe was less concerned with sex than with parenting. At first the legislation in EU countries explicitly excluded equal adoption and fostering rights – until 2005, even Belgium's granting of same-sex marriage excluded these. Children, childcare, remained a last taboo. Whatever their limitations, however, European countries had proceeded down the recognition path, with Britain as a notorious laggard in these changes. With civil partnership and adoption rights granted, Britain suddenly leapt ahead. In effect, the linking of the two aspects, namely partnership and parenting, did allow same-sex couples to form families in the most traditional sense if they wished. At the same time, however, marriage and/or heterosexuality were no longer requirements for unmarried couples to adopt children. There was now formal equality for straights and gays alike.

The British legislation, moreover, had an ideological colouring that fitted into a wider social agenda. The Blair government had long been concerned with the future of the family, and of the role of marriage as the linchpin of family life. Its 1998 consultation document, *Supporting Families*, had been one of the most comprehensive and liberal statements of family policy ever issued by a British government (Home Office 1998; Weeks 1999). Its very use of the plural 'families' signified its recognition of a diversity of family formations, and it made clear that there existed many 'strong and mutually assertive families outside marriage', though it conspicuously failed to mention non-heterosexual families. At the same time it declared its ambition to promote marriage as 'the most reliable framework for raising children' and proposed a raft of measures to do so, in part through providing advice and training for parenthood. All this was fully in line with the communitarian commitments that underpinned the government's social philosophy, which stressed the importance of strengthening family and community life as a way of combating societal dissolution and the weakening of social capital (cf. Etzioni 1995). In practice, the emphasis was increasingly on supporting parents, especially those facing poverty, regardless of their marital status (Williams 2005), but marriage as a focus of both rights and responsibilities remained a powerful, if elusive, talisman for the Blair government. From this perspective, granting of strong guaranteed rights and agreed responsibilities to same-sex couples who entered legal partnerships fulfilled communitarian principles about building stable relationships (which up to this point in the wider debate initiated by Etzioni and his followers had signally ignored same sex relationships) while not immediately undermining the legal status of marriage. As the consultation document on civil partnerships issued in 2003, which immediately preceeded the introduction of legislation, set out, the legal recognition of same-sex partnerships was 'an important equality measure' intended to 'give legitimacy' to those wishing to have 'interdependent' couple relationships that are 'intended to be permanent' (Shipman and Smart 2007). Diversity in relationships was no longer seen as a problem, but instability in relationships was.

This left in abeyance the wider question about the future of marriage itself: could it retain a special status when in practice it was indistinguishable from civil partnership in terms of legal rights and social benefits? It is difficult to avoid the logic that marriage and civil partnerships are likely eventually to merge into a single status. This is a possibility strongly implied in 2006 when the Law Commission proposed introducing new rights for heterosexual and same-sex couples alike who did not enter into marriage/civil partnerships. The proposals included rights to claim maintenance and a share of property and pensions following the breakup of cohabiting relationships, whether straight or gay, and the aim was to provide some sort of protection for people who had made a conscious decision not to marry or enter into a civil partnership – akin possibly to the limited arrangements of the Pacs. The clear assumption here was that marriage and civil partnerships constituted a common status, qualitatively different from simple cohabitation (Dyer 2006: 1). The communitarian passion for strengthening relationships whether heterosexual or non-heterosexual is, it seems, taking precedence over the defence of traditional heterosexual marriage, while marriage or marriage-like relationships are seen as one, but not the only, part of the armoury for achieving this.

Civil partnership arrangements confer new rights and entitlements, and from the point of view of those who have struggled long and hard for these rights they can justifiably see them as a major step towards full citizenship. As Angela Mason, who as leader of the gay rights lobby group Stonewall campaigned vigorously for civil partnerships, and as director of the government's Women and Equality Unit saw through the negotiation of the legislation, put it, 'I've been involved in the campaign for a long time. You wondered if it would make a difference; the answer is yes. What's been heartening is the welcome from the rest of society' (Dyer 2005: 9). This was a major step towards inclusion. But at the same time that the right to enter a civil partnership may be interpreted as a new positive freedom, it is also a new form of regulation (Halley 2001: 108–11), which produces new types of subjects: the legalized and legitimized couple. Butler has critically remarked on the dangers of the 'normalizing powers of the state' in defining same-sex marriage

(2004: 104) as the right way to live intimacy for lesbians and gays, and there is no doubt that the civil partnership and related legislation carries with it the danger of separating off the respectable gay from the unrespectable, the stable couple from the promiscuous, and of imprinting new normativities on to the gay community. While marriage and domestic partnerships should certainly be available as options, Butler (2005: 59) has argued, 'to install either as a model for sexual legitimacy is precisely to constrain the sociality of the body in acceptable ways'.

There is no doubt that the Blair government was anxious to support some patterns of relationships over others. However, its ultimate preoccupations were not about stigmatizing relationships it disliked – its general tone in relationship to consensual activities, whether heterosexual or same-sex, was broadly permissive – but about supporting types of relationship that worked. Fiona Williams has argued that 'A new normative family is emergent, which . . . revolves around the adult couple whose relationship is based on their parenting responsibilities, and whose priorities are rooted in work, economic self-sufficiency, education and good behaviour' (2005: 244). It is easy to see how this model could fit in closely with simultaneously supporting strong gay relationships, especially as they embrace parenting experiences. However, we must be careful not to try to fit everything together too neatly into a preordained explanatory framework. It is tempting for radical critics of initiatives such as civil partnerships to attempt to place them within the frameworks they are familiar with: we live in a neo-liberal climate; the Blair government supports neo-liberal economic reforms; ergo, civil partnerships must be a manifestation of neo-liberal sexual governance. Civil partnerships may indeed express values which are complementary to a form of neo-liberalism, but they are also rooted, I have argued, in a form of communitarianism, and beyond that in an older, social democratic tradition based on a combination of mutuality and self-sufficiency. Values of reciprocity and strong communities underpin these developments as much as neo-liberal rationalism.

It is even more difficult to agree with critics who have argued that new citizenship claims, including same-sex marriage, are complicit with neo-liberal strategies (Richardson 2004) when looked at from a wider international perspective. The USA, the most neo-liberal of states, has been, on an official level, the most hostile of all Western nations to same-sex citizenship rights, while the country most hostile to globalization, and to Americanization, France, has pioneered partnership rights via Pacs, but is similarly reluctant to go down the road of same-sex marriage, though for different reasons (Fassin 2001, 2005; Jackson 2006). The legalization of same-sex relationships as a process has many roots in different late modern societies, and cannot be reduced to an adjunct of wider socio-economic processes. Too much energy has been spent by activists in campaigning for sexual change to justify such a deterministic position. Richardson (2004: 405) makes the point that though many contemporary campaigns for lesbian and gay citizenship rights may seem to mimic the cautious homophile movements of the 1950s and 1960s in seeking acceptance into existing value structures, their real purpose is elsewhere. Their focus is no longer on demanding the right to exist in private, 'where the boundaries of private are marked by the limits of tolerance, but on the right to public recognition *and* the right to privacy' (ibid.: 405). Far from creating new types of relationships as an imposed norm, the new legislation confirmed existing relationships. As Shipman and Smart (2007) show in their pioneering study of those who had engaged in some form of commitment ceremony prior to the introduction of civil partnerships, most people seeking legal recognition were already in stable partnerships with shared obligations and mutual responsibilities.

Governments and legislators may seek to develop, even shape new normative frameworks, but there can never be a one-to-one fit between intention and effect, and the unintended effects of state action are usually more potent than the intended in relation to sexual and intimate life – which is why governments by and large stop short at anything that looks too obviously like moral engineering. The future of civil partnerships and same-sex marriage will depend ultimately on how the subjects of these policies respond. Radical critiques of the new civil partnerships range from rejection of any legislative framework for same-sex relationships through a desire to see new legal rights for all types of relationships, including polyamorous ones, to a rejection of the separation of marriage and civil partnerships. Kitzinger and Wilkinson (2004: 132), senior academics as well as lesbian activists, regard equal access to marriage as 'a straightforward human right and a simple matter of justice', and see civil partnerships as a form of apartheid – equal but separate. Legally married in Canada, they fought in the English courts in 2006 to gain recognition under UK law of their status (Doward 2006b: 12; Woolcock 2006b; 26). They shared the feminist and queer critiques of marriage, but as long as marriage existed, they argue, it is 'pragmatically expedient' and politically important to engage with it (Kitzinger and Wilkinson 2004: 131). In the judgement against them they were in a sense proved right when the judge indicated that civil partnerships were different from marriage, which retained a special, heterosexual status (Woolcock 2006c: 12). By creating a separate status for same-sex couples the law was apparently upholding an essential difference between homosexuality and heterosexuality that other realities – not least the existence of bisexuality, and the growing overlap of life experiments – have long been undermining (Klesse 2006). Similarly, the new law has created an anomalous situation for transgendered people, especially for married couples who include a partner who has transitioned. Under the Gender Recognition Act the trans person can now gain legal status in their new gender, thus creating a same-sex couple. But if they wish to maintain a legal bond, they will now have to divorce and then enter into a civil partnership (Kitzinger and Wilkinson 2006: 174). In other words, by essentializing both the heterosexual/homosexual binary and gender, the

Civil Partnership Act is in danger of storing up legal tangles for itself. The danger is that the legal fiction of a difference between civil partnership and marriage will become a material as well as a symbolic divide (Harding and Peel 2006: 134).

But on the ground something more radical was stirring. For most people who in these early days contracted a civil partnership the motives were less political than the Kitzinger/Wilkinson position, but equally pragmatic. For them civil partnerships were already marriages in all but name, and soon they were applying the name as well, not least in the near universal use of the language of 'weddings' and 'marriage' by people and media alike (only senior politicians maintained the formal proprieties and avoided the term). In practice new meanings and realities were being created on the ground as LGBT people began to formulate their own norms of acceptable behaviour, and to articulate their motivations for seeking legal recognition of partnerships. These varied, as I found in a series of interviews I conducted in the first half of 2006. For Meg, a 70-year-old lesbian activist who had entered into a civil partnership with her lover of twenty-five years, 'you'd be daft not to do it'. Although ideologically critical of marriage as an institution, and reluctant to use the term 'marriage' for her civil partnership, there was an acceptance of the protection that a legal status would give to her younger partner, especially in relation to inheritance and pension rights. A similar pragmatism had encouraged John, aged 60, to 'marry' his long-term but younger partner Martin. 'I've been worried for a long time about what would happen to Martin if I died before him. None of my pension would go to him, and would he have to sell the house to pay the inheritance tax? Although we had wills and deeds of trust and so on, this makes it much easier, and safer.' For Sally and Jane, a lesbian couple in their thirties, a civil partnership was a guarantee of the security of their 3-year-old son Jamie, who had been conceived by Jane through donor insemination. 'I've been having kittens about what would happen to Jamie if I suddenly dropped dead. We've done everything we could to make sure Sally would be able to look after him, but now she has full parenting rights.'

Such instrumentalist explanations are common but in many cases they seem to be the immediate spark for discussing entering into a civil partnership rather than the underlying motivating factor. Shipman and Smart (2007) found that the 'everyday responses' of their interviewees fed into five distinct categories: (1) love; (2) acknowledging mutual responsibility; (3) the importance of family recognition; (4) legal rights and recognition; (5) public commitment (see also Smart *et al.* 2006). These broadly echo my own findings, but it is useful to bring them into three broader categories: rights, commitment and recognition.

The rights agenda is implicit in some of the instrumentalist comments above, and resonates with the larger claims to full citizenship that is the prime motivation for LGBT activism. For Keith, a 45-year-old who had married his Singaporean partner, it was a way of concluding a long and convoluted immigration process. His partner Timmy already had the right to stay in the UK, but a civil partnership seemed to make it more believable and final. A civil partnership, however, is more than a list of entitlements; it involves parallel responsibilities. They have implications for social security benefits and pensions, for example, where a civil partnership union would be treated as a couple for assessment purposes. The dissolution of the union has implications for dividing property. There are implications for joint parenting, and mutual care in health. So the responsibilities are real and ongoing. 'I don't believe in saying something like "till death us do part" and all that sort of thing,' said Keith, 'but when we signed the register I knew I was in this for the long term. I always felt that, I suppose, but that piece of paper somehow made it different.' It is worth mentioning here that civil partnerships did not invent new rights; by and large they transferred existing individual entitlements to the couple. And in a welfare society such as the UK some of the passion behind the campaign for same-sex marriage was diminished. For example, the claim that marriage was important for securing spousal health care protection that Butler felt to be important in the USA diminished in a society which took for granted free health care for all (Butler 2004: 109). Nevertheless, the new entitlements were considerable, and provided a very material motivation to enter into a civil partnership.

Important as the rights (and mutual responsibilities) were to my interviewees, the underlying motivation was the desire to signify commitment. Jane Lewis (2001: 124ff.) identifies three forms of commitment: personal – wanting the relationship to continue; moral – the relationship ought to continue; and structural – the relationship has to continue, for material reasons, for the sake of the children and so on. The structural demands are perhaps less potent for LGBT people than heterosexual, though childcare responsibilities and immigration issues do become structuring factors. Moral commitment is certainly strong among many, especially those of a religious turn of mind. But the most potent today is probably the strong personal desire to affirm a commitment, the confirmation of an ongoing sense of mutual responsibilities and love. Long before civil partnerships seemed likely, gay couples had been finding various ways of marking commitment: from the exchange of rings and gifts, celebrating significant events such as date of first meeting or first sex, birthdays or Christmas, to participating in full-scale commitment ceremonies (Weeks *et al.* 2001: 127–32): 'We see the act of celebrating a same-sex union in the absence of legal recognition as an opportunity to create symbolic transformation', write Liddle and Liddle (2004: 53). That symbolic transformation is a way of claiming legitimacy for the relationship, and in changing individual attitudes, but clearly is potentially more for the couple. The lesbian and gay Christians who supported same sex marriage in Yip's research saw their partnership in religious terms as a symbolic confirmation, or covenant before God of commitment and love (Yip 2004a: 177). But even for those of an ardently secular disposition, the affirmation of commitment was a critical moment. Paul and Donny are a couple in their forties who had hesitated, after ten years of living together, about entering into a civil partnership. Their relationship is based on a strong emotional commitment, but they have a sexually open relationship. 'I was afraid that a legal tie would somehow be the end of our own openness to other people,' Paul admitted, 'and that we would just become another couple of boring old farts.' But, he went on, their simple ceremony had been more emotionally affirming than he expected. 'When I said those words about my commitment to Donny a shiver went down my back, I was in tears, and I really felt there was no turning back.' For many, civil partnership did involve a firm commitment to traditional monogamy – 'forsaking all others'. For others, however, as we saw earlier, the really important commitments were emotional, with sexual monogamy a matter of negotiation rather than prescription (Heaphy *et al*. 2004).

Beck and Beck-Gernsheim (1995: 1–2) argue that in the new era of choice love becomes an essential integrating glue. 'For individuals who have to invent or find their own social settings, love becomes the central pivot giving meaning to their lives' (1995: 170). As we noted in *Same Sex Intimacies* (Weeks *et al*. 2001: 70–1), British lesbians and gays seem to be less open than, for example, their American sisters and brothers in using the language of love as a legitimizing or authenticizing value (cf. Lewin 1998: ch. 6). 'I just couldn't get the words out about love', says Keith. 'I choked. But I suppose I meant them all the same.' But though ideas of eternal, romantic love tend to be absent from narratives of relationships, a quieter version is implicit. In its broadest sense it embraces a range of emotions, including care, responsibility, respect and mutual knowledge – 'mutual recognition between equal subjects, and an awareness of the necessity, yet delicacy, of reciprocal relationships' (Weeks *et al*. 2001; 124; see also Weeks 1995). We can compare this with Giddens' (1992) notion of confluent love, an 'active, contingent love' which jars with eternal, once-and-for-all notions of love, but is also without the highly gendered and power-ridden implications of high romance. 'Confluent love presumes equality in emotional give and take, and . . . only develops to the degree to which each partner is prepared to reveal concerns and needs to the other and to be vulnerable to the other' (Giddens 1992: 62). This has its own passion. John commented,

> 'Unlike Prince Charles, I do know what love is, but I never
> trusted the fairy tale princess version. It didn't quite fit my
> experience as a gay man first coming out in the sixties, and
> then experiencing gay liberation. But getting married for me
> was an act of love. I've never felt more open and free than in
> declaring my love in that ceremony, and I feel quite weepy
> in just saying this now.'

Affirming commitment and love in the civil partnership is usually an intensely private experience – often those who I interviewed had held a very private ceremony, sometimes with the barest minimum of formal activity above signing the register (Shipman and Smart (2007) found the same). But it had a necessary public resonance, which in the end was the real purpose of the event: public recognition of a private transaction, but also public recognition of LGBT citizenship. Meg felt 'a bit embarrassed I suppose, after all those years of going on about the iniquities of marriage. And at my age every one knows I'm a dyke, so we didn't make any sort of fuss at all'. But for Martin the fuss was important. 'We deliberately didn't ask our families, we wanted it to be just us and a couple of our closest friends. But when we told our parents they were, like, why didn't you tell us before, so we could have come down'.

The stories of same-sex unions suggest very clearly the importance of public affirmation. For some it 'was like a second coming out', as John put it. Not simply a declaration of one's gayness, but an affirmation of one's most intimate commitments, and for some this was as challenging as the first moves out of the closet (Shipman and Smart 2007). Janet, now in her late thirties, admitted that in some ways she found it even more difficult than when she first came out:

> I sort of popped out when I was 16, and had this thing for a girl
> down the street. In a mad explosion in the head I told my mother
> and father I was a lesbian. They were a bit taken aback, to say
> the least, and my dad said, basically, we love you but keep it to
> yourself. I have for twenty years or so now. They've always
> known I was still gay, and they've met most of my girlfriends,
> but nothing was said. Now that Bren and I are getting married,
> no secret love any more! We've invited them to the do – and
> they're coming. So we'll wait and see what happens.

Here, getting married is another fateful moment which disorders previous life narratives, and requires new scripts, a reshaped life story and new possibilities.

Recognition by families and friends is one thing. But recognition has a wider resonance, as Charles Taylor especially has discussed in the context of a multicultural society (1992a, 1992b; see also Plummer 2003: 111). A muted tolerance of homosexuality does not necessarily entail acceptance, while simply to laud choice and to say that being lesbian or gay is no more important than the colour of one's hair, that it is just one lifestyle among others in the hypermarket of contemporary consumerism, is subtly to downgrade the purpose of LGBT politics, which is to affirm the significance and equal worth of the homosexual choice, and the often difficult paths needed to gain recognition for that (Taylor 1992a, 1992b: 37; Weeks 1995: 63–4). The denial of legal rights for same-sex unions may be seen, in Nancy Fraser's famous phrase, as one of the 'injustices of recognition' that mark contemporary society (Fraser 1997; see also Adkins 2002: 27ff.). The bringing of LGBT people into full citizenship is therefore not a trivial act. In the end, if it is to mean anything, it must also entail confronting the forces that have inhibited full recognition. The goal of legitimizing civil partnerships or same-sex marriages, I suggest, is better seen as a form of struggle for recognition than a ruse of power. They are, of course, legally binding commitments, and inevitably that must have an implication for wider norms and values. Whether the impact of this is, in Yep *et al.*'s (2003) categorization, assimilationist or radical will depend ultimately on the degree to which the practice of same-sex unions can transform both the normative meanings of marriage, and everyday practices of LGBT people themselves. But within a very short time in the LGBT community within the UK, as elsewhere, civil partnerships are rapidly becoming normalized as one option among others: not the only or necessary choice, but a new possibility among many. As Yvette, one of Shipman and Smart's interviewees put it, 'surely that is what it is all for, so that you can lead an ordinary life on a par with everybody else'. The very ordinariness of recognized same-sex unions in a culture which until recently cast homosexuality into secret corners and dark whispers is surely the most extraordinary achievement of all.

8

Sexual wrongs and sexual rights
Globalization and the search for justice

When we start putting all these global changes together, we can come up with starkly different scenarios of the future . . . From a utopian perspective, the world is becoming more democratic. Intimacies are guided by an overarching ethic of equality, and there is greater openness and acceptance of differences. According to the dystopian view, however, the world is becoming ever more brutal.

(Plummer 2003: 126)

While the spread of global capitalism has exacerbated social inequalities, fragmented families, and severed individuals from traditional social ties, it has also given rise to transnational feminist activism, a burgeoning lesbian–gay–bisexual–transgender–queer (LGBTQ) movement, a renewed commitment to international human rights, and myriad new forms of eroticism and community.

(Bernstein and Schaffner 2005: xi)

Having the right to say no to unwanted sexual and/or romantic overtures, and the liberty to form a sexual and/or emotional relationship (however fleeting or long lasting) with a willing partner are utterly central ingredients to our ability to live dignified and meaningful lives.

(Bamforth 2005: 12)

But what does it mean to respect the dignity of a human being?

(Nussbaum 1999: 5)

Let us face it. We are undone by each other.

(Butler 2005: 51)

Global connections

I began this book by emphasizing that we live in a world of connections and live connected lives. I want to conclude it by exploring some of the implications of those connections for questions of sexual rights and sexual justice. Connected lives are both global and local. What happens in far distant parts of the world can affect us, wherever we are. The horrors of war bring this home to us in a spectacular way. In mid-2006 I was drawn to a newspaper headline: 'Gays flee Iraq as Shia death squads find a new target' (Copestake 2006: 31). In the years following the US-led invasion of Iraq in 2003, many forces were unleashed, some hopeful and democratic, others dark, violent and authoritarian. The forces of radical Shia-ism, long held in restraint within Iraq but now part of a wave of transnational Islamic revivalism, are finding an object for their fervour and urge for certainty and meaning, in targeting the 'immorals': in this case men suspected of being homosexual, and children who have been sold to criminal gangs for same-sex prostitution. Eleven-year-old Ameer Hasoon was kidnapped by policemen from the front of his house. His father found him three days later, shot in the head. In another case the mutilated, burnt body of 38-year-old Kara Oda was found following his kidnapping by the Badr Brigade, the armed wing of the Supreme Council of Islamic Revolution in Iraq. Kara Oda's family were given an arrest warrant signed by the Ministry of the Interior, which said that their son deserved to be arrested and killed for immorality. Homosexuality is apparently seen by Shia fundamentalists as so immoral that it qualifies as an honour killing to murder someone who is believed to be homosexual, and the murderers believe they can find sanction in the new Iraqi penal code which offers protection from murder charges when the victims are acting against Islam.

Such horrors are part of a wave of homophobic violence across the world, which may reflect a wider increase of conservative sexual moralities operating in both familiar and new ways (Hemmings et al. 2006: 1), and which must be set in the balance against the real gains in some more privileged and wealthy parts of the world that I have documented thus far. Across large parts of Africa and the Caribbean homosexuality has been denounced by post-colonial régimes as a Western import and imposition (Phillips 2000, 2003; Alexander 2003). Lesbian and gay people who try to form or join organizations are being violently persecuted in Uganda, Zambia, Zimbabwe and Jamaica. Transgender people are being murdered in the streets of some Latin American countries, with Argentina, Brazil and Venezuela having particularly bad records, but also evident elsewhere (Baird 2004: 8). Researchers have seen violence against bisexuals, gays and lesbians in Mexico as deeply rooted, especially when associated with transgressive gender behaviour (Ortiz-Hernandez and Granados-Cosme 2006). But this is not simply a problem of the global South. In post-Soviet Russia the formal legalization of homosexuality has not changed the attitudes of conservative moral forces, and attempts to hold a gay pride rally in early 2006 were met by vitriolic opposition from Russian Orthodox, Muslim and Jewish leaders. The Chief Mufti proposed that those who came out on to the streets should be flogged. An Orthodox bishop likened homosexuality to leprosy, while extreme nation-alists attacked a gay club, chanting, 'Death to pederasts' and 'Russia for Russians' (McLauglin 2006: 40). Even in the European Union ostensible heartland of the new liberalism, anti-homosexual feelings swept across the new accession countries, with a Catholic fundamentalist régime in Poland led by the Kaczynski twins being denounced by Human Rights Watch as presiding over 'official homophobia' (Page 2006: 43).

These are just random examples of one strand of what I am going to call 'sexual wrongs', but are sufficient to temper any easy optimism generated by the world we have won. Characteristically, declarations of conservative sexual morality are targeted particularly at women and sexual minorities, often to police the boundaries of nation or faith, and of gender and heterosexuality. A case of gang rape by fourteen Muslim men in Sydney, Australia of an 18-year-old woman led the Mufti of Australia, Sheikh Taj Aldin al-Hilali, to comment:

> If you take uncovered meat and place it outside . . . and the cats
> come to eat it . . . whose fault is it, the cats' or the uncovered
> meat's? The uncovered meat is the problem. If she was in her
> room, in her home, in her hijab, no problem would have occurred.
> (cited in Sieghart 2006: 7)

Women's autonomy is experienced both as a shock and a perennial temp-tation to male sexual needs, and beyond that, to gendered identities (Anthias and Yuval Davis 1992). Everyday practices of subordination, from compulsory wearing of the veil through domestic confinement to cliterodectomy, stoning for adultery, and the easy acceptance of violence against women keep them in line, maintaining the integrity of gender difference. In a similar way, the global circulation of the idea of non-heterosexual, non-familial life choices as essentially Western operates to keep people in post-colonial societies in line (Hemmings et al. 2006: 2). The 'persecution of people because of their sexual orientation' is, Bishop Desmond Tutu has written, every bit as immoral as that acknowledged crime against humanity, apartheid. To oppose it is a 'matter of ordinary justice' (Tutu 2004: 5; Baird 2004). But ordinary justice is what is so often lacking when questions of sexuality and intimacy come to the fore, and the fears, anxieties, threats and risk are compounded when the local feeds into the global, and the global in turn feeds back into the local.

Sexuality, like every other human and social experience, is subject to the forces of globalization, which are bringing into contestation and confrontation different beliefs and assumptions, and in the process are reshaping the context and meanings of intimacy and the erotic. 'What we now call intimacy, and its importance in personal relations,' Giddens (1994: 95) argues, 'has been largely created by globalizing influences.'

Detraditionalizing and individualizing processes have made possible, as we have seen, a variety of life patterns which combine opportunity and risk, pleasure and danger, greater freedoms and new inequities. To take just one example, in a country in many ways at the crossroads of a globalizing world, China provides a case study of the implications of rapid sexual transformation (Watts 2005). The conservatism of the 'Cultural Revolution' of the 1960s and early 1970s, where men and women were frequently segregated, and overt sexuality in dress or action was vigorously condemned, is melting under the impact of a new affluence and gradual liberalization, especially in the cities (Evans 2003). A survey by the Family Planning Agency found that almost 70 per cent of Chinese had sex before marriage, compared to 16 per cent in the early 1980s. Prostitution, famously prevalent in the pre-communist era but condemned under Mao, has again become big business. Lesbian and gay bars now exist in larger cities. The first 'adult health retailer', selling sex toys, opened in Beijing in 1993. Now there are 2000 such shops in the capital alone. Meng Yu, manager of the G Shop sex shop in Shenzen is quoted as saying, 'I feel my business is standing on the frontlines of a sexual revolution. I believe all adults have the same right to enjoy sexual pleasure. There should be no difference between the orient and the west on this point.' But it has its downside:

> At the Shaki factory, there is no excited talk about sexual
> revolution, nor even the slightest titillation or shocked
> giggles. The workers labour in near silence for eight hours a
> day for £50–£66 per month, knocking out so many cheap thrills
> for the world that they become numb to what they are doing.
> (Watts 2005: 20)

Across the newly industrializing countries and what used to be called the developing world we see similar patterns of rapid sexual transformations and new patterns of exploitation, which are in large part determined by Western needs and desires in the global marketplace.

A globalized world is one in which Western norms, values, behaviours and categorizations of sexuality increasingly interact and interpenetrate with, and are challenged by, the often very different ones operating in other sexual cultures, and in which new patterns emerging worldwide – whether being universalized or asserted in opposition to one another – are increasingly interconnected across cultures, and are bound up with the global circulation of both sexual goods and services, and differences and inequalities. Sexuality has a 'central significance within global régimes of power' as Hemmings et al. (2006:1) argues, and this is manifest in persistent inequities between cultures, and in continuing sexual injustices, especially against women, children and lesbian, gay or transgendered identified peoples. At the same time, we see the emergence of global standards of what constitutes justice. We can learn to accept difference and human variety, various ways of being sexual, and this has become a new imperative as we get to know more and more about other cultures. We can understand the power differentials that underpin difference. But increasingly, in a world not just of different but of conflicting values, many people are also seeking common standards by which to measure, and even judge, behaviours and values to avoid a hopeless, pluralist swamp. In the process, new human sexual values and rights are emerging.

What is happening to gays in Iraq matters to us not simply because we can see one set of values in conflict with another, but because we know what is happening is wrong, wrong not simply by the standards of Western liberalism and possible post-colonial paternalism, but wrong by emerging values of human solidarity. We have become aware of sufferings across the world where 'before they might have gone unnoticed' (Baird 2004: 8). We can no longer easily fail to notice when the survivors of injustices can tell us of their sufferings across the globalized media, from the internet to television, and when waves of people begin to appear at our own doorsteps, seeking refuge from persecution. The Shia threat, for example, 'has led to a rapid increase in the numbers of Iraqi homosexuals now seeking asylum in the UK because it has become impossible for them to live safely in their own country' (Copestake 2006: 31). Globalization has made us aware of sexual wrongs across the world, has swept us up in global flows, and has awakened us to the significance of sexual rights. As Giddens (1994: 97) writes, 'A world where no-one is "outside" is one where pre-existing traditions cannot avoid contact not only with others but also with many alternative ways of life . . . The point is not only that the other "answers back", but that mutual interrogation is possible' – if often also impossibly difficult.

Globalizing the sexual

Globalization is not new in the field of sexuality any more than it is in wider economic and cultural relations. Peter Laslett (1965: 4) notes in *The World We Have Lost* that the 'England of the Tudors and Stuarts already knew of social structures and sexual arrangements, existing in the newly discovered world which were alarmingly different from their own'. The conquests and exploitation of the 'new lands' to the west and the east since the sixteenth century in many ways established abiding beliefs and stereotypes about the other which have been constitutive in the shaping of European gendered subjectivities. Perhaps, suggests Connell (2003: 49), 'the first group who became defined as a recognizable "masculine" cultural type, in the modern sense, were the conquistadors'. Displaced from customary social relationships, engaged in routine acts of violence, to a large extent out of control of imperial authority, they defined a rough masculinity in direct opposition to the colonized other. This had a long resonance. An 'implicit racial grammar', Stoler (1995: 12) argues, underpinned the emerging bourgeois culture of the West from the start, and was crucial from the sixteenth to the nineteenth century in shaping a sense of (respectable) selfhood, and in defining boundaries between virtue and vice, respectable and unrespectable, Western and non-Western behaviour. Images of Asian men as both corrupting and effeminate, and of Asian women as passive and submissive, have persisted in orientalist discourse, as have the more aggressive portrait of African (and subsequently American slave) male hypersexuality and female immorality (Anthias and Yuval-Davis 1992).

The dubious other marked the limits and shaped the norms, and these were embodied in the anthropological texts that increasingly portrayed the diversity of sexual lives. From the 'sodatic zones', where homoerotic activity was believed to be rife, described by the explorer Richard Burton, to the twentieth century ethnographies of Westermarck, Malinowski and Mead, the global dimensions of sexual difference have been both described and constituted, feeding the erotic imaginary (Weeks 1985: ch. 5). Globalization has from its earliest days contributed both to the building of ethnic communities and their dissolution through increased opportunities for ethnic intermingling through settlement, tourism, trade and invasion. In this way, suggests Nagel, 'we can think of globalization as an important part of the process whereby race is sexed and sex is raced' (Nagel 2003: 228). But these processes produced resistances that were not only local but increasingly international.

Already in the nineteenth century, inspired in part by the long campaigns to abolish the slave-trade, an international dialogue around sexual wrongs was developing. Josephine Butler, the British feminist campaigner against the state regulation and support of prostitution, founded an international organization to campaign against it (later known as the International Abolitionist Federation) in 1875 (Summers 2006: 216). An international conference on the prevention of sexual trafficking was held in Paris as early as 1885, and the effort to control the 'white slave-trade' became a powerful motif in feminist campaigns against sexual exploitation. In other areas, too, there were attempts to impose new international standards. The Hague Convention of 1907 prohibited rape as an act of war (Altman 2001: 114, 123), a cause, alas, still alive a century later. By the end of the First World War an international discourse was emerging around common sexual issues. Magnus Hirschfeld's World League for Sexual Reform in the 1920s and early 1930s brought together people not only from the industrialized countries in Western Europe and America but also from Asia, Africa and Latin America. The agenda that then developed – for example, over the sexual exploitation of young children, the recognition and rights that should be accorded self-defined homosexuals, the control of sexual disease, liberalizing attitudes to birth control and abortion, marriage and divorce – strikingly resemble the issues that have become central to contemporary debates about globalization and sexuality (Weeks 1990: 139–42). Those early hopes for civilized discourse on sexual reform, in the interests of science and justice, were, however, to die as fascism and then war gripped Europe and the world. Sexuality *per se* was noticeably absent from the new declarations of Universal Human Rights that signalled the birth of the post-war world, despite the ostensible protection of rights to family life and privacy (Petchesky 2000). These were interpreted very narrowly, and in very traditional terms. It was to take the transformations from the 1970s to reawaken concern with sexual wrongs and rights on a global scale.

The context now is a heightened, more extensive and intensified wave of globalization. As Plummer (2003: 116) has noted, 'its precise meaning remains far from clear', and it is a highly contested term, full of ambiguities. At one level it is a neutral term to describe transformations in global interactions as a result of ever increasing economic and social change. But since the 1990s it has also been seen as a transnational political and cultural project which in turn has generated anti-capitalist and anti-globalization movements. It seems most useful to me as an attempt to encapsulate a series of interlinked processes which together are transforming the context and meanings of human interactions at all levels. Following Held *et al.* (2000: 54–5), I would include the following key elements in a general description of globalization. In the first place it may be defined as a *stretching* of social, political, cultural and economic relations across frontiers, so that activities and activities in one part of the globe have a potential impact on individuals and communities in every other part of an interconnected world. It is most obviously linked to the latest phase of capitalist expansion since the 1970s, to post-Fordist economic and social restructuring, to US hegemony and the development of neo-liberal forms of governance, with incalculable effects on personal life.

It implies, second, an *intensification* and growing strength of global interconnectedness, interactions and flows which go beyond the various societies and state forms that make up the world order. This has implications for the role of traditional boundaries between communities, states and international structures, in the solidity of traditional identities and structures (including structures of family life and the gender and sexual order), and for the potential emergence of new transnational identities, organizations and social, cultural and political movements. Third, there is a *speeding up* of global interactions, especially through the development of more rapid and accessible transportation, media and information technologies, and circulation of goods, capital and peoples. What happens in New York, Sydney, London or Istanbul is instantaneously known, and can be replicated in Baghdad, Kabul, Jerusalem or Beijing. Tourism, especially sexual tourism, dissolves barriers but eases new patterns of exploitation. Ways of being hybridize, and cross-national relationships are made easier, though fears of 'swamping' by accelerating migration can lead to new barriers being erected. All this in turn leads to a deepening entanglement of the global and the local so that the *impact* of distant events is hugely increased, while even the most local of events – the sentencing to death of an adulterous women in the Saudi Kingdom or Nigeria, the incidence of AIDS in sub-Saharan Africa – may have huge global implications, and the boundaries between the domestic and the worldwide become ever more blurred.

But while these processes – measured in terms of their extensity, intensity, velocity and impact – affect all parts of the globalizing world, their impact is uneven on individuals, groups, states and regions of the world, because they are enmeshed in huge disparities of power and gross inequalities. As Povinelli and Chauncey (1999: 442) comment, 'The range and speed of an object's (or a subject's) circulation depend on a variety of institutionally mediated power relations.' Members of new global élites have more in common with each other than with the poor in their own nation-states. People with the latest hi-tech gadgets rub shoulders with people who have nothing. The new technologies may create new forms of inequality, new desires, wants and needs, while people lose the comforts of their lost worlds, and are forced, defenceless or ill-equipped, into a global marketplace. Structural readjustment policies endorsed by the International Monetary Fund (IMF) and the World Bank and Western governments have huge unintended consequences on patterns of everyday life in some of the most disadvantaged countries of the world. Globalization, Altman suggests, does not abolish difference so much as redistribute it: styles, consumer patterns and identities are internationalized while class divides, often across national boundaries, are strengthened and solidified (Altman 2001: 21). At the same time, global perspectives produce new opportunities for transcending the limits and restrictions of tradition, offering a new imaginary of transnational and cosmopolitan minglings. Sexuality is a vital aspect of this new phase of globalization. What is different from earlier patterns of global connecting is a far denser and faster system for diffusing ideas, values and perceptions, 'so that a certain self-consciousness about and understanding of sexuality is arguably being universalised in a completely new way' (Altman 2001: 38). It has become necessary to think globally in order to understand social change and its impact on issues of sexuality (Waites 2005a: 40–1).

The world of sexuality is being transformed by global connections and flows. I list below some obvious ones:

- Flows of men and women leaving their traditional homes seeking work and new opportunities, moving from country to towns and cities (for example, in China and Africa as part of what is probably the largest migration of peoples in human history), from country to country (from the global South to the affluent West), and even within the West (from the former Soviet bloc to Britain and Ireland). The separation of men from their families, the involvement of some women and men in the global sex trade (O'Connell Davidson 1998), the possibility of HIV infection and transmission, vast numbers of orphaned children – all these disrupt settled family and sexual patterns and open the way to new opportunities and forms of exploitation.

- Flows of war, with soldiers crossing countries, causing disruption, committing sexual abuses and rape, and possibly transmitting STIs; people fleeing war and extreme violence; the disruption of families, economies, cultures; 'the intimate violence' of genocides and civil wars (Bourke 2000).
- Flows of people escaping from persecution for their sexualities (Bamforth 2005), or seeking access to reproductive choice. Altman reminds us of women seeking abortion by travelling from Ireland to the UK, from Eastern Europe to the Netherlands, or fleeing strict abortion policies in China (Altman 2001: 42).
- Flows of sexually transmitted infections, including HIV, of community-based organizations to combat them, and of international mobilization (Altman 2001).
- Flows of pornography and sexually explicit materials in a multi-billion-dollar global industry, with the 'pornographication' of the mainstream and the expansion of the 'pornosphere' (Attwood 2006: 82).
- Flows of drugs with erotic connotations, both illicit (marihuana, cocaine, ketamine) and licit (Viagra, Cialis).
- Flows of tourism, transforming economies, transporting millions to once exotic and mysterious foreign places, and the explosion especially of sex tourism (O'Connell Davidson and Sanchez Taylor 2005).
- Flows of media that make sexual information, news, gossip, styles, scandals, personalities, stereotypes, role models, personal dramas, legal changes, reactionary pronouncements, crimes and misdemeanours instantly and simultaneously known everywhere.
- Flows of popular culture: in films, television, games, music, the internet (blogs, chat rooms, audio and video downloads and uploads).
- Flows of consumption, of everything from clothes and gadgets to sex toys. China now supplies 70 per cent of all 'adult toys' across the world (Watts 2005).
- Flows of religion, and their associated moralities, especially of neo-traditionalist or fundamentalist colour (Bhatt 1997; Ruthven 2004).
- Flows of sexual stories that circulate sexual secrets and confessions, desires, practices, hopes, fears, identities and aspirations, and through their interaction shape new meanings, communities and possibilities (Plummer 1995, 2003).
- Flows of science that try to interpret and categorize the sexual world, and increasingly to remake it via new technologies, especially reproductive techniques (Lancaster 2003).
- Flows of social movements, such as global feminist and lesbian, gay and transgender movements (Threlfal 1996; Adam *et al.* 1999a).
- Flows of identities and ways of being, and especially the globalization of lesbian and gay and transgendered subjectivities, networks of people living with HIV, sado-masochists, sex workers, paedophiles and the like: positive, negative, life-enhancing, abusive, all offering

forms of subjectivity and self-realization that can shift the terms of being sexual.

- Flows of concern about children – their exploitation, their protection, their rights – and flows of children themselves, through displacement, migration, adoption and sale (O'Connell Davidson 2005; Waites 2005b: 40–59).
- Flows of campaigns, from NGOs, international agencies, lobby groups, grass-roots organizations, on everything from sexual abuse to sexual infections.
- Flows of conferences, seminars, academics, activists, experts, medics, psychologists, therapists, all adding to the flow of words, the proliferation of stories, the shaping of discourses and new subjectivities.
- Flows of sport, including the Gay Games and from 2006 the Outgames as well.
- Flows of literature: ancient, contemporary, Mandarin, populist, pornographic, educational, instructional, academic, scientific, religious, moralistic, scandalous, titivating, biographical, historical, political – in millions of books, magazines, journals, pamphlets, in print, online.
- Flows through cyberspace – in ways already too vast to enumerate and list.
- Flows of reproductive necessities, to prevent and promote births: the Pill, condoms, sperm, donated eggs, adoption, surrogacy.
- Flows of regulation: on the exploitation of children, marriage rights, sex work, crimes, sexual health, medicines, drugs, pornography, internet posting or downloading. National boundaries can no longer contain the flows; but nor do international agencies know much better how to control the protean world that contemporary sexualities now occupy.
- Flows of discourse around rights: human sexual rights, reproductive rights, relational rights, love rights (Petchesky 2000).
- Flows of transnational friendship and relationships. Living apart together is no longer about living in different cities in one country. It is a transnational phenomenon, ranging from partners kept apart by restrictive and suspicious immigration rules to couples united by jumbo jets. Then there are the diasporic flows, as younger people mainly (but not exclusively) migrate across the globe in search of pleasures, partners, employment, wealth, freedoms, justice, home (Patton and Sanchez-Eppler 2000).
- And then there are flows of mourning. By 1999 the annual candlelight memorial to remember those who had died from AIDS, started in 1983, had participants in fifty countries (Altman 2001: 83) – a reminder of the costs as well as the gains, the agonies as well as the joys of global connectedness.

Sexual wrongs

These massive flows, these dense connections across distance and difference, this tangled mass of opportunities and threats, create the context in which sexual norms and values are being rewritten, new knowledges created and new self-perceptions generated. But they also highlight sexual injustice, sexual wrongs. Some of these are the results of prejudice, deliberate discrimination, historically loaded oppressions. Others are not intentional or anticipated, certainly not planned, but the inevitable consequences of other injustices. I want to look in a little more detail here at some of the most significant intersections, especially as they reveal what Altman (2001) calls the 'political economy' of 'global sex'. Take the impact of the forbiddingly titled 'Structural adjustment programmes'.

From the 1980s structural adjustment programmes were enforced on debtor countries in the 'developing world' by the IMF and the World Bank as a condition of continued financial support. In essence these amounted to a thorough liberalization of the local economy through the ending of subsidies, abolishing import controls, floating their currencies, and balancing the budgets, largely achieved by savage cutbacks in welfare budgets – health, education and other social services. These cuts inevitably had a massive impact on the poorest, with women and children particularly affected, with often devastating effects. The international agencies, backed by leading Western governments, ignored the unpaid labour of women, and their role in upholding everyday life. Okin (2005), for example, has suggested that the cutting back on educational opportunities for women has had a major impact on population policies, inhibiting women's opportunities to control their own fertility. Similarly, cutbacks in health spending have not helped in the efforts to curb the spread of HIV/AIDS in sub-Saharan Africa. 'It may be hard to believe,' Okin (2005:115) argues,

> but for two crucial decades at the close of the twentieth century, the world's chief financial institutions were not just advocating but forcing on the less developed world policies that increased women's work, facilitated the spread of AIDS, and reduced the chances of population control.

Economic restructuring, whether through external imposition or the search for new markets, has had often drastic effects on delicate local sexual cultures. Tourism has had a major impact here. Many countries have adopted active policies to encourage not only Western tourism but sexual tourism, helping in the process to create what O'Connell Davidson and Sanchez Taylor (2005: 84) have called 'sexual Disneylands'. In these, Western (usually male) punters can explore their fantasies to the limits of their imaginations and pockets, and distance themselves from their discontents with contemporary civilization (see also Seabrook 2001). This is both a heterosexual and a queer phenomenon (see *GLQ* 2002), though with different implications. O'Connell Davidson (2001) has explored the discourse of male heterosexual tourists in the Dominican Republic, and finds that their desire for the other is less a wish to love them for themselves but rather to proclaim what they feel they have lost: a certain form of male privilege. In contrast, 'In the third world, even the "third rate" American or European tourist is king or queen' (O'Connell Davidson and Sanchez Taylor 2005: 87). The early stages of the Thai economic miracle were fuelled by its role as a 'rest and recuperation' centre for US troops in the Vietnam War, and whatever the formal government policy now, easy sex has become a major element in Thailand's allure (see Renton 2005). But it is not just so-called developing countries that welcome the sex tourist. Manchester and London in the UK have both focused on the gay positive attractions of their cities. European cities such as Amsterdam have long been magnets for sex tourists, with others such as Rome and Madrid (and other attractions such as Lesbos) rapidly following suit (Whittle 1994; Giorgi 2002; Kantsa 2002; Luongo 2002).

Sex tourism, despite its bad name, is not necessarily exploitative, but it can potentially unbalance fragile economies, with complex impacts on local populations. Alexander (1991: 63–100; 2003: 180) has analysed the way in which the Bahamas has restructured its own economy as a service economy, with a large part of its capital invested now in the tourist industry (hotels, airlines, services and tour operators, international finance capital, real estate). She asks, 'How does one prepare citizens for self determination by depending on its antithesis – tourism – the practice of servility and serviceability, the production of maids, washers, cooks . . . Difference is exotically and fleetingly adopted' (Alexander 2003:181). Such difference remains predicated on huge disparities of power and opportunity, and in these circumstances the formal tourist economy slips easily into a more informal, sexualized economy, involving not just women servicing men, but men servicing women (Sanchez Taylor 2006: 43).

Lesbian and gay tourism has generally been seen as more progressive, challenging colonial patterns and striving for new forms of identification across distance. Yet there has been an insistent note of sexual colonialism throughout modern gay history (see Weeks 1990) and recent writers have seen a continuing trend (Binnie 2004: 86–104) in which the entitlement to travel, and to resist homophobic pressures has to be balanced by an ethical concern for the local cultures which have become desirable destinations. Some indigenous pro-gay organizations, as in Hawaii, have questioned 'the "hidden" or "unnoticed" violence of tourism', which depends on low-waged labour which exploits many workers, especially women and young people, and which in the long run displaces poor peoples from their own lands and neighbourhoods (AFSC 2002: 211). Even the internationally famous Sydney Mardi Gras has been challenged for its marginalization of working-class gays and lesbians, people of colour, and of bisexuals, transgendered people and queers (Markwell 2002: 81–100).

The sexual exploitation of children and young people has been a particular object of international concern. An important signal of this has been the emergence of the acronym 'CSEC' – the Commercial Sexual Exploitation of Children' – to bring together the varying forms of child exploitation, including child prostitution, child pornography and trafficking in children. The new definition was the result of two decades of work, culminating in two World Congresses, in 1996 and 2001. It is based on the belief that childhood is fundamentally different from adulthood, and should be protected from commerce and sexual activity. It produces children as victims of exploitation, and while this has been an advance from the former stigmatizing labels (which as we have seen are having a disastrous effect in Iraq), and has encouraged children to be change-agents, it produces new problems. Saunders (2005: 176) suggests that it flounders when faced with young people who reject the idea that they are victims, and who do not see the harm supposedly done to them in the same way as their NGO advocates. For example, they often reject suggestions that they had been forced into prostitution, preferring analogous language such as 'having guests' or 'meeting with foreigners' (see O'Connell Davidson 2005).

The 'white slave-trade' has always been an evocative image in moral discourse about prostitution, implying an exploitative relationship between client and supplier cultures. 'Trafficking', largely involving children and young adults, usually though not invariably female, has been described as 'a $7 billion a year business' (O'Connell Davidson 2006: 5). No one can doubt that the sex industry can be the site of sometimes extreme forms of exploitation, but the implications are far from clear. At the centre of contemporary debates has been the question of the extent to which prostitutes can consent to a client's sexual command over them. For Kathleen Barry, and the US-based Coalition Against Trafficking of Women with which she has been strongly associated, there can be no doubt that prostitution is exploitation, and therefore a violation of the human right to dignity, whether a prostitute has consented or not. There can be no distinction between forced and free prostitution, only 'sex slavery'. This position has had a major impact on the attitudes of NGOs and of many governments. On the other hand, this position has infuriated other feminists who see a sharp distinction between a child forced into prostitution and women who make a choice to enter the sex trade for economic reasons, and who see themselves as 'sex workers' (for a summary see O'Connell Davidson 1998, 2003). Here the challenge is less a moral crusade against prostitution than a struggle against legal systems and hypocritical moral codes that penalize the sex worker (see e.g. Agustin 2005a, 2005b, 2007). This in turn has produced international movements of sex workers. An international Committee for Prostitutes' Rights was founded in the 1970s by the US-based COYOTE group (Call Off Your Tired Old Ethics) and the English Collective of Prostitutes, with the first world meeting held in Washington in 1975. At the Second World Whores' Congress held in Brussels in 1986 delegates demanded that prostitution 'should be redefined as legitimate work and the prostitutes should be redefined as legitimate citizens' (Altman 2001: 101). Defining the conditions under which the work can be legitimized has, however, proved more difficult. The Trafficking Victims Protection Act passed in the USA in 2000 gives protection to victims of trafficking (VoT) but relies heavily on a distinction between victims and 'guilty' sex workers, a distinction which has had a wide currency (O'Connell Davidson 2006: 14–15), including in the UK. Such distinctions do nothing to protect those deemed to be guilty.

The distinction between innocent and guilty victims is one that has also coloured responses to the AIDS pandemic, and underlines the deep ambiguities and anxieties that have dogged its history since the 1980s. As the first new global health crisis in the age of heightened globalization, both the spread of the syndrome, the variety of moral, cultural and social responses, and the possibility of international mobilization against it, all make AIDS the exemplar of the connections that both bring us together and tear us apart. Linking globalization and AIDS throws new light on the epidemiology of a sex-related set of diseases; on the processes of mobilization which have combated the epidemic on a transnational scale; and on the dominance of certain ways of understanding the epidemic which are gendered, ethnicized and embody certain assumptions about sexuality. AIDS has also sexualized identities, or at least has led to a gradual shift towards conceptualizing sexuality as a central aspect of identity in parts of the world where HIV programmes have played a prominent role. AIDS provides a reminder of the uneven development of societies, of the fragility of political borders, and of the necessity for both international and specific local responses that this engenders (Altman 2001).

It is the sheer size of the pandemic that terrifies and threatens to overwhelm any hope for social justice. By the end of 1985, in the midst of the first panic around AIDS, there were just over 20,000 cases reported. By the end of 2005 there were over 40 million reported cases of HIV infection worldwide, and 25 million people had died, from North America, where the HIV epidemic had been first documented, through Latin America, Europe, to Asia and Africa. Five million new cases had been reported in the previous year alone. There were 14,000 new infections every day, and 8000 deaths. Over eleven million children in sub-Saharan Africa have lost at least one parent to AIDS, projected to reach twenty million by 2010. South Africa, a beacon of hope after the end of apartheid, had more HIV citizens than any other country, over five million out of a population of forty-five million. It was likely that up to half of the population could die of AIDS in some other African countries, though by 2006 there was some evidence that the rate of infection was levelling off on that continent, home to 64 per cent of world cases, largely due to behavioural changes, while increasing elsewhere. At a UN conference in 2006 world leaders were told that the epidemic was spreading rapidly in Asian countries such as China, Indonesia, Papua New Guinea and

Vietnam (*The Economist* 2003: 115–17; Roedy 2005: 2; Bone 2006: 51). AIDS is a truly global disaster, with incalculable consequences.

The potential of international cooperation to combat the epidemic was evident early on, both in the grass-roots, community-based mobilization of forces (Altman 1994, 2001) and at international level, through the World Health Organization programmes from the 1980s, then through UNAIDS. But the response was continually shaped by the inequalities of power across the globe. While, by the end of 2003, 800,000 people with AIDS worldwide were on anti-viral combination therapies, three-fifths of these were in the rich countries, where the epidemic as a result was largely under control. In other countries gross poverty, entrenched sexual moralities (which subordinated women and castigated homosexuality), religious scruples (most notably the refusal of the Roman Catholic Church to contemplate the use of condoms) and in some cases, as in South Africa under Thabo Mbeki, ideological opposition, blocked the easy distribution of the new, potentially life-saving drugs. HIV/AIDS stigma remains a key driver of the epidemic in sub-Saharan Africa, including South Africa, with particular impact on women and children (Campbell *et al.* 2006: 132–8).

The UN conference in 2006 promised to double the money going to combat AIDS, to reach US\$20 to 23 billion by 2010. But the difficulty of reaching a final agreement underlined the continuing differences. The UN Secretary-General Kofi Annan lobbied unsuccessfully for a mention in the final declaration of vulnerable and stigmatized groups, such as sex workers, intravenous drug-users and 'men who have sex with men', but this was blocked by conservative Islamic countries. Female delegates failed to gain any full discussion of the plight of women. The USA lobbied (though unsuccessfully) to limit the references to sex education. And the attempt to set a goal that 80 per cent of people with HIV/AIDS should have access to anti-viral medicines by 2010 was blocked (Bone 2006: 51).

Regulating sex in an age of globalization

These examples of sexual wrongs, heightened by globalization, pose immense questions about regulation, and especially the development of common standards. The regulation of sexuality – its production, categorization, organization, directing, governance – is always overdetermined; that is, it is shaped and reshaped by a variety of forces rather than monocausal (Bernstein and Schaffner 2005). It is in the first place, of course, regulated at a national level, through national legal systems – directly through statute, but also through diffuse and indirect state practices, such as those governing welfare provision, educational practices, housing and planning provision, and immigration policies (Weeks 2003). International regulation of sexuality is less well established, but the pace is increasing in intensity and influence, with sex tourism a particular focus due to the effectiveness of NGO campaigns to protect children (Waites 2005b: 53–4) The result of this has been the widespread enactment of laws which allow for the prosecution of offences committed outside the territorial jurisdiction of a state. The UK government, for example, has introduced legislation which permits prosecutions relating to paedophilia where an action that is illegal in the UK is committed abroad. A 66-year-old retired concert pianist was jailed in 2004 for two years under this law for attempting to commission sexual activity via the internet with a 15-year-old Sri Lankan boy, the first successful prosecution under this act (Cowan 2004: 7).

Increasingly, international or transnational structures are shaping a global discourse with incalculable effects. As we have seen, international organizations such as the IMF and World Bank impose policies that may have dramatic effects on intimate life. NGOs – concerned with children, women, trafficking, HIV/AIDS, LGBT issues, reproductive rights, human rights – develop international campaigns which can focus world attention on sexual issues, and shape national and international strategies. The sheer weight of mobilization is often impressive. Three thousand NGOs were accredited to the 1995 World Conference on Women in Beijing, and 40,000 delegates attended the parallel NGO forum (Altman 2001: 125). Transnational bodies such as the European Union and other European institutions such as the Court of Human Rights are increasingly involved in shaping sexuality, in relation to homosexual or transgender rights, working practices, and the cross-national trade of sexually explicit materials (Bell 1998). The UN has intervened in relation to the role of women and children, and on homosexuality (Hari 2003: 17).

Religious organizations remain powerful players in regulating sexual behaviour and establishing sexual moralities across national boundaries, though they are themselves not immune to the stresses and strains of sexual change. If secularization has been a touchstone for sexual liberalization in Western Europe, in other parts of the world the traditional forces of religion are fighting a fierce rearguard action. The Anglican Community, ostensible conveyer of human compassion and religious moderation, faces a global split due to the fierce hostility to homosexuality in African, as well as some British and American, dioceses (Bates 2004a; see also Nagel 2003: 124). Deep moral conservatism, as we know, is not confined to the global South. The Roman Catholic Church confirms the 'evil' of homosexual practice (Hooper 2005), and sets its face rigidly against more liberal birth control and abortion policies, despite its injunctions being largely ignored in the West. Conflicts over sexuality have, as we have observed previously, become integral to the emergence of fundamentalist politics both within Western societies and elsewhere around the world (Bhatt 1997). The relativization of sexual values that has accompanied the recognition of a plurality of sexualities in Western societies has led to issues of the family, traditional gender relations, sex education and homosexuality becoming central preoccupations of fundamentalist movements. Many of these movements are transnational with identities organized around the great religious faiths such as

Hinduism and Islam that have bridged divisions between the North and the South in global terms. Radical Islamicists are less gripped, perhaps, by the seductions of late modernity than other faiths; on the contrary their moral codes in relation to family, gender and sexual identity are violently reactionary. Yet the flirtation with aspects of modernity are part of the complex mix of contemporary fundamentalism, which thrive precisely on the mobilizing energies of modern technologies and means of communication.

Churches across the world are themselves feeling the effects of detraditionalization and are losing much of their former protection. During 2005 the robustly traditionalist Greek Orthodox Church was buffeted by sex and corruption scandals. A newspaper published photographs of a 91-year-old bishop naked in bed with a young woman. Rampant homosexuality was exposed among senior churchmen. Another leading churchman was accused of drug-dealing in a notorious nightclub. The head of Greece's richest diocese was suspended from his duties following allegations of 'lewd exchanges with young men' and charges that he had embezzled over US$4 million for his old age. For the first time, a majority of the Greek population was prepared to see the full separation of the state from the church, the traditional guarantor of Greek national identity (Smith 2005). This echoed the long-running scandal of the Catholic Church and paedophile priests which has wracked the church across the world, from the USA to Australia, the UK and Ireland. The crisis in the Irish church was particularly dramatic: a church that like the Greek one had been central to national identity during years of colonial dependency, and had imposed the strictest moral standards on its flock, was revealed as riddled with sexual abuse (McKittrick 2002: 13).

The apparently most religious of affluent countries, the USA, has been particularly riven by culture wars that have had international implications – such as the USA opposing population control policies that might endorse abortion – and religious conservatism has been a major factor in foreign as much as domestic policies. But there is a curious set of paradoxes in American religion. While the vast majority of Americans state that religion is important in their lives (60 per cent say very important, 26 per cent say fairly important) this is actually a decline from half a century ago: in 1952 the figures were 75 per cent and 20 per cent. The USA seems more religious in comparison to heavily secularized Europe, and the religious Right is far more important, largely due to the decline of liberal Protestantism, the rise of evangelical fervour among Protestants, their better organization skills, and their new-found common cause with Catholicism in support of social conservatism (*The Economist* 2005: 29–32). Yet at the same time, American behaviour is much less conservative than its moralities, as the number of leading evangelicals caught with their trousers down or secretly embroiled with men underlines. By age 15, only half of American children live with both biological parents, compared with roughly two-thirds of Swedish,

German and French children, and 95 per cent of children in Italy and Spain. And the American states with the highest rates of divorce are precisely those with the most fervent religious Right politics. The Bible Belt divorce rate is about 50 per cent higher than the national average. Nearly a quarter of married born-again Christians have been divorced twice or more. Even more striking: America has one of the highest rates of teenage pregnancy in the Western world, and three times as many abortions per 1000 women as the notoriously liberal Dutch (Sullivan 2004). Perhaps it is precisely the regular encounter with 'sin' that feeds religious fervour. Perhaps there is another explanation. Alan Wolfe (2004: 57) has suggested that the religion of the American Right is less about wrestling with the soul than with individual salvation and well-being: 'America's conservative Christians are as American as they are Christian and conservative . . . If they have to choose between old-time religion and the seductions of modernity, they are more likely to opt for the latter.' The privatization of morality seems to be racing ahead even in the most religious and moralistic of Western societies.

These tensions between tradition and modernity, national charac-teristics and global trends, secular and religious values, individual aspirations towards greater freedom and collective pressures towards conformity and social discipline, are characteristic of contemporary sexual régimes, and bedevil attempts at global regulation. Globalization has accentuated the conflicts of values that always live alongside, and shape, the erotic. None of us can finally escape taking a stand.

Cosmopolitan possibilities and human sexual rights

The myriad forces now in play in a globalizing culture – international organizations, the new global players in NGOs, the cross-national move-ments, the traditional universalisms of various faiths, the new fervour of fundamentalist movements, the culture wars in the world superpower flowing into the rest of the world – all pose once again, but now on a global scale, the fundamental question posed by living in a complex, diverse world: how to find agreed common standards by which to measure indi-vidual and particularist needs and to find ways of living harmoniously with difference. This is, for Beck (1999: chs 1 and 2, 2002), the challenge that the cosmopolitan perspective can meet by offering 'an alternative imagination, an imagination of alternative ways of life and rationality, which includes the otherness of the other' (Beck 2002: 18). This implies a breakaway from a perspective that freezes and reifies different cultures, identities and ways of being, and that welcomes the conviviality of intermingling. The cosmopolitan citizen is someone who is capable of working across different national traditions, communities of fate and alternative ways of life, and of engaging in dialogue with the discourses of others in order to expand the horizons of meanings that trap us in our own prejudices, anxieties and fears (Held 2000: 425). But these near utopian hopes have to confront the harsh realities of continuing and in some contexts accentuating disparities of power, and the difficulties of living them amidst complex multicultural and multi-faith societies. There is no consensus about ways forward, even among key progressive theorists – for example, see Gilroy's (2004) scepticism concerning contemporary cosmopolitan claims, compared with the more optimistic position adopted by McGhee (2005: 163–85), both in the British context.

That is not to say, however, that there is no point in trying. Cosmopolitan citizenship has its pioneers in the new sexual subjects that have moved on to the stage of history since the 1970s. Among these the 'global gay' (Altman 2001) shows the potential and the difficulties, the challenge and the opportunities. He or she can potentially feel at home in all parts of the world where a similar repertoire of cafés, bars, clubs, saunas, cruising areas, local neighbourhoods, styles of dress, modes of behaviour provide the material base for a 'queer cosmopolitanism' (Binnie 2004: 126 ff.), an ability and willingness to engage with others and to develop a sense of common being. Globalization has helped create an international lesbian and gay identity which goes beyond the boundaries of the West (Altman 2001: 86ff.). Yet this very Western notion of what it is to be gay or lesbian is ever refracted through different ways of living homosexuality and gender. As Patton and Sanchez-Eppler (2000: 3) comment in their collection on 'queer diasporas':

> 'being' gay, homosexual, lesbian, joto, internacional, tortillera, like that, battyman, bakla, katoi, butch, et cetera, entails answering or not answering to those terms and the desires they purport to index, in a given place, for a given duration. When a practitioner of 'homosexual acts', or a body that carries any of many queering marks moves between officially designated spaces – nation, region, metropole, neighbourhood, or even culture, gender, religion, disease – intricate realignments of identity, politics, and desire take place.

Globalization has produced the opportunity for recognition across distance, and for the development of elements of a common life and common cause. But it has also exposed the particularities, the specifics, of lived experience, the 'intricate realignments' that determine the local identifications and distancing, the constant making and remaking of subjectivities. Similarly, while it is possible and necessary to recognize the common elements of homophobia and enforced normalization that circle the globe, it is also necessary to be sensitive to the different tempos and rhythms of oppression, the different régimes of sexuality that govern individual ways of being. The privileges enjoyed by Western gays provide models and ideals that LGBT people in other parts of the world may envy or aspire to – though it also has to be acknowledged that most of their legal rights are very recent, and that these gains have in part been built on material comfort. Of the nineteen countries with some recognition of same-sex relational rights or 'love rights' in 2003, all were ranked in the top twenty-four OECD countries for GDP per capita (Wintermute 2005: 218). But the Western gay is not seated at the top of an evolutionary tree, the only model of development, and notions of what it is to be sexually different are likely to be radically modified as the 'perverse dynamic' at the heart of so many cultures (Sinfield 2005: 144) confronts the imperatives of global interconnectedness.

Historians and anthropologists have sought to detect patterns of homosexual and cross-gendered interaction on a global scale, and have basically identified three overarching forms which apply largely to men. An intergenerational pattern has been most famously documented by Herdt (1994) among the Sambia of New Guinea, where boy-insemination by an older man is an essential ritual in acquiring manhood. It does not imply lifelong homosexuality; indeed the concept is entirely absent. In various forms it remains common across many parts of the world. The second pattern, of gender inversion, the hijras in India, the bantut in Philippines, the transgendered culture of Latin America (Kulick 1998; *Sexualities* 1998; Johnson 2003; Boyce 2006) sees generally the emergence of something equivalent to a third sex, which often acts to keep the rest of the population pure by becoming the repository of sex work. Again, this does not necessarily imply any notion of homosexuality as a distinct experience. In a modified form it might permit homoerotic activity as long as the main interaction is between an active man and a passive youth or effeminate man, so that the gender is not betrayed or undermined. The third pattern, most common in the West since the 1970s, is the would-be egalitarian model, which assumes a high degree of similarity in terms of status, sexual tastes and choice between peers, with a distinctive identity and complex ways of life.

All of these models today coexist across most cultures, and older, traditional patterns are being weakened through global connections. But the encounter between different cultural manifestations of male-to-male or female-to-female relations provides new forms and patterns. Mark Johnson (2003) notes how in the Philippines the term 'gay' is being used by bantut, effeminate or transgenderally identified men, to distance themselves from the negative connotations of the old term, but embraces a locally determined range of meanings rather than simply echoing the Western usage. In India, a complex culture of sex between men has evolved which both ignores the hijra and more Western notions of a gay identity, developing only among a more educated and affluent élite, giving rise to a form of sexuality without subjectivity (Seabrook 1999; Boyce 2006). The strength of cultures built around traditional family life, governed by deeply gendered beliefs and practices, inhibits the development of distinctive same sex identities and ways of life, or leads to real tensions between Western and local subjectivities. These require complex negotiations, as in Taiwan and Hong Kong with a deeply embedded confuscianism and a celebration of familial values (Ernie and

Spires 2001: 41; Shiu-Ki 2004), or modern Turkey with a mixture of rapid modernization, embedded Islamic values and cultural conservatism (Bereket and Adam 2006).

But while many differences are being recognized, and in the process helping to dissolve the idea of a single universal lesbian or gay identity, a sense of common being has been encouraged by the growing awareness of various forms of discrimination against same-sex and transgendered activities (Graupner 2005; Graupner and Tahmindjis 2005). The promotion of positive LGBT identities has been taken up by organizations such as the International Gay and Lesbian Association (ILGA), the International Gay and Lesbian Human Rights Commission (IGLHRC), ACT-UP, and transgender groupings such as the International Gender Transient Affinity and Gender Freedom International, and the International Foundation for Gender Organization (IFGE). Implicit in this cross-national mobilization is the awareness that cosmopolitan aspirations are meaningless without the achievement of widely recognized rights.

The work of these international organizations has been crucial in shaping LGBT rights as human rights, and in putting them on the global agenda. The UN Commission on Human Rights' call in 2003 upon all states 'to promote and protect the human rights of all persons regardless of their sexual orientation' (Hari 2003:17) was a major breakthrough, long fought for. The intervention of other NGOs alongside LGBT organizations was also very important. Two reports in the early 2000s made a major impact. Amnesty International's *Breaking the Silence* (1997) examined the various ways in which individuals can be targeted for their sexual orientation – real or alleged – and how a rights framework can be developed. A further report, *Crimes of Hate, Conspiracy of Silence: Torture and Ill-treatment based on Sexual Identity* (2001a) provided further detail.

These are part of a growing agenda concerned with human sexual rights more broadly that are transforming the global debate. Two further reports by Amnesty International, *Broken Bodies, Shattered Minds: Torture and Ill-treatment of Women* (2001b) and *It's in Our Hands: Stop Violence Against Women* (2004) explored the position of women. These built on the work of grass-roots women's organizations across the globe which have documented women's experience, with 'autobiographical documentary' playing an enormous role in bringing that experience to a wider audience (Okin 2005: 84–5). The reports and experiential accounts document an endless stream of stories of violence and abuse, ranging from harassment, enforced female circumcision, forced marriages to rape and murder. Bamforth (2005: 3–10) has observed five commonalities. First, the acts of violence they highlight are intimately related to social conceptions of gender and appropriate gender roles. This involves the denial of basic human rights to individuals simply because they are women, and often extreme violence to LGBT people and women when they are seen to infringe locally enforced norms. Second, the violence inflicted on minorities and women itself has strongly sexual dimensions – notably in the high incidence of rape. Third, these actions are often justified by reference to local religious or cultural factors. Fourth, many of the laws in countries where violence and abuse of human rights are rife often play a role in justifying abuse, and state agents, especially the police, often play a part in inflicting violence. Finally, although the role of the state is critical in permitting violence, much of the violence against women and sexual minorities is conducted by private actors, in the home or the locality.

Cosmopolitanism as the ideal of establishing dialogue across chasms of difference and of establishing some sort of democracy in interpersonal as well as political life depends on breaking down the structures that separate people off and inhibit the development of a common framework of rights. And yet struggles over human rights are themselves not unproblematic. A recognition of the human rights of women, for example, does not mean that as yet it is possible to develop a common assumption about what those rights mean in practice, as controversies over the legitimacy of women wearing the veil, enforced or arranged marriages, access to birth control and the like underline. Okin (2005: 84) warns of the dangers in a multiculturalism or cultural relativism that protects different cultures in West and South that discriminate against women. She challenges the claim that women's human rights are 'justifiably limited by the right of people to the protection of their cultures or to the freedom of religious practices' in the name of a developing framework of human rights. Yet others see dangers in imposing what are seen as 'Enlightenment values' on the global South (Rajan 2005). The work on international campaigns about reproductive rights suggests that there is a double push in this global movement around rights: for bodily integrity and the right of women to control their own bodies; but also for challenging wider social, economic and cultural inequalities, without which rights may become meaningless. While a common discourse on reproductive rights is emerging, particularly in the language of international human rights, the meanings vary across different societies, dependent on different traditions, circumstances and relations of power (see e.g. Petchesky and Judd 1998).

This is true of all claims to specific rights as well as ambitious assertions of universalistic or human sexual rights. If sexual cultures are multifarious and have specific historical formations, how do we distinguish those claims to right that have a universal resonance, and those which are highly culturally specific – and possibly distasteful to large numbers of citizens around the globe? One answer lies in the necessary realization that human rights do not exist in nature. They are not there to be discovered written on tablets of stone. They have to be invented, in complex historical conjunctures and contestations, as part of the making of minimal common values (Weeks 1995). They are the result of sustained dialogue. And in a divided, often violently polarized world, that is not an easy task.

As Petchesky (2000) observes, prior to the early 1990s, sexuality was absent from international human rights discourse. The Universal Declaration of Human Rights, adopted by the UN General Assembly in 1948, famously declared the 'inherent dignity' and 'equal and inalienable rights' of all members of the human family. Gradually this universal subject has been seen as having different racial or ethnic origins, with different faiths or none, has different health needs, is gendered in complex ways and has different sexual preferences or orientations; yet for a long time the UN (or rather its diverse members) proved reluctant to acknowledge issues of sexual diversity or trangender. The international argument for a wider agenda began to emerge with the Vienna Conference on Human Rights in 1993, the UN declaration of the Elimination of Violence against Women later that year, the world population conference in Cairo in 1994, and the women's conference in Beijing in 1995. The groundwork had been going on quite clearly since the 1970s, with the various campaigns of second-wave feminism and the internationalizing of the LGBT movement. The global HIV/AIDS epidemic further helped to force sexuality on to the international sexual agenda. And as I mentioned above, the precursor movements were much older, going back at least to the early twentieth century. But as Petchesky (2000) again notes, while the claim to rights can be enabling, it can as easily lead to an intensification of conflict over which rights and whose rights have priority. Rajan (2005: 134) has argued that conflicting rights are 'the major obstacle to ensuring women's human rights in the South'.

Sexuality to a large extent has been brought into human right discourses by debates over privacy and reproduction (Waites 2005a: 55), while the Beijing conference coalesced around questions of violence against women (Okin 2005: 86). Clearly there are strong links between them, especially in relation to core themes such as bodily integrity or control over one's own body, personhood, equality and diversity (Correa and Petchesky 1994). But reproductive rights and sexual rights can never be coextensive, though international agencies often find it easier to deal with the former (conflictual as these may be) than to confront the wider questions raised by sexuality: of the integrity and transparency of the body, concerning pleasure (and the diverse forms that pleasure may take) and the very validity of homosexuality (Petchesky 2000). Conflating reproductive and sexual rights can lead to the disenfranchisement of non-reproductive sex in general, and non-heterosexual sex and questions of transgender in particular (Miller 2000). Yet, as Butler (2005) argues, issues raised globally by LGBT campaigners are not just particularist claims: they pose profound questions about what it means to be human in a globalized world which in many parts still seeks to deny the humanity of non-heterosexual or gender challenging people. To assert sexual rights means that 'when we struggle for rights we are not simply struggling for rights that attach to my person, but we are struggling *to be conceived as persons*' (Butler 2005: 69). Sexuality is more than simply an attribute of an individual. It has come to define a relationship with the self and with others, one's very humanity. LGBT people *have* to raise questions about the injustices they face because if they did not do so their very humanness would continue to be questioned. Thus the central challenge of international gay and lesbian rights is to assert the reality of homosexuality, not as inner truth, not as sexual practice, 'but as one of the defining features of the social world in its very intelligibility' (ibid.: 64–5). To assert the value of LGBT identities and ways of life is to challenge existing realities, and to show that there are many different ways of being sexual – and of being human. The struggle over sexual rights is in the end a struggle about what it is to be human. Just as discrimination, prejudice, oppression and exploitation are denials of full humanity, so a positive claim for rights is an assertion of the rich diversity of human possibilities.

The rights we are discussing affirm the importance of both negative and positive freedoms. Negative freedoms (freedom from violence, legal oppression, the criminalization of sexual behaviour, harassment, the denial of free speech, and association) provide the essential preconditions for an autonomous life. Positive freedoms (the right to privacy, to engage in consensual sexual practices, to individual autonomy, to control of one's own body, the recognition of different ways of life, to freedom of choice in relationships and 'love rights') (Wintermute 2005) are the building blocks of a worthwhile life, as long as these rights do not conflict with, or cause harm to, the rights of others (see e.g. Declaration of Montreal 2006). These are the same claims that have been central to the debates about intimacy and the erotic since the 1960s that I have traced in this book. Because of the processes we have come to know as globalization they have become part of the discourse of human rights. That does not, as I have stressed, make them unproblematic, nor has it led to their easy acceptance. In Britain 'human rights' have entered political discourse to an unprecedented way following the passing of the Human Rights Act in 1998, but the balance sheet is mixed: the new law has not come close to the hopes of reformers for a new benchmark of rights, nor the fears of opponents that human right claims would clog up the legal system (*The Economist* 2004: 31–2). Whether in international discourse or at a national level human rights remain contested. Yet, I suggest, without them we are in no position to weigh in the balance the losses and gains of the period of extraordinary change on a global scale that we are living through. They remain standards by which we can challenge both the absolutism which can find only good in traditional ways of life that have irrevocably gone, and a relativism, either descriptive or normative, that refuses to make distinctions at all. As Nussbaum (1999: 8) has persuasively argued, a universal account of human justice need not be insensitive to the variety of traditions that shape human lives, nor is it a mere projection of particularist Western values on to parts of the world with different concerns. The evolution of human sexual rights has been a process that engages the Other, that has involved a dialogue across differences, and the concept of sexual rights that is emerging provides space and opportunity for difference to flourish within a developing discourse of our common humanity.

Conclusion

Like Beck (1999: 13) I do not believe this to be an age that is seeing a decline of values; on the contrary, it is an age *of* values, in which uncertainty forces us to be creative, inventive and generative of values (see Weeks 1995). The very insecurities and contingencies that are so characteristic of the contemporary world have produced, as we have seen, acute conflicts of values – culture wars and fundamentalisms have dramatized these but they permeate almost every aspect of everyday life. Yet in an age where pessimism – about wars, climate change, poverty, economic insecurity, ethnic clashes, racism, conflicts of religion, and random terror – is in danger of becoming endemic, it is important to remember what we have gained in the past half-century or so. The discourse of human sexual rights codifies many of the gains, and takes them on to a new plain. They signal the gap between aspiration and achievement, the chasm that sometimes seems to exist between ideal and reality. But compared to the silence around the power relationships and oppressions that enveloped sexuality and intimacy half a century ago, today's babel signals a vital, and necessary, change. And if we find in this chaotic confusion of voices a real challenge to our hopes, it also reminds us, as Nussbaum puts it, that cultures are not monolithic (Nussbaum 1999: 14). Even in the most hierarchical society men and women can develop relationships of equality and mutuality. Even in a homophobic society, men and men, women and women can find love and respect. Even in the most individualistic of cultures, people still manage to find sources of community and solidarity.

In an earlier work, *Invented Moralities* (Weeks 1995: 76–81), I argued that in the contemporary world difference is the starting point for thinking about constructing solidarity. Solidarity implies care and responsibility for others, a belief in the dignity of the other, a curiosity to learn about others, and a willingness to support those who seek to reduce violence and domination in private relationships as well as public institutions. It implies too a recognition of equality and interdependence, and a commitment to resolving conflict democratically, through dialogue rather than open warfare.

This is the terrain of the new cosmopolitanism which I have outlined in this chapter, and of a related concept, that of a new or radical humanism which Plummer (2003: 162, n. 1) among others has signalled: 'The humanism I would like to see developed would encourage a view of human beings as an "embedded", dialogic, contingent, embodied, universal self with a moral (and political) character.' This is humanism as a 'regulative ideal' rather than a metaphysical concept, with 'humanity' as a project of political construction not something that has always been there (Weeks 1995: 77). Solidarity has to be created through a growing realization of the pain and humiliation of others: 'The progress of human solidarity is the ability to see more and more traditional differences as unimportant when compared with similarities with regard to pain and humiliation. Ability to feel pain is all we have in common, but that can be the core around which solidarity is built' (Rorty 1989: xvii). Surely one of the less obvious but most vital features of globalization, and of the discourse of human sexual rights, is this growing sense of what Butler (2005: 54) calls vulnerability to others? It involves making the 'human gesture', affirming the human bond which links us beyond the chasms of difference.

This has taken us a long way from 1945, and the peculiar history of a small mining community with its particular social, economic, political and sexual culture. I painted a picture of intense solidarity but also of deep sexual and cultural conservatism, especially regarding family life, gendered divisions and sexual autonomy. But in closing this book I want to recall some words from Martha Nussbaum, which puts that picture into some perspective:

> people are not stamped out like coins by the power machine
> of social convention. They are constrained by social norms, but
> norms are plural and people are devious. Even in societies
> that nourish problematic roles for men and women, real men
> and women can also find spaces in which to subvert these
> conventions, resourcefully creating possibilities of love and joy.
> (Nussbaum 1999:14)

Many of the problematic roles have been successfully challenged, and those spaces have vastly increased as a result of the changes that have remade erotic and intimate life since the 1940s. But what has not changed are the possibilities of love and joy that link individual to individual, generation to generation. That is the golden thread which links the past that has irretrievably gone to this world we have won.

Bibliography

Aaron, J. (1994) 'Finding a Voice in Two Tongues: Gender and Colonization', in Aaron *et al.* (eds) 1994, 183–98.

Aaron, J., Rees, T., Betts, S. and Vincentelli, M. (eds) (1994) *Our Sisters' Land: The Changing Identities of Women in Wales*, Cardiff: University of Wales Press.

Aaronovitch, D. (2006) 'The Paedophile Panic: Why We Have Reached Half Way to Bonkers Island', *The Times* , 12 January, 21.

Abse, L. (1973) *Private Member*, London: Macdonald.

Adam, B.D. (1992) 'Sex and Caring Among Men', in Plummer (ed.) 1992.

Adam, B.D. (1998) 'Theorising Homophobia', *Sexualities* 1 (4), November, 387–404.

Adam, B.D. (2006) 'Relationship Innovation in Male Couples', *Sexualities* 9 (1), February, 5–26.

Adam, B.D., Duyvendak, J.W. and Krouwel, A. (eds) (1999a) *The Global Emergence of Gay and Lesbian Politics: National Imprints of a Worldwide Movement*, Philadelphia, PA: Temple University Press.

Adam, B.D., Duyvendak, J.W. and Krouwel, A. (1999b) 'Gay and Lesbian Movements Beyond Borders? National Imprints of a Wordwide Movement', in Adam *et al.* (eds) 1999a, 344–71.

Adams, T. (2002) 'What Happened to the Romance?', *The Observer*, 'Sex Uncovered' Supplement, 27 October, 4.

Adkins, L. (2002) *Revisions: Gender and Sexuality in Late Modernity*, Buckingham: Open University Press.

AFSC (American Friends Service Committee) (2002) 'AFSC Hawai'i Gay Liberation Program: Activist Materials Addressing Tourism', *GLQ: A Journal of Lesbian and Gay Studies* 8 (1–2), 207–26.

Aggleton, P., Davies, P. and Hart, G. (eds) (1994) *AIDS: Foundations for the Future*, London, and Bristol, PA: Taylor & Francis.

Agustin, L.M. (2005a) 'At Home in the Streets: Questioning the Desire to Help and Save', in Bernstein and Schaffler (eds) 2005, 67–82.

Agustin, L.M. (2005b) 'The Cultural Study of Commercial Sex', *Sexualities* 8 (5), December, 618–31.

Agustin, L.M. (2007) *Sex at the Margins: Migration, Labour Markets and the Rescue Industry*, London: Zed Books.

Alexander, M.J. (1991) 'Erotic Autonomy as a Politics of Decolonization: An Anatomy of Feminist and State Practices in the Bahamas Tourist Economy', in Mohanty *et al.* (eds) 1991, 63–100.

Alexander, M.J. (2003) 'Not Just (Any) Body can be a Citizen: The Politics of Law,

Sexuality and Postcoloniality in Trinidad and Tobago and the Bahamas', in Weeks *et al.* (eds) 2003, 174–82.

Ali, T. (1996) *We are Family: Testimonies of Lesbian and Gay Parents*, London and New York: Cassell.

Alibhai-Brown, Y. and Montague, A. (1992) *The Colour of Love: Mixed Race Relationships*, London: Virago.

Allan, G. (1989) *Friendship: Developing a Sociological Perspective*, Boulder, CO: Westview Press.

Allan, G. (1996) *Kinship and Friendship in Modern Britain*, Oxford: Oxford University Press.

Allan, G. (ed.) (1999) *The Sociology of the Family: A Reader*, Oxford: Blackwell.

Allan, G. (2004) 'Being Unfaithful: His and Hers Affairs', in Duncombe *et al.* (eds) 2004, 121–40.

Allan, G. and Jones, G. (eds) (2003) *Social Relations and the Life Course*, Basingstoke: Palgrave.

Allen, L. (2003) 'Girls Want Sex, Boys Want Love: Resisting Dominant Discourses of (Hetero)sexuality', *Sexualities* 6 (2), May, 215–36.

Allen, S. and Harne, L. (1988) 'Lesbian Mothers – The Fight for Child Custody', in Cant and Hemmings (eds) 1988, 181–94.

Allen, S., Sanders, L. and Wallis, J. (1974) *Conditions of Illusion: Papers from the Women's Movement*, Leeds: Feminist Books.

Almarck, K. (2005) 'What's in a Name? The Significance of the Choice of Surname Given to Children Born Within Lesbian parent families', *Sexualities* 8(2), April, 239–54.

Altman, D. (1979) *Coming Out in the Seventies*, Sydney and Eugene: Wild & Woolley.

Altman, D. (1982) *The Homosexualization of America, The Americanization of the Homosexual*, New York: St Martin's Press.

Altman, D. (1989) 'AIDS and the Reconceptualization of Homosexuality', in Van Kooten Niekerk, A. and van der Meer, T. (eds) *Homosexuality? Which Homosexuality?*, Amsterdam: An Dekker/Schorer; London: GMP.

Altman, D. (1993) *Homosexual: Oppression and Liberation* (1st edn 1971), this edition with a new Introduction by Jeffrey Weeks, New York: New York University Press.

Altman, D. (1994) *Power and Community: Organizational and Cultural Responses to AIDS*, London, and Bristol, PA: Taylor & Francis.

Altman, D. (2001) *Global Sex*, Chicago, IL: University of Chicago Press.

Amnesty International (1997) *Breaking the Silence: Human Rights Violations Based on Sexual Orientation*, London: Amnesty International.

Amnesty International (2001a) *Crimes of Hate, Conspiracy of Silence: Torture and Ill-treatment based on Sexual Identity*, London: Amnesty International.

Amnesty International (2001b) *Broken Bodies, Shattered Minds: Torture and Ill-treatment of Women*, London: Amnesty International.

Amnesty International (2004) *It's in Our Hands: Stop Violence Against Women*, London: Amnesty International.

Amos, V. and Parma, P. (1984) 'Challenging Imperial Feminism', *Feminist Review* 17, Autumn, 3–20.

Amos, V., Lewis, G., Mama, A. and Parmar, P. (1984) 'Editorial', *Feminist Review* 17, autumn, 1–2.

Anthias, F. and Yuval-Davis, N. (1992) *Racialized Boundaries: Race, Nation, Gender, Colour and Class, and the Anti-racist Struggle*, London: Routledge.

Attwood, F. (2006) 'Sexed Up: Theorising the Sexualization of Culture', *Sexualities* 9 (1), February, 77–94.

Bailey-Harris, R. (2001) 'Same Sex Partnership in English Family Law', in Wintermute and Andenaes (eds) 2001, 605–22.

Bainham, A. and Brooks-Gordon, B. (2004) 'Reforming the Law on Sexual Offences', in Brooks-Gordon *et al.* (eds) 2004, 261–96.

Baird, V. (2004) *Sex, Love and Homophobia: Lesbian, Gay, Bisexual and Transgender Lives*, London: Amnesty International.

Bamforth, N. (2005) *Sex Rights*, Oxford Amnesty Lectures, Oxford and New York: Oxford University Press.

Barker, M. and Langdridge, D. (2006) 'Editorial', *Lesbian and Gay Psychology Review* 7 (2), 115–19.

Barney, S. (2005) 'Accessing Medicalized Donor Sperm in the US and Britain: An Historical Narrative', *Sexualities* 8(2), April, 205–20.

Barrett, M. and McIntosh, M. (1982) *The Anti-social Family*, London: Verso.

Bates, S. (2004a) *A Church at War: Anglicans and Homosexuality*, London and New York: I.B. Tauris.

Bates, S. (2004b) 'Vatican Birth Control Policy Spurned', *Guardian*, 30 June, 12.

Bauman, Z. (1998) 'On Postmodern Uses of Sex', *Theory, Culture and Society* 15 (3–4), 19–33.

Bauman, Z. (2003) *Liquid Love: On the Frailty of Human Bonds*, Cambridge: Polity Press.

Bauman, Z. (2005) *Liquid Life*, Cambridge: Polity Press.

Bech, H. (1992) 'Report from a Rotten State: "Marriage" and "Homosexuality" in "Denmark"', in Plummer (ed.) 1992, 134–50.

Bech, H. (1997) *When Men Meet: Homosexuality and Modernity*, Cambridge: Polity Press.

Bech, H. (1998) 'City Sex: Representing Lust in Public', *Theory, Culture and Society* 15 (3–4), 215–41.

Bech, H. (1999) 'After the Closet', *Sexualities* 2 (3), August, 343–6.

Beck, U. (1992) *Risk Society: Towards a New Modernity*, London: Sage.

Beck, U. (1994) 'The Reinvention of Politics: Towards a Theory of Reflexive Modernization', in Beck *et al.* 1994, 1–55.

Beck, U. (1999) *World Risk Society*, Cambridge: Polity Press.

Beck, U. (2002) 'The Cosmopolitan Society and its Enemies', *Theory, Culture and Society* 19 (1–2), 17–44.

Beck, U. and Beck-Gernsheim, E. (1995) *The Normal Chaos of Love*, Cambridge: Polity Press.

Beck, U. and Beck-Gernsheim, E. (2002) *Individualization: Institutionalized Individualism and its Social and Political Consequences*, London, Thousand Oaks and New Delhi: Sage.

Beck, U. and Beck-Gernsheim, E. (2004) 'Families in a Runaway World', in Scott *et al.* (eds) 2004, 499–514.

Beck, U., Giddens, A. and Lash, S. (1994) *Reflexive Modernization: Politics, Tradition and Aesthetics in the Modern Social Order*, Cambridge: Polity Press.

Beck-Gernsheim, E. (1998) 'On the Way to a Post-familial Family: From a Community of Need to Elective Affinities', *Theory, Culture and Society* 15 (3–4), 53–70.

Beddoe, D. (1991) 'Munitionettes, Maids and Mams: Women in Wales 1914–1939', in John (ed.) 1991, 189–209.

Beddoe, D. (2000) *Out of the Shadows: A History of Women in Twentieth-century Wales*, Cardiff: University of Wales Press.

Beddoe, D. (ed.) (2003) *Changing Times: Welsh Women Writing on the 1950s and 1960s*, Dinas Powys: Honno.

Bell, Daniel (1996) *The Cultural Contradictions of Capitalism* (20th Anniversary edn), New York: Basic Books.

Bell, David (2006) 'Bodies, Technologies, Spaces: on "Dogging"', *Sexualities* 9(4), October, 387–408.

Bell, D. and Binnie, J. (2000) *The Sexual Citizen: Queer Politics and Beyond*, Cambridge: Polity Press.

Bell, D. and Binnie, J. (2002) 'Sexual Citizenship: Marriage, the Market and the Military', in Richardson and Seidman 2002, 443–458.

Bell, M. (1998) 'Sexual Orientation and Anti-discrimination Policy: The European Community', in Carver and Mottier (eds) 1998, 58–67.

Bell, V. (2003) 'The Vigilantt(e) Parent and the Paedophile: The News of the World Campaign 2000 and the Contemporary Governmentality of Child Sex Abuse', in Reavey and Warner (eds) 2003, 108–28.

Benhabib, S. (1987) 'The Generalized and the Concrete Other: The Kohlberg-controversy and Feminist Theory', in Benhabib, S. and Cornell, D. (eds) *Feminism as Critique: Essays on the Politics of Gender in Late Capitalist Societies*, Cambridge, MA, and London: MIT Press.

Benkov, L. (1994) *Reinventing The Family: The Emerging Story of Lesbian and Gay Parents*, New York: Crown.

Bennett, A. (2000) *Telling Tales*, London: BBC Worldwide.

Bereket, T. and Adam, B.D. (2006) 'The Emergence of Gay Identities in Contemporary Turkey', *Sexualities* 9 (2), April, 131–51.

Bernauer, J. and Rasmussen, D. (eds) (1988) *The Final Foucault*, Cambridge, MA, MIT Press.

Bernstein, E. and Schaffner, L. (eds) (2005) *Regulating Sex: The Politics of Intimacy and Identity*, New York and London: Routledge.

Bernstein, G.L. (2004) *The Myth of Decline: The Rise of Britain since 1945*, London: Pimlico.

Bernstein, M. (2005) 'Liberalism and Social Movement Success: The Case of United States Sodomy Laws', in Bernstein and Schaffner (eds) 2005, 3–18.

Berridge, V. (1996) *AIDS in the UK: The Making of Policy, 1981–1994*, Oxford: Oxford University Press.

Berridge, V. and Strong, P. (eds) (1993) *AIDS and Contemporary History*, Cambridge: Cambridge University Press.

Berthoud, R. (1999) *Young Caribbean Men and the Labour Market*, London: Joseph Rowntree Trust.

Bettinger, M. (2005) 'Polyamory and Gay Men: A Family Systems Approach', *Journal of GLBT Family Studies* 1 (1), 97–116.

Betts, S. (1994) 'The Changing Family in Wales', in Aaron *et al.* (eds) 1994, 17–30.

BHAN (Black HIV and AIDS Network) (1991) *AIDS and the Black Communities*, London: Grosvenor.

Bhatt, C. (1997) *Liberation and Purity: Race, New Religious Movements and the Ethics of Postmodernity*, London: University College London Press.

Bi-Academic Intervention (ed.) (1997) *The Bisexual Imaginary: Representation, Identity and Desire*, London and Verndon, VA: Cassell.

Binnie, J. (2004) *The Globalization of Sexuality*, London, Thousand Oaks, CA, New Delhi: Sage.

Binnie, J. and Skeggs, B. (2004) 'Cosmopolitan Knowledge and the Production and Consumption of Sexualized Space: Manchester's Gay Village', *The Sociological Review* 52 (1), February, 39–61.

Birch, K. (1988) 'A Community of Interests', in Cant and Hemmings (eds) 1988, 51–59.

Bland, L. (2001) *Banishing the Beast: Feminism, Sex and Morality*, London: Penguin.

Blasius, M. (1994) *Gay and Lesbian Politics: Sexuality and the Emergence of a New Ethic*, Philadelphia, PA: Temple University Press.

Blasius, M. (1998) 'Contemporary Lesbian, Gay, Bisexual, Transgender, Queer Theories, and their Politics', *Journal of the History of Sexuality* 8 (4), April, 642–74.

Blumstein, P. and Schwartz, P. (1983) *American Couples*, New York: William Morrow.

Bone, J. (2006) 'Leaders Pledge to Double AIDS Cash', *The Times*, 3 June, 51.

Borrillo, D. (2001) 'The *"Pacte Civil de Solidarite"*: in France: Midway Between Marriage and Cohabitation', in Wintermute and Andenaes (eds) 2001, 475–92.

Borrillo, D. and Lascoumes, P. (2002) *Amours egales? Le Pacs, les homosexuals et la gauche*, Paris: Editions la Decouverte.

Boseley, S. (2006a) 'Birth Rate at Highest Level for 13 Years, But Still Off Target', *Guardian*, 19 May, 5.

Boseley, S. (2006b) 'HIV Prevention Policy is Failing', *Guardian*, 7 June, 12.

Boswell, J. (1994) *Same Sex Unions in Pre-modern Europe*, New York: Villard Books.

Bourke, J. (2000) *An Intimate History of Killing: Face-to-face Killing in Twentieth-century Warfare*, London: Granta.

Boyce, P. (2006) 'Moral Ambivalence and Irregular Practices: Contextualizing Male-to-male Sexualities in Calcutta/India', *Feminist Review* 83, 79–98.

Boyes, R. (2006) 'Cannibalism is Murder – Even if the Victim Requests to be Eaten', *The Times*, 10 May, 3.

Bozett, F.W. (ed.) (1987) *Gay and Lesbian Parents*, New York: Praeger.

Brandzel, A.L. (2005) 'Queering Citizenship? Same-sex Marriage and the State', *GLQ: A Journal of Lesbian and Gay Studies* 11 (2), 171–204.

Brannen, J. and Nilsen, A. (2006) 'From Fatherhood to Fathering: Transmission and Change among British Fathers in Four Generation Families', *Sociology* 40 (2), April, 335–52.

Braun, V., Gavey, N. and McPhillips, K. (2003) 'The "Fair Deal"? Unpacking Accounts of Reciprocity in Heterosex', *Sexualities* 6 (2), May, 237–61.

Bray, A. (1981) *Homosexuality in Renaissance England*, London: Gay Men's Press.

Bredstrom, A. (2005) '"Love in Another Country": "Race", Gender and Sexuality in sexual Education Material Targeting Migrants in Sweden', *Sexualities* 8 (4), October, 517–35.

Brighton Ourstory Project (1992) *Daring Hearts: Lesbians and Gay Lives of 1950s and 1960s Brighton*, Brighton: Brighton Ourstory Project.

Brooks, D. (2000) *Bobos in Paradise: The New Upper Class and How They Got There*, New York and London: Simon & Schuster.

Brooks-Gordon, B., Gelsthorpe, L., Johnson, M. and Bainham, A. (eds) (2004) *Sexuality Repositioned: Diversity and the Law*, Oxford, and Portland, OR: Hart Publishing.

Browne, A. (2006) 'I Would Prefer Women Not to Wear the Veil at all, Says Straw', *The Times*, 7 October, 6.

Budgeon, S. (2006) 'Friendship and Formations of Sociality in Late Modernity: The Challenge of "Post Traditional Intimacy"', *Sociological Research Online* 11 (3), at: http://www.socresonline.org.uk/11/3/budgeon.html.

Buonfino, A. and Mulgan, G. (2006) *Porcupines in Winter: The Pleasures and Pains of Living Together in Modern Britain*, London: The Young Foundation.

Burchill, J. (1998) *Diana*, London: Weidenfeld & Nicolson.

Butler, J. (1990) *Gender Trouble: Feminism and the Subversion of Identity*, London: Routledge.

Butler, J. (1993) *Bodies that Matter: On the Discursive Limits of Sex*, New York and London: Routledge.

Butler, J. (2004) *Undoing Gender*, New York and London: Routledge.

Butler, J. (2005) 'On Being Besides Oneself: On the Limits of Sexual Autonomy', in Bamforth 2005, 48–78.

Cahill, S. (2005) '"Welfare Moms and the Two Grooms": The Concurrent Promotion and Destruction of Marriage in US Public Policy', *Sexualities* 8(2), April, 169–89.

Callender, C. (1987) 'Women Seeking Work', in Fineman, S. (ed.) *Unemployment: Personal and Social Consequences*, London and New York: Tavistock Publications, 22–46.

Campbell, B. (1972) 'Sexuality and Submission', in Allen *et al.* 1974, 99–109.

Campbell, B. (1998) *Diana, Princess of Wales: How Sexual Politics Shook the Monarchy*, London: The Women's Press.

Campbell, C., Nair, Y. and Maimane, S. (2006) 'AIDS Stigma, Sexual Moralities and the Policing of Women and Youth in South Africa', *Feminist Review* 83, 132–8.

Campbell, D. (2006a) 'Sex: Britain's Quiet Revolution', *Observer*, 21 January, 16–17.

Campbell, D. (2006b) 'What teens really think about sex', *Observer*, 21 May, 16.

Cant, B. (ed.) (1997) *Invented Identities? Lesbians and Gays Talk about Migration*, London, and Herndon, VA: Cassell.

Cant, B. and Hemmings, S. (eds) (1988) *Radical Records: Thirty Years of Lesbian and Gay History, 1957–1987*, London and New York: Routledge.

Carballo-Dieguez, A. and Bauermeister, J. (2004) '"Barebacking": Intentional Condomless Anal Sex in HIV-risk Contexts. Reasons for and Against It', *Journal of Homosexuality* 43 (1), 1–16.

Carrington, C. (1999) *No Place like Home: Relationships and Family Life among Lesbians and Gay Men*, Chicago, IL and London: The University of Chicago Press.

Carver, T. and Mottier, V. (eds) (1998) *Politics of Sexuality: Identity, Gender, Citizenship*, London and New York: Routledge.

Castells, M. (1983) *The City and the Grassroots: A Cross Cultural Theory of Urban Social Movements*, London: University of California Press/Edward Arnold

Castells, M. (1996) *The Information Age: Economy, Society and Culture. Volume 1: The Rise of Network Society*, Oxford: Blackwell.

Castells, M. (1997) *The Information Age: Economy, Society and Culture. Volume 2: The Power of Identity*, Oxford: Blackwell.

Castells, M. (1998) *The Information Age: Economy, Society and Culture. Volume 3: End of Millennium*, Oxford: Blackwell.

Chamberlain, M. (2005) *Family Love in the Diaspora: Migration and the Anglo-Caribbean Experience*, New York and London: Transaction Publishers.

Charles, N. (1994), 'The Refuge Movement and Domestic Violence', in Aaron *et al.* (eds) 1994, 48–60.

Charles, N. (2002) *Gender in Modern Britain*, Oxford: Oxford University Press.

Charles, N. and Aull Davies, C. (2005) 'Studying the Particular, Illuminating the General: Community Studies and Community in Wales', *Sociological Review* 53 (4), November, 672–90.

Charter, D. (2006) 'Promiscuous Britons "ignoring AIDS"', *The Times*, 3 October, 22.

Chauncey, G. (1994) *Gay New York: Gender, Urban Culture, and the Making of the Gay Male World, 1890–1940*, New York: Basic Books.

Clark, D. (ed.) (1991) *Marriage, Domestic Life and Social Change: Writings for Jacqueline Burgoyne*, London and New York: Routledge.

Clark, D. and Haldane, D. (1990) *Wedlocked? Intervention and Research in Marriage*, Cambridge: Polity Press.

Clarke, V. and Kitzinger, C. ' "We're not Living on Planet Lesbian": Construction of Male Role Models in Debates about Lesbian Families', *Sexualities* 8(2), April, 137–52.

Clarke, V., Burgoyne, C. and Burns, M. (2006) 'Just a Piece of Paper? A Qualitative Exploration of Same Sex Couples' Multiple Conceptions of Civil Partnership and Marriage', *Lesbian and Gay Psychology Review* 7 (2), 141–61.

Clarkson-Freeman, P.A. (2004) 'The Defense of Marriage Act (DOMA): Its Impact on Those Seeking Same-sex Marriages', *Journal of Homosexuality* 48 (2), 21–44.

Coates, J. (1997) *Women Talk: Conversations Between Women Friends*, Oxford: Blackwell.

Cohler, B.T. (2005) 'Life Course Social Science Perspectives on the GLBT Family', *Journal of GLBT Family Studies* 1 (1), 69–95.

Collins, M. (2003) *Modern Love: An Intimate History of Men and Women in Twentieth-Century Britain*, London: Atlantic Books.

Collins, M. (2005) *The Likes of Us: A Biography of the White Working Class*, London: Granta.

Conekin, B., Mort, F. and Waters, C. (eds) (1999) *Moments of Modernity: Reconstructing Britain 1954–1964*, London: Rivers Oram Press.

Connell, R.W. (1987) *Gender and Power*, Cambridge: Polity Press.

Connell, R.W. (1995) *Masculinities*, Cambridge: Polity Press.

Connell, R. W. (2002) *Gender*, Cambridge: Polity Press.

Connell, R.W. (2003) 'The Big Picture: Masculinities in Recent World History', in Weeks *et al.* (eds) 2003, 46–56.

Connolly, H. and White, A. (2006) 'The Different Experiences of the United Kingdom's Ethnic and Religious Populations', in ONS (Office of National Statistics) 2006, 1–8.

Connolly, K. (2001) 'Germans Flock to Tie the Knot after Law Change', *Observer*, 22 July, 19.

Cook, H. (2005a) *The Long Sexual Revolution: English Women, Sex, and Contraception 1800–1975*, Oxford: Oxford University Press.

Cook, H. (2005b) 'The English Sexual Revolution: Technology and Social Change', *History Workshop Journal* 59, spring, 109–28.

Cook, M. (2003) *London and the Culture of Homosexuality, 1885–1914*, Cambridge: Cambridge University Press.

Cooke, R. (2002) 'There's Gold in Them There Pills . . .', *Observer*, 'Sex Uncovered' Supplement, 27 October, 24–31.

Cooper, A. (2006) *Identity Work: Negotiating Gay Male Identity in a Changing World*, unpublished Ph.D. thesis, London: London South Bank University.

Cooper, D. (1994) *Sexing the City: Lesbian and Gay Politics within the Activist State*, London: Rivers Oram Press.

Cooper, D. (2001) 'Like Counting Stars? Re-structuring Equality and the Socio-legal Space of Same-sex Marriage', in Wintermute and Andenaes (eds) 2001, 75–96.

Cooper, D. (2004) *Challenging Diversity: Rethinking Equality and the Value of Difference*, Cambridge: Cambridge University Press.

Copestake, J. (2006) 'Gays Flee Iraq as Shia Death Squads Find a New Target', *Observer*, 6 August, 31.

Correa, S. and Petchesky, R.P. (1994) 'Reproductive and Sexual rights: A Feminist Perspective', in Sen, G., Germain, A. and Chen, L.C. (eds) (1994) *Population Policies Reconsidered: Health, Empowerment, and Rights*, Boston, MA: Harvard Center for Population and Development Studies, and New York: International Women's Health Coalition, 107–123.

Cowan, R. (2004) 'Pianist Jailed for Sex Tourism', *Guardian*, 3 June, 7.

Coward, R. (1992) *Our Treacherous Hearts: Why Women let Men get their Way*, London, and Boston, MA: Faber and Faber.

Crisp, Q. (1998) *How to Have a Lifestyle*, Boston, MA: Alyson Publications.

Curtis, P. (2006) 'Twice as Many Men as Women Start Civil Partnerships', *Guardian*, 23 February, 14.

David, H. (1997) *On Queer Street: A Social History of British Homosexuality 1895–1995*, London: HarperCollins.

Davies, C. (2006) *The Strange Death of Moral Britain*, New York: Transaction Publishers.

Davies, R. (1969) *Print of Hare's Foot: An Autobiographical Beginning*, London: Heinemann.

Davies, T.A. (1980) 'Impressions of Life in the Rhondda Valley', in Hopkins (ed.) 1980, 11–21.

Davis, M.D.M. (2005) *Treating and Preventing HIV in the Post-crisis Situation: Perspectives from the Personal Experience Accounts of Gay Men with HIV*, unpublished Ph.D. thesis, London: Institute of Education, University of London.

Declaration of Montreal (2006) International Conference on LGBT Human Rights, Montreal: 1st Outgames.

Dench, G. (1996) *The Place of Men in Changing Family Attitudes*, London: Institute of Community Studies.

Dench, G., Gavron, K. and Young, M. (2006) *The New East End: Kinship, Race and Conflict*, London: Profile Books.

Dennis, N. and Erdos, G. (1993) *Families without Fatherhood*, London: Institute for Economic Affairs, Health and Welfare Unit.

Dennis, N., Henriques, F. and Slaughter, C. (1956/1969) *Coal is Our Life: An Analysis of a Yorkshire Mining Community* (2nd edn 1969), London: Tavistock Publications.

Department of Constitutional Affairs (2004) 'Gender Recognition Act 2004', News Release, 2 July.

Dibbell, 'Let us Spray' (2006) *Observer Magazine*, 23 April, 14–19.

Dodd, P. (2006) 'Grimethorpe', in Buonfino and Mulgan 2006, 33–6.

Donald, J. and Rattansi. A. (eds) (1992) 'Race', Culture and Difference, London, Newbury Park, CA, and New Delhi: Sage.

Donovan, C. (2004) 'Why Reach for the Moon? Because the Stars aren't Enough', Feminism and Psychology 14 (1), February, 24–9.

Donovan, C., Heaphy, B. and Weeks, J. (1999) 'Citizenship and Same Sex Relationships', Journal of Social Policy 28 (4), 689–709.

Doward, J. (2006a) 'Sex Scandal that Engulfed Kelly', Observer, 15 January, 8–9.

Doward, J. (2006b) 'Accept it: We're Married, Lesbian Couple tell Judge', Observer, 28 May, 12.

Drucker, J. (1998) Families of Value: Gay and Lesbian Parents and Their Children Speak Out, New York: Insight Books, Plenum Press.

Duggan, L. and Hunter, N.D. (1995) Sex Wars: Sexual Dissent and Political Culture, New York and London: Routledge.

Duncan, S. (2005) What's the Problem? Teenage Parents: A Critical Review, Families and Social Capital ESRC Research Group, Working Paper 15, London: London South Bank University.

Duncan, S. and Edwards, R. (1999) Lone Mothers, Paid Work and Gendered Moral Rationalities, Basingstoke and London: Macmillan.

Duncan, S. and Smith, D. (2006) 'Individualisation Versus the Geography of "New" Families', C21st Society: Journal of the Academy of Social Sciences 1 (2), November, 167–90.

Duncombe, J. and Marsden, D. (1999) 'Love and Intimacy: The Gender Division of Emotion and "Emotion Work"', in Allan (ed.) 1999, 91–110.

Duncombe, J. and Marsden, D. (2004a) '"From Here to Ephiphany . . .": Power and Identity in the Narratives of an Affair', in Duncombe et al. (eds) 2004, 141–66.

Duncombe, J. and Marsden, D. (2004b) 'Affairs and Children', in Duncombe et al. (eds) 2004, 187–202.

Duncombe, J., Harrison, K., Allan, G. and Marsden, D. (eds) (2004) The State of Affairs: Explorations in Infidelity and Commitment, Mahwah, NJ and London: Lawrence Erlbaum Associates.

Dunne, G.A. (1997) Lesbian Lifestyles: Women's Work and the Politics of Sexuality, London: Macmillan.

Dunne, G.A. (1999) 'A Passion for Sameness?: Sexuality and Gender Accountability', in Silva, and Smart, (eds) 1999, 66–82.

Durham, M. (1991) Sex and Politics: The Family and Morality in the Thatcher Years, Basingstoke: Macmillan.

Durham, M.G. (2004) 'Constructing the "New Ethnicities": Media, Sexuality, and Diaspora Identity in the Lives of South Asian Immigrant Girls', Critical Studies in Media Communication 21 (2), June, 140–61.

Dworkin, A. (1981) Pornography: Men Possessing Women, London: The Women's Press.

Dworkin, A. (1989) Intercourse, New York: The Free Press.

Dyer, C. (2005) 'Thousands Prepare to Tie the Knot', Guardian, 5 December, 9.

Dyer, C. (2006) 'Unmarried Couples to get New Rights', Guardian, 31 May, 1.

Dyer, R. (1997) White: Essays on Race and Culture, London and New York: Routledge.

Economist, The (2003) 'A Mixed Prognosis', 29 November, 115–17.

Economist, The (2004) 'Human Rights Law: The Menace that Wasn't', 13 November, 31–2.

Economist, The (2005) 'Special Report: America's Religious Right', 25 June, 29–32.

Economist, The (2006a) 'The Fertility Bust', 11 February, 46.

Economist, The (2006b) 'Cupidity', 18 February, 73.

Eder, F.X., Hall, L.A. and Hekma, G. (1999) *Sexuality in Europe: Themes in Sexuality*, Manchester: Manchester University Press.

Edwards, T. (2006) *Cultures of Masculinity*, London and New York: Routledge.

Edwards, R. (2004) 'Present and Absent in Troubling Ways: Families and Social Capital Debates', *The Sociological Review* 52 (1), February, 1–21.

Edwards, R. and Gillies, V. (2004) 'Support in Parenting: Values and Consensus Concerning Who to Turn to', *Journal of Social Policy* 33 (4), 627–47.

Edwards, R., Franklin, J. and Holland, J. (2003) *Families and Social Capital: Exploring the Issues*, Families and Social Capital ESRC Research Group, Working Paper 1, London: London South Bank University.

Edwards, R., Franklin, J. and Holland, J. (eds) (2007) *Assessing Social Capital: Concept, Policy and Practice*, Cambridge: Cambridge Scholars Publication.

Edwards, R., Hadfield, L., Lucey, H. and Mauthner, M. (2006) *Sibling Identity and Relationships: Sisters and Brothers*, London and New York: Routledge.

Ekins, R. and King, D. (eds) (1996) *Blending Genders: Social Aspects of Cross-dressing and Sex-change*, London and New York: Routledge.

Ekins, R. and King, D. (2006) *The Transgender Phenomenon*, London, Thousand Oaks, CA, and New Delhi: Sage.

Elford, J. (2002) 'Surfing for Sex', *AIDS Focus* 17, 1–3.

Elias, N. (2000) *The Civilizing Process*, Oxford: Blackwell.

Elliott, A. (2004) 'Love in the Time of Consumption', *Times Literary Supplement*, 2 January, 24.

Elliott, A. and Lemert, C. (2006) *The New Individualism: The Emotional Costs of Globalization*, London and New York: Routledge.

Epstein, D., Johnson, R. and Steinberg, D.L. (2004) 'Thrice Told Tales: Modernising Sexualities in the Age of Consent', in Steinberg and Johnson (eds) 2004, 96–113.

Epstein, S. (1990) 'Gay Politics, Ethnic Identity: The Limits of Social Constructionism', in Stein, E. (ed.) (1990) *Forms of Desire: Sexual Orientation and the Social Constructionist Controversy*, New York and London: Garland Publishing.

Epstein, S. (1998) *Impure Science: AIDS Activism and the Politics of Knowledge*, Berkeley: University of California Press.

Epstein, S. (1999) 'Gay and Lesbian Movements in the United States: Dilemmas of Identity, Diversity, and Political Strategy', in Adam *et al.* (eds) 1999a, 30–90.

Epstein, S. (2003) 'Sexualizing Governance and Medicalizing Identities: The Emergence of "State Centred" LGBT Health Politics in the United States', *Sexualities* 6 (2), May, 131–71.

Ernie, J.N. and Spires, A.J. (2001) 'Glossy Subjects: G and L Magazines and "Tonghzi" Cultural Visibility in Taiwan', *Sexualities* 4 (1), February, 25–49.

Escoffier, J. (ed.) (2003) *Sexual Revolution*, New York: Thunder's Mouth Press.

Estlund, D.M. and Nussbaum, M.C. (eds) (1997) *Sex, Preference and Family: Essays on Law and Nature*, New York and Oxford: Oxford University Press.

Etzioni, A. (1995) *The Spirit of Community: Rights, Responsibilities and the Communitarian Agenda*, London: Fontana.

Evans, H. (2003) 'Sex and the Open Market', in Weeks *et al.* (eds) 2003, 216–26.

Eves, A. (2004) 'Queer Theory, Butch/Femme Identities and Lesbian Space', *Sexualities* 7 (4), November, 480–96.

Farquhar, C. (2000) '"Lesbian" in a Post-lesbian World? Policing Identity, Sex and Image', *Sexualities* 3 (2), 219–36.

Fassin, E. (2001) 'Same Sex, Different Politics: "Gay Marriage" Debates in France and the United States', *Public Culture* 13 (2), 215–32.

Fassin, E. (2005) *L'Inversion de la Question Homosexuelle*, Paris: Editions Amsterdam.

Feminist Anthology Collective (eds) (1981) *No Turning Back: Writings from the Women's Liberation Movement 1975–80*, London: The Women's Press.

Fenton, K.A., Mercer, C.H., McManus, S., Erens, B., Wellings, K., Macdowall, W., Byron, C.L., Copas, A.J., Nanchahal, K., Field, J. and Johnson, A.M. (2005) 'Ethnic Variations in Sexual Behaviour in Great Britain and Risk of Sexually Transmitted Infections: A Probability Survey', *The Lancet* 365 (9466), 2 April, 1246–55.

Finch, J. (1989) *Family Obligation and Social Change*, London: Polity Press.

Finch, J. and Mason, J. (1993) *Negotiating Family Responsibilities*, London: Routledge.

Finch, J. and Summerfield, P. (1991) 'Social Reconstruction and the Emergence of Companionate Marriage, 1945–59', in Clark (ed.) 1991, 7–32.

Firestone, S. (1971 *The Dialectic of Sex*, London: Paladin.

Fisher, K. (1999) '"Didn't Stop to Think, I Just Didn't Want Another One": The Culture of Abortion in Inter-war South Wales', in Eder *et al.* 1999, 213–32.

Fisher, K. (2006) *Birth Control, Sex and Marriage in Britain 1918–1960*, Oxford and New York: Oxford University Press.

Florida, R. (2004) *The Rise of the Creative Class, And How It's Transforming Work, Leisure, and Everyday Life*, New York: Basic Books.

Ford, R. (2006) 'Curb on Sham Weddings Ruled Illegal', *The Times*, 11 April, 14.

Ford, R. and Frearn, A. (2004) 'Census Gives First Official Gay Map', *The Times*, 4 February, 3.

Foucault, M. (1979) *The History of Sexuality: Volume 1: An Introduction*, Harmondsworth: Penguin.

Foucault, M. (1988) 'The Ethic of Care for the Self as a Practice of Freedom', in Bernauer and Rasmussen (eds) 1988.

Frankenberg, R. (1993) *White Women, Race Matters: The Social Construction of Whiteness*, London: Routledge; Minneapolis: University of Minnesota Press.

Frankham, J. (2006) 'Sexual Antinomies and Parent/Child Sex Education: Learning from Foreclosure', *Sexualities* 9 (2), April, 236–54.

Fraser, N. (1997) *Justice Interruptus: Critical Reflections on the Postsocialist Condition*, London and New York: Routledge.

Frearn, A. (2005) 'Age of Consent "Confuses Young"', *The Times*, 18 June, 34.

Frearn, A. (2006a) 'Chance to Pick and Choose and Still Remain in Control', *The Times*, 5 January, 6.

Frearn, A. (2006b) 'Black Girls to be the Targets of Plan to Cut Teen Pregnancy', *The Times*, 21 July, 4.

Fukuyama, F. (1995) *Trust: The New Foundations of Global Prosperity*, New York: The Free Press.

Fukuyama, F. (1999) *The Great Disruption: Human Nature and the Reconstitution of Social Order*, London: Profile Books.

Furedi, F. (2004) *Therapy Culture: Cultivating Vulnerability in an Uncertain Age*, London and New York: Routledge.

Furstenberg, F.F. and Kaplan, S.B. (2004) 'Social Capital and the Family', in Scott *et al.* (eds) 2004, 218–232.

Gabb, J. (2004) 'Critical Differentials: Querying the Incongruities within Research on Lesbian Parent Families', *Sexualities* 7 (2), May, 167–82.

Gabb, J. (2005) 'Lesbian M/Otherhood: Strategies of Familial-linguistic Management in Lesbian Parent Families', *Sociology* 39 (4), October, 585–604.

Gagnon, J. and Simon, W. (1974) *Sexual Conduct. The Social Sources of Human Sexuality*, London: Hutchinson.

Gardiner, J. (2003) *From the Closet to the Screen: Women at the Gateways Club, 1945–85*, London, Sydney, Chicago, IL: Pandora.

Garner, S. (2006) 'The Uses of Whiteness: What Sociologists Working on Europe can Draw from US Research on Whiteness', *Sociology* 40 (2), April, 257–75.

Garton Ash, T. (2006) 'What Young British Muslims Say Can be Shocking – Some of it is also True', *Guardian*, 10 August, 25.

Gavron, K. (1996) 'Du Mariage Arrange au Mariage d'Amour: Nouvelle Strategies chez les Bengali d'East London', *Terrain* 27, September, 15–26.

Geppert, A.C.T. (1998) 'Divine Sex, Happy Marriage, Regenerated Marriage: Marie Stopes's Marital Manual *Married Love* and the Making of a Best-seller, 1918–1955', *Journal of the History of Sexuality* 8 (3), January, 389–433.

Gibson, O. (2006) 'More Likely to Have a Mobile, Use the Net, Listen to Radio, Read Papers: It's the Girls', *Guardian*, 3 May, 3.

Giddens, A. (1990) *The Consequences of Modernity*, Cambridge: Polity Press.

Giddens, A. (1991) *Modernity and Self-identity*, Cambridge: Polity Press.

Giddens, A. (1992) *The Transformation of Intimacy: Sexuality, Love and Eroticism in Modern Societies*, Cambridge: Polity Press.

Giddens, A. (1994) 'Living in a Post-traditional Society', in Beck *et al.* 1994, 56–109.

Gillam, A. (2006) 'Britons put Work and Fun before Babies', *Guardian*, 2 May, 1.

Gillies, V. (2005) 'Raising the "Meritocracy": Parenting and the Individualization of Social Class', *Sociology* 39 (5), December, 835–53.

Gilligan, C. (1982) *In A Different Voice: Psychological Theory and Women's Voice*, Cambridge, MA, and London: Harvard University Press.

Gilroy, P. (2004) *After Empire: Melancholia or Convivial Culture*, Abingdon: Routledge.

Giorgi, G. (2002) 'Madrid *en Transito*: Travelers, Visibility, and Gay Identity', *GLQ: A Journal of Lesbian and Gay Studies* 8 (1–2), 57–80.

GLQ (1998) Special Issue on 'The Transgender Issue', *GLQ: A Journal of Lesbian and Gay Studies* 4 (2).

GLQ (2002) Special Issue on 'Queer Tourism: Geography of Globalization', edited by J.K. Puar, *GLQ: A Journal of Lesbian and Gay Studies* 8 (1–2).

Goldstein, R. (2003) *Homocons: The Rise of the Gay Right*, London and New York: Verso.

Gorer, G. (1955) *The English Character*, London: The Cresset Press.

Gorer, G. (1971) *Sex and Marriage in England Today: A Study of the Views and Experiences of the Under-45s*, London: Nelson.

Gorna, R. (1996) *Vamps, Virgins and Victims: How Women Can Fight AIDS*, London: Cassell.

Goss, R.E. (1997) 'Queering Procreative Privilege: Coming Out as Families', in Goss and Strongheart (eds) 1997.

Goss, R.E. and Strongheart, A.S. (eds) (1997) *Our Families, Our Values: Snapshots of Queer Kinship*, Binghampton, NJ: The Harrington Park Press.

Goulbourne, H. and Chamberlain, M. (eds) (2001a) *Caribbean Families in Britain and the TransAtlantic World*, London and Oxford: Macmillan Education.

Goulbourne, H. and Chamberlain, M. (2001b) 'Caribbean Families in the TransAtlantic World', in Goulbourne and Chamberlain (eds) 2001a, 2–11.

Graupner, H. (2005) 'Sexual Autonomy – A Human Rights Issue', *Pukaar* 48, January, 8–10.

Graupner, H. and Tahmindjis, P. (eds) (2005) *Sexuality and Human Rights: A Global Overview*, Special Edition of *Journal of Homosexuality* 48 (3/4), New York: Harrington Park Press.

Green, R. and West, D.J. (eds) (1997) *Socio-legal Control of Homosexuality*, New York and London: Plenum Press.

Greer, G. (1970) *The Female Eunuch*, London: MacGibbon & Kee.

Grewal, I. and Kaplan, C. (2001) 'Global Identities: Theorizing Transnational Studies of Sexuality', *GLQ: A Journal of Lesbian and Gay Studies* 7 (4), 663–79.

Griffin, K. and Mulholland, L. (eds) (1997) *Lesbian Mothers in Europe*, London: Cassell.

Gurney, P. (1997) '"Intersex" and "Dirty Girls": Mass Observation and Working-class Sexuality in England in the 1930s', *Journal of the History of Sexuality* 8 (2), October, 256–90.

Halberstam, J. (1998) *Female Masculinity*, Durham, NC, and London: Duke University Press.

Halberstam, J. (2005) *In a Queer Time and Place: Transgender Bodies, Subcultural Lives*, New York and London: New York University Press.

Hall, L.A. (1991) *Hidden Anxieties: Male Sexuality, 1900–1950*, Cambridge: Polity Press.

Hall, L.A. (2000) *Sex, Gender and Social Change in Britain since 1880*, Basingstoke and London: Macmillan.

Hall, R., Ogden, P.E. and Hill, C. (1999) 'Living Alone: Evidence from England and Wales and France for the Last Two Decades', in McRae (ed.) 1999, 265–96.

Hall Carpenter Archives (1989a) *Walking after Midnight: Gay Men's Life Stories*, Gay Men's Oral History Group, London: Routledge.

Hall Carpenter Archives (1989b) *Inventing Ourselves: Lesbian Life Stories*, Lesbian Oral History Group, London: Routledge.

Halley, J. (2001) 'Recognition, Rights, Regulation, Normalisation: Rhetorics of Justification in the Same-sex Marriage Debate', in Wintermute and Andenaes (eds) 2001, 97–112.

Halperin, D.M. (2003) 'The Normalization of Queer Theory', *Journal of Homosexuality* 45 (2/3/4), 339–43.

Hamblin, A. (1974) 'The Suppressed Power of Female Sexuality', in Allen *et al.* 1974, 86–98.

Hamer, E. (1996) *Britannia's Glory: A History of Twentieth Century Lesbianism*, London and New York: Cassell.

Hammersley, B. (2002) 'Porn.com', *Observer*, 'Sex Uncensored' Supplement, 27 October, 34–40.

Hanscombe, G. and Forster, J. (1983) *Rocking the Cradle: Lesbian Mothers. A Challenge in Family Living*, London: Sheba Feminist Publishers.

Haour-Knipe, M. and Rector, R. (1996) *Crossing Borders: Migration, Ethnicity and AIDS*, London and Bristol, PA: Taylor & Francis.

Harding, R. and Peel, L. (2006) '"We Do"? International Perspectives on Equality,

Legality and Same-sex Relationships', *Lesbian and Gay Psychology Review* 7 (2), 123–40.

Harding, S. (1988) 'Trends in Permissiveness', in Jowell *et al.* 1988, 35–52.

Hari, J. (2003) 'At Last the UN Recognises the Need for Gay Rights', *Independent*, 25 April, 17.

Haritaworn, J. (2005) *Thai Multiculturalism in Britain and Germany: An Intersectional Study*, Unpublished Ph.D., London: London South Bank University.

Harne, L. and Rights of Women (1997) *Valued Families: The Lesbian Mothers' Legal Handbook*, London: The Women's Press.

Harrison, K. (2004) 'The Role of Female Friends in the Management of Affairs', in Duncombe *et al.* (eds) 2004, 203–22.

Hawkes, G. (2004) *Sex and Pleasure in Western Culture*, Cambridge: Polity Press.

Hazleden, R. (2004) 'The Pathology of Love in Contemporary Relationship Manuals', *The Sociological Review*, 52 (2), May, 201–17.

Heaphy, B., Donovan, C. and Weeks, J. (1999) 'Sex, Money and the Kitchen Sink: Power in Same-sex Couple Relationships', in Seymour and Bagguley (eds) 1999, 222–45.

Heaphy, B., Donovan, C. and Weeks, J. (2004) 'A Different Affair? Openness and Nonmonogamy in Same Sex Relationships', in Duncombe *et al.* (eds) 2004, 167–84.

Heaphy, B., Weeks, J. and Donovan, C. (1999) 'Narratives of Love, Care and Commitment: AIDS/HIV and Non-heterosexual Family Formations', in Aggleton, P., Hart, G. and Davies, P. (eds) (1999) *Families and Communities Responding to AIDS*, London: UCL Press, 67–82.

Heaphy, B., Yip, A. and Thompson, D. (2003) *Lesbian, Gay and Bisexual Lives over 50: A Report on the Project 'The Social and Policy Implications of Non-heterosexual Ageing'*, Nottingham: York House Publications, Nottingham Trent University.

Heath, J. and Potter, A. (2005) *The Rebel Self: How the Counterculture Became Consumer Culture*, Albany, OR: Capstone Publishing.

Heinz, E. (1995) *Sexual Orientation: A Human Right. An Essay on International Human Rights Law*, Dortrecht, Boston, MA, and London: Martinus Nijhoff.

Hekma, G. (2005) 'How Libertine is the Netherlands?: Exploring Contemporary Dutch Sexual Cultures', in Bernstein and Schaffner (eds) 2005, 209–24.

Held, D. (1987) *Models of Democracy*, Cambridge: Polity Press.

Held, D. (2000) 'Regulating Globalization?, in Held and McGrew (eds) 2000, 420–30.

Held, D. and McGrew, A. (eds) (2000) *The Global Transformations Reader: An Introduction to the Globalization Debate*, Cambridge: Polity Press.

Held, D., McGrew, A., Goldblatt, D. and Perraton, J. (2000) 'Rethinking Globalization', in Held and McGrew (eds) 2000, 54–60.

Hellen, N. (2005) 'Navy Signals for Help to Recruit Gay Sailors', *Sunday Times*, 20 February, 12.

Heller, A. and Feher, F. (1988) *The Postmodern Political Condition*, Cambridge: Polity Press.

Hemmings, C., Gedalof, I. and Bland, L. (2006) 'Sexual Moralities', *Feminist Review* 83, 1–3.

Henderson, M. (2004) 'So it is Down to Mother: Gay Gene Survives Because it Boosts Fertility', *The Times*, 13 October, 5.

Henderson, M. (2006) 'Drug Companies "Inventing Diseases" to Boost their Profits', *The Times*, 11 April, 5.

Henderson, S., Holland, J., McGrellis, S., Sharpe, S. and Thomson, R. (2007) *Inventing Adulthoods: A Biographical Approach to Youth Transitions*, London: Sage.

Hennessy, P. (2006a) *Never Again: Britain 1945–51*, London: Penguin Books.

Hennessy, P. (2006b) *Having it so Good: Britain in the Fifties*, London: Allen Lane.

Hennessy, R. (2000) *Profit and Pleasure: Sexual Identities in Late Capitalism*, New York and London: Routledge.

Hennink, M., Diamond, I. and Cooper, P. (1999) 'Young Asian Women and Relationships: Traditional or Transitional?', *Ethnic and Racial Studies* 22 (5), September, 867–91.

Herdt, G. (1994) *Guardians of the Flutes, Idioms of Masculinity*, Chicago, IL: Chicago University Press.

Herman, D. (1997) *The Anti Gay Agenda: Orthodox Vision and the Christian Right*, Chicago, IL: University of Chicago Press.

Herman, D. and Stychin, C. (eds) (1995) *Legal Inversions: Lesbians, Gay Men and the Politics of Law*, Philadelphia, PA: Temple University Press.

Heron, L. (ed.) (1985) *Truth, Dare or Promise: Girls Growing Up in the 1950s*, London: Virago.

Hicks, S. (2005) 'Is Gay Parenting Bad for the Kids? Responding to the "Very idea of Difference" in Research on Lesbian and Gay Parents', *Sexualities* 8(2), April, 153–68.

Higgins, P. (1996) *The Heterosexual Dictatorship*, London: Fourth Estate.

Higgs, D. (ed.) (1999) *Queer Sites: Gay Urban Histories Since 1600*, London and New York: Routledge.

Himmelfarb, G. (1995) *The De-moralization of Society: From Victorian Values to Modern Values*, London: Institute of Economic Affairs.

Hines, S. (2006) 'Intimate Transitions: Transgender Practices of Partnering and Parenting', *Sociology* 40 (2), April, 353–71.

Hinsliff, G. and Martin, L. (2006) 'How the Baby Shortage Threatens our Future', *Observer*, 19 February, 8–9.

Hitchens, P. (2002) *The Abolition of Britain: From Winston Churchill to Princess Diana*, London: Encounter Books.

HMSO (1957) *Report of the Committee on Homosexual Offences and Prostitution* ('The Wolfenden Report'), Command 147, London: Her Majesty's Stationary Office.

Hobsbawm, E. (1994) *Age of Extremes: The Short Twentieth Century 1914–1991*, London: Michael Joseph.

Hochschild, A.R. (2003a) *The Managed Heart: Commercialization of Human Feeling* (20th Anniversary edn), Berkeley, Los Angeles and London: University of California Press.

Hochschild, A.R. (2003b) *The Commercialization of Intimate Life: Notes from Home and Work*, Berkeley and Los Angeles: University of California Press.

Holden, A. (2004) *Makers and Manners: Politics and Morality in Post-war Britain*, London: Politico's.

Holland, J., Weeks, J. and Gillies, V. (2003) 'Families, Intimacy and Social Capital', *Social Policy and Society* 2 (4), 339–48.

Holland, J., Ramazanoglu, C., Sharpe, S. and Thomson, R. (1998) *The Male in the Head*, London: The Tufnell Press.

Holland, J., Thomson, R., Henderson, S., McGrellis, S. and Sharpe, S. (2000)

'Catching Up, Wising Up, and Learning from Your Mistakes: Young People's Accounts of Moral Development', *International Journal of Children's Rights* 8: 271–94.

Holmes, M. (2004) 'An Equal Distance? Individualization, Gender and Intimacy in Distance Relationships', *The Sociological Review* 52(2), May, 180–200.

Holt, M. (2004) '"Marriage-like" or Married? Lesbian and Gay Marriage, Partnership and Migration', *Feminism and Psychology* 14 (1), February, 30–5.

Home Office (1998) *Supporting Families: A Consultation Document*, London: HMSO.

Hooper, J. (2005) 'Pope's Edict Prohibits Gay Priests', *Guardian*, 24 November, 19.

Hopkins, K.S. (ed.) (1980) *Rhondda Past and Future*, Ferndale: Rhondda Borough Council.

Houlbrook, M. (2005) *Queer London: Perils and Pleasures in the Sexual Metropolis, 1918–1957*, Chicago, IL and London: University of Chicago Press.

Hoyle, B. (2006) 'Why Today's Singles are Logging on in the Search for Love at First Byte', *The Times*, 5 January, 6.

Hubbard, P. (2001) 'Sex Zones: Intimacy, Citizenship and Public Space', *Sexualities* 4 (1), February, 51–71.

Humphries, S. (1988) *A Secret World of Sex: Forbidden Fruit. The British Experience 1900–1950*, London: Sidgwick & Jackson.

Inglehart, R. (1997) *Modernization and Postmodernization: Cultural, Economic and Political Change in 43 Countries*, Princeton, NJ: Princeton University Press.

Irvine, J.M. (2002) *Talk about Sex: The Battles over Sex Education in the United States*, Berkeley: University of California Press.

Jack, D. (2006) 'Stigma is the Real Assassin', *Guardian*, 3 August, 25.

Jackman, M. (2006) 'I Was Smitten', *The Times* 2, 25 May, 5.

Jackson, J. (2006) 'Sex, Politics and Morality in France, 1954–1982', *History Workshop Journal* 61, spring, 77–102.

Jackson, S. (1998) 'Sexual Politics: Feminist Politics, Gay Politics and the Problem of Heterosexuality', in Carver and Mottier 1998, 68–78.

Jackson, S. (2000) *Heterosexuality in Question*, London, Thousand Oaks, CA, New Delhi: Sage.

Jackson, S. and Scott, S. (2004a) 'Sexual Antinomies in Late Modernity', *Sexualities* 7 (2), May, 233–48.

Jackson, S. and Scott, S. (2004b) 'The Personal *is* still Political: Hetero-normativity, Feminism and Monogamy', *Feminism and Psychology* 14 (1), February, 151–7.

Jakobsen, J.R. and Kennedy, E.L. (2005) 'Sex and Freedom', in Bernstein and Schaffner (eds) 2005, 247–70.

Jamieson, L. (1998) *Intimacy: Personal Relationships in Modern Societies*, Cambridge: Polity Press.

Jamieson, L. (1999) 'Intimacy Transformed: A Critical Look at the "Pure Relationship"', *Sociology* 33 (3): 447–94.

Jamieson, L. (2004) 'Intimacy, Negotiated Monogamy, and the Limits of the Couple', in Duncombe *et al.* (eds) 2004, 35–58.

Jay, M. (1973) *The Dialectical Imagination: A History of the Frankfurt School and the Institute of Social Research*, London: Hutchinson.

Jeffreys, S. (1990) *Anti-climax: A Feminist Perspective on the Sexual Revolution*, London: The Women's Press.

Jeffreys, S. (1993) *The Lesbian Heresy*, London: The Women's Press.

Jenkins, P. (1998) *Moral Panic: Changing Concepts of the Child Molester in Modern America*, New Haven, CT: Yale University Press.

Jennings, R. (2004) 'Lesbian Voices: The Hall Carpenter Oral History Archive and Post-war British Lesbian History', *Sexualities* 7 (4), November, 430–45.

Jennings, R. (2006) 'The Gateways Club and the Emergence of a post-Second World War Lesbian Subculture', *Social History* 31 (2), May, 206–25.

John, A.V. (ed.) (1991) *Our Mother's Land: Chapters in Welsh Women's History 1830–1939*, Cardiff: University of Wales Press.

Johnson, A.M., Mercer, C.H. and Erens, B. (2001) 'Sexual Behaviour in Britain: Partnerships, Practices, and HIV Risk Behaviours', *The Lancet*, vol. 358 (9296), 1 December, 1835–42.

Johnson, M. (2003) 'Anomalous Bodies: Transgenderings and Cultural Transformation', in Weeks *et al.* (eds) 2003, 105–18.

Johnson, M.H. (2004) 'A Biological Perspective on Human Sexuality', in Brooks-Gordon *et al.* (eds) 2004, 155–86.

Johnson, P. (2004) 'Haunting Heterosexuality: The Homo/Het Binary and Intimate Love', *Sexualities* 7 (2), May, 183–200.

Johnson, P. (2005) *Love, Heterosexuality and Society*, Abingdon and New York: Taylor & Francis.

Jones, C. (2005) 'Looking Like a Family: Bio-genetic Continuity in British Lesbian Families using Licensed Donor Insemination', *Sexualities* 8(2), April, 221–38.

Jones, D. (1991) 'Counting the Cost of Coal: Women's Lives in the Rhondda, 1881–1911', in John (ed.) 1991, 109–34.

Jones, S. (2002) Y: *The Descent of Men*, New York and London: Little, Brown.

Journal of Homosexuality (2002) 'The Drag King Anthology', 43 (3/4).

Journal of Homosexuality (2004) 'The Drag Queen Anthology: The Absolutely Fabulous but Flawlessly Customary World of Female Impersonators', 46 (3/4).

Jowell, R., Witherspoon, S. and Brook, L. (eds) (1988) *British Social Attitudes: The 5th Report*, Aldershot: Gower.

Kantsa, V. (2002) '"Certain Places Have Different Energy": Spatial Transformations in Eresos, Lesvos', *GLQ: A Journal of Lesbian and Gay Studies* 8 (1–2), 35–56.

Katz, J.N. (1995) *The Invention of Heterosexuality*, New York: Dutton.

Kaufmann, E. (2006) 'Breeding for God', *Prospect*, November, 26–30.

Khan, S. (2006) 'Why Muslim Women Should Thank Straw', *The Times*, 9 October, 21.

King, D. (2003) 'Gender Migration: A Sociological Analysis (or The Leaving of Liverpool)', *Sexualities* 6 (2), May, 173–94.

King, E. (1993) *Safety in Numbers: Safer Sex and Gay Men*, London and New York: Cassell.

Kinsey, A., Pomeroy, W.B. and Martin, C. (1948) *Sexual Behavior in the Human Male*, Philadelphia, PA: W.B. Saunders.

Kinsey, A., Pomeroy, W.B., Martin, C. and Gebhard, P.H. (1953) *Sexual Behavior in the Human Female*, Philadelphia, PA: W.B. Saunders.

Kitzinger, C. and Wilkinson, S. (2004) 'The Re-branding of Marriage: Why We got Married Instead of Registering a Civil Partnership', *Feminism and Psychology* 14 (1), February, 127–50.

Kitzinger, C. and Wilkinson, S. (2006) 'Genders, Sexualities and Equal Marriage Rights', *Lesbian and Gay Psychology Review* 7 (2), 174–9.

Klesse, C. (2005) 'Bisexual Women, Non-monogamy and Differentialist Anti-promiscuity Discourses', *Sexualities* 8 (4), October, 445–64.

Klesse, C. (2006) 'Heteronormativity, Non-monogamy and the Marriage Debate in the Bisexual Movement', *Lesbian and Gay Psychology Review* 7 (2), 162–73.

Knowles, C. and Mercer, S. (1992) 'Feminism and Antiracism: An Exploration of Political Possibilities', in Donald and Rattansi (eds) 1992, 104–25.

Kulick, D. (1998) *Travesti: Sex, Gender and Culture Among Brazilian Transgendered Prostitutes*, Chicago, IL and London: University of Chicago Press.

Kulick, D. (2005) 'Four Hundred Thousand Swedish Perverts', *GLQ: A Journal of Lesbian and Gay Studies* 11 (2), 205–35.

Lancaster, R. (2003) *The Trouble with Nature: Sex in Science and Popular Culture*, Berkeley, Los Angeles and London: University of California Press.

Langdridge, D. and Butt, T. (2004) 'A Hermeneutic Phenomenological Investigation of the Construction of Sadomasochistic Identities', *Sexualities* 7 (1), February, 31–53.

Lasch, C. (1985) *The Minimal Self: Psychic Survival in Troubled Times*, New York: W.W. Norton.

Laslett, P. (1965) *The World We Have Lost*, London: Methuen.

Leap, W.L. (ed.) (1999) *Public Sex, Gay Space*, New York: Columbia University Press.

Lewin, E. (1984) 'Lesbianism and Motherhood: Implications for Child Custody', in Dary, T. and Potter, S. (eds) *Women-identified-women*, Palo Alto, CA: Mayfield Publishing.

Lewin, E. (1993) *Lesbian Mothers: Accounts of Gender In American Culture*, Ithaca and London: Cornell University Press.

Lewin, E. (1998) *Recognizing Ourselves: Ceremonies of Lesbian and Gay Commitment*, New York: Columbia University Press.

Lewis, E.D. (1980) 'Population Changes and Social Life 1860 to 1914', in Hopkins (ed.) 1980, 110–128.

Lewis, J. (1980) *The Politics of Motherhood: Child and Maternal Welfare in Britain, 1900–1939*, London: Croom Helm.

Lewis, J. (1982) *Women in England 1870–1950*, Brighton: Harvester Press.

Lewis, J. (2001) *The End of Marriage? Individualism and Intimate Relations*, Cheltenham, and Northampton, MA: Edward Elgar.

Lexington (2006) 'Deconstructing the God Squad', *The Economist*, 21 October, 66.

Liddle, K. and Liddle, B.J. (2004) 'In the Meantime: Same-sex Ceremonies in the Absence of Legal Recognition', *Feminism and Psychology* 14(1), February, 52–6.

Lister, D. (2006) 'Boy Charged over 11-year-old's Pregnancy', *The Times*, 13 May, 23.

Loe, M. (2004) *The Rise of Viagra: How the Little Blue Pill Changed Sex in America*, New York and London: New York University Press.

London Gay Liberation Front (1971) *Manifesto*, London: Gay Liberation Front.

Long, S. (2005) 'A Letter from Scott Long', *Pukaar* 49, April, 13.

Loseka, D.R. (2003) '"We hold these Truths to be Self-evident": Problems in Pondering the Paedophile Priest Problem', *Sexualities* 6 (1), February, 6–14.

Luongo, M. (2002) 'Rome's World Pride: Making the Eternal City an International Tourist Destination', *GLQ: A Journal of Lesbian and Gay Studies* 8 (1–2), 167–82.

Lusher, T. (2006) 'Straight Talk', *Guardian 2*, 7 June, 7.

Mabry, J.B. and Bengtson, V.L. (2004) 'Generations, the Life Course, and Family Change', in Scott *et al.* (eds) 2004, 87–108.

McCreery, P. (2004) 'Innocent Pleasures? Children's Sexual Politics', *GLQ: A Journal of Lesbian and Gay Studies* 10 (4), 617–30.

McGhee, D. (2001) *Homosexuality, Law and Resistance*, London and New York: Routledge.

McGhee, D. (2003) 'Moving to "Our" Common Ground – A Critical Examination of Community Cohesion Discourse in Twenty-first Century Britain', *The Sociological Review* 51 (3), 376–404.

McGhee, D. (2004) 'Beyond Toleration: Privacy, Citizenship and Sexual Minorities in England and Wales', *The British Journal of Sociology* 55 (3), 357–75.

McGhee, D. (2005) *Intolerant Britain: Hate, Citizenship and Difference*, Berkshire: Open University Press.

McIntosh, M. (1981) 'The Homosexual Role', in Plummer (ed.) 1981, 30–49.

Mackenzie, G.O. (1999) '50 Billion Galaxies of Gender: Transgendering the Millennium', in More and Whittle (eds) 1999, 193–218.

McKittrick, D. (2002) 'Child Sex Abuse Scandals Risk Meltdown of Irish Church', *Independent*, 9 November, 13.

McLaren, A. (1999) *Twentieth-century Sexuality: A History*, Oxford: Blackwell.

McLaughlin, D. (2006) 'Homophobia seeps across new EU', *Observer*, 12 March, 40.

McRae, S. (ed.) (1999) *Changing Britain: Families and Households in the 1990s*, Oxford: Oxford University Press.

McWhirter, D. and Mattison, A.M. (1984) *The Male Couple: How Relationships Develop*, Princeton, NJ: Prentice Hall.

Maffesoli, M. (1995) *The Time of Tribes: The Decline of Individualism in Mass Society*, London and New Delhi: Sage.

Magee, B. (1966) *One in Twenty*, London: Secker & Warburg.

Mansfield, P. and Collard, J. (1988) *The Beginning of the Rest of Your Life: A Portrait of Newly Wed Marriage*, London: Macmillan.

Marcuse, H. (1969) *Eros and Civilization*, London: Sphere Books.

Marcuse, H. (1972) *One-dimensional Man*, London: Abacus.

Markwell, K. (2002) 'Mardi Gras Tourism and the Construction of Sydney as an International Gay and Lesbian City', *GLQ: A Journal of Lesbian and Gay Studies* 8 (1–2), 81–100.

Marshall, T.H. (1950) *Citizenship and Social Class, and Other Essays*, Cambridge: Cambridge University Press.

Martin, J.I. (2006) 'Transcendence among Gay Men: Implications for HIV Prevention', *Sexualities* 9 (2), April, 214–35.

Marwick, A. (1998) *The Sixties: Cultural Revolution in Britain, France, Italy, and the United States, c. 1958–c. 1974*, Oxford and New York: Oxford University Press.

Mason, J. (2004) 'Personal Narratives, Relational Selves: Residential Histories in the Living and Telling', *The Sociological Review* 52 (2), May, 162–79.

Melucci, A. (1989) *Nomads of the Present: Social Movements and Individual Needs in Contemporary Society*, London: Radius.

Mendes-Leite, R. and Banens, M. (2006) *Vivre avec le VIH*, Paris: Calman-Levy.

Mercer, K. (1994) *Welcome to the Jungle: New Positions in Black Cultural Studies*, London and New York: Routledge.

Merin, Y. (2002) *Equality for Same Sex Couples*, Chicago, IL: Chicago University Press.

Miller, A. M. (2000) 'Sexual but not Reproductive: Exploring the Junctions and Disjunctions of Sexual and Reproductive Rights', *Health and Human Rights* 4 (2), 68–109.

Mirza, H.S. (1997) *Black British Feminism: A Reader*, London and New York: Routledge.

Mitchell, J. (1973) *Women's Estate*, Harmondsworth: Penguin.

Mohanty, C.T., Russo, A. and Torres, L. (eds) (1991) *Third World Women and the Politics of Feminism*, Bloomington: Indiana University Press.

Moran, L. (1995) 'The Homosexualization of English Law', in Herman and Stychin (eds) 1995, 3–28.

Moran, L. and Skeggs, B., with Tyrer, P. and Corteen, K. (2004) *Sexuality and the Politics of Violence and Safety*, London and New York: Routledge.

More, K. and Whittle, S. (eds) (1999) *Reclaiming Genders: Transsexual Grammar at the fin de siecle*, London and New York: Cassell.

Morgan, D. (1999) 'What Does a Transsexual Want? The Encounter between Psychoanalysis and Transsexualism', in More and Whittle (eds) 1999, 219–239.

Morgan, D.H.J. (1996) *Family Connections*, Cambridge: Polity Press.

Morgan, D.H.J. (1999) 'Risk and Family Practices: Accounting for Change and Fluidity in Family Life', in Silva and Smart (eds) 1999, 13–30.

Morgan, D.H.J. (2004a) 'Men in Families and Households', in Scott *et al.* (eds) 2004, 374–94.

Morgan, D.H.J. (2004b) 'The Sociological Significance of Affairs', in Duncombe *et al.* (eds) 2004, 15–34.

Morgan, P. (1995) *Farewell to the Family? Public Policy and Family Breakdown in Britain and the USA*, London: Institute of Economic Affairs, Health and Welfare Unit.

Morgan, P. (2006) 'Where Marriage is a Dirty Word', *Sunday Times*, 'News Review', 19 February, 7.

Mort, F. (1996) *Cultures of Consumption: Masculinities and Social Space in late Twentieth-century Britain*, London and New York: Routledge.

Mort, F. (1999) 'Mapping Sexual London: The Wolfenden Committee on Homosexual Offences and Prostitution, 1954–7', *New Formations* 37, 92–113.

Mowbray, N. (2006) 'Now We can All Play Happy "Framilies"', *Observer*, 9 April, 19.

Muir, H. (2006) '6500 Couples Opt for Civil Partnerships but Ceremony Creates New Problems', *Guardian*, 8 August, 7.

Munson, M. and Stelboum, J.P. (eds) (1999) *The Lesbian Polyamory Reader: Non-monogamy and Casual Sex*, New York and London: Harrington Park Press. Published simultaneously as a special issue of *Journal of Lesbian Studies* 3 (1/2) 1999.

Nagel, J. (2003) *Race, Ethnicity and Sexuality: Intimate Intersections, Forbidden Frontiers*, New York and Oxford: Oxford University Press.

Nardi, P. (1992) 'That's What Friends Are For: Friends As Family In The Lesbian And Gay Community', in Plummer (ed.) 1992.

Nardi, P. (1999) *Gay Men's Friendships: Invincible Communities*, Chicago, IL: Chicago University Press.

Neale, P.R. (1998) 'Sexuality and the International Conference on Population and Development. The Catholic Church in International Politics', in Carver and Mottier (eds) 1998, 147–57.

Nussbaum, M. (1999) *Sex and Social Justice*, New York and Oxford: Oxford University Press.

Observer (2002) 'The Uncovered Poll', *Observer*, 'Sex Uncovered' Supplement, 27 October, 10–19.

O'Connell Davidson, J. (1998) *Prostitution, Power and Freedom*, Cambridge: Polity Press.

O'Connell Davidson, J. (2001) 'The Sex Tourist, the Expatriate, his Ex-wife, and her "Other": The Politics of Loss, Difference and Desire', *Sexualities* 4 (1), 6–24.

O'Connell Davidson, J. (2003) 'Power, Consent and Freedom', in Weeks *et al.* (eds) 2003, 204–15.

O'Connell Davidson, J. (2005) *Children in the Global Sex Trade*, Cambridge: Polity Press.

O'Connell Davidson, J. (2006) 'Will the Real Sex Slave Stand Up?', *Feminist Review* 83, 4–22.

O'Connell Davidson, J. and Sanchez Taylor, J. (2005) 'Travel and Taboo: Heterosexual Sex Tourism to the Caribbean', in Bernstein and Schaffler (eds) 2005, 83–100.

Okin, S.M. (2005) 'Women's Human Rights in the Late Twentieth Century: One Step Forward, Two Steps Back', in Bamforth 2005, 83–118.

O'Leary, P. (2004) 'Masculine Histories: Gender and the Social History of Modern Wales', *Welsh History Review* 22 (2), 252–77.

ONS (2006) *Social Trends* 36, London: Office of National Statistics/Palgrave.

Oosterhuis, H. (2000) *Stepchildren of Nature: Krafft-Ebing, Psychiatry and the Making of Sexual Identity*, Chicago, IL, and London: University of Chicago Press.

O'Riordan, K. (2005) 'From Usenet to Gaydar: A Comment on Queer Online Community', *ACM SIDDROUP Bulletin* 25 (2), 28–32.

Ortiz-Hernandez, L. and Granados-Cosme, J. A. (2006) 'Violence against Bisexuals, Gays and Lesbians in Mexico City', *Journal of Homosexuality* 50 (4), 113–40.

Page, J. (2006) 'Gay Pride Takes a Fall amid Fears and Threats', *The Times*, 27 May, 43.

Pahl, R. (2000) *On Friendship*, Cambridge: Polity Press.

Pant, S. (2005) 'Traffiking of Boys', *Pukaar* 50, July, 5.

Parker, R. (1991) *Bodies, Pleasures and Passions: Sexual Culture in Contemporary Brazil*, Boston, MA: Beacon Press.

Parker, R. (1999) *Beneath the Equator: Cultures of Desire, Male Homosexuality and emerging Gay Communities in Brazil*, London and New York: Routledge.

Parker, R. and Aggleton, P. (eds) (1999) *Culture, Society and Sexuality: A Reader*, London: UCL Press.

Parker, R., Barbosa, R.M. and Aggleton, P. (eds) (2000) *Framing the Sexual Subject: The Politics of Gender, Sexuality, and Power*, Berkeley, Los Angeles and London: University of California Press.

Parnell, M. (1997) *Laughter from the Dark: A Life of Gwyn Thomas*, Bridgend: Seren.

Patton, C. (2000) 'Migratory Vices', in Patton and Sanchez-Eppler (eds) 2000, 15–37.

Patton, C. and Sanchez-Eppler, B. (eds) (2000) *Queer Diasporas*, Durham, NC, and London: Duke University Press.

Petchesky, R. (2000) 'Sexual Rights: Inventing a Concept, Mapping an International Practice', in Parker *et al.* (eds) 2000, 81–103.

Petchesky, R. (2003) 'Negotiating Reproductive Rights', in Weeks *et al.* (eds) 2003, 227–40.

Petchesky, R. and Judd, J. (eds) (1998) *Negotiating Reproductive Rights: Women's Perspectives Across Countries and Cultures*, London: Zed Books.

Phelan, S. (2001) *Sexual Strangers: Gays, Lesbians, and Dilemmas of Citizenship*, Philadelphia, PA: Temple University Press.

Phillips, C. (2004) 'Kingdom of the Blind', *Guardian Review*, 17 July, 4–6.

Phillips, M. (1999) *The Sex-change Society: Feminised Britain and Neutered Male*, London: The Social Market Foundation.

Phillips, M. (2006) *Londonistan: How Britain is Creating a Terror State Within*, London: Gibson Square Books.

Phillips, O. (2000) 'Constituting the Global Gay: Issues of Individual Subjectivity and Sexuality in Southern Africa', in Stychin and Herman (eds) 2000, 17–34.

Phillips, O. (2003) 'Zimbabwean Law and the Production of a White Man's Disease', in Weeks *et al.* (eds) 2003, 162–73.

Phillipson, M. (1989) *In Modernity's Wake: The Ameurunculus Letters*, London: Routledge.

Pilcher, J. (1994) 'Who Should Do the Dishes? Three Generations of Welsh Women Talking about Men and Housework', in Aaron *et al.* (eds) 1994, 31–47.

Playdon, Z-J. (2004) 'Intersecting Oppressions: Ending Discrimination Against Lesbians, Gay Men and Trans People in the UK', in Brooks-Gordon *et al.* (eds) 2004, 131–54.

Plummer, K. (1975) *Sexual Stigma: An Interactionist Account*, London: Routledge & Kegan Paul.

Plummer, K. (ed.) (1981) *The Making of the Modern Homosexual*, London: Hutchinson.

Plummer, K. (ed.) (1992) *Modern Homosexualities: Fragments of Lesbian and Gay Experience*, London and New York: Routledge.

Plummer, K. (1995) *Telling Sexual Stories: Power, Change and Social Worlds*, London: Routledge.

Plummer, K. (1999) 'The Lesbian and Gay Movement in Britain: Schism, Solidarities and Social Worlds', in Adam *et al.* (eds) 1999a, 133–57.

Plummer, K. (2003) *Intimate Citizenship: Private Decisions and Public Dialogues*, Seattle: University of Washington Press.

Plummer, K. (2004) 'Social Worlds, Social Change and the Rise of the New Sexualities Theories', in Brooks-Gordon *et al.* (eds) 2004, 39–64.

Porter, R. and Hall, L. (1995) *The Facts of Life: The Creation of Sexual Knowledge in Britain, 1650–1950*, New Haven, CT, and London: Yale University Press.

Porter, R. and Teich, M. (eds) (1994) *Sexual Knowledge, Sexual Science: The History of Attitudes to Sexuality*, Cambridge: Cambridge University Press.

Povinelli, E.A. and Chauncey, G. (1999) 'Thinking Sexuality Transnationally: An Introduction', *QLQ: A Journal of Lesbian and Gay Studies* 5 (4), 439–49.

Power, L. (1995) *No Bath But Plenty of Bubbles: An Oral History of the Gay Liberation Front 1970–73*, London: Cassell.

Probert, R . (2001) 'From Lack of Status to Contract: Assessing the French Pacte Civil de Soldarite', *Journal of Social Welfare and Family Law* 23 (3), 257–69.

Prosser, J. (1999) 'Exceptional Locations: Transsexual Travelogues' in More and Little (eds) 1999, 83–114.

Putnam, R.D. (2001) *Bowling Alone: The Collapse and Revival of American Community*, New York, London, Toronto, Sydney and Singapore: A Touchstone Book, Simon & Schuster.

Rahman, M. (1998) 'Sexuality and Rights: Problematizing Lesbian and Gay Rights', in Carver and Mottier (eds) 1998, 79–90.

Rahman, M. (2000) *Sexuality and Democracy*, Edinburgh: Edinburgh University Press.

Rajan, R. S. (2005) 'Women's Human Rights in the Third World', in Bamforth 2005, 119–36.

Rajasingham, D. (1995) 'On Mediating Multiple Identities: The Shifting Field of Women's Sexualities within the Community, State and Nation', in Schuler, M.A. (ed.) *From Basic Needs to Basic Rights: Women's Claim to Human Rights*, Washington, DC: Women, Law and Development International, 233–48.

Raymond, J. (1979) *The Transsexual Empire*, Boston, MA: Beacon Press.

Reavey, P. and Warner, S. (eds) (2003) *New Feminist Stories of Child Sexual Abuse: Sexual Scripts and Dangerous Dialogues*, London and New York: Routledge.

Rees, T. (1994) 'Women and Paid Work in Wales', in Aaron *et al.* (eds) 1994, 89–106.

Reiche, R. (1979) *Sexuality and the Class Struggle*, London: New Left Books.

Renton, A. (2005) 'Learning the Thai Sex Trade', *Prospect*, May, 56–62.

Reynolds, R. (1999) 'Postmodernizing the Closet', *Sexualities* 2 (3), August, 346–9.

Reynolds, R. (2002) *From Camp to Queer: Remaking the Australian Homosexual*, Melbourne: Melbourne University Press.

Reynolds, T. (2001) 'Caribbean Fathers in Family Lives in Britain', in Goulbourne and Chamberlain (eds) 2001a, 133–54.

Reynolds, T. (2004) *Caribbean Families, Social Capital and Young People's Diasporic Identities*, Families and Social Capital ESRC Research Group, Working Paper 11, London: London South Bank University.

Reynolds, T. (2005) *Caribbean Mothers: Identity and Experience in the UK*, London: Tufnell Press.

Ribbens McCarthy, J., Edwards, R. and Gillies, V. (2003) *Making Families: Moral Tales of Parenting and Step-parenting*, Durham: Sociology Press.

Rich, A. (1984) 'On Compulsory Heterosexuality and Lesbian Existence', in Snitow *et al.* (eds) 1984, 212–41.

Richards, M. (2004) 'Assisted Reproduction, Genetic Technologies', in Scott *et al.* (eds) 2004, 478–98.

Richardson, D. (1987) *Women and the AIDS Crisis*, London: Pandora.

Richardson, D. (ed.) (1996) *Theorising Heterosexuality: Telling it Straight*, Buckingham, and Philadelphia, PA: Open University Press.

Richardson, D. (2000a) *Rethinking Sexuality*, London, and Thousand Oaks, CA: Sage.

Richardson, D. (2000b) 'Claiming Citizenship? Sexuality, Citizenship and Lesbian/Feminist Theory', *Sexualities* 3 (2), May, 255–72.

Richardson, D. (2004) 'Locating Sexualities: From Here to Normality', *Sexualities* 7 (4), 391–411.

Richardson, D. and Seidman, S. (2002) *Handbook of Lesbian and Gay Studies*, London, Thousand Oaks, CA, and New Delhi: Sage.

Riddell, P. (2004) 'On God and Sex there is a Moral Divide between Britain and US', *The Times*, 10 November, 17.

Ridge, D.T. (2004) '"It was an Incredible Thrill": The Social Meanings and Dynamics of Younger Men's Experiences of Barebacking in Melbourne', *Sexualities* 7 (3), August, 259–79.

Ridley, M. (2003) *Nature via Nurture*, London: Fourth Estate.

Rights Of Women Custody Group (1986) *Lesbian Mothers' Legal Handbook*, London: The Women's Press.

Riley, D. (1988) '*Am I That Name?' Feminism and the Category of 'Women'*, London: Macmillan.

Roberts, G. (1994) 'The Cost of Community: Women in Raymond Williams's Fiction', in Aaron *et al.* (eds) 1994, 214–27.

Robinson, K., Taher, A. and Elliott, J. (2006) 'A Veiled Threat?', *Sunday Times*, 8 October, 13.

Robinson, P.A. (1972) *The Sexual Radicals: Reich, Roheim, Marcuse*, London: Paladin.

Robinson, P.A. (2005) *Queer Wars: The New Gay Right and its Critics*, Chicago, IL, and London: University of Chicago Press.

Rodgerson, G. and Wilson, E. (eds) (1991) *Pornography and Feminism: The Case Against Censorship, by Feminists against Censorship*, London: Lawrence and Wishart.

Roedy, B. (2005) 'Global Effort to Beat the HIV Pandemic', *Guardian Media*, 5 December, 2.

Rorty, R. (1989) *Contingency, Irony and Solidarity*, Cambridge: Cambridge University Press.

Rose, D. (2006) 'Sex with many Partners? No Thanks, we're British', *The Times*, 1 November, 29.

Rose, H. (1996) 'Gay Brains, Gay Genes, and Feminist Science Theory', in Weeks and Holland (eds) 1996, 53–72.

Rose, H., Rose, S. and Jencks, C. (eds) (2001) *Alas, Poor Darwin: Escaping Evolutionary Psychology*, New York and London: Vintage Press.

Rose, N. (1998) *Inventing Our Selves: Psychology, Power and Personhood*, Cambridge: Cambridge University Press.

Rose, N. (1999) *Governing the Soul: The Shaping of the Private Self* (2nd edn), London and New York: Free Associations Books.

Roseneil, S. (2000) 'Queer Frameworks and Queer Tendencies: Towards an Understanding of Postmodern Transformations of Sexuality', *Sociological Research Online* 5 (3) at http://www.socresonline.org.uk/5/3/roseneil.html.

Roseneil, S. (2004) 'Why We Should Care About Friends: An Argument for Queering the Care Imaginary in Social Policy', *Social Policy and Society* 3 (4), 409–19.

Roseneil, S. (2006) 'On Not Living with a Partner: Unpicking Coupledom and Cohabitation'. *Social Research Online* 11 (3) at http://www.socresonline.org.uk/11/3/roseneil.html.

Roseneil, S. and Budgeon, S. (2004) 'Beyond the Conventional Family: Intimacy, Care and Community in the 21st Century', *Current Sociology* 52 (2), 135–59.

Rothblum, E.D. (2005) 'Same-sex Marriage and Legalized Relationships: I do, or do I?', *Journal of GLBT Family Studies* 1 (1), 21–31.

Rowbotham, S. (1973) *Women's Consciousness, Man's World*, Harmondsworth: Pelican.

Rowbotham, S. (2001) *Promise of a Dream: Remembering the Sixties*, London and New York: Verso.

Rowlingson, K. and McKay, S. (2005) 'Lone Motherhood and Socio-economic Disadvantage: Insights from Quantitative and Qualitative Evidence', *The Sociological Review* 5 (1), February, 30–49.

Rubin, G. (1984) 'Thinking Sex: Notes for a Radical Theory of the Politics of Sexuality', in Vance (ed.) 1984, 267–319.

Rubin, H.S. (1999) 'Trans Studies: Between a Metaphysics of Presence and Absence', in More and Whittle (eds) 1999, 174–92.

Rubin, L. (1985) *Just Friends. The Role of Friendship in Our Lives*, New York: Harper & Row.

Rutherford, J. (2005) 'How We Live Now', *Soundings: A Journal of Politics and Culture* 30, summer, 9–14.

Ruthven, M. (2004) *Fundamentalism: The Search for Meaning*, Oxford: Oxford University Press.

Ryan, A. (2001) 'Feminism and Sexual Freedom in an Age of AIDS', *Sexualities* 4 (1), February, 91–107.

Ryan-Flood, R. (2005) 'Contested Heteronormativities: Discourses of Fatherhood among Lesbian Parents in Sweden and Ireland', *Sexualities* 8 (2), April, 189–204.

Saffron, L. (1994) *Challenging Conceptions: Planning a Family by Self-insemination*, London and New York: Cassell.

Saffron, L. (1996) *What About the Children? Sons and Daughters of Lesbians and Gay Parents Talk about their Lives*, London and New York: Cassell.

Sanchez Taylor, J. (2006) 'Female Sexual Tourism: A Contradiction in Terms?', *Feminist Review* 83, 42–58.

Sandbrook, D. (2005) *Never Had It So Good: A History of Britain from Suez to the Beatles*, London: Little, Brown.

Sandbrook, D. (2006) *White Heat: A History of Britain in the Swinging Sixties*, London: Little, Brown.

Saunders, P. (2005) 'Identity to Acronym: How "Child Prostitution" became "CSEC"', in Bernstein and Schaffler (eds) 2005, 167–188.

Savage, J. (2006) 'Meek by Name, Wild by Nature', *Observer Music Monthly* 39, November, 66–74.

Scheper-Hughes, N. and Devine, J. (2003) 'Priestly Celibacy and Child Sex Abuse', *Sexualities* 6 (1), 15–40.

Schlichter, A. (2004) 'Queer at Last? Straight Intellectuals and the Desire for Transgression', *GLQ: A Journal of Lesbian and Gay Studies* 10 (4), 543–64.

Schneider, S.J. (ed.) (2005) *1001 Movies You Must See Before You Die*, London: Cassell Illustrated.

Schofield, M. (1973) *The Sexual Behaviour of Young Adults*, London: Allen Lane.

Schuster, L. and Solomos, J. (2004) 'New Directions or "The Same Old Story"? New Labour's Policies on Race Relations, Immigration and Asylum', in Steinberg and Johnson (eds) 2004, 81–95.

Scott, J. (1998) 'Changing Attitudes to Sexual Morality: A Cross-national Comparison', *Sociology* 32, 815–45.

Scott, J. (1999) 'Family Change: Revolution or Backlash in Attitudes?', in McRae (ed.) 1999, 68–99.

Scott, J., Treas, J. and Richards, M. (eds) (2004) *The Blackwell Companion to the Sociology of the Family*, Oxford, and Malden, MA: Blackwell.

Scott-Clark, C. and Levy, A. (2005) 'Where it's Really Hurting', *Guardian Weekend*, 10 September, 24–33.

Scruton, R. (2005) *Gentle Regrets: Thoughts from a Life*, London and New York: Continuum.

Scruton, R. (2006) *England: An Elegy*, London and New York: Continuum.

Seabrook, J. (1999) *Love in a Different Climate: Men who have Sex with Men in India*, London and New York: Verso.

Seabrook, J. (2001) *Travels in the Skin Trade: Tourism and the Sex Industry* (2nd edn), London: Pluto Press.

Sedgwick, E.K. (1990) *Epistemology of the Closet*, Berkeley and Los Angeles: University of California Press.

Segal, L. (1987) *Is the Future Female? Troubled Thoughts on Contemporary Feminism*, London: Virago.

Segal, L. (1990) *Slow Motion: Changing Masculinities, Changing Men*, London: Virago.

Segal, L. (1999) *Why Feminism?*, Cambridge: Polity Press.

Segal, L. (2003) 'Only the Literal: The Contradictions of Anti-pornography Feminism', in Weeks *et al.* (eds) 2003, 95–104.

Segal, L. (2004) 'New Battlegrounds: Genetic Maps and Sexual Politics', in Brooks-Gordon *et al.* (eds) 2004, 65–84.

Segal, L. (2006) Contribution to 'Seven Ages of Women', *Guardian G2*, 27 March, 18.

Segal, L. and Mcintosh, M. (eds) (1992) *Sex Exposed: Sexuality and the Pornography Debates*, London: Virago.

Seidman, S. (ed.) (1999) *Queer Theory/Sociology*, Oxford: Blackwell.

Seidman, S. (2002) *Beyond the Closet: The Transformation of Gay and Lesbian Life*, London and New York: Routledge.

Seidman, S. (2005) 'From Outsider to Citizen', in Bernstein and Schaffner (eds) 2005, 225–46.

Seidman, S., Meeks, C. and Traschen, F. (1999) 'Beyond the Closet? The Changing Social Meanings of Homosexuality in the United States', *Sexualities* 2 (1), February, 9–34.

Sennett, R. (1992) *The Fall of Public Man*, New York: W.W. Norton.

Sennett, R. (2003) *Respect: The Formation of Character in a World of Inequality*, London: Allen Lane.

Sevenhuijsen, S. (1998) *Citizenship and the Ethics of Care: Feminist Considerations on Justice, Morality and Politics*, London and New York: Routledge.

Sexualities (1998) 'Transgender in Latin America', Special Issue edited by D. Kulick, *Sexualities* 1 (3), August.

Sexualities (2006a) 'Viagra Culture', special issue edited by A. Potts and L. Tiefer, *Sexualities* 9 (3), July.

Sexualities (2006b) Special Issue on Polyamory, *Sexualities* 9 (5), December.

Seymour, J. and Bagguley, P. (eds) (1999) *Relating Intimacies: Power and Resistance*, Basingstoke: Macmillan.

Shakespeare, T. (2003) '"I Haven't Seen that in the Kama Sutra": The Sexual Stories of Disabled People', in Weeks *et al.* (eds) 2003, 143–52.

Sharrock, D. (2006) 'Outrage of Old Guard Fails to Rain on First "Gay Wedding" Day', *The Times*, 20 December, 14.

Shaw, A. (2004) 'Immigrant Families in the UK', in Scott *et al.* (eds) 2004, 270–86.

Sherman, J. and Bennett, R. (2006) 'Affluent Suburbs Show Fastest Rise in Teenage Pregnancy', *The Times*, 12 September, 14.

Sherwin, A. (2006) 'Gay Means Rubbish', *The Times*, 6 June, 5.

Shipman, B. and Smart, C. (2007) '"It's Made a Huge Difference": Recognition, Rights and the Personal Significance of Civil Partnership', *Sociological Research Online* 12 (1), January, accessed at http://www.socresonline.org. uk/12/1shipman.html.

Sieghart, M.A. (2003) 'The Culture War is Over: The Shoulder Shruggers have Won', *The Times*, 4 July, 22.

Sieghart, M.A. (2005) 'Happily, Everyday is Father's Day for more Families Now', *The Times*, T2, 16 June, 2.

Sieghart, M.A. (2006) 'Can't Muslim Men Control their Urges', *The Times, T2,* 2 November, 7.

Shiu-Ki, T.K. (2004) 'Queer at your own Risk: Marginality, Community and Hong Kong Gay Male Bodies', *Sexualities* 7 (1), February, 5–30.

Silva, E.B. and Smart, C. (eds) (1999) *The New Family?*, London: Sage.

Simon, W. (1996) *Postmodern Sexualities*, London and New York: Routledge.

Simon, W. (2003) 'The Postmodernization of Sex', in Weeks *et al.* (eds) 2003, 22–32.

Sinfield, A. (1989) *Literature, Politics and Culture in Postwar Britain*, Oxford: Blackwell.

Sinfield, A. (2005) 'Rape and Rights: *Measure for Measure* and the Limits of Cultural Imperialism', in Bamforth 2005, 140–58.

Skeggs, B. (1997) *Formations of Class and Gender: Becoming Respectable*, London, Thousand Oaks, CA, and New Delhi: Sage.

Smart, C. (2006) 'Children's Narratives of Post-divorce Family Life: From Individual Experience to an Ethical Disposition', *The Sociological Review* 54 (1), February, 155–70.

Smart, C. and Neale, B. (1999) *Family Fragments?*, Cambridge: Polity Press.

Smart, C., Mason, J. and Shipman, B. (2006) *Gay and Lesbian Marriage: An Exploration of the Meanings and Significance of Legitimating Same-sex Relationships*, Manchester: Morgan Centre for the Study of Relationships and Personal Life, University of Manchester.

Smith, A.M. (1994) *New Right Discourse on Race and Sexuality: Britain, 1968–1990*, Cambridge: Cambridge University Press.

Smith, B.G. (ed.) 2000 *Global Feminisms Since 1945: Rewriting Histories*, New York and London: Routledge.

Smith, D. (1980) 'Leaders and Led', in Hopkins (ed.) 1980: 37–65.

Smith, D. (2006) 'Foreword', in Williams 2006.

Smith, David (2005) 'Women's Lib Owes it All to the Pill', *Sunday Times*, 17 July, accessed at http://www.timesonline.co.uk/article/0,,2087-1697247,00.html.

Smith, H. (2005) 'Sex and Fraud Woe for Greek Church', *Guardian*, 19 February, accessed at http://www.guardian.co.uk/international/story/0,,1417 874,00.html.

Snitow, A., Stansell, C. and Thompson, S. (eds) (1984) *Desire: The Politics of Sexuality*, London: Virago.

Sontag, S. and Hodgkin, H. (1991) *How We Live Now*, with illustrations by Howard Hodgkin, London: Jonathan Cape.

Soundings (2006) 'Convivial Cultures', edited by Jonathan Rutherford, *Soundings* 33, Summer.

Spencer, L. and Pahl, R. (2006) *Rethinking Friendship: Hidden Solidarities Today*, Princeton, NJ, and Woodstock: Princeton University Press.

Stacey, J. (1996) *In the Name of the Family: Rethinking Family Values in the Postmodern Age*, Boston, MA: Beacon Press.

Stacey, J. (2006) 'Gay Parenthood and the Decline of Paternity as We Knew It', *Sexualities* 9 (1), February, 27–53.

Stack, C. (1974) *Allow Kin*, New York: Harper & Row.

Stanley, L. (1995) *Sex Surveyed 1949–1994: From Mass-Observation's 'Little Kinsey' to the National Survey and the Hite Reports*, London and Bristol, PA: Taylor & Francis.

Steedman, C. (1986) *Landscape for a Good Woman: A Story of Two Lives*, London: Virago.

Steinberg, D.L. and Johnson, R. (eds) (2004) *Blairism and the War of Persuasion: Labour's Passive Revolution*, London: Lawrence & Wishart.

Steinberg, D.L. and Kear, A. (eds) (1999) *Mourning Diana: Nation, Culture and the Performance of Grief*, London: Routledge.

Stephens, M. (ed.) (2001) *Rhys Davies: Decoding the Hare. Critical Essays to Mark the Centenary of the Author's Birth*, Cardiff: University of Wales Press.

Stoler, A.L. (1995) *Race and the Education of Desire: Foucault's History of Sexuality and the Colonial Order of Things*, Durham, NC, and London: Duke University Press.

Storr, M. (1999) 'Postmodern Bisexuality', *Sexualities* 2 (3), August, 309–25.

Strang, J. and Stimson, G. (1990) *AIDS and Drug Misuse: The Challenge for Policy and Practice in the 1990s*, London and New York: Routledge.

Strasser, M. (1997) *Legally Wed: Same-sex Marriage and the Constitution*, Ithaca, NY: Cornell University Press.

Stychin, C. and Herman, D. (eds) (2000) *Sexuality in the Legal Arena*, London: Athlone Press.

Sullivan, A. (1995) *Virtually Normal: An Argument about Homosexuality*, London: Picador.

Sullivan, A. (ed.) (1997) *Same-sex Marriage: Pro and Con. A Reader*, New York: Vintage Books.

Sullivan, A. (1998) *Love Undetectable: Reflections on Friendship, Sex and Survival*, London: Chatto & Windus.

Sullivan, A. (2004) 'Where the Bible Bashers are Sinful and the Liberals Pure', *Sunday Times*, 28 November, accessed at http://www.timesonline.co.uk/tol/comment/article.396496.ece.

Sullivan, N. (2003) *A Critical Introduction to Queer Theory*, Edinburgh: Edinburgh University Press.

Summers, A. (2006) 'Which Women? What Europe? Josephine Butler and the International Abolitionist Federation', *History Workshop Journal* 62, autumn, 214–31.

Summerskill, B. (ed.) (2006) *The Way We are Now: Gay and Lesbian Lives in the 21st Century*, London and New York: Continuum.

Szreter, S. (1999) 'Failing Fertilities and Changing Sexualities in Europe Since c.1850: A Comparative Survey of National Demographic Patterns', in Eder *et al.* 1999, 159–94.

Szreter, S. (2002) *Fertility, Class and Gender in Britain, 1860–1940*, Cambridge: Cambridge University Press.

Tatchell, P. (2006) 'Watch Out! Left-wing Homophobia is on the March again', *Fyne Times*, April, 7.

Taylor, C. (1992a) *Multiculturalism and the Politics of Recognition*, edited by Amy Gutmann, Princeton, NJ: Princeton University Press.

Taylor, C. (1992b) *The Ethics of Authenticity*, Cambridge, MA, and London: Harvard University Press.

Thane, P. (1999) 'Population Politics in Post-war British Culture', in Conekin *et al.* (eds) 1999, 114–33.

Thompson, B. (1994a) *Soft Core: Moral Crusades against Pornography in Britain and America*, London: Cassell.

Thompson, B. (1994b) *Sadomasochism: Painful Perversion or Pleasurable Play?*, London: Cassell.

Thomson, R. (2004) '"An Adult Thing"? Young People's Perspectives on the Heterosexual Age of Consent', *Sexualities* 7 (2), May, 133–49.

Thomson, R. and Holland, J. (2004) *Youth Values and Transitions to Adulthood*, Families and Social Capital ESRC Research Group, Working Paper 4, London: London South Bank University.

Thomson, R., Bell, R., Holland, J., Henderson, S., McGrellis, S. and Sharpe, S. (2002) 'Critical Moments: Choice, Chance and Opportunity in Young People's Narratives of Transit', *Sociology* 36 (2), 235–54.

Thomson, R., Holland, J., McGrellis, S., Bell, R., Henderson, S. and Sharpe, S. (2004) 'Inventing Adulthoods: A Biographical Approach to Understanding Youth Citizenship', *The Sociological Review* 52 (2), May, 218–39.

Threlfal, M. (ed.) (1996) *Mapping the Women's Movement*, London and New York: Verso.

Tiefer, L. (1995) *Sex is Not an Unnatural Act, and Other Essays*, Boulder, CO, San Francisco, CA, and Oxford: Westview Press.

Tiefer, L. (2006) 'The Viagra Phenomenon', *Sexualities* 9 (3), July, 273–94.

Times, The (2006) 'Swinging Pensioners need Sex Education', 19 July, 5.

Toynbee, P. (2006) 'Only a Fully Secular State can Protect Women's Rights', *Guardian*, 17 October, 33.

Trezise, R. (2006a) *In and Out of the Goldfish Bowl*, Cardigan: Parthian.

Trezise, R. (2006b) *Fresh Apples*, Cardigan: Parthian.

Trumbach, R. (1999) 'London', in Higgs (ed.) 1999.

Trumbach, R. (2003) 'Sex and the Gender Revolution', in Weeks *et al.* (eds) 2003, 14–21.

Turkel, S. (1995) *Life on the Screen: Identity in the Age of the Internet*, New York: Simon & Schuster Paperbacks.

Turkle, S. (2004) *The Second Self: Computers and the Human Spirit* (2nd edn) (1st edition 1984), Cambridge, MA: MIT Press.

Turner, M.W. (2003) *Backward Glances: Cruising the Queer Streets of New York and London*, London: Reaktion Books.

Tutu, D. (2004) 'Foreword', in Baird 2004, 5–6; also published as 'Homophobia is as Unjust as that Crime against Humanity, Apartheid', *The Times*, 1 July, 21.

Tyler, M. (2004) 'Managing Between the Sheets: Lifestyle Magazines and the Management of Sexuality in Everyday Life', *Sexualities* 7 (1), February, 81–106.

Valentine, G. (ed.) (2000) *From Nowhere to Everywhere: Lesbian Geographies*, New York, London and Oxford: Harrington Park Press.

Vance, C.S. (ed.) (1984) *Pleasure and Danger: Exploring Female Sexuality*, London, and Boston, MA: Routledge & Kegan Paul.

Velu, C. (1999) 'Faut-il "pactiser" avec l'universalisme? A Short History of the PACS', *Modern and Contemporary France* 7(4), 429–42.

Vernon, M. (2005) *The Philosophy of Friendship*, Basingstoke: Palgrave Macmillan.

Verrill-Rhys, L. and Beddoe, D. (eds) (1992) *Parachutes in Petticoats: Welsh Women Writing on the Second World War*, Dina Powys: Honno.

Vincentelli, M. (1994) 'Artefact and Identity: The Welsh Dresser as Domestic Display and Cultural Symbol', in Aaron *et al.* (eds) 1994, 228–41.

Waaldijk, K. (2001a) 'Towards the Recognition of Same-sex Partners in European Union Law: Expectations Based on Trends in National Law', in Wintermute and Andenaes (eds) 2001, 635–52.

Waaldijk, K. (2001b) 'Small Change: How the Road to Same-sex Marriage Got Paved in the Netherlands', in Wintermute and Andenaes (eds) 2001, 437–464.

Wainwright, M., Branigan, T., Vasager, J., Taylor, M. and Dodd, V. (2006) 'Dangerous Attack or Fair Point? Straw Veil Row Deepens', *Guardian*, 7 October, 4.

Waites, M. (2003) 'Equality at Last? Homosexuality, Heterosexuality and the Age of Consent in the United Kingdom', *Sociology* 37 (4), November, 637–55.

Waites, M. (2004) 'The Age of Consent and Sexual Consent', in Cowling, M. and Reynolds, P. (eds) (2004) *Making Sense of Sexual Consent*, Aldershot: Ashgate.

Waites, M. (2005a) *The Age of Consent: Young People, Sexuality and Citizenship*, Basingstoke and New York: Palgrave Macmillan.

Waites, M. (2005b) 'The Fixity of Sexual Identities in the Public Sphere: Biomedical Knowledge, Liberalism and the Heterosexual/Homosexual Binary in Late Modernity', *Sexualities* 8 (5), 53–69.

Wajcman, J. (2004) *TechnoFeminism*, Cambridge: Polity Press.

Wakeford, N. (2002) 'New Technologies and "Cyber-queer" Research', in Richardson and Seidman 2002, 115–144.

Walkerdine, V. (2005) 'Freedom, Psychology and the Neo-liberal Worker', *Soundings: A Journal of Politics and Culture* 29, 47–61.

Walter, N. (1999) *The New Feminism*, London: Virago.

Walter, N. (2005) 'Prejudice and Evolution', *Prospect*, June, 34–9.

Wandor, M. (ed.) (1972) *The Body Politics: Writings from the Women's Movement 1969–1972*, London: Stage 1.

Ward, L. (2006) 'More than 15,000 Civil Partnerships Prove Popularity of Legislation', *Guardian*, 5 December, 9.

Warner, M. (ed.) (1993) *Fear of a Queer Planet: Queer Politics and Social Theory*, Minneapolis and London: University of Minnesota Press.

Warner, M. (1999) *The Trouble with Normal: Sex, Politics and the Ethics of Queer Life*, New York: The Free Press.

Waters, C. (1999) 'Disorders of the Mind, Disorders of the Body Social: Peter Wildeblood and the Making of the Modern Homosexual', in Conekin *et al.* (eds) 1999, 134–51.

Watney, S. (1987) *Policing Desire: Pornography, AIDS and the Media*, London: Comedia/Methuen.

Watney, S. (1994) *Practices of Freedom: Selected Writings on HIV/AIDS*, London: Rivers Oram Press.

Watney, S. (2000) *Imagine Hope: AIDS and Gay Identity*, London and New York: Routledge.

Watts, J. (2005) 'Sex is China's Latest Boom Industry', *Guardian*, 25 June, 20.

Weatherburn, P., Reid, D., Hickson, F., Hammond, G. and Stephens, M. (2005) *Risk and Reflexion: Findings from the United Kingdom's Gay Men's Sex Survey 2004*, London: Sigma Research.

Webb, J. (2002) 'A Date with Hate', *Observer*, 'Sex Uncovered' Supplement, 27 October, 49–53.

Weeks, J. (1990) *Coming Out: Homosexual Politics in Britain from the Nineteenth Century to the Present* (1st edn 1977), London: Quartet.

Weeks, J. (1989) *Sex, Politics and Society: The Regulation of sexuality since 1800* (1st edn 1981), Harlow: Longman.

Weeks, J. (1985) *Sexuality and its Discontents: Meanings, Myths and Modern Sexualities*, London: Routledge & Kegan Paul.

Weeks, J. (1991) *Against Nature: Essays on History, Sexuality and Identity*, London: Rivers Oram Press.

Weeks, J. (1993) 'AIDS and the Regulation of Sexuality', in Berridge and Strong (eds) 1993, 17–36.

Weeks, J. (1995) *Invented Moralities: Sexual Values in an Age of Uncertainty*, Cambridge: Polity Press.

Weeks, J. (1998) 'The Sexual Citizen', *Theory, Culture and Society* 15 (3–4), 35–52.

Weeks, J. (1999) 'Supporting Families', *Political Quarterly* 70 (2), April–June, 225–30.

Weeks, J. (2000) *Making Sexual History*, Cambridge: Polity Press.

Weeks, J. (2003) *Sexuality* (2nd edn) (first published 1986), London and New York: Routledge.

Weeks, J. (2004a) 'The Rights and Wrongs of Sexuality', in Brooks-Gordon *et al.* (eds) 2004, 19–38.

Weeks, J. (2004b) 'Labour's Loves Lost? The Legacies of Moral Conservatism and Sex Reform', in Steinberg and Johnson (eds) 2004, 66–80.

Weeks, J. (2005a) ' Remembering Foucault', *Journal of the History of Sexuality* 14 (1/2), January/April, 186–201.

Weeks, J. (2005b) 'Fallen Heroes: All About Men', *Irish Journal of Sociology* 14 (2), 53–65.

Weeks, J. (forthcoming) *The Languages of Sexuality*, London: Routledge.

Weeks, J. and Holland, J. (eds) (1996) *Sexual Cultures: Communities, Values and Intimacy*, Basingstoke and London: Macmillan.

Weeks, J., Heaphy, B. and Donovan, C. (2001) *Same Sex Intimacies: Families of Choice and other Life Experiments*, London: Routledge.

Weeks, J., Heaphy, B. and Donovan, C. (1999a) 'Families of Choice: Autonomy and Mutuality in Non-heterosexual Relationships', in McRae (ed.) 1999, 297–316.

Weeks, J., Heaphy, B. and Donovan, C. (1999b) 'Partners by Choice: Equality, Power and Commitment in Non-heterosexual Relationships', in Allan (ed.) 1999, 111–28.

Weeks, J., Heaphy, B. and Donovan, C. (1999c) 'Partnership Rites: Commitment and Ritual in Non-heterosexual Relationships', in Seymour and Bagguley (eds) 1999, 43–63.

Weeks, J., Heaphy, B. and Donovan, C. (2004) 'The Lesbian and Gay Family', in Scott *et al.* (eds) 2004, 340–55.

Weeks, J. and Porter, K. (1998) *Between the Acts: Lives of Homosexual Men 1885–1967*, London: Rivers Oram Press.

Weeks, J., Holland, J. and Waites, M. (eds) (2003) *Sexualities and Society: A Reader*, Cambridge: Polity Press.

Weeks, J., Taylor-Laybourn, A. and Aggleton, P. (1994) 'An Anatomy of the HIV Voluntary Sector in Britain', in Aggleton *et al.* (eds) 1994, 1–19.

Weinstock, J.S. and Rothblum, E.D. (eds) (1998) *Lesbian Friendships: For Ourselves and Others*, New York and London: New York University Press.

Wellings, K. (2005) *The Seven Deadly Sins*, Swindon: Economic and Social Research Council.

Wellings, K., Field, J., Johnson, A. M. and Wadsworth, J. (1994) *Sexual Behaviour in Britain: The National Survey of Sexual Attitudes and Lifestyles*, London and Basingstoke: Macmillan.

Wellings, K., Collumbien, M., Slaymaker, E., Singh, S., Hodges, Z., Patel, D. and Bajos, N. (2006) 'Sexual Behaviour in Context: A Global Perspective', *The Lancet*, 1 November, online at http://www.thelancet.com?journals/lancet/article/PIISO14073606694798/fulltext, 1–32.

West, D. (1955) *Homosexuality*, Harmondsworth: Pelican.

Weston, K. (1991) *Families We Choose: Lesbians, Gays, Kinship*, New York: Columbia University Press.

Westwood, G. (1952) *Society and the Homosexual*, London: Victor Gollancz.

White, E. (1980) *States of Desire: Travels in Gay America*, New York: E.P. Dutton.

Whittle, S. (ed.) (1994) *The Margins of the City: Gay Men's Urban Lives*, Aldershot, and Brookfield, VT: Ashgate.

Whittle, S. (1999) 'The Becoming Man: The Law's Ass Brays', in More and Whittle (eds) 1999, 15–33.

Whittle, S. (2002) *Respect and Equality: Transsexual and Transgender Rights*, London, Sydney and Portland, OR: Cavendish Publishing.

Wildeblood, P. (1957) *Against the Law*, Harmondsworth: Penguin.

Wilkinson, C. (2002) 'The Net Effect. How to Corrupt and the Changing Definition of Obscenity', *Observer*, 'Sex Uncovered' Supplement, 27 October, 37.

Williams, F. (2004) *Rethinking Families*, ESRC CAVA Research Group, London: Calouste Gulbenkian Foundation.

Williams, F. (2005) 'A Good Enough Life. Developing the Grounds for a Political Ethic of Care', *Soundings: A Journal of Politics and Culture* 30, summer, 17–32.

Williams, R. (2006) *Border Country* (first published 1960), (Library of Wales edn), Cardigan: Parthian.

Wilson, A. (2006) *Dreams, Questions, Struggles: South Asian Women in Britain*, London, and Ann Arbor, MI: Pluto Press.

Wilson, E. (1974) 'Gayness and Liberalism', in Allen *et al.* 1974, 110–27.

Wilson, E. (1977) *Women and the Welfare State*, London: Tavistock.

Wilson, E. (1980) *Only Halfway to Paradise: Women in Postwar Britain*, London and New York: Tavistock.

Wilson, E. (1982) *Mirror Writing: An Autobiography*, London: Virago.

Wilson, E. (1983) *What is to Be Done about Violence Against Women?*, Harmondsworth: Penguin.

Wilson, E. (1986) *Prisons of Glass*, London: Methuen.

Wilson, G. and Rahman, Q. (2005) *Born Gay: The Psychobiology of Sex Orientation*, London and Chester Springs: Peter Owen.

Wilton, T. (2004) *Sexual (Dis)orientation: Gender, Sex, Desire and Self Fashioning*, Basingstoke: Palgrave Macmillan.

Wintermute, R. (2005) 'From "Sex Rights" to "Love Rights": Partnership Rights as Human Rights', in Bamforth 2005, 186–224.

Wintermute, R. and Andenaes, M. (eds) (2001) *Legal Recognition of Same-sex Partnerships: A Study of National, European and International Law*, Oxford, and Portland, OR: Hart Publishing.

Wolfe, A. (2004) 'Dieting for Jesus', *Prospect*, January, 52–7.

Wolmark, J. (ed.) (1999) *Cybersexualities: A Reader on Feminist Theory, Cyborgs and Cyberspace*, Edinburgh: Edinburgh University Press.

Woolcock, N. (2006a) 'Figures for Births to Immigrants in Britain reaches Record Level', *The Times*, 5 January, 32.

Woolcock, N. (2006b) 'Lesbian Partners Fight for Right to be Married', *The Times*, 7 June, 26.

Woolcock, N. (2006c) 'Lesbians Lose their Battle for Foreign Marriage to be Legalised', *The Times*, 1 August, 12.

Wouters, C. (1986) 'Formalization and Informalization: Changing Tension Balances in Civilizing Processes', *Theory, Culture and Society* 3 (2), 1–18.

Wouters, C. (1998) 'Balancing Sex and Love since the 1960s Sexual Revolution', *Theory, Culture and Society* 15 (3–4), 187–214.

Wouters, C. (2004) *Sex and Manners: Female Emancipation in the West, 1890–2000*, London, Thousand Oaks, CA, and New Delhi: Sage.

Yeoman, F. and Bannerman, L. (2006) 'Divorce on the Decline as Couples Wait Longer to Tie the Knot', *The Times*, 1 September, 35.

Yep, G.A., Lovanas, K.E. and Pagonis, A.V. (2002) 'The Case of "Riding Bareback": Sexual Practices and the Paradoxes of Identity in the Era of AIDS', *Journal of Homosexuality* 42 (4), 1–14.

Yep, G.A., Lovanas, K.E. and Elia, J.P. (2003) 'A Critical Appraisal of Assimilationist and Radical Ideologies Underlying Same-sex Marriage in LGBT Communities in the United States', *Journal of Homosexuality* 45 (1), 45–64.

Yip, A. (2003) 'Sexuality and the Church', *Sexualities* 6 (1), February, 60–4.

Yip, A. (2004a) 'Same-sex Marriage: Contrasting Perspectives among Lesbian, Gay and Bisexual Christians', *Feminism and Psychology* 14 (1), February, 173–80.

Yip, A. (2004b) 'Negotiating Space with Family and Kin in Identity Construction: The Narratives of British Non-heterosexual Muslims', *The Sociological Review* 52 (3), August, 336–50.

Young, M. and Willmott, P. (1957) *Family and Kinship in East London*, London: Routledge & Kegan Paul.

Young, M. and Willmott, P. (1973) *The Symmetrical Family: A Study of Work and Leisure in the London Region*, London: Routledge & Kegan Paul.

Yuval-Davis, N. (2005) 'Racism, Cosmopolitanism and Contemporary Politics of Belonging', *Soundings: A Journal of Politics and Culture* 30, summer, 166–78.

Index